'We Need Two Worlds'

'We Need Two Worlds'

Chinese Immigrant Associations in a Western Society

Li Minghuan

Amsterdam University Press

Cover illustration: ANP, 's-Gravenhage

Cover design: Crasborn Grafisch Ontwerpers, bNO, Valkenburg a/d Geul
Lay-out: Bookman, Leiden (www.bookman.nl)

ISBN 90 5356 402 0

© Amsterdam University Press, Amsterdam, 1999

Contents

Foreword

The presence in most western countries of ethnic minorities from faraway parts of the world clearly demonstrates that globalization is not a new phenomenon at all. The investigations carried out by Dr. Li Minghuan concern the Chinese migrants who have settled down in some of the major cities in the Netherlands from the beginning of the twentieth century onwards, what used to be a small colony initially, has rapidly grown in size during the last twenty-five years in particular. The more specific theme of study is the collective action taken by the people of Chinese origin to solve their problems as newcomers in the Netherlands, a type of society with which they were not familiar since early youth. The associations which they started to establish already at an early date did not only seek to promote a wide range of activities within the community of immigrants but also to represent their members vis-à-vis Dutch government and non-government agencies. These organizational efforts have certainly helped to raise the visibility of the Chinese community.

The University of Xiamen, of which Dr. Li Minghuan is a senior staffmember, agreed to send her to the Netherlands for the purpose of this study. Although it has been standard practice since a long time for scholars in the Atlantic region of the world to visit and study societies and civilizations in the non-western parts of the world, it is until now only on rare occasions that scholars from those countries are given the opportunity to investigate structural and cultural dynamics in the West. We do hope that the commendable and inspiring work done by Dr. Li Minghuan will also in this respect set a trend for the future of cross-cultural investigations within a collaborative framework. She has managed to bring out in her book in great detail the life and work of the present-day Chinese immigrants as a community-in-between. While, on the one hand, the country in which they have chosen to settle down enables them to become full-fledged citizens of the Dutch welfare state, there is pressure from the other side to remain economically, socially and culturally loyal to the country of origin. Caught in between? Not really, because the migrants themselves insist that they want to chart a dual course, that is, to be considered as belonging to both worlds. As a matter of fact, they aim to live and operate beyond the nation-state and that is also how their multi-national networks are constituted. It is a way of life that comes close to what global citizenship is all about.

Prof.dr. Jan Breman
Center for Asian Studies Amsterdam (CASA)
Amsterdam School of Social Sciences

Acknowledgements

This book is based on my Ph.D dissertation. Looking back on the initiating stages and the carrying out of the whole research project, memories of many persons and issues directly or indirectly related to the entire research and writing process well up in my mind: accomplishments and disappointments, joys and sorrows, support and disturbances. I know from the bottom of my heart that I would never have completed this study without many people's generous support. However, since there is no room to name them all individually, only a few will be acknowledged here.

Between 1986 and 1988, I was initially sent by Xiamen University (located in Fujian Province, China) to the University of Amsterdam as a visiting scholar. At that time, Dr. Gregor Benton encouraged me to start researching the Chinese immigrants in the Netherlands. Between 1986 and 1988, three books focussing on the Chinese in the Netherlands were published (Wubben, 1986; Benton & Vermeulen, 1987; Pieke, 1988). These publications, although all written in Dutch of which I only have a rudimentary knowledge, became my first textbooks and stimulated me for years. In October of 1988, I returned to Xiamen University with regrets: my own research on the Chinese in the Netherlands was just in its elementary stage.

After determining that my dissertation project would be on the Chinese immigrants' associations in the Netherlands, Prof. Dr. Jan Breman and Prof. Dr. Selma Leydesdorff soundly supported the project and kindly agreed to be my supervisors. I have, in various ways, benefitted from my supervisors' comprehensive inspiration, insightful advice, and timely admonitions. That they were always willing to share my cares and burdens helped me to get over loneliness and encouraged me to overcome difficulties. My sincere thanks are also due to my supervisors' continuous encouragement to improve the manuscript and convert it into a book.

I gratefully acknowledge the financial support provided by WOTRO (the Netherlands Foundation for the Advancement of Tropical Research) and NWO (the Netherlands Organization for Scientific Research). In 1995, my dissertation project was chosen for funding by WOTRO. Then, between 1995 and 1998, its financial support enabled me to conduct my research both in the Netherlands and in China. In 1998, a small grant provided by NWO helped me to make a two-month study trip to Harvard University and University of California in Berkeley, which expanded my knowledge on the topic. Then, another grant from NWO covered the English editing cost of this book. As a foreigner, as a Chinese, it has impressed me deeply how Dutch foundations have positively functioned in improving academic studies. Moreover, I appreciate their equal treatment to their applicants regardless of their ethnic background.

Throughout the entire research period (1995-1998), I was affiliated with the Center for Asian Studies Amsterdam (CASA) in the Amsterdam School for Social Science Research and the Belle van Zuylen Institute (BvZI) at the University of Amsterdam. I appreciated the institutional facilities provided by CASA and BvZI. Diversified academic activities such as lectures, seminars, and regular meetings of the Promotion Club have challenged and prodded me. Since the beginning of 1999, I have been attached to the International Institute for Asian Studies (IIAS) as a research fellow. I owe thanks to the head of the project on which I am working, Prof. Dr. L. Blussé, for allowing me time in 1999 to finish the task of converting the manuscript to a book. For the publication of this book, I am grateful for the support provided by the IIAS. Meanwhile, I would like to express my heartfelt thanks for the contributions made by Chinees restaurant Sea Palace in Amsterdam, Leo Haks, Edgar van Lokven, and Netwerk Chinese Vrijwilligers.

This study is meanwhile my way of repaying hundreds of interviewees: they gave their attention and time, and they provided substance to construct the basis of this study. Since oral accounts are an essential source of this study, it would never have reached fruition without the sincere cooperation of my interviewees. I listed the names of my interviewees after I had finished writing. Unexpectedly, I was shocked since only then did I recognize that up to eight of my interviewees had passed away in the last few years, although their voices and appearances were still vividly present. I remember very clearly how late Mr. Liu agreed to my interviews while he was suffering from lung cancer. Moreover, he persuaded me to move up his interviewing dates when he was informed by the doctor that his sickness was becoming serious and he suddenly might not be able to talk. Mr. Liu passed away only one month after the last interview. There were many impressive experiences during my interviews. I owe much to all of my interviewees. I would like to take this opportunity to express my deepest gratitude to all of them. I hope all of the interviewees will be pleased by the efforts of this study; after all, my sincerest wish is that it helps improve the understanding between Chinese immigrants and the Dutch.

It is a great challenge for me to write a dissertation in English. I would not have succeeded in it without the assistance kindly provided by Mr. Z. R. Zhuang and Mr. Zachariah Silk. My wholehearted thanks must go to Mr. Zhuang in particular for coaching me in English writing. Moreover, the value of his efforts on checking my translations between English, Dutch and Chinese deserves special acknowledgment. I am pleased with the editing work done by Mr. Silk, a professional English editor. He worked very hard to perfect this dissertation.

There are many people who gave comments and suggestions in various stages of the research process. I wish to thank all of them. Particular thanks must go to Edgar Wickberg, Otto van den Muijzenberg, Gregor Benton, Frank Pieke, Edgar van Lokven, Leo Douw, Hong Liu, and Go Gien Tjwan.

Social scientists are after all normal human beings. It is beyond description how much I owe to my dear friends Christianne Borghouts, Maylie Siauw and her family. I will never forget their generous hospitality, kindness and thoughtful care. I cannot imagine how difficult my stay in the Netherlands would have been without their invaluable friendship.

Finally, my greatest debt is undoubtedly to those most beloved to me: my mother, husband and son. I owe much to my mother since I cannot accompany her when she is old and sick. I owe much to my husband since I am always busy doing research, writing and being absent now and then. For my little son I owe a lot in particular for not being able to enrich his childhood with profound maternal love. However, I am very lucky: the complete understanding and full support of my mother and husband always accompanies and encourages me.

Altogether, I have completed this study to repay those who are concerned about me; I regard this dissertation as a conclusion of the past; moreover, I take this study as a starting point toward the future.

CHAPTER I

Introduction

The Chinese, with their ubiquitous restaurants, form a socially visible immigrant sector in the Netherlands. On the one hand, especially since the 1980s, their migration history, their cultural background and, more importantly, their internal social structure and the path their future development will take have been attracting some attention from Dutch society. On the other hand, as an immigrant group that has settled in the Netherlands but still maintains various contacts with their home community, their function as a broker for international trade and mutual cooperation between their receiving and sending societies has also been seriously taken into account in their country of origin.

Ethnic migrants in alien surroundings, like the Chinese in the Netherlands, often forge a sense of collectivity. Despite individual differences in training and experiences before and after their arrival, they have identified themselves, and are always identified by non-Chinese people, at the aggregate level by their shared ethnic background. To ensure a better future in their receiving country, the immigrants organize themselves through visible and invisible links. The emergence of associations is recognized as an important collective symbol.

Chinese abroad recognize that their associations form one of three pillars that support Chinese communities in alien surroundings. More precisely, the Chinese associations, together with the Chinese schools, newspapers and journals that have been established or published by and for the Chinese abroad, have formed a collective strength to promote the cohesion and continuity of the Chinese community in their respective receiving countries.

The first Chinese association in the Netherlands can be traced back to the early 1910s. Then, in the 1920s and the 1930s, ten-odd Chinese associations emerged, most of them established on the basis of shared provenance. Among them, the *Wah Kiu Wei Kun* is the best known. However, all Chinese associations had to disband themselves when the Netherlands was occupied by Nazi Germany during the Second World War. The first well-organized Chinese association that was set up after the Second World War was the *Algemene Chinese Vereniging in Nederland*, which was established in 1947. Interestingly, only after the 1980s does the general organizational trend among Chinese immigrants in the Netherlands show a clear increase in the total number of Chinese associations. More precisely, between 1984 and 1997, over five new Chinese associations were founded on average each year. Thus, by the end of 1997, more than one hundred Chinese associations have been organized among the Chinese immigrants in the Netherlands (cf. Appendix III). They organize and finance distinct and varied public activities now and then, which are attended mostly by Chinese audiences but sometimes by local audiences as well. The social profile of the Chinese immigrant community in the Netherlands as a whole has been greatly highlighted by these activities.

Meanwhile, although most Chinese immigrants have, more or less, directly or indirectly, beneffitted from the Chinese organizational movement, it is worth noting that the percentage of the ordinary Chinese immigrants that bother to register as formal Chinese association members remains relatively low. This situation is in need of exploration. It should be stressed, however, that the social significance of the Chinese associations should be studied from a comprehensive perspective, rather than focussing exclusively on the number of registered members. Moreover, the clearly highlighted social profile of the Chinese associations in today's Dutch society is in itself a telling social phenomenon, which to a great degree mirrors the history of how Chinese immigrants adjust themselves to a Western world.

Given these reasons, I have taken the associations organized by and for Chinese immigrants in the Netherlands as the foundation on which to build up the study.

1 *Aim of the study*

When and why did Chinese people begin to settle down in the Netherlands? How did the Chinese immigrant community grow? When did Chinese immigrants in the Netherlands begin to set up their own associations and why? How have their organizational activities developed going along with their efforts to adjust themselves to the Dutch society? What factors have shaped their organizational structures? And, moreover, what is the social significance of these associations?

Starting from an outline of the Chinese immigration process and the development of their associations in the Netherlands and making an analysis of its characteristics, the purpose of this study is to portray the collective social features of the Chinese immigrants in the Netherlands. More specifically, the objectives of this study are:

(i)   to trace the history of the Chinese immigration process and organizational activities in the Netherlands;
(ii) to discuss the diversity and unity within the Chinese immigrant community;
(iii) to explore their attempts to develop an identity while caught in the gap between their sending and receiving societies.

A general characteristic of Chinese immigrants in the Netherlands is that they are living between two worlds: one is the world of their origin, which is a physically distant but psychologically familiar world; the other is the world of their everyday life, which remains psychologically distant despite its physical presence. Taking the social significance of the Chinese associations as a special angle to start the research, this study aims to explore two aspects: how the Chinese immigrants, consciously or unconsciously, use their social resources from their country of origin to survive and develop themselves in a Western society; and, how their experiences in the West, regardless of whether or not they have realized their dreams, have affected their social status in their original world.

One of my major arguments in this study is that the Chinese associations are regarded as both barriers and bridges that function between the Chinese immigrants and their receiving society. Some studies have argued that the Chinese associations have only acted as boundary markers and barriers to closer relations with mainstream societies (e.g., Coughlin, 1960: 62, 66; Mcbeath, 1973: Chapter 3); while others have stressed that associations indicate a trend towards integration (Wickberg, 1988:313). Although Chinese immigrant associations — as they are set up, shaped and reshaped — are undoubtedly influenced by their Western surroundings, they are fundamentally derived out of aspects of their original culture, e.g., values, habits or ideas. Thus, instead of following the traditional approach of discussing whether the Chinese organizational movement has retarded the assimilation or integration of the Chinese immigrants into the host society, this study will explore its basic functions as an organizational approach to straddling the two worlds and, furthermore, its attempt to benefit from being the bridge between them.

Generally speaking, through the activities organized by the Chinese associations, their social functions can be considered the following:

(i) their manifest function is to form an invisible *wall* by accentuating the we-group feeling and differentiating their members from outsiders; on the other hand, they have built a *bridge* to the wider society by acting as a representative agent and as an intermediary towards the authorities and the general population;

(ii) meanwhile, a latent function has been the construction of an ethnic *niche*; that is, a cultural and social space that is distinct from both the receiving and sending societies.

In fact, some of those immigrants who are familiar with both new and old worlds have developed a sense of superiority because they are able to benefit from straddling the two worlds.

This is a localized study that primarily focusses on the Chinese immigrants in a western society — the Netherlands. To a certain degree, however, I have attempted to study the general concerns through this local case. A Chinese immigrant community has existed in the Netherlands for about one century. Especially since the Second World War, Chinese immigration into the Netherlands has been on the increase, and their combined assets have become considerable when compared with that of many larger immigrant communities in the Netherlands. Moreover, they have organized themselves to call for proper attention to their significance and particularly to highlight their human and economic potential for both the sending and receiving societies. Their process of socio-economic adaptation collectively reflects how Chinese immigrants have developed themselves in a relatively peaceful and lenient environment.

This study, rather than being limited to merely historical evidence from written sources, deals with a number of emotive social issues that Chinese immigrants in the Netherlands currently face. Therefore, by reviewing Chinese settlement patterns and exploring the association development in the Netherlands, this study is concerned with the effects of migration on both receiving and sending societies. It also focusses on the individual's and the community's sense of ethnic or national identity. Moreover, it explores their efforts to benefit rather than suffer from the marginal social position that often follows a long-distance transnational migration.

As a researcher, I never think that I am capable of solving any puzzles faced by my interviewees and their peers. Rather, I will be satisfied if the study presented here not only makes my findings available to the wider public but also eliminates the mystery of the Chinese community and helps to improve understanding between the Dutch and the Chinese immigrants.

2 *A review of literature*

Since this study focusses on *Chinese immigrants in the Netherlands* and *their voluntary associations*, an overview of the relevant studies done to date will be delineated into three groups: Chinese immigrant studies in the Netherlands; studies on the Chinese in the Netherlands done in China; and the relevant studies of the Chinese associations abroad.

A *Chinese immigrant studies in the Netherlands*

The migration studies in the Netherlands paid little attention to the existence of Chinese migrants before the 1980s. Only seldom did the migration process of the Chinese immigrants, the social structure of their community, their difficulties and their expectations of a future in the Netherlands attract attention from either Dutch sinologists or Dutch scholars of migration (cf. Pieke & Benton, 1998).

Before the Second World War, apart from some scattered news reports that appeared in various Dutch newspapers, the first and only comprehensive academic investigation report about early Chinese settlers in the Netherlands was published in 1936. The restricted purpose of the investigation was to provide information for the policy-makers of the Dutch government. F. van Heek, a sociologist from Amsterdam, conducted the investigation. The research was officially published in a report entitled *Chineesche Immigranten in*

Nederland (Chinese immigrants in the Netherlands) (van Heek, 1936). This is an important historical record for anyone who wants to study the early history of Chinese immigrants in the Netherlands, although the depth of the study was limited because the researcher did not have the language abilities necessary to contact the Chinese directly.

In the 1950s, in order to explore the religious background of the Chinese immigrants in the Netherlands, the *Katholiek Sociaal-Kerkelijk Instituut* (Catholic Social-Ecclesiastical Institute) in The Hague carried out a research project. According to the researchers, they aimed to make a sociological portrait of the Chinese immigrants in the Netherlands. The resulting report, *De groep van Chinese afkomst in Nederland* (The group of Chinese descent in the Netherlands), was presented in February 1957 as a little booklet. The report considers three groups: Chinese immigrants that were born in China; Chinese immigrants that were born in Indonesia, Surinam and the Antilles; and students of Chinese origin. The major sources of the first part came from van Heek's book. The second part was simple and extended only five pages. To make up for this weakness, an introduction about the relevant research on the Chinese in Southeast Asia was added as a reference. The third part dominated the report and related the history of Chinese students in the Netherlands: their general situation, their mentality and their religious background. Most students came from Chinese immigrant families of the second group. The researchers clearly recognized the big differences, socially and culturally, between the Chinese immigrants of the first group and the others.

In the 1960s, two sociology students of Amsterdam University carried out one research project on the Chinese immigrants in Amsterdam. Their report, *de Chinezen van Amsterdam: de integratie van een ethnische minderheidsgroep in de Nederlandse samenleving* (The Chinese of Amsterdam: the integration of an ethnic minority group in Dutch society), was presented in 1966 as their MA thesis (Vellinga & Wolters 1966). It should be noted that at least the following three points determined the boundaries of the researchers' understanding of the Chinese immigrant community in the Netherlands. First, this research was carried out during a period when the Chinese catering business was booming, but there were few new immigrants from mainland China. Second, at that time most Chinese immigrants preferred to lead their social lives out of the sight of the Dutch society. Often their contacts with the Dutch were limited to inside Chinese restaurants. They remained a silent group, suggesting that all problems were supposed to be solved among themselves. Finally, having made most of their contacts with "the Chinese descendants from Chinese fathers and Dutch mothers" rather than the immigrants of the first-generation because of the language barrier, the researchers were deeply impressed that the new generation identified themselves overwhelmingly with the culture of their Dutch mother. Therefore, they conceived the near future of the Chinese immigrants as "the integration of an ethnic minority group in Dutch society."

In the 1980s there is a clear increase in research on Chinese immigrants in the Netherlands. Among others, Gregor Benton, a sinologist and historian at

Amsterdam University, played an important role in initiating the trend to study this topic. In the early 1980s he together with Hans Vermeulen set up a project to study the history of the Chinese in the Netherlands and urged some scholars to work on the topic from different perspectives. Since then, a number of serious studies have been published. These include the book on the Chinese immigrants' history before the Second World War written by Henk J. J. Wubben (1986), the comprehensive introductory book on the Chinese in the Netherlands edited by Gregor Benton and Hans Vermeulen (1987), and an investigative report by Frank Pieke (1988). Yet all of these contributions, and the books or booklet mentioned earlier, were printed exclusively in Dutch. Consequently, its readership has undoubtedly remained rather limited.[1]

Soon after publication, however, the studies done by Wubben and Pieke met with sharp criticism from the Chinese community. There is a variety of intriguing reasons for this.

As early as 1932, a Dutch official once vulgarly called the Chinese in the Netherlands "*Chineezen en ander Aziatisch ongedierte*" [Chinese and other Asian vermin] (cf. Chapter III). Obviously, this reflected a pronounced sense of racial superiority. Many decades later, this quotation was used as the title of Wubben's book and printed in large characters on the front cover. Although Wubben stresses that his book displays sympathy for the Chinese if read carefully, there was an obvious and immediate aversion from the Chinese community.[2]

The criticism to Pieke's report was even stronger. For instance, one Chinese newspaper put out by CCRM, a well-known Chinese association in the Netherlands, published an article with the following title: "A vicious intention hidden in Pieke's Report: the Chinese in the Netherlands will be regarded as a backward minority" (INFO Krant, 17 June 1988). Under this title, a collective protest against Pieke's report was lodged in the name of a joint meeting held by about ten Chinese associations. Although the result of this report turned out to be positive for the Chinese community in the Netherlands,[3] many Chinese leaders did not associate this consequence with the contribution of Pieke's report and have maintained a hostile attitude. In 1994, six years after Pieke's report was presented, the chairperson of one Chinese association criticized Pieke's report again: how can a Dutch reporter draw conclusions on the social status of the Chinese in the Netherlands simply by interviewing about 20 Chinese (CCRM, 1994: 5-6).[4]

Both of the above-mentioned instances exemplify the gap between Dutch researchers and Chinese immigrants. However, in the 1990s, three new phenomena related to Chinese studies in the Netherlands have emerged and are worth noting.

The first phenomenon is the change of research emphasis in the Netherlands. The migration studies in the Netherlands began to pay some attention to the existence of the Chinese immigrant community, although compared with the extent of their influence, the research still lags behind. For instance, the problem of Chinese immigrants as a whole has been more or less touched upon in a recent book that discussed the impact of international migration on the Netherlands. This book identifies the following general characteristics of Chinese immigrants in the Netherlands at the present time: it is difficult to estimate their demographic size and development because of their diverse origins; they have a very high naturalization rate; their fertility levels are probably low; and they are possibly the most geographically dispersed ethnic group (Penninx et al., 1993). Compared with the book's contents on other ethnic immigrant communities in the Netherlands, however, the paragraphs that concern Chinese immigrants are too short to give a clear picture.

Another phenomenon is related to the coordination of European-wide studies. One example is the publication of the book *The Chinese in Europe* at the beginning of 1998 (Benton & Pieke, eds., 1998). This book brings together for the first time studies on Chinese immigrants across Europe, both in their national settings and ones more continental in scope. Among others, the book includes one article on The Chinese in the Netherlands (Pieke & Benton, 1998). This is the first article written in English that gives a comprehensive introduction to Chinese immigrants in the Netherlands.

A final phenomenon involves the increase in research projects and publications that explore the situation of the Chinese in the Netherlands; interestingly, the Chinese associations themselves have sponsored this recent research.

For instance, in 1991, *Chun Pah*, a nationwide association for the Chinese elders, issued a Chinese booklet entitled *Helan Huaren jianshi* (A brief history of the Chinese in the Netherlands). This is a booklet of personal reminiscences. The author draws on personal experience to illustrate certain important events for Chinese immigrants in the Netherlands between the 1930s and the 1980s (Chen, 1991). In October 1998, in the name of celebration of its tenth anniversary of establishment, *Chun Pah* published another investigative report titled *Wo xin anchu jiu jiaxiang* (*Waar ik me prettig voel, noem ik mijn thuis*; Where I feel comfortable, there is my home). On the basis of 555 questionnaires distributed throughout the organization of the seven *Chun Pah* regional branches, the report describes the dilemmas faced by most Chinese elders in the Netherlands: they are willing to live in the Netherlands since they regard the Netherlands as a rich and peaceful country; however, mainly due to the language barrier, they have hardly made any contacts with the relevant Dutch authorities or the Dutch people, and few have the knowledge necessary to fuction in Dutch society. The report asks that the Dutch government pay more attention to the Chinese elders and help them to enjoy their lives in the Netherlands (Chun Pah, 1998).

In the early 1990s, the Chinese association CCRM worked together with the *Wetenschapswinkel* (Scienceshop) of Erasmus University of Rotterdam to conduct research on Chinese women, Chinese elderly, and Chinese residents in Rotterdam. The results were circulated as three publications: *Leefwereld van Chinezen in Rotterdam* (The views and ways of living of the Chinese in Rotterdam), *Chinese vrouwen en arbeid* (Chinese women and labour), and *Zorg voor de Chinese ouderen* (Providing care for the Chinese elders).

Because the ethnic Chinese economy in the Netherlands is heavily skewed toward the catering business, many investigations since the 1980s have reported about it (cf. Sijde, 1983; Bedrijfschap HORECA, 1992; Rijkschroeff, 1998). In early 1997, initiated by HCS, a Chinese restaurateurs' association, a group organized by the students of the *Hoge Hotelschool Maastricht* (Hotel Academy of Maastricht) investigated the current situation of Chinese-Indonesian restaurants in the Netherlands. The report, entitled *Imago Chinees Indische Bedrijven, Een onderzoek naar het imago van de Chinees Indische restaurants in Nederland* (Image of Chinese-Indonesian business, a study of the image of Chinese-Indonesian restaurants in the Netherlands), was presented in October of the same year.

In December 1996, two Chinese associations, the European-wide EFCO and the nationwide LFCON, initiated an investigation project on the Chinese community in Europe. The report, entitled *The Chinese Community in Europe*, was completed in June 1998 and presented to the European Commission on 6 July, 1998.[5] In May 1999, the revised English version was published through the sponsorship of the Dutch Ministry of Public Health, Wellbeing and Sports (EFCO, 1999).

The aforementioned investigative results do present significant issues for further study from various perspectives. Moreover, the projects themselves begin to highlight the social position of the Chinese community in Dutch society; something dearly desired by the Chinese association leaders. Furthermore, since I have taken the Chinese associations as my study target, these results, as well as the initiating and organizing processes of this phenomenon, have unique meaning for my studies.

To highlight the social position of the Chinese in Dutch society, the Chinese association leaders present the Dutch Queen a Chinese handicraft article — an exquisitely drawn portait of the Dutch Queen (Photo by Liu Bing).

B *Studies on the Chinese in the Netherlands done in China*

In China itself, until recently, the scholars working on overseas Chinese have focussed almost exclusively on Southeast Asia, although some attention has been paid to North America as well. Few studies, however, have looked at the Chinese immigrants in Europe.

One book is *Ouzhou Huaqiao jingji* (Overseas Chinese Economy in Europe) published in 1956 by Xu Bin. Based upon the materials collected by the embassies or representative offices set up by the government of Taiwan in European countries, the author has generalized scattered information and outlined the Chinese economy in European countries during the early 1950s.[6] Another documentary publication is the *Huaqiao jingji nianjian* (Overseas Chinese Economy Year Book), sponsored by the OCAC (Overseas Chinese Affairs Commission) in Taiwan. A part of this annual series concerns the Chinese in Europe: the structure of the Chinese business in European countries and a brief introduction to their immigration history. In the late 1980s, a series of books about overseas Chinese in their respective countries were published by Zhengzhong Publishing House in Taiwan. In this series, a booklet on the Chinese in the Netherlands is included. Furthermore, the investigative report conducted by Frank Pieke on the social status of the Chinese in the Netherlands was translated into Chinese and published in Taiwan in 1992.

However, all aforementioned books were published in Taiwan. When there was tension between mainland China and Taiwan, few scholars in mainland China could read these publications. Hence, in 1989, when my first paper on Chinese immigrants in the Netherlands, *Amsterdam Tangrenjie de lishi bianqian* [A history of Chinatown Amsterdam], was published in Beijing, some readers, including scholars working on Chinese overseas, told me that, except for some Chinese communist pioneers who once organized the work-study programs in France in the 1920s, they hardly knew anything about the history of Chinese migrants to Europe, let alone the story of the Chinese in the Netherlands. Since then, I have published more than ten papers on Chinese immigrants in Western Europe, focussing on the migration process, structural characteristics, economic activities, identity ambivalence, or cultural traits. It seems that they form a considerable part of the publications on the Chinese in Europe by Chinese scholars in mainland China.

Since the 1990s, the studies on Chinese immigrants in Europe have attracted more attention in their home areas. In Zhejiang province — especially in the two most important source-communities of Chinese immigrants in the Netherlands, Wenzhou and Qingtian districts — some studies on their emigrants to Europe have been carried out on various levels. In Jinhua, a city of Zhejiang province, a Center for Overseas Chinese Studies was set up in 1995. Its sponsors are two institutions: Zhejiang Provincial Federation of Returned Overseas Chinese and Zhejiang Normal University. It is worth noting that besides some local scholars who have done studies on the topic, two Zhejiang Chinese in the Netherlands have been invited to be its honorary members.[7]

In Wenzhou, there is also a Wenzhou Overseas Chinese Research Institute, which was initiated by a couple of retired cadres who had been in charge of overseas Chinese affairs before their retirement. In accordance with the requests of some native clans or families whose members now have widely settled down abroad and want to trace their roots, several clan or lineage genealogies have been edited and published in the name of the institute. In February 1997, in order to set up a research foundation in the name of the institute, two leading cadres of the institute went to visit their fellow provincials in Europe. They visited all associations headed by their co-villagers and asked for donations for the foundation.[8]

In addition, when I was doing research in the villages of Wenzhou and Shenzhen, I found various official or unofficial publications — including booklets, folders and newsletters — on their emigrants abroad. These are local chronicles about their emigrants. In Yuhu, a distant *zhen* under the jurisdiction of Wenzhou municipality, many of whose inhabitants are now in the Netherlands, I met an elderly villager. For dozens of years he has been recording the contributions (i.e., donations) made by the emigrants to their native village. These original records, both the contents (what have been recorded) and the special significance (why they have been recorded), have provided valuable documents for the research in this area.

C *Studies on the Chinese associations abroad*

As was pointed out at the beginning, Chinese associations, together with Chinese schools and Chinese newspapers, are regarded as one of the three pillars that support Chinese communities in alien surroundings. Nowadays, the Chinese voluntary associations can be found wherever a Chinese immigrant society exists. A vast but loosely knit web of Chinese voluntary associations extends around the world, providing numerous possibilities for communication, mutual help, and organized activities for Chinese immigrants. These associations range from large to small and from ephemeral and informal to firmly established and tightly organized. Therefore, comprehensive studies on Chinese immigrants abroad would have to focus on their associations to some degree. What follows is a brief review of the publications that have taken the Chinese organizations as the major topic for study.

First, as was mentioned above, the scholars working on overseas Chinese have focussed their attention almost exclusively on Southeast Asia and somewhat on North America, and so the studies related to Chinese associations abroad concentrated on the same areas. Up to this point, the only book in English that has provided even a quasi-introduction to Chinese immigrant associations in Europe is the recently published *The Chinese in Europe* (Benton & Pieke, eds., 1998). Many of the articles on Chinese immigrants in various European countries contained in this book have also more or less superficially mentioned their associations; these articles just give a brief picture of the Chinese associations in Europe.[9]

Of the limited number of publications, more have focussed on the history

of associations before the Second World War than on their current developments (e.g., Tien, 1953; Skinner, 1957, 1958; Freedman, 1967; Yen, 1986,
1993); and some are collections of documents rather than intensive studies.
For instance, among the relevant publications written in Chinese, the books
written or edited by Guo et al. (1960), Wu (1975-1976, 1980) and Peng
(1983) are well known. Yet their major contribution is the rich documents
they have collected and sorted on the Chinese associations in Thailand,
Singapore or Malaysia.

Among the relevant publications written in English, one of the leading
studies concerns the Chinese community in Thailand and was conducted by
Skinner (1957, 1958). While studying the leadership and power structures
present within the Chinese immigrant community, he noted the history and
social functions of their various organizations in Thailand before the mid-
1950s. Another leading scholar on the subject worth mentioning is Freedman. As an anthropologist specialising on Chinese traditional society, Freedman has made a profound contribution in his study of Chinese lineage and
clan, not only in Fujian and Guangdong provinces, but also regarding their
emigration to parts of Southeast Asia. His study has provided useful insights
into the Chinese associations in Singapore in the 19th century "before they
were affected by modern political and cultural developments" (1967:41). He
studied how Chinese in Singapore "group themselves" to establish "their
rights *vis-à-vis* one another and attempted to deal with non-Chinese authority" (ibid.).

Skinner and Freedman are pioneers among Western scholars who have
focussed on the study of the Chinese immigrant societies in Southeast Asia.
Their anthropological approaches have influenced many followers.

The books or articles written by Comber (1959), Crissman (1967), Blythe
(1969), Mak (1981), and Yen (1986, 1993) are also directly concerned with
the Chinese immigrant organizations or social structures. Having concentrated on the secret societies among the Chinese immigrants in Southeast Asia in
the 19th century, their studies, especially Yen (1986), have helped readers to
understand the early Chinese associations that were established based on
common surname, shared provenance, or shared dialect.

Since the 1970s, as a consequence of the rapid growth of the Chinese
immigrant communities in their respective receiving countries, the development of Chinese associations has attracted more attention from scholars. For
instance, in mainland China, the *Shijie Huaqiao Huaren cidian* (Dictionary of
Overseas Chinese), a large-scale reference book, is a collection of contributions from dozens of Chinese scholars. It covered more than one thousand
Chinese associations abroad (Zhou, ed., 1993).

Although a book in English focussed on Chinese associations abroad has
yet to be published, many have touched upon the topic to some degree.
Edgar Wickberg is the first Western scholar to target his studies on the
Chinese organizations in the Philippines after World War II. In a series of
articles (e.g., 1988, 1992, 1993, 1994, 1996), Wickberg presented a comprehensive study of the recent developments of the Chinese associations in the

Philippines, especially in Manila. He examined how the following points affect Chinese associations: population movements, economic activities, relevant government policies, relations between the Philippines and China. His findings are beneficial to my work since his study is among the few that are close to my current study, not only in terms of the topic but also the period; however, a clear gap exists because of the completely different political and cultural backgrounds of the two host societies — the Philippines and the Netherlands.

In summary, the study presented here concentrates on the Chinese associations in the Netherlands, which until now has not been systematically researched either in the Netherlands or in China. Based on careful fact-finding, this study will put forward arguments resulting from comparison and analysis. The study is expected to make some contributions to the topic of the Chinese immigrants in the Netherlands and broaden the scope of research in this area. Undoubtedly, all relevant studies done by other scholars have helped me to deepen my current study through comparison.

3 Defining central concepts

This study applies an interdisciplinary approach. My early training in China was as a historian. However, since 1995, when I began this study under the supervision of the Amsterdam School and Belle van Zuylen Institute, I have been strongly influenced by Western anthropological and sociological approaches. Meanwhile, I have also had intensive training in the tradition of oral history. Therefore, the oral sources collected and used to build up the study, the classification systems, and explanatory treatments presented in this study are organized in a way that combines some current Western and Chinese ideas and practices. What follows are definitions for some of the study's central concepts.

A Immigrants: the general attributes of the Chinese in the Netherlands

In China, the common terms used to name their compatriots abroad are *Huaqiao, Huaren* or *Huaqiao-Huaren*; sometimes *Huayi* is included. In this study, however, I prefer to use the concept of *Chinese immigrants* to label my study target. To help Western readers understand the differences between the terminology mentioned above, a brief definition would not go amiss.

Having gone through the documents issued by the relevant Chinese authorities, the brief definitions are as follows:

> *Huaqiao*: Originally, this term meant those Chinese who spend some time abroad, but it does not include settlers. Nowadays, it simply refers to Chinese who have the permanent right to reside in their adopted country but retain their Chinese citizenship, either the citizenship of the People's Republic of China, the Republic of China (Taiwan), the Hong Kong

Special Administration Region or Macao.

Huaren: This refers to the Chinese who have settled down somewhere outside China and have also obtained foreign citizenship.

Huaqiao-Huaren: A general term to combine the above-mentioned two groups of people together.

Huayi: Chinese descendants who were born and have grown up outside of China or have been educated and socialized in the country that their parents or ancestors have adopted.

Discussions are continually cropping up as to the exact definitions of the concepts listed above, although Professor Wang Gungwu, a leading scholar in this area, concludes that "correct usage [of the above mentioned concepts] is clearer today than in the past" (Wang, 1998:16; Cf. Wang 1981, 1991; Pieke, 1987; Cushman & Wang eds. 1988; Zhou, 1993; Tu, 1994; Yang, 1996; Zhujia, 1996 [10]).

In December 1994, during the keynote lecture of The Last Half Century of Chinese Overseas conference, Wang put forth his most recent opinion on the Chinese overseas: since all countries which receive migrants have similar expectations of their new citizens, neither *Huaqiao* nor *Huaren* would adequately convey the idea of migrants who have been accepted as nationals of their new countries (cf. Wang, 1998, a revised version of the lecture). This argument immediately drew criticism from several scholars in China, who stressed that neither *Huaqiao* nor *Huaren* are dated; instead, there is no concept better than these two to portray the general characteristics of the Chinese abroad (Yang, 1996; Zhujia, 1996).

This debate is complicated by a new concept that is becoming popular among some Western scholars: the *Chinese diaspora*. The term overseas Chinese is avoided by some scholars because it "touches on political sensitivities if extended to include Taiwan and Hong Kong." When they "are not concerned with the boundaries of sovereignty claims or with distinctions of citizenship or with whether the sojourn abroad is seen as temporary or permanent," the term Chinese diaspora is selected (Lever-Tracy et al, 1996). One representative example is the newly published book *Ungrounded Empire* (Ong & Nonini, 1997). Diaspora as a pattern has been defined with an affirmative view, which is central to this book. According to the authors, while separated by space and travelling across and throughout the regions of dispersion, the Chinese diaspora is characterized by multiplex and varied connections of family, kinship, commerce, sentiments about their native place in China, shared memberships in transnational organizations, and so on (ibid., 18). In additing, Joel Kotkin calls the Chinese outside of mainland China, together with Jews, British, Japanese and Indians, "global tribes." According to him, the global tribe is defined by their strong ethnic identity and sense of mutual dependence, a global network and a passion for technical and other knowledge from all possible sources. He predicts that in the new era such cosmopolitan groups will "play an ever more important role in the emerging world economy" (1993, 4-5; 262).

In my opinion, it is questionable to use either diaspora or tribe to define the ethnic Chinese abroad. To a certain degree, the concept of Chinese diaspora may be adopted when the study concentrates on the border-crossing network among the Chinese abroad. However, it is worth noting that the ethnic Chinese who have been involved in such a network are limited to a few transnational Chinese entrepreneurs, business people or highly qualified professionals. Most Chinese abroad are settlers, and rank and file citizens to boot, in a certain country, such as millions upon millions of ethnic Chinese in today's Southeast Asia.[11] It is not simple for them to migrate from their settled country to another one whenever they want.[12]

The selection of a concept and its corresponding term mirrors the user's principal opinion of the general characteristics of the Chinese abroad. Therefore, rather than limiting the discussions to terminology definitions, I shall explain why I have selected the term *Chinese immigrants* even though *Huaqiao* has been a common self-assumed image of the Chinese in the Netherlands.

My studies have shown that, although few cherish short-term sojourning, many Chinese in the Netherlands, whether they have become naturalized Dutch citizens or retained their Chinese nationality, prefer to call themselves *Huaqiao*. When asked why they have identified themselves as *Huaqiao*, very often the interviewee would ask me in reply "Why not?" This is an interesting phenomenon that caught my attention from the very beginning because it shows clear contrasts with the popular reaction of most ethnic Chinese in Southeast Asia. The latter had given up the concept of *Huaqiao* decades ago. The reasons behind this phenomenon can be enumerated as follows.

Firstly, it is a reflection of the dominance of first-generation immigrants in Chinese communities in the Netherlands (cf. Chapter II). Before they emigrated, many knew from their own experiences that all government administration in China (both on the mainland and in Taiwan) that deals with the affairs of overseas Chinese uses the label *Huaqiao*. Therefore, it is logical that they simply identify themselves as *Huaqiao* because they are now abroad. Many do not know, and do not care, about the differences between *Huaqiao*, *Huaren* and *Huayi*.

Secondly, it is a reflection of the tolerant social surroundings in which the Chinese in the Netherlands live. The Netherlands has a tradition of tolerance towards diverse opinions, various religions, and other cultures. In addition, the Chinese immigrants in the Netherlands have only formed an insignificant part of the population, and their share of the Dutch economy is negligible. Or, to put it differently, the Chinese in the Netherlands have never become an ethnic, economic, or cultural strength that would be able to affect the mainstream of the dominant society, like their peers in some Southeast Asian countries.

Finally, it is a reflection of *flexible citizenship* (Ong, 1993:41). According to the definition made by Ong, flexible citizenship is a product of the current trend of globalization, which has made economic calculation a major element in diasporic subjects' choice of citizenship. Nowadays, the citizenship to

Chinese "nationalism" redefined

a certain degree has become a popular strategy that some migrants are using to take advantage of political and economic conditions in different parts of the world. In the case of the Chinese in the Netherlands, it is worth noting that some Chinese associations in the Netherlands not only have their associations titled *Huaqiao*, but publicly proclaim that they are a "patriotic overseas Chinese association" (cf. ACV, 1997). However, the fact that they are living in the Netherlands and remembering their home country is certainly nostalgia, but it is not the Chinese nationalism that some scholars warned of (Zhujia, 1996). Their patriotic complex is nothing more than an imaginary sense that, in Anderson's words, is just "a politics without responsibility or accountability" or "long-distance nationalism" (1992:11).[13] In effect, the members of these associations prefer to live in the Netherlands rather than in China. Regardless of whether they are committed to it or not, the political situation in the Netherlands affects them and their families much more directly. Undoubtedly, it is true that their hopes regarding the prosperity of China are indeed stronger than that cherished by most Dutch people, and their happiness about the progress made by China is indeed greater. Nevertheless, it is important to recognize the potential meaning of this phenomenon: they want to gain social elevation in the Netherlands from the strength and prosperity of China.

In my study presented here, however, I have selected neither *Huaqiao* nor *Huaren*, but have opted instead for the concept of *Chinese immigrants* because it is based on an important consideration that the phenomenon of the Chinese immigrant group is hereinafter examined from the starting point of the receiving country.

First, it is a comprehensive concept that includes all of the Chinese in the Netherlands; that is, not only those who emigrated straight from China (mainland, Taiwan, Hong Kong and Macao) to the Netherlands, but also the Chinese offspring who re-emigrated from Indonesia, Surinam, Indo-China or somewhere else. To a certain degree, it also includes the three groups mentioned above: *Huaqiao*, *Huaren* and *Huayi*.

Secondly, this concept clearly reflects a feature of the Chinese community in the Netherlands: it is still dominated by first-generation immigrants (cf. Chapter II). That is, because this study focusses on the association activities organized by the Chinese of the first generation, adopting the concept of Chinese immigrants is even more appropriate.[14]

B *Community: a "we-group" to identify the members from "outsiders"*

In this study, the term *community* has been attached to three social groups: the Chinese immigrant community, the original community of Chinese immigrants and the Dutch community.

The concept of community has attracted many different interpretations and has been subjected to widespread use and abuse. Moreover, the idea of a Chinese community arouses many different responses (Crissman, 1967: 188-191; Wang, 1993:9). With regard to my study target, undoubtedly, the

Chinese in the Netherlands can only in a very limited sense be identified as one community. Rather, one can say that below the surface there is a whole series of relatively independent communities and networks. Several transnational Chinese communities also exist that extend to their respective home communities in China. However, at the same time, living in an alien environment indeed gives all Chinese immigrants in the Netherlands the image of a cohesive ethnic community. With regard to the Dutch, the existence of ethnic immigrant groups next to them also awakens their community consciousness. Given its vagueness, community is the preferred, and most convenient, term: its boundary can be defined to identify members of any group. Yet, to avoid misunderstanding, it is necessary to make a clear definition of the way this concept will be used here.

In this study the term community is not relegated to its strict meaning — i.e., all members sharing a common living area — nor simply to portray the target as close-knit and as facilitating cooperation and mutual aid among all members. For instance, I clearly point out that, in contrast to an idealized harmonious existence, the Chinese immigrants in the Netherlands are divided by various dialects, dissimilar hometowns or living areas before emigration, differing political orientations towards China, as well as exhibiting their own class structure. I give a detailed description of the sub-groups among the Chinese immigrant community in the Netherlands in Chapter II.

Further, the relevant communities mentioned in this study can only be named for the sake of contrast; it "depends primarily on a recognized difference in ethnicity or origin" (Crissman, 1967:188). In this sense, the term community properly reflects the fact that the relevant people as a whole have formed "a section of the population" (maybe something like *bevolkingsgroep* in Dutch). The label of community in this study applies to a we-group whose members are identified with each other on the basis of their common physical appearance and shared culture, which they stress, consciously or unconsciously, to differentiate themselves and their peers from others or outsiders. In other words, either the Chinese or the Dutch will act or are acted upon as a community when co-ethnic cooperation is of particular need. For instance, the emergence of economic competition between ethnic groups very often encourages many to gain competitive advantage through fellow-ethnic resources, which hastens a kind of community loyalty being stressed.

In general, the community exists in both a real and an imaginary sense. It is real because the collective characteristics of each community can be illustrated, and moreover, the members of each one can be identified and recognized to a certain degree. At the same time, however, it is imaginary because it has been framed by invisible links. This is especially the case for the Chinese immigrant community in the Netherlands, where community has been framed along national margins and is in reality far from being a strong and integrated entity.

C *Constructing a new identity: benefits from the two worlds*

By taking the development of the Chinese associations in the Netherlands as a case study, I attempt to show in this project how the Chinese immigrants in the Netherlands have made efforts to benefit from their special position instead of simply suffering from the painful experiences of being "nowhere at home." Moreover, when considered in conjunction with global migration trends, I believe a localized study has important general implications.

Many studies have made acute analyses of the consequence of cultural hybridization on transnational or transcultural migrants. The migrants who have left one society and its culture without making a satisfactory adjustment to another find themselves on the margin of each society and a member of neither (Stonequist, 1965). In some cases new cultural and relational patterns, which are neither wholly from the receiving society nor wholly from the sending society, have developed over time (Watson, 1977). Under these circumstances the immigrants must unite the qualities of "nearness and remoteness, concern and indifference" (Park & Burgess, 1921: 322-327). They are a group that stands in the borderland between two worlds and two eras, akin to both but nowhere at home (Kohn, 1929: 117).

This being the case, what are the responses of the migrants? Do they feel pitiful about their marginal position? Do they try to change this position?

Some studies have shown that the relevant migrants have made efforts to change the situation itself, i.e., to promote acculturation (Stonequist, 1965: 221-222). Others, however, have their emotional life and political psychology nostalgically oriented toward their home country (Anderson, 1992). While admitting that these two possibilities have reflected basic orientations of the Chinese immigrant communities in their adopted countries, I shall consider the consequences of marginal positions from another perspective.

The processes of globalization are changing the world. Among other things, the increase of all media of exchange among countries — such as capital, trade, technology, and tourism — has given rise to international migration. Someone has even predicted that "the last decade of the twentieth century and the first of the twenty-first century will be the age of migration" (Castles & Miller, 1993:3). This rapid growth in international population movements calls for a new understanding of the marginal positions created between societies. By now there is a considerable body of literature about transnationalism, globalization, and migration, which are hot topics at the moment (e.g., Sassen, 1988; Fox 1991; Robertson 1992; Kotkin 1993; Bottomley et al, 1994; Kearney 1995; Lever-Tracy et al, 1996; Sinn, 1998). Instead of joining these comprehensive discussions, my considerations are based upon empirical findings of a localized case.

The establishment of Chinese voluntary associations in Western societies is in itself a consequence of the distance between the two worlds: the economic and cultural differences between the immigrants' original society and their receiving society. The development of the relevant associations has, from a certain perspective, collectively reflected the efforts made by the immigrants to benefit from the two worlds. Thus, the symbolic power that the Chinese associations have created must be understood in order to comprehend their social significance. It is worth noting that this symbolic power is becoming more and more necessary for all societies with immigrant populations.[15]

More precisely, the Chinese associations as a whole have formed a socially visible, representative strength. The Dutch authorities, which have aimed at bringing all Chinese immigrants into a socially controlled orbit, need the associations. Meanwhile, the Chinese associations act to tie Chinese immigrants more closely together. An important wish cherished by many immigrants is to move from marginality to assertion. When a demand, no matter how important, is heard through a million separate voices, the result is cacophony; consequently, the associations seek instead to create a concert of purpose by channelling these voices into one body (Cf. Menton, 1982: 207-8).

For instance, the public activities held by the associations — such as the Chinatown festival and Chinese New Year's party — where Chinese immigrants are hosts and the Dutch are attentive customers, have helped to quell their outsider feelings. This is accomplished because the Chinese immigrants are recognized by the dominant society as a social force with its own distinct culture.

To the society in their region of origin, many emigrants also want to become and believe they should be respected as a new force at the core. Because, individually, they have made contributions to their respective families or clans through remittances or by having brought over someone else to their new world; collectively, they have made generous contributions to their hometown, moreover, they believe that their experiences in a developed Western country have given them a wiser and more advanced view on their country of origin. They may take into account the distance between themselves and their native people created by their emigration; however, many regard this more as a symbolic capital than as a weakness.

Those immigrants who are able to preserve the best in their ancestral heritage while reaching out for the best that the Dutch society can offer have become the finest examples of those who have successfully straddled two worlds. They need two worlds: the successful experiences in one can be used to climb up ladders in the other. If immigrants lose their own cultural or ethnic characteristics, they lose the most valuable treasure they have.

The last important point that should be added is that the combination of the best from both worlds can only be realized within tolerant and harmonious social surroundings, especially when the official relationship between their sending and receiving societies is friendly. Experience shows how immigrants become victims of the contradictions between their sending and receiving countries. With the recent developments in the global economy and the rapid movement of capital and labour, the migrants who have developed an integrated relationship with their new world, while enhancing their own cultural and social capital, possess unique attributes to gain competitive advantage. Although at present such an updated identity is found mainly among the elite and well-educated immigrants, its potential is significant.

4 *Operationalizing the research*

As a pilot study on the Chinese associations in the Netherlands, this research is exploratory in nature. It combines the approaches of individual case analysis and general investigation. While selecting three associations with their respective characteristics to give a detailed illustration, this study also involves many more associations from a comparative perspective. To a certain degree, I try to point out the general implications of the current localized study and suggest more popular conclusions.

This study is comparative, however, more in the sense that it compares the structural and functional differences between the Chinese associations. Lacking the necessary knowledge and access, I could not manage to study other ethnic immigrant associations in the Netherlands. Therefore, in this study, the comparison between the Chinese immigrant associations and the associations organized by other ethnic immigrants, although it seems rather important and interesting, remains limited and superficial.

Some methodological considerations and definitions are presented below.

A *Definitions of this study*

First, this study has focussed on the associations organized by the Chinese immigrants who directly emigrated from China (including mainland, Hong Kong and Taiwan) to the Netherlands. The Chinese appeared as an immigrant group in the Netherlands in the early 20th century. Among them, there are two great sub-groups who emigrated from the former Netherlands East Indies and Surinam, two former colonies of the Netherlands. As two distinctive groups that require an independent study, their associations, except when it might be of value to mention them for the purpose of comparison, will not be included here.

Second, this study has concentrated on the associations organized by and for the first generation of Chinese immigrants. As by the end of 1997 there were more than one hundred Chinese associations all over the Netherlands (cf. Appendix III), it would be too ambitious to present an exhaustive study of all of them. Among others, the children of the Chinese immigrant parents, i.e., the Holland-born or Holland-educated Chinese descendants, have formed a new section within the Chinese community in the Netherlands. Since their expectations and behaviour are rather different from their parents, it is an interesting topic that needs a separate investigation. Therefore, in this study, their activities will be touched upon only a few times when they have some relation with other associations.

Third, this study has targeted Chinese *voluntary* associations. Hence, the associations that were organized for the purpose of making profits will not be included, but a few cases where the leaders or initiators have used the name of a voluntary organization for some hidden purpose will be discussed as a special phenomenon. In addition, certain secret or illegal organizations that exist among the Chinese community are not my study targets since there are too many differences between the legal and illegal ones, and the latter in itself needs an independent study.

Finally, it should be pointed out that this study mainly focusses on Chinese immigrants whose social lives still remain at the core of the Chinese community or are mainly bound to the Chinese community. There are some people who should be studied but are difficult to reach because they are out of sight from the Chinese perspective, e.g., those who have completely assimilated into the Dutch society; those who had played an active role but have passed away; or those who have re-migrated to other countries; etc.

B *Oral accounts are an essential source for the study*

This study to a certain degree relies on the oral data from nearly 200 interviews in total, although the study of archives and the collections of written documents have also formed one part of the necessary basis. The reasons why oral accounts are so essential here should be viewed from at least the following four perspectives.

First, having set up this study on the basis of interviews, I have attempted to fill in gaps and weaknesses in the written sources by tracing the psychological processes that coincide with the settlement of these immigrants in their receiving country. As was pointed out earlier, no systematic research on the development of the Chinese associations in the Netherlands has been done. This is surprising considering the fact that more than one hundred Chinese associations have been founded since the end of the Second World War. In view of the few books on the Chinese in the Netherlands, the gap between the writers, who are Western scholars, and their subjects, the Chinese immigrants, is wide and obvious. It is also clear that a comprehensive study on the topic cannot ignore the voice of ordinary Chinese immigrants.

On the Chinese side, there have been some publications — such as newspapers, periodicals, and reports — edited and published by a few of the Chinese associations in the Netherlands. From these written sources, the activities of Chinese associations can be gleaned, especially after the 1980s. In addition, some articles written by Chinese immigrants show their feelings about living in a strange country, their personal life stories, their psychological ambivalence, and their expectations for the future. Nevertheless, such articles are few in number, and the writers are limited to a few well-educated persons. On this point, oral sources can be used to fill in gaps and weaknesses in the written sources.

Just as Alessandro Portelli has pointed out: the first thing that makes oral history different is that "they tell us not just what people did, but what they wanted to do, what they believed they were doing, what they now think they did. Oral sources may not add much to what we know of, for instance, the material cost of a given strike to the workers involved; but they tell us a good deal about its psychological costs" (1981:99-100; 1991:50). Elizabeth Tonkin argues that "the past" is not only a resource to deploy or support a case or to assert a social claim, it also enters memory in different ways and helps to structure it; therefore, "we are our memories" (1992:1). Also, she argues that personal narratives cannot be taken as accurate historical documents but should be approached "as literature" that itself is "part of social action" (ibid:3), and "it is a dynamic process and also a situational one" (ibid:51).

Elsewhere, Selma Leydesdorff illustrates the strong nostalgia orientation of the Jewish proletariat of Amsterdam (1994); Dorothy Louise Zinn describes the contradictory feelings of staying or returning to Senegal among Senegalese immigrants in Italy (1994); Gadi Ben-Ezer analyzes the identity problem that Ethiopian Jews have encountered after their migration to Israel (1994). All of these researchers provide examples of how to use oral sources to trace the migrants' psychology in their respective strange countries, which of course is important for the construction of their history.

In this study, the organizational motivations and the social significance of the Chinese associations cannot be studied without rich oral data collected from interviews. Many examples can be read from the ensuing chapters, but the following is a representative case.

Mr. MH is a successful Chinese restaurateur and a leading member of several Chinese associations. During an interview, when I expressed my appreciation for his achievements after emigrating from China, his response was as follows:[16]

> Yes, I am a successful restaurateur now. I have a big restaurant, a nice house, savings maybe even enough for another lifetime if I can have it [...] Yet, what is the meaning of these things to me? I was a historian before I emigrated. Many of my classmates are now professors. When I met them, they gave me their books. That is their achievement. What can I give to them? Of course, they all appreciated my achievements in the Netherlands, but I really feel ashamed when I tell them that I am a Chinese restaurateur, I have to worry about the value of business everyday and I have to smile with customers around the tables [...] I would be much happier if I were a scholar, although I would have lived in a poorer way.[17]

The contradiction between the interviewee's economic gains and psychological losses is clear. Also, I noted that he did not directly mention how he thought about his leading position within the Chinese associations. Based on what he has said, however, it may be considered that seeking psychological balance became a basic motivation to be active within the Chinese associations and win a sense of achievement from such activities. In addition, this oral account is helpful to obtain an insight into the following event: while visiting his old university in China, this interviewee donated twenty thousand Dutch guilders to support the publication of one historical issue edited by his ex-classmates; then his name as a special sponsor was printed on the top of the cover page.

The second perspective on oral accounts is that the use of interviews as a research approach provides a practical way to allow more Chinese immigrants to express their part in history; in this way, the construction of history can be more comprehensive.

During the relevant interviews, in addition to their responses that directly related to a certain Chinese association, I heard a lot of life stories. These life stories, as the narrator's personal experiences both in their home country and abroad, form the vital basis on which to study their personal attitudes towards the relevant associations on the one hand and the deep or latent social significance of the associations on the other.

For example, up through mid-1998, Chinese immigrants in Europe had organized about forty various European-wide Chinese associations. Why has the idea of organizing transnational associations been realized and developed among the European Chinese? One factor can be drawn from oral sources: Europe or rather Western Europe is like a single entity in their mind. From the life stories of my interviewees, I found it is quite common for them to transfer from one country to another and then to a third or fourth country, especially just after their arrival. The following examples illustrate this:

Mr. Chen. In 1929, Mr. Chen emigrated from Qingtian in Zhejiang province to Paris. With the help of a cousin, he left for Berlin in 1930. In 1933, he crossed the border into the Netherlands.

Mr. A. Mr. A jumped ship in London in 1946 and worked in a fellow villager's restaurant for about two years before he returned to Hong Kong. In 1967 he jumped ship again in Denmark and used his savings to buy a small fast-food store in Copenhagen. He then sold the store and emigrated to Sweden in 1969. At last in 1975 he decided to join his daughter's business in the Netherlands when he was 55 years old.

Mr. G. Mr. G emigrated to Italy in 1962. Having saved some money, he re-emigrated to the Netherlands in 1968 after hearing about the Chinese restaurant boom there. Then, in the late 1980s, when the competition among the Chinese catering businesses in the Netherlands became intensive, while the limitation on trading business is more flexible in Italy than in the Netherlands, he went to register an import-export trading company in Italy.

Mrs. N. Mrs. N left mainland China to join her husband in Hong Kong in the 1960s. After being divorced by her husband, she tried to find a better future in Europe in the 1980s. Because she has a brother, a couple of cousins and friends who have settled down in France, Belgium and the Netherlands respectively, she then lived in these three countries in succession for several years before she married a Dutchman and finally settled down in a Dutch city.

Mr. C. Mr. C went to the Netherlands in 1985 on a tourist visa. He was sent back to Wenzhou in 1988 after being picked up by the Amsterdam police as an illegal immigrant. Less than one year later, he left for Italy, again on a tourist visa. This time, he was lucky, for he was granted permanent residence when the Italian government announced an amnesty for illegal residents.

These life stories show that Europe is the equivalent of one single "country" in the minds of these people. Their experience of emigration from one country to another made the idea of organizing transnational associations acceptable for ordinary European Chinese. For instance, Mr. Chen, Mr. G. and Mrs. N mentioned above are among the active initiators of transnational Chinese associations in Europe.

The third reason for the use of oral data is that oral sources to a certain degree may provide profound meanings to some well-known facts based on unconscious memories cherished by the speakers. Certainly, it is clear that the oral sources collected from the interviews are not always fully reliable in point of fact. Nevertheless, "rather than being a weakness, this is however, their strength: errors, inventions, and myths lead us through and beyond facts to their meanings" (Portelli, 1991:3). The following is an interesting example of my experience.

When asked about the initiating process of a Netherlands-wide Chinese association, CSFN, the relevant interviewees told me at least three different stories and in total gave me six names of its key initiators. Since there are short of original documents to show the early period of the association, it is impossible to bring the real initiator(s) of CSFN to light simply on the basis of the interviews. This is a shortcoming of the oral sources: the informants cannot completely get rid of their subjectivity. Yet, at least two other constructive meanings can be drawn from the superficially contradictory oral sources. On the one hand, the oral sources show that this association has enjoyed great prestige among the Chinese community; so much so, that people regard it as an honour to be its initiator. On the other hand, from the phenomenon that there are some differences — areas of origin and political orientations towards China — among the six possible initiators, it can be seen clearly that CSFN shows neither political orientations nor any bias according to different places of origin. Therefore, a conclusion can be reached based on the relevant oral sources that CSFN is a united association that opens its door to all Chinese immigrants in the Netherlands (cf. Chapter V).

The fourth and final reason for using oral accounts is that there is a lack of reliable qualitative statistics dealing with the Chinese immigrants in the Netherlands. On the one hand, some Chinese immigrants do not want to or do not know how to go through formal registration; on the other hand, the Dutch authorities did not have the capacity to control Chinese immigrants, whose languages they rarely understand. Oral sources may not add many data to what the researcher can find out from the written sources, such as how many meetings or public activities have been organized by a certain association; instead, they tell us a good deal about its effects. Thus, a vivid history can be portrayed with the fresh materials provided by interviewees and under the logical "reconstruction" of the researcher (cf. Thompson, 1988).

In sum, written and oral accounts do not exist in separate worlds. Instead of being mutually exclusive, oral and written sources may be mutually complementary. Also, the assumption that written sources are objective and oral sources are subjective is not always correct. In contrast, by utilizing comparative studies of relevant oral and written sources, the history can be constructed in a richer and deeper way.

To define the current study, I follow the development of the Chinese immigrant community in the Netherlands from the mid-1980s. As a visiting scholar to the University of Amsterdam between 1986 and 1988, I set up my contacts with the relevant Chinese associations and made dozens of pilot interviews with the Chinese immigrants in the Netherlands. However, the major oral data of this study, drawn from 156 in-depth interviews, was collected between 1995 and 1998, after I had undergone intensive training on oral history-taking in the Belle van Zuylen Institute of Amsterdam University in the spring of 1995. Among these in-depth interviews, 97 were conducted among the Chinese immigrants in the Netherlands, while the other 59 were done in their hometowns of Wenzhou and Shenzhen in China.

The selection of interviewees is largely arbitrary. Among those in the Netherlands, there are Chinese association initiators, leaders and backbone elements; in addition, there are also some Chinese who proclaimed that they were completely uninterested in any organizational activities. In the immigrants' hometowns of Wenzhou and Shenzhen, my interviewees included local cadres who are in charge of overseas Chinese affairs, relatives of the Chinese emigrants, and some returned migrants who had made their living in the Netherlands. Their responses regarding the Chinese associations in the Netherlands, as well as their memories or indirect impressions (imaginations) about the Netherlands, expanded my understanding. Some responses were not merely different but sometimes antagonistic to certain facts, which helped me to correct some of my lopsided views. Meanwhile, it is worth mentioning that the number of people with whom I had conversations on their experiences in the Netherlands is much higher than the number of official interviewees. I was often present on occasions where people interacted socially, for instance at home, in a restaurant, in an association's weekly meeting, or during festivals. I have imbibed valuable information from such unofficial interviews.

Since I am working in my own community, I know how difficult it is to maintain my perspective as a complete outside observer. For example, during the period of my research, I was very often asked to offer certain help, e.g., to act as an interpreter, to write a report for a certain organization, to fill in a form for an illiterate elderly person, to be a Chinese language teacher, or to help with the arrangement of meetings. I have attempted to complete the requests as a volunteer, although I have, consequently, spent rather a lot of time and energy. As a response, however, I have been regarded as a member of the we-group and very often enjoyed my interviewee's personal trust or friendship and benefitted from that. Sometimes I almost forgot that I was a researcher and often shared the narrator's joys and sorrows. I know it is my weak point that I quite often stand too close to my fellow country people, but I cannot thoroughly control my sentiments. "Few can claim to be 'detached' or 'dispassionate' no matter where they work; anthropologists are, after all, only human" (Watson, 1977: 15). Nevertheless, as a Chinese who has been trained in a Western school and tries to study her own community from the inside, the study has benefitted from my insider's perspective because I believe I have a better understanding of the situation.

C *Field experience at both ends of the migration chain*

A methodological preparation for this study is that I have carried out my field experience at both ends of the migration chain, i.e., in the Netherlands and in Wenzhou and Shenzhen, the hometowns of a great part of Chinese migrants in the Netherlands.[18]

Voluntary associations by and for the Chinese immigrants in the Netherlands have been organized and are developed in concert with the Chinese immigration process. Moreover, the organizing process itself has formed one of their responses to having settled down in the Netherlands while remaining nostalgically connected to their communities of origin. As Watson has rightly pointed out, "it is impossible to gain a true picture of immigration as a *process* without investigating the people and their families on both sides" (1977: 2, italics in original).

Being a Chinese scholar familiar with the original background of Chinese migrants, I started, and basically focussed, this project in the Netherlands. Between 1986 and 1988, then carrying on again from 1995, I took an approach of participant observation to follow all important activities organized by the Chinese associations in the Netherlands. During the early months of 1996 and of 1997, I made specific trips first to Wenzhou and then to Shenzhen to conduct another part of my fieldwork. Having visited some *qiaoxiang* (or emigrant communities), I am impressed by the striking interdependent influences between the two geographically distant worlds.

The comparative studies on the responses — which are based on posing similar questions to interviewees either in their receiving or sending societies — are used to develop a more comprehensive understanding of the social significance of the Chinese associations.

In general, none of the other studies related to Chinese immigrants in the Netherlands had been conducted from both ends of their migration chain. I hope the dual perspective will also increase the value of this study.

5 *Structure of the text*

This book begins with an examination of the process of settlement of the Chinese in the Netherlands. Then, once the history of the Chinese voluntary associations has been traced in detail, different types of associations are distinguished. In Chapter IV, three Chinese associations with their respective characteristics are studied. The three substantial chapters that contain my major arguments focus on three principal topics:

(i)   To have dreams come true: organizational motivations;
(ii) Leadership and membership: organizational structures;
(iii) A bridge and a wall between the two worlds: organizational functions.

Finally, some conclusions are drawn from a comparative perspective to give an outlook on the future development of the Chinese associations in the Netherlands.

"We need two worlds!" When one interviewee said this to me in a mild tone, I was deeply impressed at first and afterwards tried to explore its potential or deeper meaning. Many contemporary immigrants with updated identities want to and believe they can benefit from their marginal position. Their organizational activities are a result of this desire. Therefore, one of my important explorations is the two-worlds perspective, that is, how an achievement in one society has been converted into capital for upward mobility in another society.

The study presented here is the result of my exploration.

CHAPTER II

The Settlement of Chinese Immigrants in the Netherlands

Presenting a comprehensive historical overview of the settlement of Chinese immigrants in the Netherlands is an indispensable way to prepare for a more detailed study on the activities and structures of their associations.

1 *Chinese migration to the Netherlands in the 20th century*

When and how did the Europe-oriented migration occur from some areas of China?[1] How have these areas been historically selected? How has this migration wave been shaped and reshaped in the 20th century?

According to the documents I have studied, written from a Chinese perspective and focussing on different stages throughout the 20th century, the pattern of Chinese immigration to the Netherlands can be divided into three phases:

(i)   The inception of the first Europe-oriented migration tide: before 1949;
(ii) The Chinese emigration tide from outside of mainland China: 1950 – 1975;
(iii) A sudden rising tide of emigration from mainland China: after 1976.

A *The inception of the first Europe-oriented migration tide (before 1949)*

From a historical perspective, the Dutch presence in China occurred much earlier than that of the Chinese in the Netherlands. As early as the 17th century, the Dutch had control of Taiwan, the biggest island of China, lasting for nearly 40 years (1624 – 1662). Since then, for almost four centuries, the Dutch have been described in official Chinese publications as "barbarians with red hair [...] They have deep-set eyes and long noses. All their hair, eyebrows, and beards are red. They have big feet, as long as forty centimeters.[2]" The book carrying this description was officially published in 1739. It is obvious that until the eighteenth century the Netherlands was an alien place even among the Chinese intellectuals.

Similarly, in the Netherlands (with the exception of the former Netherlands Indies), to the majority of native Dutch until the middle of the 19th century, the Chinese were a strange people.[3] All the materials that I have collected show that the Chinese as a foreign immigrant group did not appear in the Netherlands until the early 20th century. In other words, since the beginning of the 20th century, the Netherlands has changed in perception from a country of "barbarians with red hair" to an ideal destination for some Chinese.

How did this change come about? Why did the Chinese make such a long and arduous journey to settle down in the Netherlands?

The earliest ethnic Chinese immigrants who appeared in the Netherlands can be divided into two groups: one was a re-emigrant group which came from the former Netherlands East Indies; the other group came directly from China. Although both of them were ethnic Chinese, there were large differences between them with regard to the general motivations behind their migration, their original backgrounds, and their social position in the Netherlands. Since this study focusses on the Chinese emigrants from China, the accounts related to the Chinese immigrants from the former Netherlands East Indies to the Netherlands will be introduced briefly and only for comparative purposes.

The majority of this latter migrant group were students, who were also known as Peranakan Chinese.[4] Although some Chinese businessmen in the Netherlands East Indies had conducted business in the Netherlands since the end of the 19th century, their number was always very limited, as few of them could compete with Dutch entrepreneurs operating in their Dutch homeland. Education, however, was another matter. In 1908, the so-called Holland-Chinese school was established in the Netherlands East Indies. Since

Table 1 *Registration of occupations of 331 Chinese entering the Netherlands (January 1937)*

Birthplace[*]	Sailor[**]	Hawker[***]	Cook	Restaurateur	Others[****]	Total
Guangdong	97	4	6	3	1	111
Zhejiang	31	158			4	193
Fujian	1	2				3
Shanghai	1	11				12
Hong Kong	2				1	3
Jiangsu		4				4
Anhui	1	2			1	4
Shandong		1				1
Total	133	182	6	3	7	331

[*]   Shanghai and Hong Kong are cities. The other names of birthplaces are provinces of China.
[**]   11 registered as stoker, others registered as sailors.
[***] Among the hawkers from Zhejiang, one was female.
[****] "Others" include the following occupations: 1 laundry-man, 1 bookkeeper, 3 artists, 1 boarding-house keeper, 1 peasant.

Table 2 *Changes in the occupations of above-mentioned Chinese (January 1937)* *

Changing From	To	Zhejiang	Guangdong	Fujian	Shanghai	Anhui	Total
hawker	peanut-cake seller**	49	3		4	2	58
sailor	peanut-cake seller**	18	1			1	20
hawker	clothes seller	9					9
sailor	clothes seller	4					4
hawker	shopkeeper	1					1
sailor	hawker	1	5				6
hawker	boarding-house keeper	3	1				4
hawker	sailor	10	1				11
hawker	bookkeeper	1					1
hawker	cook			1			1
hawker	laundry-man	1					1
sailor	cook		3				3
sailor	waiter		3				3
Total		97	17	1	4	3	122

*   Among the 331 registered Chinese, 122 changed their occupations after arrival. These changes are shown in this table.

**   As we shall see, around the beginning of the 1930s, many Chinese in the Netherlands had to sell a kind of peanut-cake to make a living.

Source: the above two tables are systematized and calculated from Chineezen, verblijf houdende op terrein N. V. Stoomvaart Maatschappij 'Nederland' op 26 Januari 1937. The original document number: No. A 376 / 75 / 1937.

the early 1900s, with the increase of local-born Chinese descendants who grew up in the Netherlands East Indies and received a Dutch education, entry into the Netherlands for secondary and tertiary education became an overriding ambition for some literate Chinese, even though it was a very expensive and difficult undertaking.[5] According to available statistical data, there were about 20 Peranakan Chinese students studying in the Netherlands in 1911. This number increased to about 50 in 1920 and to about 150 in 1930. In the aftermath of the world economic crisis of the 1930s, this number decreased to about 100 in the mid-1930s. At the end of the 1930s, aware that war might break out any time in Europe, Peranakan Chinese families were afraid to send their offspring to the Netherlands. The number of Peranakan Chinese students decreased rapidly to a few dozen. In sum, according to the statistical data offered by *Chung Hwa Hui*,[6] there were about 900 Peranakan Chinese who studied in the Netherlands between 1911 and 1940 (van Galen, 1987:136; Tan, 1986:2; 7).

The Chinese pioneers who came directly from China to the Netherlands were people from the provinces of Guangdong and Zhejiang.[7] More precisely, the majority of Chinese in the Netherlands came from the following two areas: Bo On district[8] of Guangdong province and Wenzhou and Qingtian districts of Zhejiang province. Tables 1 and 2 show some basic details about the Chinese in the Netherlands in the 1930s.

The first Chinese group that came directly from China to make their living in the Netherlands was the Guangdong or Bo On group. The majority of this group were seafarers when they first arrived in the Netherlands, who had been employed and brought over to the Netherlands by Dutch shipping companies (van Heek, 1936; Wubben, 1986; Chen, 1991; Pieke & Benton, 1998). Going back to the beginning, I shall sketch the historical background from the Chinese side.

Bo On was a county that was established by the central government of the Jin Dynasty in 331 AD.[9] It is located in the area around the mouth of the Pearl River. Before the cession of Hong Kong to Great Britain in the Nanking Treaty of 1842, Hong Kong fell under the administrative jurisdiction of Bo On. Therefore, with the development of Hong Kong as an international port and the concomitant labour shortage this entailed, the natives of the less developed areas of Bo On began going to Hong Kong to make their living.

By the early part of this century, ocean-shipping enterprises were already a well-entrenched economic sector of Britain, the Netherlands, and some other Western European countries. From the middle of the 19th century, after the cession of Hong Kong, in a bid to seek higher profits, British shipping companies, followed by the Dutch and other Western companies, began to hire cheap Chinese labour on ships leaving from Hong Kong. This began the practice of strong, healthy Bo On peasants working as seafarers.[10]

This history can also be viewed from the Dutch side. As their way of life always entailed all kinds of difficulties and dangers, the sailors of Western European countries had developed a strong trade union to protect their rights. Protective of their profits, ship owners at that time began employing poor Chinese peasants instead of Western labour. An investigation by the Dutch seamen's trade union in the 1930s showed that the wage accepted by Chinese seamen was only about two-thirds of the pay that was offered to their Dutch counterparts.[11]

In 1898, there were 11 Chinese seamen registered as foreign employees in Amsterdam. This figure grew to 109 the next year and 335 the year after. In the first ten years of the 20th century, the number of Chinese seamen registered in Amsterdam remained between 100 and 300. This, however, changed during a Dutch seamen's strike in 1911, when hundreds of Chinese were employed simultaneously to break the strike.[12] At this time, the total number of Chinese seamen jumped from 196 in 1910 to 765 in 1911 and kept rising to reach 2,165 in 1915. Through 1930, the number of Chinese seamen registered in Dutch shipping companies remained at a level of between two and three thousand each year.[13]

The increase of Chinese seamen working for Dutch companies meant that due to sickness, waiting for a new berth or simply being tired of the sea-faring life, many Chinese jumped ship to make a living ashore; thus, more and more Chinese seamen spent a longer and longer period of time in the Netherlands. By doing so, they had become to a certain degree foreign residents of Dutch harbour cities, first in Rotterdam and soon afterwards in Amsterdam. They usually lived in a cluster, each one renting a bed in a boarding house run by a so-called Chinese shipping master (van Heek, 1936; Meyer, 1983; Chen, 1991; Li, 1989). With the establishment of many such Chinese boarding houses in a certain street or corner, the first two Chinatowns in the Netherlands began to emerge, i.e., in Rotterdam's *Katendrecht* district and in the *Buitenbantammerstraat* of Amsterdam. During the 1920s and 1930s, the name of Bo On appeared in Dutch publications and police reports now and then.

The other important district group among early Chinese immigrants in the Netherlands came from the Wenzhou and Qingtian districts, an area located in the south part of today's Zhejiang province.[14] The Qingtian people are very proud of the fact that the mountains in Qingtian county supply the valuable resource of a pale-coloured soapstone, which is ideally suited for carving knickknacks. Some written sources found in Qingtian show that Qingtian carved stone had found a market in Europe at least as early as the end of the 19th century (Chen, 1990). This has given rise to a legend. It is said that in the spring of 1914, while selling Qingtian carved stone in Europe, a Qingtian man luckily had a chance to present a piece to the Dutch Queen: an incense burner with two lively lions playing with a pearl. The Queen liked the article very much and praised it highly. This set a fashion, and many Dutch aristocrats subsequently bought such Qingtian stone ornaments. As a result, this Qingtian man earned a lot of money and was regarded as a hero in his hometown (Lin & Chen, 1986). Of course, this is only hearsay;[15] however, it is one of many such legends widespread in the Qingtian and Wenzhou districts. Not surprisingly, such legends stimulated the imaginations of the people in the region. The motivation of selling Qingtian carved stone in Europe to get rich quick spurred Qingtian people to find their way to Europe. Carrying Qingtian stones, Qingtian people voyaged to Europe by sea, and amazingly others even crossed Siberia on foot to reach the continent of legend.[16]

The tide of emigration out of Qingtian had a strong impact on its neighbouring villages and towns, which fell under the jurisdiction of Wencheng or Rui'an county. Beginning in the early 20th century, the wave of emigration gained momentum in these areas as well. According to an investigation in Yuhu — a little *xiang*[17] in Wencheng county adjacent to the emigration area of Qingtian — the first villager who went to make his living in Europe did so in 1905. It was said that he was brought over by his uncle — a stone carver from Qingtian. Following this example, up until the end of the 1930s, there were 391 Yuhu people living in Europe, and 75 of them settled in the Netherlands (Li, 1996).[18]

The following chart shows the emigration waves from Qingtian county and its neighbouring county Wencheng from 1900 to 1949. It is worth noting

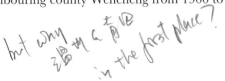

that the emigration wave from Wencheng rose and dropped after that happened in Qingtian. Moreover, toward the end of the 1930s, when Japan began its war against China and the Second World War broke out in Europe, few Qingtian and Wencheng people wanted to pursue their dreams of advancement abroad.

Chart 1 *Emigration of Qingtian and Wencheng people abroad (1900-1949)*

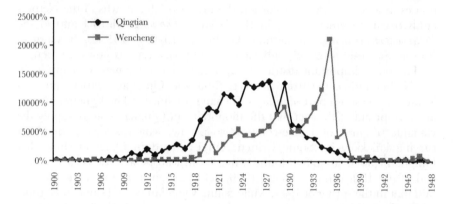

Sources: Qingtian xian zhi [Qingtian county chronicles] & Wencheng xian zhi [Wencheng county chronicles].

It should also be pointed out that among the migrants of this first period, many were sojourners. For instance, by the end of the 1940s, of the 196 Wencheng emigrants who once made their living in France, only 16, i.e., less than ten per cent of the total, were still living in the country. 52 had died while128 had resettled in their hometown (Zhu, 1996: 225). Some of them came back with broken dreams. But some returnees were able to use the money brought back from Europe to buy houses and/or land in their home-town.[19]

Life was not easy for most Chinese in the Netherlands during the first half of the 20th century. Almost all of these Wenzhou and Qingtian people (hereafter the Zhejiang group) were pedlars selling cheap ties, necklaces, or little toys from door to door. The seamen from Guangdong, who were very often hired as coal-stokers, found their lives affected by the advances in marine engineering. When more and more ships switched from using coal to oil, there was no longer a big demand for Chinese stokers in Dutch shipping companies (van Heek, 1936: 20-21). Lacking any special skills, they had to join the Zhejiang pedlars selling cheap goods in the streets to make a living. Not surprisingly, the market for the Chinese pedlars was very restricted. They not only had to face discrimination from the host society, but relations between the Zhejiang group and the Guangdong group were sometimes also strained because of competition among themselves.

The situation grew even worse during the period of economic depression in the 1930s. To survive, the Chinese pedlars in the Netherlands had to make and sell what were called peanut-cakes from door to door.[20] As they describe it:

> We said we were salesmen. But, in fact we were nothing like salesmen, we were just like beggars.[21]

> Some Dutch threw coins to us but didn't pick up any peanut-cakes. I knew they treated us just like beggars.[22]

> I remember very clearly that at that time, very often when I took a seat in the train, the Dutchman who sat beside me would stand up and leave immediately. We were regarded as dirty people. We were looked down upon.[23]

From some elderly interviewees' reluctance to talk about their experiences at that period, I could infer that they had attempted to erase the memory of the hardships endured in that time of deprivation.

At the end of the 1930s, the number of Chinese people in the Netherlands had clearly decreased. While some had returned home by their own means with their dreams shattered, several hundred "economically useless" Chinese were deported by the Rotterdam Police. The Chinatown in Rotterdam's Katendrecht, which was recognized as the biggest Chinatown in Europe in the 1920s, completely disappeared around the beginning of the 1940s (Meyer, 1983:32-44; Wubben, 1986:174; Zeven, 1987:62).

In May 1940, Germany attacked the Netherlands. Within five days the Germans had occupied the whole country. Sharing their hardship with the Dutch people, the Chinese in the Netherlands suffered from the ensuing privations: shortages of food and clothes, which was exacerbated by living in constant fear of Nazi persecution. Although the Chinese hated Japanese fascism, some Chinese during that dangerous period had to pretend that they were Japanese in order to survive the racial policies of Germany. Their suffering was made even more painful because during the war the Chinese lost all contacts with their families in China, some of them forever.

There are many such harrowing stories:

> In 1934, my father left for Europe when I was only three months old. He told my mother that he would be back as soon as he had earned some money [...] Before the war, my father had sent some money back to his parents and my mother. However, the war stopped the correspondences between my father and mother. My mother died during the war. My father could not know this until he found his way back home in 1956. His heart was broken [...] He often said to me in his later life that he felt so sorry for my mother that the pain in his heart could never be alleviated.[24]

> I jumped ship in Holland just before the war broke out. Of course I didn't know a war was imminent, otherwise I would have stayed together with

my family in our hometown. After the war broke out, I lost contact with
my wife and my three children. During that difficult period, however, I
took up whatever hard, dirty work there was to make a living since I
always thought that my wife and children were waiting for me in my
hometown [...] As soon as the war ended, I tried to contact my family. At
last, I got a letter from one of my relatives. But all he could tell me was
that my wife and three children had all died on one and the same occasion
when the Japanese bombed the city [...] If I were at home, I would have
been able to help them find a place to shelter, they would not have died
[...] The last half of my life has been full of failures, I know that I am being
punished [...][25]

Like that of the Dutch people, the history of the Chinese in the Netherlands
during the Second World War is full of blood, tears, and hatred of fascism.

B *Chinese emigration from outside of mainland China (1950-1975)*

The end of the Second World War brought an economic rebirth to the
Netherlands and its people. With this rejuvenation, the Chinese in the Neth-
erlands successfully found a new approach to earn a living: developing the
Chinese catering business.

The 1960s and 1970s were the never-had-it-so-good years for the Chinese
catering business in the Netherlands. It seemed as if Chinese restaurants had
been scattered all over the Netherlands in just one night. In 1947, there were
only 23 Chinese restaurants in the whole of the Netherlands (Chen, 1991:29).
Towards the end of the 1970s, the total number had reached about two
thousand. Moreover, business was excellent for almost every one. They were
so popular that shortages of cooks and workers became a serious problem.
Where could those Chinese restaurateurs find suitable workers for their restaurants?

It is a well-known phenomenon of Chinese chain-migration that established migrants bring over their *qin peng hao you*[26] from their hometown whenever they need them. However, during that golden age of Chinese restaurants, this tradition did not hold. The reasons for this can be traced to the
political changes that took place in mainland China.

The People's Republic of China was established in 1949. Since then,
Chinese nationals have been educated to dedicate their entire life to the
construction of a prosperous, new China. For quite a long period, both this
patriotic education and the strict control of emigration proved highly effective all over mainland China. Under such circumstances, it became very
difficult for the Chinese settled in the Netherlands to bring over workers
directly from their hometowns in mainland China. For instance, Wencheng,
a *qiaoxiang* county in Wenzhou district, has had a emigration tradition since
the beginning of the 20th century. By the end of the Second World War,
there were about 420 villagers making their living in Europe. Though more
and more Wencheng people were developing businesses in Europe and were

in need of more labourers, emigration from Wencheng remained very low. More precisely, during the 20 years between 1950 and 1969, only 130 Wencheng people were able to go abroad.[27]

In order to augment their manpower, the Chinese restaurateurs in the Netherlands had to switch to promising areas outside mainland China. Therefore, Chinese immigration in this period was characterized by thousands of Chinese, in pursuit of work in Chinese restaurants, migrating or re-migrating from outside mainland China into the Netherlands. As a result, the Hong Kong Chinese became the largest Chinese immigrant group among the Chinese immigrant community in the Netherlands. During this period, the emigration tide from Hong Kong surged upward twice.

The first tide appeared around the turn of the 1960s. Closer examination shows that these people from Hong Kong could be divided into two sub-groups. One group included the native peasants of Hong Kong. For instance, during the period from 1958 to 1961, the so-called "vegetable revolution" took place in the New Territories of Hong Kong. Vegetable cultivation and industrial parks quickly replaced the traditional rice economy. As a result, because many native peasants had to look for alternative means of livelihood, the highest emigration tide after the Second World War was provoked. Many peasants grabbed the opportunity to find their future in Britain because of the special relationship between Hong Kong and that country and, more-over, because the Chinese restaurant trade was flourishing in Britain at this time. Their dream was to use a low-paid job, such as dishwasher or cook, in a Chinese restaurant as a stepping stone to becoming a Chinese restaurateur. With thousands of new job-seekers arriving in Britain, the opportunities became limited. Since there were more and better opportunities to achieve their goals in the Netherlands, some immigrants quickly altered their plans and focussed on this possibility.

Another sub-group among the Hong Kong migrants was composed of newcomers from mainland China, who had arrived in Hong Kong either around or after the period of the birth of the People's Republic of China. Among these newcomers, Bo On people constituted an attractive pool of labourers. After 1950, the border between the People's Republic of China and Hong Kong was closed.[28] It became a criminal offense to escape from communist Bo On county to capitalist Hong Kong. Disregarding severe retributions, from 1951, due to the wide gap in the economic situation between the two areas, clandestine escapes from Bo On to Hong Kong happened and did not stop completely until the end of the 1970s. Thanks to the initiative and help of the pioneer settlers in the Netherlands, some of these migrants re-emigrated from Hong Kong to the Netherlands. When facing outsiders, these new immigrants, rather than identifying themselves as Bo On people, preferred to be known as Hong Kong people.[29] The reason can be traced to two causes. Firstly, the "reach-base policy" pursued by the Hong Kong government meant that almost all of those Bo On people had in fact become Hong Kong citizens when they re-emigrated to the Netherlands.[30] Therefore, they are *Hong Kong ren* (Hong Kong people or Hong Kong citizens) rather than *Bo*

On ren (Bo On people). Secondly, to proclaim that they are *Hong Kong ren* was also a normal reflex of the attempt to erase their illegal actions while the strict injunctions were still in force in their hometown.[31]

During the late 1960s, there was another emigration wave from Hong Kong. In 1967, as a sort of spillover from the Cultural Revolution in mainland China, a large riot was triggered in Hong Kong that scared many residents and caused others to take flight.[32] Although most of them emigrated to the United States and Canada, some also found their way to the Netherlands.

After some Hong Kong people had settled down in the Netherlands, a new chain-migration was set in motion. In fact, some Zhejiang interviewees commented that, because the only workers they could recruit were Hong Kong people, the Zhejiang restaurateurs had to learn the Hong Kong dialect (i.e., Cantonese) to be able to communicate with their employees. Consequently, the Hong Kong culture has since then dominated the Chinese community in the Netherlands. Other chapters will discuss this further.

During the same period, the Chinese immigrants who re-emigrated from Southeast Asia formed another labour source for the Chinese catering business in the Netherlands. This group of people can be roughly divided into two types: one seeking employment as Chinese restaurant workers; the other one re-emigrating for political reasons.

The first type of emigrants came mainly from Singapore and Malaysia. As early as the first quarter of the 20th century, Singapore was another principal emigration destination of Wenzhou people (Wang, 1985; Zhang, 1987; Li, 1996). According to the trade segmentation among the Singapore Chinese, Wenzhou immigrants were labelled a carpenter group.[33] Attracted by their co-villagers' persuasion and stories about the much better economic opportunities in the Netherlands, a few hundred Wenzhou people came to the Netherlands in the 1960s. As one man put it, "it is quicker to earn money by cooking than by woodworking."[34]

Another re-emigrated group included Peranakan Chinese from Indonesia and political refugees from Indochina. After the independence proclamation of Indonesia in 1945, some Chinese who had worked for the Dutch colonial government left for the Netherlands with their families. Meanwhile, others who had no confidence in the new national government of Indonesia also took up their Dutch citizenship and tried to find a way to emigrate. Thus, in 1948 there were about 400 Peranakan Chinese in the Netherlands; this number rose to about 1,400 in 1957 (van Galen, 1987:144).[35] After the massacre on 30 September, 1965 (the persecution of communists and presumed leftists in Indonesia), the Netherlands once more became a destination for many Dutch-speaking Chinese who once had studied in the Netherlands or had learned the language in the Netherlands Indies.

Between 1975 and 1982, the Dutch government accepted about 6,500 Vietnamese as political refugees. Among them, about one-fourth were *Hoas*, or ethnic Chinese (Kleinen, 1987:177). This group migrated to the Netherlands, straddling both this and the next period of immigration.

Finally, the Surinamese-Chinese formed a large ethnic group who emigrated from outside of China to the Netherlands in this period as well. Surinam was a Dutch colony but proclaimed its independence in 1975. There are approximately 4,000 Surinamese-Chinese now living in the Netherlands; most of them arrived during the mid-1970s (Tseng, 1983: 63-68).

In sum, after the above-mentioned new immigrant groups arrived in the Netherlands, their diverse original backgrounds played a role in the degree to which distinctions within the Chinese immigrant community were felt or even stressed.

C *A sudden rising tide of emigration from mainland China (after 1976)*

In the last quarter of the 20th century, from those well-known *qiaoxiang* areas, such as the Wenzhou and Qingtian districts, the flow of emigration to Europe has been far greater than anything experienced during the first three-quarters of the century. For instance, according to an unofficial statistic, more than 70000 Wenzhou people emigrated between 1984 and 1995, most of whom went to Europe.[36] The following chart clearly shows the incomparably high emigration wave from *qiaoxiang* Wencheng that rose in the 1980s.

Chart 2 *Emigration waves rising in Wencheng county (1910-1990)*

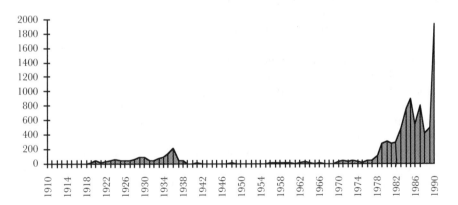

Source: Wencheng xian zhi [Wencheng county chronicles].

What are the factors behind the latest emigration wave from mainland China? Wenzhou is a good example to illuminate the factors from a Chinese perspective. During the last quarter of the 20th century, the motivation behind the going abroad mania in Wenzhou can be studied from at least three perspectives.

First, the social position of *Huaqiao* has shifted from a "betraying one's motherland" label to a term of actual admiration. After the establishment of the People's Republic of China, the position of *Huaqiao* in mainland China was delicate. On the one hand, the central government officially honoured well-known patriotic overseas Chinese, such as Tan Kah Kee.[37] On the other hand, the socialist revolution regarded most overseas Chinese as bourgeoisie or petty-bourgeoisie and targetted them for remolding.[38] The following story told by one of my interviewees is representative of the consequences of this ambiguity:[39]

> My father went abroad when I was only a few months old. Then he lost contact with my mother. I was brought up by my mother, in very difficult circumstances [...] During the early 1950s, I joined the People's Army. I had done excellent work in the army. I was told that I had been selected as a prospective officer and I was full with a sense of pride [...] Suddenly, all of my life changed. My father appeared! He came back from the Netherlands to find his only son whom he had left behind [...] Very soon, I was asked to leave the army since I had become a person with so-called *haiwai guanxi* [overseas relations]. I tried to explain that my father was a patriotic overseas Chinese, that he loves communist China; however, it was useless. I was demobilized from the army. I could not enjoy the Party's trust any more.

Although there are no public documents from the central government indicating that all of the *Huaqiao* were suspected of betraying one's motherland, the *Huaqiao*, as well as their relatives, would often come under suspicion: few of them could join the army; few of them could become cadres of government; and even fewer still could pass the repeated strict examinations to become a member of the Chinese Communist Party. Particularly during the period of the so-called Cultural Revolution, people having *haiwai guanxi* or, in other words, those with relatives or contacts abroad were regarded as a kind of reactionary social source.[40] Because of heavy social pressure, many Chinese who returned from overseas dared not to keep up any contact with their relatives abroad. Any one receiving a letter from abroad was supposed to immediately give a report to the officials concerned. Thus, at that time, being labelled as having *haiwai guanxi* was extremely dangerous; more so if one openly expressed a desire to go abroad, which would undoubtedly be regarded as treason, and against Chinese nationalism and patriotism. This situation has changed since the end of the Cultural Revolution.

In 1977, the late Deng Xiaoping pointed out:[41]

> There is a saying that overseas relations make things complicated and the people with overseas relations cannot be trusted. Such a saying is reactionary [...] Now we have too few overseas relations rather than too many. [Having overseas relations] is something excellent, which can help us to establish contacts abroad from various perspectives.

In 1992, Deng said again:[42]

China is different from other countries all over the world. We have our specific opportunities. For instance, we have several tens of millions of patriotic Chinese abroad. They have made great contributions to their motherland.

Since then, special departments have been set up to implement the policies regarding the care of *Huaqiao* and *qiaowu*. Protecting the rights and interests of overseas Chinese and their relatives has been stressed repeatedly. All returned *Huaqiao* or their relatives who were punished because of their *haiwai guanxi* have been rehabilitated. And the private property (houses, stocks, gold, jewelry or savings) confiscated during the Cultural Revolution has been returned to the owners. The social position of *Huaqiao* has risen since then.

As Western countries developed more friendly relations with China, as China opened its door to the outside world by strengthening its links with Western countries, and as more and more Chinese from abroad became investors or intermediaries for foreign investment, the social position of *Huaqiao* rose even higher. In fact, *Huaqiao* as a whole have been thought of as enjoying both fame and wealth. Conjunctively, younger Chinese view Western countries as rich, strong, prosperous, and full of opportunities to realize their dreams. Many are particularly curious about and yearn for experiences abroad — especially in the developed Western countries, and thus the emigration tide has risen.

Secondly, the fact that the Chinese government has softened its severely defined emigration policies to conform to international rules has lowered an emigration barrier. In China, applying for a private passport is the first step for emigrating or going abroad. During the 1950s and 1960s, only a very limited number of direct family members of the Chinese abroad were allowed to go through the strictly defined procedure of applying for a passport. There were unwritten rules that influenced emigration as well. For example, attempts were made to *persuade* at least a couple of persons from the remaining emigrants' families to stay in the hometown.[43]

The government did not revise this policy until the 1980s. Then, in those *qiaoxiang* areas, the relevant policies of applying for a private passport were revamped. In short, a private passport could now be issued to the following people: those who hold official documents to prove that they can be accepted by another country, i.e., for family reunion, for visiting relatives or for further study, and those who have already possessed a working permit from the destination country.

Wenzhou city is a good example of the effects of those policies. Between 1950 and 1956, there were only 20 persons who were permitted to get passports and join their family member(s) abroad. Since 1980, each year more than four thousand Wenzhou people have been issued a private passport. In some years, like 1987, 1989, and from 1990 to 1993, the number of people who received passports was more than seven thousand. Investigations carried out in Wenzhou city in 1982 and 1983 show that 80 per cent of the passport applicants did indeed receive a passport.[44] Since the early 1990s, going on a holiday tour abroad could be an acceptable reason for applying for a passport. Obviously, the government's updated emigration policies benefit prospective migrants.

The last important cause for the emigration mania in Wenzhou is that since the pursuit of material well-being is no longer taboo in mainland China, potential economic betterment in wealthy countries has effectively pushed the Chinese into going abroad.

This motivation is a direct result of the economic reform movement itself. For instance, Wenzhou, the first potential source area for large-scale emigration flows to the Netherlands, belongs to the experimental zone of China, and economic progress there has been greater than in many other parts of China. However, another related phenomenon deserves attention: one of the economic reform movement's results is that many persons' expectations and value orientation have changed. The wish for material prosperity cherished by some people has grown in a very short period to unrealistic proportions. People quickly accepted increases in incomes and other rewards which were the benefits of the economic reform as normal. In other words, although the living standards are rising, the aspirations and expectations of the people are rising even more quickly. This is suggestive of the well-known concept of relative deprivation (Merton & Kitt, 1950). In the words of Robin Williams:

> [R]aising the incomes of all does not increase the happiness of all [...]Individuals assess their material well-being, not in terms of the absolute amount of goods they have, but relative to a social norm of what goods they ought to have [...] [W]hen levels of real income received are rising for a majority of a population over a substantial period, there will be increases in expected levels, in aspirations, and in feelings that the achieved levels are appropriate and deserved (that is, an increase in levels of normative claim). (Williams, 1976:360-361)

In Zhejiang *qiaoxiang*, conscious or unconscious feelings of relative economic deprivation provided the people with stronger incentives to become still richer; correspondingly, the so-called *conspicuous consumption* exhibited by some returned migrants resulted in a heightening of the esteem of all *Huaqiao*.[45] During my research in Wenzhou district, I saw returned migrants or their relatives display some signs of conspicuous consumption. For instance, there are commodious houses in the suburbs and the countryside. Also, extravagant mausoleums are scattered across the countryside. Interestingly, many owners of those houses and family mausoleums are still living in Europe. In fact, some tombs have been prepared for the younger generation who were born abroad and are still children. Both the migrants and local villagers regard commodious houses and extravagant family mausoleums as symbols of wealth and social status.[46] It is safe to say that high expectations about Europe — and not the poor living conditions in the *qiaoxiang* areas like Wenzhou — provoked the emigration wave (Li, 1996).

Now let us turn to an overview of the Dutch and Western European perspective. As was noted at the beginning, instead of only focussing on the Netherlands itself, it is important to look around at its neighbouring countries and sometimes to look at Western Europe as a whole.

Because it is composed of highly developed countries, Western Europe is highly attractive to people from the Third World. For instance, in Wenzhou *qiaoxiang*, whenever asked about their personal knowledge of Europe, the interviewees would without exception immediately talk about how high the wages are there. Many interviewees know rather precisely that the average wage of a cook in a Chinese restaurant in the Netherlands is about 2,500 guilders a month. In the early 1990s, this amount of income was 75 times the average income of a peasant in Wenzhou, or about 60 times that of a peasant in Rui'an and nearly 140 times that of a peasant in Wencheng.[47] Without relating this wage to the cost of living in the Netherlands, in the eyes of Wenzhou people, this salary seems astonishingly high. Moreover, the most attractive point — regardless of its validity — is that you can expect a high income in any European Chinese restaurant, without any special skill,[48] without any investment capital, and even without any knowledge about the host society, if only you are a hardworking person.

Another cluster of causes is related to the lenient immigrant policies of some West European countries, many of which have significantly lowered their entrance barriers. This point can be seen from both sides.

First, almost all West European countries have kept doors open for migration through the family reunion principle. For Chinese, however, family (*jia*) is a broad concept whose boundary is not clearly defined (Fei 1992b). For instance, all brothers and sisters, either married or not yet married, belong to one family. Their children also belong to the family. Sometimes even only sharing the same family name will be taken as sufficient evidence for membership of one great family.

Second, in the 1960s and 1970s, many Western European countries recruited guest workers, and thus lenient immigration policies were in place. The same period was also the golden time for Chinese restaurants in Europe, which desperately needed large numbers of cheap workers. Many Chinese immigrants remember distinctly that up through the first years of the 1980s as long as you could *prove* you were a certified Chinese cook, you could easily get a work permit and visa for European countries such as the Netherlands or France.

Since the late 1980s, several European countries have tightened their immigration policies. Consequently, illegal migration to Europe has become an issue. One of the crucial factors behind illegal immigration is that the policies of Western European countries offer illegal immigrants some hope. For instance, potential migrants in Wenzhou are told by *shetou* (black migration brokers) that regardless of whether you are legally or illegally in a Western European country, you can expect to receive a residence permit from the government if you can prove that you are a victim of the family planning policy or political movements in China.

Illegal immigrants also hope for the occasional reprieve that allows illegal immigrants to legalize their stay: the regularization law. In January 1996, as soon as I settled down in Wenzhou to begin my research there, I found that a hot topic of conversation among my interviewees was the most recent regularization law in Italy. After successively putting three such laws into effect that directly involved the Chinese (i.e., in 1981, 1986 and 1990; cf. Montanari & Cortese, 1993: 280-281; Tomba, 1997; Carchedi and Ferri, 1998), Italy promulgated its fourth regularization law at the end of 1995. More or less like the first three laws, this new law regularized immigration by legalizing the stay of irregular immigrants who were either in paid employment or self-employed. Although the procedures stipulated by the law would be very costly, many families of illegal migrants throughout Europe were excited about this law. As I mentioned earlier, the Chinese tend to look at Western Europe as a single entity, and the internal borders between most European Union countries are known to be hardly guarded. Illegal immigrants are confident that they can easily leave any Western European country where they have temporarily settled and go to Italy to apply for a residence permit. Many also believe that what has happened today in Italy might also happen in some other European countries tomorrow.[49]

It is clear that the motivations analyzed above are interrelated. The Chinese emigration to the Netherlands, like all other human migrations, is a social process which has been historically conditioned. In the principal *qiaoxiang* of European Chinese, one can clearly observe that a kind of *culture of emigration*[50] has emerged: as *qiaoxiang* people, they are proud of their special social position and that their family life and expectations can be closely connected with the wealth of Europe. They believe that *getting rich quickly in Europe* is their common destiny.[51]

2 *Changes of size and composition*

The size and composition of the Chinese community in the Netherlands have clearly changed because of the developments in the last decades of the 20th century. There are a number of explanatory trends that need to be explored.

First, the general population of Chinese immigrants in the Netherlands has consistently and strongly risen since the Second World War. The following is a chart to portray the development of the Chinese population in the Netherlands.

There are, however, estimated statistics that vary somewhat. During my interviews between 1986 and 1988, I was often told that there were about 60,000 Chinese in the Netherlands. By 1995, when I began my second study on the Chinese in the Netherlands, the population had obviously increased. By conservative estimates there are about 80,000 Chinese in the Netherlands. Some Chinese association leaders, and sometimes the diplomatic officials of the Chinese Embassy in the Netherlands as well, usually say that there are 100,000 ethnic Chinese in the Netherlands. According to a source book published by the Overseas Chinese Affairs Commission of ROC, however, in

Chart 3 *General population of Chinese immigrants in the Netherlands*

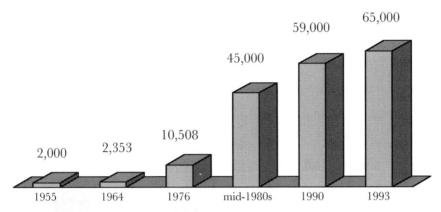

Sources
1955:   ZGQZXH, 1956:79, 85;
1964:   OCEYB, 1968:452. The editor points out that the statistics were supplied
            by the Dutch Minister of Justice on 13 June 1964;
1976:   Voets & Schoorl, 1988:130. But the number only includes the ethnic
            Chinese who emigrated from PRC, Hong Kong and Singapore;
mid-1980s: Benton & Vermeulen, 1987:10;
1990:   Pieke & Benton, 1998:137;
1993:   ACB & LFCON, 1994:10.

the mid-1990s there were up to 120,000 ethnic Chinese residing in the Netherlands. The editor of the book proclaims that the relevant statistics were provided by the Dutch Ministry of the Interior (OCEYB, 1996:619).

It is not possible to trace the exact number of Chinese immigrants living in the Netherlands today since the census statistics dealing with migrants are notoriously difficult to verify. The numbers quoted above, however, are at least clear enough to give a general profile to show the changing demography of the Chinese in the Netherlands during the second half of the 20th century.

A second trend is that the gender ratio of Chinese immigrants became balanced. According to one investigative document written by the Rotterdam Police in 1932, while there were about 1,200 Chinese living in dozens of Chinese boarding houses located in Katendrecht in Rotterdam, there was not one Chinese woman among them (van Heek, 1936:61). One of my informants, Mr. ChB, confirmed that the first Chinese female migrant from China (not including the Peranakan Chinese) did not arrive in the Netherlands until as late as 1936.[52] Another informant, Mr. LK, also mentioned that until 1946, only four Chinese women came directly from China and settled down in the Netherlands.[53] An investigation in *qiaoxiang* Wencheng shows that among the 1,309 Wencheng people who went abroad before 1948, only eight of them were women.[54] As an anecdote, I possess about ten historical photos of Chinese living in the Netherlands before the Second World War. The people in these photos, with the exception of diplomatic officials' wives from the Chinese Embassy, were exclusively male.

Since the 1950s, this remarkable gender has slowly changed, but it did not reach an almost equal level until the 1980s. In 1985, some volunteers sent by a Chinese association (CCRM) visited 392 Chinese in the Netherlands. The following chart is the result of their investigation, although the samples for investigation were limited and the interviewing volunteers were not professionals (cf. INFO Krant, 22 November 1985).

Chart 4 *Gender ratio among the new Chinese immigrants*

In 1988, two Dutch scholars of the Dutch Interuniversity Demography Institute published a report on demography development and composition of the Chinese in the Netherlands (Voets & Schoorl, 1988). From the figures given by this report, the changing process of gender ratio among the Chinese immigrants in the Netherlands can be calculated. It shows that, in 1956, of all Chinese from the People's Republic of China living in the Netherlands, only 25 per cent were women. This figure rose to about 46 per cent in 1975, indicating that the gender ratio became almost equal (ibid., 1988:12 & 16).[55]

As the gender ratio became more balanced, more and more Chinese made a home in the Netherlands. In 1987, CCRM investigated the composition of its INFO Krant's readers through its distribution network. The result indicated that there were 7,709 Chinese families in the Netherlands.[56] Another census showed that among the Chinese immigrants, 61 per cent lived within families (Pieke, 1988:33).

In short, with its population growing in size and its composition changing, the Chinese community in the Netherlands as a whole changed from a single-male society to a society composed of individual families. This transition marked the beginning of a new historical period of the Chinese migration process to the Netherlands. This indicates that Chinese immigrants in the Netherlands have changed from an exclusively male group to a community composed of thousands of family units; from a sojourning group to a community composed of settlers.

The third important trend that relates to the demographic changes in the Chinese immigrant population is the composition of their nationality. Some scholars have pointed out that the tendency of the Chinese to become naturalized as a Dutch citizen is surprisingly strong (Penninx et al. 1993:88). One Dutch scholar advanced some explanations for the tendency:

(i) the desire to escape from the political and/or socio-economic situation in China;
(ii) the uncertainty about the future of Hong Kong and the limited rights associated with the British Hong Kong passport;
(iii) the anxiety about the restrictive policies of the Dutch government towards further recruitment of Chinese (Groenendijk, 1987).

According to my study, some very practical motives may also be added. For instance, some Chinese are afraid that having non-Dutch nationality could affect the security of their business or chances of promotion. Others applied for naturalization to make travelling more convenient. And recently, some Chinese businessmen were motivated by their desire to share China's preferential treatment to foreign investors.

Massive changes of nationality have profound implications. Once more and more Chinese have become naturalized Dutch citizens, the idea of the Chinese community as a temporary and sojourning group becomes a thing of the past. Their present life and their future are rooted in the host society rather than in their original country. This is reflected in the registration patterns of Chinese organizations. For instance, those associations organized before the Second World War would register at the Chinese Embassy first, and now newly founded Chinese associations only register with the Dutch authorities.

The change of nationality brings with it a kind of identity crisis, which became a new issue for Chinese immigrants. Those who are naturalized Dutch citizens know they will spend most of their life in this Western country. Nevertheless, they are not, and can never be, *really* Dutch in their own mind nor in the eyes of the Dutch. This ambivalence will be studied again in the discussion of organizational motivations.

3 Sub-groups within the Chinese immigrants

Now that the common features of Chinese immigrants have been discussed, let us turn to their differences. Though sharing similar appearances and the same cultural roots, which clearly distinguish the Chinese immigrants from other ethnic groups, are there any recognized internal divisions within the Chinese community in the Netherlands today?

Before going into a detailed study of the Chinese immigrants' associations, it is necessary to delineate the sub-groups that exist within the Chinese community in the Netherlands. Generally speaking, the two groups that have dominated the community are labelled as Guangdong people (or Hong Kong people or Cantonese-speaking group) and Zhejiang people (or Wenzhou and Qingtian group). Their organizational activities are the primary subject of this study. Besides them, a number of smaller groups make up about one-third of the Chinese community.

A *The Guangdong people*

The Guangdong group is the largest sub-group among the Chinese immigrants in the Netherlands. The Chinese immigrants themselves believe that the Guangdong group has always comprised more than one-third of the Chinese immigrants in the Netherlands.

After the 1960s, because of the migration process described above, the Guangdong or Hong Kong group has greatly increased its influence among the Chinese immigrants. It is worth pointing out that the people identifying themselves as belonging to this group not only include those whose original hometowns are in Guangdong or Hong Kong, but also those who had settled down in Hong Kong for a while before they came to the Netherlands. The common feature of this group is that their first language is Cantonese. Since Cantonese has become the dominating market language within the Chinese immigrants in the Netherlands, the dialect does not produce subgroup cohesion. Moreover, different political orientations — such as whether they are more oriented towards Beijing or Taiwan — have also weakened the cohesion.

This group includes most of the richest Chinese restaurateurs. As was mentioned earlier, many people of this group arrived in the blooming period of the Chinese catering trade and have benefitted greatly from it. The people of this group own a major part of the big Chinese restaurants in major Dutch cities, such as Amsterdam, The Hague and Rotterdam. Moreover, some also grasped the opportunities to expand their business in establishing grocery shops, travel agencies, accounting and bookkeeping firms, import and export firms, computer companies and so on. Currently, most Chinese ethnic services business in the Netherlands are run by people of this group.

In addition, this group is dominated by Hong Kong culture. From the glossaries found in their publications to the textbooks used in their after-school Chinese schools, from the videotape rentals in the video shops to the organizing of feasts and parties, the imprints of Hong Kong culture are easily recognizable.

This is a group that needs more social attention. Since a great part of this group arrived in the 1960s and the 1970s, more and more have found themselves at the heart of problems towards the end of the 20th century; problems such as how to help oneself when becoming older and sick, how to bridge the generation gap when children have grown up in the Western world, whether to spend the rest of their life in the host country or return to their hometown; etc.

The last characteristic of this group is their special relations with their hometown. Since 1979, the Shenzhen Special Economic Zone, the former centre of the Bo On, has been developed as the economic example of China. This development greatly benefitted the natives of Shenzhen. Since Shenzhen was designed as a special zone of China, a vast amount of money from all over China has been invested in industrial enterprises and commercial buildings. Consequently, the price of land in Shenzhen has consistently risen over a long period. Based on this development, the native residents of Shenzhen, who were mostly peasants, easily made profits from their private land.

For example, the several million people who rushed to Shenzhen because of the economic boom needed to find places for accommodation, and thus about 300,000 native Shenzhen people became the landlords to 3,000,000 newcomers. To build houses on their private land and then rent them out has become the most popular method for many native Shenzhen people to make higher profits. In addition, some use their land as an investment in their shares from the enterprise(s) which have been established on their land. Some even have established their own workshops on their land to become the new entrepreneurs. Such big changes affected the Shenzhen expatriate's opinions about their emigration. Some interviewees told me that now they regret emigrating. The perception is that if they were still living in Shenzhen, they would have had many more opportunities than what they can find as an outsider in the Netherlands. The changing relations between the emigrants and their hometown is one of the key topics of Chapter VII.

B *The Zhejiang people*

Due to their common district of origin, people from the Wenzhou and Qingtian districts have formed another greatly visible sub-group among the Chinese immigrants in the Netherlands. They are named Zhejiang *ren* (i.e., Zhejiang people), according to the name of their original province, or just Wenzhou *ren* or Qingtian *ren*, because the people from the Wenzhou and Qingtian areas are strongly represented in this group.

This is the second largest sub-group of the Chinese immigrants in the Netherlands. According to the figures offered by the Dutch Central Bureau of Statistics, on 1 January 1993 there were about 14,000 Chinese immigrants in the Netherlands who had been born in the People's Republic of China (ACB & LFCON 1994:18), i.e., about one-fifth of the Chinese community. According to the *Overseas Chinese Economy Year Book* published in 1996, there are 25,000 migrants from mainland China residing in the Netherlands (OCEYB, 1996:619). Yet, according to the census statistics conducted by *qiaowu ganbu* from the Wenzhou area, there are 35,000 Wenzhou people living in the Netherlands, including both the Wenzhou emigrants and their children who were born abroad.[57]

The Zhejiang group has been regarded as a closely knit group by other Chinese in the Netherlands, although among them the people from Qingtian county, Wencheng county, Rui'an county or Wenzhou city each has, more or less, its own smaller group. The similar dialect used by Wenzhou and Qingtian people is a strong cohesive factor.[58] Any outsider, even native Chi-

nese, will be impressed by that peculiar dialect: its pronunciation is completely different from either *Putonghua* or other dialects widely used in south China.[59] Both Wenzhou and Qingtian people prefer to use their own dialect, in
spite of the fact that most of them can speak *Putonghua* very well.

As was mentioned above, most of the earliest Zhejiang migrants came as
pedlars, selling goods along the streets. Nevertheless, at the end of the 20th
century, a great part of the Zhejiang group consisted of mid- or small-scale
restaurateurs. Their restaurants are usually scattered in middle-sized or small
towns in the Netherlands. Furthermore, the high tide of emigration from the
Wenzhou and Qingtian districts to the Netherlands happened during the last
decades of the 20th century, when the golden period of the Chinese catering
business was already over. Therefore, some newcomers are still in the difficult
initiation period.

Zhejiang immigrants usually have maintained close ties with their home
community and have a strong desire to climb up the socio-economic ladder
not only in their adopted country but in their areas of origin as well. In
Wenzhou and Qingtian districts, *qiaoxiang* is a highly visible and respectable
social unit. *Qiaoxiang* people have been labelled as "a rich and lucky group."
The migrants' families left in the village have a favourable image of themselves and feel proud of the social mobility they have achieved.

Finally, this is a group with a clear mainland China background. With
their hometown located in mainland China, they are paying closer attention
to what is going on there. Some have made or are trying to make contributions to their respective home communities. This feature leaves a clear mark
on their organizational activities, which will be specifically discussed in Chapter VII.

C *Peranakan Chinese*

Another separate subgroup is the Peranakan Chinese. Even though they
clearly identify themselves as Chinese, they usually do not identify themselves
as equal to other "restaurant Chinese." At the same time, other Chinese
groups do not accept them as "real Chinese." To explain this, we must look
at differences between their social and cultural backgrounds. Socially speaking, many Peranakan Chinese are professionals that hold relatively higher
status than other Chinese do. Culturally speaking, the identity of Peranakan
Chinese has been modified by both cultural loss as well as cultural persist-
ence. Hereinafter, I am going to examine the group's distinguishing features
that set them apart in such a boundary position.

First, the differences in class status between Peranakan Chinese and other
"restaurant Chinese" are significant and carry their own implications. As
described above, their special migration background made the Peranakan
Chinese in the Netherlands a group with a noticeably higher level of education. Although some Peranakan Chinese who arrived before or soon after the
Second World War were rather poor, they have been successful in elevating
their social position from one generation to another. While most members of

other Chinese groups attain their means of livelihood in the Netherlands through the Chinese catering business, many of the adult Peranakan Chinese are professionals. For example, in the mid-1980s one Dutch writer found from the telephone lists that about one-third of the Peranakan Chinese have academic titles. Among them, there are at least five hundred people with full university degrees working in the medical sector as doctors, dentists, pharmacists and acupuncturists, about two hundred are engineers, and more than one hundred have graduated from law institutes (van Galen, 1987:145). From the 1950s up to the early 1980s, about 20 Chinese in the Netherlands were appointed to a professorship in either a university or an academic centre. Almost all of them were Peranakan Chinese (Li, 1995:45).[60]

A second distinguishing factor is that they are ethnic Chinese who were more familiar with the Indonesian culture than the Chinese culture. This is a group composed of a sprinkling of the first generation (China-born); some are third-, fourth-, or even fifth-generation Sino-Indonesians. *Peranakan* means children of the soil. To a certain degree, the Peranakan Chinese are the Chinese children of Indonesian soil. In Indonesia, many of them speak a modified form of the Indonesian language, prepare their food in Indonesian fashion, and maintain social relations with native people. In fact, most do not even speak Chinese any more. China is a distant and strange world to them. Few have had experience with China, except for maybe a short visit as a tourist. The Peranakan Chinese in the Netherlands have in fact more contacts with Indonesia than with China, since most of them still have family members, relatives and friends there.

Finally, China's assent toward global influence has acted as an impetus for the Peranakan Chinese to develop a sense of being Chinese. As was described above, the unfair treatment of the ethnic Chinese minority in Indonesia forced many of the Peranakan Chinese to re-emigrate from Indonesia to the Netherlands. This, of course, provoked those who had identified themselves as Indonesians to re-identify themselves. Living and working in the Netherlands has presented few adjustment problems for them, and many are Dutch citizens. However, because of their unchangeable physical appearance, the Dutch always look upon them as Chinese. Moreover, current developments in China have drawn a great deal of attention all over the world. The achievements of China in the last couple of decades have been highly praised. This situation doubtlessly encouraged some of the Peranakan Chinese to reassert their Chinese identity.

In sum, the differences in class status, level of education, and cultural background cannot be easily covered by the common ethnic identity of all Chinese immigrants. Thus, it is difficult for the Peranakan Chinese in the Netherlands to bridge the clear gap between them and other Chinese groups.[61]

Because they are a distinct group that deserves independent study, the association activities of the Peranakan Chinese, except when it might be of value to mention them for the sake of comparison, will not be included in this study.

D *Surinamese-Chinese*

The Surinamese-Chinese comprised about four thousand people in the 1980s (Tseng, 1983:69)[62] and five thousand in the 1990s (ACB & LFCON, 1994:19). There are three basic characteristics of this group.

First, though they are another re-emigrated group, most Surinamese-Chinese in the Netherlands are, in contrast to the Peranakan Chinese, first-generation immigrants from China and their offspring. Originally, most of them were Hakka people who lived in the villages of Guangdong. Chinese indentured coolies began arriving in Surinam in 1853. After the abolition of the contract labour system, the Chinese who had survived the hardship settled there, and some, step by step, set up a kind of private business. These people became the initiators of chain-migration. In the period from the end of the Second World War up to the 1960s, the Chinese community in Surinam quickly expanded as many newcomers arrived (Tseng, 1983:16, 23-28).

Second, this group is not as economically ambitious as the Zhejiang and Guangdong groups. Before their emigration to the Netherlands, many Surinamese-Chinese ran smaller businesses and shops in Paramaribo. Unlike the Zhejiang and Guangdong migrants, who hoped for economic advancement and material betterment, the original motivation of Surinamese-Chinese to emigrate to the Netherlands was a safer life. After arriving in the Netherlands, as nationals of an ex-colony of the Netherlands, they were entitled to Dutch citizenship and have enjoyed all social welfare benefits. This caused some ex-Surinamese-Chinese business people — in the face of a language barrier and a strange environment — to give up on establishing businesses in the Netherlands.[63]

The final basic characteristic is that they are divided into more or less two parts: one bigger part is formed by the first generation, and the other part is comprised of the younger immigrants who had a Dutch-language education in Surinam. After arriving in the Netherlands, the latter, with their similar ages and education background, formed their own social circles, which has been often seen as representative of all Surinamese-Chinese. The former, who did not have the necessary knowledge about the Netherlands, had to attach themselves to an established Chinese group. Due to their common district of origin, many selected the Guangdong group.

E *Singaporean- and Malaysian-Chinese*

The Singaporean- and Malaysian-Chinese have never become an independent group within the Chinese community in the Netherlands. The reason can be traced directly from their migration process. As was mentioned previously, most Singaporean- and Malaysian-Chinese were brought over by their personal relatives, friends or co-villagers to the Netherlands as workers for Chinese restaurants. For example, many Singaporean-Chinese are Wenzhou people by origin, and some Malaysian-Chinese are Cantonese-speaking. Therefore, automatically, each has closer contacts with or has simply joined the relevant established groups.

F *Vietnamese-Chinese*

During the first decade after their arrival, the Vietnamese-Chinese formed a small but tightly knit group. Having survived horrible disasters together, they kept close mutual contacts and information exchange. With their business experiences in Vietnam plus the warrant of special government care for refugees when they had just arrived, some have successfully opened Chinese restaurants, shops, and companies, while some tried to find employment, and some just depended on Dutch social security. The common memory of the disasters in Vietnam cannot act as a cohesive agent forever. The longer they stay in the Netherlands, the lower profile they have as a special group.

G *The Chinese* liuxuesheng *group*

Originally, the term *liuxuesheng* meant Chinese students studying abroad. Since 1979, studying in a Western country has become one of the most attractive goals for a majority of Chinese university students. Now, in the Netherlands, as in other developed Western countries, an independent Chinese *liuxuesheng* group includes not only those Chinese students who are studying in that country, but also those who finished their studies and are now working there. This term even includes their family members. Instead of a simple label indicating someone's temporary and transitional status, at least by now the concept of *liuxuesheng* has come to denote a fixed social identity. Once labelled *liuxuesheng*, they are willing to keep this social identity. Few will accept the changing of their status to a *Huaqiao*, although many in truth have transferred their status from a student to an immigrant.

This is a transient group. Some have left for either China or other countries, but more keep coming. By the mid-1990s, there were more than one thousand people belonging to the *liuxuesheng* group in the Netherlands.

H *Illegal Chinese migrants*

Facing the surge of emigration from developing countries, many developed Western countries have tried to control the immigrant influx by tightening up their immigration laws. This has resulted in a growing number of illegal migrants in these countries. For the whole of the Netherlands, the number of illegal immigrants from all different countries was estimated at between 100,000 to 150,000 at the beginning of the 1990s (Vos, 1994:93). Chinese form a small part of them.

In September 1996, one Chinese official of the Chinese Embassy in the Netherlands told me about the illegal immigrant situation. According to him, in 1995, nearly seven hundred illegal Chinese immigrants had been repatriated from the Netherlands to their hometowns through cooperation between the Dutch Ministry of Justice and the Chinese Embassy in the Netherlands.[64]

Among the illegal migrants from mainland China in the 1990s, most are from the following areas: Wenzhou and Qingtian districts, north Fujian and north Guangdong.[65] Some first came to pay a visit to their relatives or just as a tourist but stayed over after their visa expired. Some enter the country through intermediaries or, very often, through international smuggling networks.[66]

According to the information from my fieldwork in those areas, the fee charged by smugglers is terribly high and is much more than the natives can afford. For instance, at the end of the 1980s, the fee for smuggling a person from Wenzhou to Europe was about 100,000 Chinese dollars. In 1996, the fee rose to between 150,000 and 200,000 Chinese dollars.[67] In other words, the fee is about two hundred times the annual average income of a peasant in Wenzhou (Li, 1996).[68] Harbouring unrealistic expectations about Europe, some took money from local usurers.[69] Normally, the potential emigrants were asked to pay a certain amount of money (usually from a few thousand to ten thousand Chinese dollars) before leaving home. When they have been successfully smuggled into the destination country, they would call their relatives or friends who had already settled down in that country and ask them to pay the rest of the amount of money. Almost every one of them is deeply in debt.[70] Therefore, they urgently need to earn money quickly. Nevertheless, as undocumented workers, many are not able to find work in the Netherlands after their arrival. Those who are lucky enough to find a job are always forced to work for very low wages, and some have turned to crime against fellow Chinese.[71]

In general, the Chinese immigrant community in the Netherlands is far from a harmonious one. The differences within the community influence the development of their associations.

CHAPTER III

A History of Chinese Associations in the Netherlands

The initiation of the Chinese voluntary association in the Netherlands can be traced back to as early as the 1910s. In reviewing the development of the Chinese associations in the 20th century, two great upsurges become clear: the first unfolded in the 1930s; the second extended from the mid-1980s to the 1990s. According to the materials I have collected, during the second half of the 20th century, more than one hundred Chinese associations have proclaimed their establishment in the Netherlands, although more than half of them are nominal or rarely organize any public activities.

How have the Chinese associations in the Netherlands developed? How does any feature of the Chinese immigrant community examined earlier affect, and how is it affected by, the associations? What are the prevailing characteristics of the Chinese associations in the Netherlands? This chapter will attempt to give answers to these questions.

1 *Chinese associations before the Second World War*

According to the documents I have collected, the first Chinese association officially set up in the Netherlands was *Chung Hwa Hui* (Chinese association), organized by some Peranakan Chinese students in 1911. After 1911, with more and more Chinese coming from China to settle down in the Netherlands, the first well-known association of Chinese-speaking workers was established in Rotterdam on 9 January 1922, named *Wah Kiu Wei Kun* (*Chineesche Vereniging in Holland*; Chinese Association in Holland).[1] Subsequently, dozens of other Chinese associations were organized in Rotterdam and Amsterdam, but no one could compete with *Wah Kiu Wei Kun*. In the late 1930s, at the time when China was suffering under Japanese aggression, the first federation of Chinese organizations in the Netherlands was set up with *Wah Kiu Wei Kun* at the core. For patriotic reasons, the Chinese in the Netherlands united for the first time.

A *The first Chinese association: Chung Hwa Hui*

In October 1911, around twenty Peranakan Chinese students met together in a hotel in Amsterdam to establish their own ethnic association *Chung Hwa Hui* (hereafter CHH). This was the birth of the first official Chinese voluntary association in the Netherlands.[2] Herewith, I will focus on the relationship between CHH and other Chinese groups in the Netherlands instead of reiterating the comprehensive descriptions of CHH given in other studies (e.g., Galen, 1989; Liao, 1986).

The birth of CHH, first of all, was an extension of the Chinese nationalist movement, which emerged in the Netherlands East Indies around the turn of the 20th century. The Chinese in the former Netherlands Indies had a very long history of organization.[3] In 1900, the first nationwide modern Chinese ethnic association, *Tiong Hoa Hwee Koan* (hereafter THHK), was set up in Batavia (now: Jakarta) and shortly after established dozens of branches all over the Netherlands Indies.[4] Instead of limiting itself to a certain dialect or clan or district group, THHK stressed its role as an all-Chinese body representing one united nation. In fact, the term of *Tiong Hoa* means China or Chinese and *Hwee Koan* means Association; thus, THHK simply means Chinese Association. As a modern nationalist association whose major purpose was to improve the social position of the Chinese, the encompassing national identity of THHK was an example to others.[5] It became popular for all newly established Chinese associations to put *Tiong Hoa* in front of the association's real name, e.g., the *Tiong Hoa* Chamber of Commerce, the *Tiong Hoa* Sports Association, and so on (Li & Huang, 1987: 313-316).

Influenced by this, the association set up in the Netherlands by Peranakan Chinese students in this period strategically named itself *Chung Hwa*. Even though *Chung Hwa* and *Tiong Hoa* are pronounced and spelled differently, if written in Chinese characters, both terms are in fact the same, meaning Chinese or China. Thus, selecting *Chung Hwa* as the association's name reflected the founders' sense of a Chinese national identity.[6]

The birth of CHH was also a result of the trend of re-Sinification among the Peranakan Chinese students in the Netherlands. This was related to a variety of conditions present in the Netherlands at that time.

One reason was their disappointment with their inferior social position in the Netherlands. When living in the Netherlands East Indies, they had a sense of superiority because their families were much richer than most Chinese immigrants or the natives. They lost such privileges when studying in the Netherlands and living amongst the Dutch. They felt very uneasy belonging to a group of colonial people. However, China — their ancestral country — was an independent country with its Embassy in The Hague. In order to restore their self-respect, they turned back to China (although it was very strange to them) and tried to identify themselves as ethnic Chinese.

In addition, the cultural atmosphere in the Netherlands encouraged the trend of re-Sinification among the Peranakan Chinese students. It is said that the Chinese traditional culture "made a conquest of Europe" during the 17th and 18th centuries (Blussé, 1989:90). And the Dutch, due to their contacts with Chinese over a long period, played the role of middlemen by introducing and spreading Chinese culture in Europe. It is interesting to note that many Dutch people agreed with the common statement "the Dutch are the European Chinese": many felt the Chinese and Dutch shared a similar enterprising spirit (ibid., 1989:8).[7] Moreover, Delft and Leiden, two cities where most of the Peranakan Chinese lived and studied, were the two places where interest in Chinese cultural affairs was most apparent. For instance, the first position for a Professor of Sinology was established in Leiden University, and the best European-made Chinese porcelain was produced in Delft. In such a cultural atmosphere, it was not surprising that the Peranakan Chinese students' interest was re-oriented toward Chinese culture.

Although what those Peranakan Chinese students wanted from their re-Sinification was to improve their own social position in the Netherlands, the Chinese national identity made them, more or less, pay attention to their compatriots who were living in the Netherlands.

The activities of CHH also indicated their re-Sinification orientation. For instance, just like other Chinese groups, CHH made great efforts to establish closer contacts with the Chinese Embassy in the Netherlands. As an indication that their emotional life remained nostalgically oriented towards China, CHH first registered as a Chinese association at the Chinese Embassy soon after the association was set up. Moreover, the committee of CHH reported to the Chinese Embassy on their own initiative whenever a new lead group was elected. When a Chinese ambassador left his post for home and a new Chinese ambassador arrived, CHH would organize the members to send off the old and welcome the new. In 1919, while organizing a Chinese study class mainly for its members, CHH invited the Chinese ambassador, some officials of the Chinese Embassy and the famous Dutch Sinologist, Prof. J. J. L. Duyvendak, to give lectures. The chairman of CHH asked the Chinese ambassador to write the association's name in Chinese characters with a Chinese brush. Then the streamer was hung in the association's office in Leiden. Above the streamer, the picture of Dr. Sun Yat-sen was hung on the wall. After Sun Yat-sen passed away in 1925, before each meeting was in full session, all in attendance had to stand up and read Sun Yat-sen's Will in Dutch (cf. van Galen, 1987: 136-138; Tan, 1987:2-3).

Another event worth noting is the relationship between CHH and the Chinese working people in the Netherlands. Generally speaking, there is a gap between these two groups (cf. Chapter II). However, some special contacts were established in the 1930s. At that time, a worldwide economic crisis burst. Many Chinese working people were reduced to desperate poverty because they had been laid off by the Dutch shipping companies and could not find work ashore. Taking their difficulties into account, CHH tried to help some Chinese ex-seamen to tide over the crisis. In 1931, adopting Rotterdam Chinatown's original name — Katendrecht, CHH set up the Katendrecht Foundation. They collected clothes and money for the unemployed Chinese, to help the sick and to bury the deceased (Zeven, 1987:56-57).

In 1937, when China was suffering under Japanese aggression, some leaders and members of CHH established the *Hulp China Comite* (Help China Committee), charged with collecting money for China's resistance efforts. At that special period, Oey Kang Soey, the chairman of CHH's Leiden branch, played a leading role in collecting donations for China, attempted to set up a collection post in Amsterdam to help poor and sick Chinese, and elicited the support of some eminent Dutch people. He consequently enjoyed prestige among the Chinese working people living in Rotterdam and Amsterdam (Chen, 1991:25).

Nevertheless, people like Oey were rare.[8] Their efforts had less practical impact than they expected. It would be useful at this point to make a few observations about how some factors maintained the gap between the CHH's members and other Chinese.

First, as described in the last chapter, the gap was created by the significant difference in social status between the members of CHH and other Chinese workers. Although the CHH's members identified themselves as Chinese, some proclaimed openly that they were deeply frustrated by the fact that many Dutch did not know there were indeed two kinds of Chinese living in the Netherlands. Some felt ashamed when the Dutch could not distinguish them from those "pitiful peanut Chinese." Among the Chinese immigrants in the Netherlands, if comparing the Peranakan Chinese with the Chinese who directly came from China (either mainland or Hong Kong), the superiority complex of the Peranakan Chinese was apparent.

Second, the linguistic differences also presented an obstacle to the mutual communication between the CHH's members and Chinese workers. Usually, the Peranakan Chinese students would use Dutch or Malay as their daily language, while some might speak more or less Hokkian dialect (a dialect used in the south Fujian province of China). All the brochures published by CHH, except for the three Chinese characters of the association's name, were written in either Dutch or English. Most Chinese workers, however, could understand none of these languages; likewise, the dialects popularly used by them were not understood by the Peranakan Chinese.

Finally, the emotional orientation towards their original home differed between the CHH's members and other Chinese workers. For the majority of CHH's members, their nostalgia was toward the Indies rather than toward China. To them, the Netherlands Indies was their country of birth and the country where their families were living; thus, any political change or economic development that happened there had direct implications for them. They could not stop following the situation in that archipelago. Most of them thought of China as a strange and distant country. In CHH's brochures, the hot topic was the future of the Netherlands Indies and the position of the Chinese in that country (Suryadinata, 1981:51-53). Therefore, many returned to the Netherlands East Indies as soon as they finished their studies in the Netherlands. Some became famous doctors, lawyers or engineers in pre- and post-independent Indonesia, while some even became statesmen.[9]

CHH stopped all activities when the Netherlands was occupied by Nazi Germany. In August 1945, when Chinese in the Netherlands held a great parade to celebrate the end of the Second World War, CHH was among the organizers. During the 1950s, CHH kept rather a low social profile. Finally, it officially disbanded itself on 15 April 1962.

In general, the founding of CHH marks the beginning of the Chinese organizational activities in the Netherlands.

B *Wah Kiu Wei Kun and its historical position*

In the history of Chinese associations in the Netherlands, *Wah Kiu Wei Kun* was the first well-known association established by Chinese who came directly from China.

As was noted previously, since the early 20th century, Chinese seamen and pedlars were increasingly brought over and stayed in the Netherlands. Almost from the beginning, these Chinese lived in gangs that related to their areas of origin. Such a situation provided a fertile environment from which the Chinese organizations were later born.

In 1912, Chinese boarding houses began to be set up in the Netherlands, first in Amsterdam and soon after in Rotterdam. It is worth noting that from the very beginning, the tenants would usually be co-villagers of the boarding house owner. This trend was related to various connections — such as the same dialect, familiar customs — and often due to chain-introduction among the co-villagers themselves. Normally, the boarding house owners acted at the same time as shipping masters: they were brokers between their tenants and Western shipping companies; in other words, the tenants depended on the shipping master's introduction to find a job. Consequently, some shipping masters became important figures among the Chinese. Having control of dozens or even hundreds of young Chinese men, the master was Number One in his gang. Then, the Bo On group, Tung Kung group and Hakka group appeared. Between the 1910s and the 1930s, among Bo On people, Ng Ri Ming, Yat Ming, and Lew Sing were the powerful Number Ones; among Qingtian people, Wang Zhinan and Xue Dagui were the leaders; and among the Hakka people Ah Tam was best known.

As described in the last chapter, in the early period of Chinese settlement in the Netherlands, the Bo On group was the largest one among all the district Chinese groups. Thus, Bo On leaders exercised some influence outside their own group. As time passed, some attempted to become the representative of all Chinese in the Netherlands. The result was the birth of *Wah Kiu Wei Kun*.

On 9 January 1922, *Wah Kiu Wei Kun* was set up in Rotterdam. To stress that it would serve all of the Chinese in the Netherlands regardless of differences related to the areas of origin, the initiators named the association *Wah Kiu Wei Kun* (*Chineesche Vereniging in Holland*; hereafter WKWK).[10] If translated into English, the association's name would be the Chinese Association in Holland — an association aimed to be an umbrella for all of the Chinese in the Netherlands.

In order to highlight its position, WKWK applied to the Chinese government for recognition as an *official overseas Chinese association* as soon as it was set up. Through the support of the Chinese Consul in Amsterdam, the Chinese government approved the application.[11] Thus, WKWK enjoyed — at least in the eyes of its organizers — an authoritative position among the Chinese in the Netherlands.

Did WKWK behave and was it accepted as the only representative of all the Chinese in the Netherlands? The answer should be drawn from a study of its organizational structure and social functions and of its social significance from both the Chinese and the Dutch perspectives.

First, let us look at the composition of WKWK. Although its initiators clearly indicated their presumption of total Chinese representation, it was obvious that Bo On people were over-represented. Table 3 is a detailed list of WKWK's committee members in 1930. From the table, it is apparent that among the nine committee members, except for Mr. William Fung, the secretary for Western languages, all were Guangdong people. Furthermore, five, including chairman and vice-chairman, were co-villagers of Bo On. In the application form of WKWK to the government in 1930, the secretary reported that WKWK had around six hundred members.[12] Among them, more than 70 per cent were Guangdong people (van Heek, 1936:32). Only a small number of Wenzhou and Qingtian people joined the association.[13]

Table 3 *Committee members of WKWK in 1930*

Name	Date of birth	Place of birth	Occupation	Position in committee	Years in NL
Kwok Shu Cheung	21/1/1892	Bo On	Chinese restaurateur	Chairman	11
Wong Sing	9/8/1881	Bo On	Boarding-house owner	Vice-Chairman	9
William Fung	12/1/1906	Batavia	Administrator	Secretary for Western Languages	6
Liong Dai	11/11/1891	Tung-kung*	Administrator	Treasurer	6
Chan Soei Chun	15/2/1883	Toi San**	Chinese drug store owner	Second Commissioner	7
Sio Man	2/1/1888	Bo On	Bookkeeper	First Commissioner	8
Lim Soei Dauw	8/5/1883	Bo On	Bookkeeper	Substitute Commissioner	10
Yuen Fong	21/9/1894	Bo On	Administrator	Secretary for Chinese language	6
Lou Kie	8/8/1894	Tung-kung*	Boarding-house owner	Substitute Commissioner	8

* Tung-kung is a county in Guangdong Province, next to Bo On.
** Toi San is a county in Guangdong Province, a well-known qiaoxiang; most emigrants from this qiaoxiang went to the United States.

Source: Application Form of WKWK to the Central Bureau of Police in Rotterdam. The Form was filled out and presented by William Fung, on 10 September 1930. Agenda No. 87 / 20 / 1930; No. 2254 / 13766.

In reviewing the committee members' occupations and comparing their social position with that of most Chinese immigrants during that period, it is obvious that all of them had climbed up to the higher rungs of the socio-economic ladder. More precisely, the majority was composed of boarding-house owners. Although there were only two people in the list who had registered their occupations as boarding-house owner, according to the relevant documents, everyone except Yuen Fong was a boarding-house owner:

> *Kwok Shu Cheung* was a well-known rich Chinese boarding-house owner. Based on the successful running of his boarding house, he had established a Chinese restaurant at Delistraat 24, Rotterdam, in 1922, which was the first Chinese restaurant in Holland;
> *Liong Dai* had a boarding house at Delistraat 14, Rotterdam;
> *Chan Soei Chun* had a boarding house at Veerlaan 36, Rotterdam;
> *Sio Man* had a boarding house at Delistraat 10, Rotterdam;
> *Lou Kie* shared ownership of a boarding house with Tchai Ah Kiu at Delistraat 16, Rotterdam;
> *Lim Soei Dauw* shared ownership of a boarding house with Cheung Kwok Shu at Delistraat 22; and shared one with Choy Sang Young at Delistraat 26, Rotterdam;
> *William Fung* once had a boarding house at Delistraat 14, Rotterdam but sold out and moved to Amsterdam.[14]

Why did they not want to report themselves as boarding house owners? No direct explanation is clear. According to my study, I believe the potential motivation may come from the two angles. First, it may come from the wish that the various occupations of the committee members could reflect the general representation of the association. Second, since the Chinese boarding-house owners had earned money from their compatriots, few enjoyed a good reputation among the Chinese; in fact, some were even thought of as greedy exploiters. Such an image, to a certain degree, might make some boarding house owners hesitate to reveal their real occupation.[15]

In brief, the composition of WKWK shows that it is an association headed by a group of Chinese boarding house owners; its membership was mainly derived from Guangdong people, among which the Bo On group is at the core.

The social functions performed by WKWK are another important issue. According to the constitution of WKWK, its intentions were as follows:

A. To promote good understanding among all Chinese staying in the Netherlands;
B. To offer help to all Chinese in the Netherlands who need support.[16]

In Article 8, there were some further explanations of the association's functions:

Every member of the association who is impecunious and who is of Chinese nationality may expect the following help from the association:
A. He may expect financial support from the association if he is sick;
B. He may expect that the association will help him to return to China if he is disabled but wishes to go back home;
C. He may expect that the association would help to arrange the funeral when a member has passed away.

In order to put its constitutional propositions into effect, WKWK set up an office located at Lombok Straat 5, Rotterdam. Often one or two staff members were arranged by WKWK committee to perform the routine duties of the association: to accept visitors and listen to their requests; to help its members to contact Dutch police or government; and to send money or gift parcels to those members who were seriously sick or living in straitened circumstances.

During the late 1920s, WKWK established a quasi-enforcement power over its members through the refusal of services. According to its regulations, whenever coming back from a sea trip, all Chinese seamen had to pay 50 cents as membership dues to the association. In addition, all Chinese boarding-house owners were also requested to make a certain donation to the association regularly. It is said that during that period no one dared to refuse paying because everyone recognized the importance of getting support from WKWK.[17]

Nevertheless, the support of WKWK to its members was far from complete, particularly during the early 1930s when the lives of both Chinese boarding-house owners and workers were hit by the Depression. For instance, in a report by the Dutch police on the Peanut Chinese Case, it is mentioned that in the early 1930s, WKWK and some influential Chinese in Rotterdam once tried to stop Chinese from selling peanut cakes along the streets because it looked like begging and would spur discrimination against the Chinese. The peanut-cake selling, however, kept mushrooming. One reason was that WKWK could not offer enough financial assistance to unemployed Chinese seamen (Rotterdam Police Report, 1933:5).

Regardless of whether WKWK could have supervised all of the Chinese in the Netherlands, viewed from the perspective of the Dutch government, WKWK's position was an ambivalent problem. On the one hand, being the only influential Chinese association at that period, WKWK was used by the Dutch police, at least the police of Rotterdam, as an intermediary to make necessary communication with the Chinese community. The relevant documents show that during the late 1920s and the early 1930s, whenever there was an issue dealing with the Chinese in general, the Dutch police would first ask cooperation from WKWK. For instance, due to the language barriers, Rotterdam police had to ask WKWK's help to register the newly arrived Chinese.

On the other hand, the Dutch authorities never recognized WKWK as a legal association. During the first years after WKWK was established, it did not try to register in the Netherlands as an official voluntary association. Neither the Dutch authorities nor the Chinese cared about this problem before 1930. Then, on 10 September 1930, at the suggestion and under direct arrangement of its new secretary, Mr. William Fung, a Peranakan Chinese intellectual, the committee of WKWK for the first time sent an application form to the Rotterdam police to register as an official voluntary association in the Netherlands. Soon after, the Rotterdam police examined all of the committee members in detail. On 29 October, the police sent a 13-page report to the Ministry of Justice in The Hague. According to the report, no committee member should be trusted: some had attended the conference held by the Communist Party of the Netherlands; some were opium dealers; and some were smugglers (Rotterdam Police Report, 1930). Interestingly, there is no explanation for why the report was pigeonholed in the Ministry for more than one year. The fact that WKWK sent its representatives repeatedly to urge a response from the police makes it clear that WKWK knew nothing about the report. On 26 January 1932, contrary to their expectations, the application was rejected. The decision signed by the Dutch Minister of Justice was based on the official report and stated that "[WKWK's] true character did not coincide with its constitution, so that its request cannot be granted." Moreover, it should be noted that on the same page of the Ministry of Justice's memorandum there was also the following comment:

If a people loses its sense of nationality, then its women would be abused by Chinese and other Asian vermin.[18]

This comment mirrors the racist attitudes of the Dutch officials at that time. It seems that, to a certain degree, the case of WKWK was judged according to racist principles. Interestingly, however, even after WKWK was rejected as a legal association in the Netherlands, the Rotterdam police still used it as an instrument to deal with cases related to the Chinese. During 1935 and 1936, when the Dutch police tried to repatriate those Chinese who were regarded by the Dutch authorities as "economically useless," the Dutch officials who were in charge of the repatriation arrangement visited WKWK office personally several times to discuss how to handle the matters efficiently (van Heek, 1936:32-35; Zeven, 1987:59-61).[19]

The last issue is to study WKWK's social position from the perspective of the ordinary Chinese people who lived during that period. Among my interviewees, seven of them had made their living in the Netherlands during the 1930s.[20] Three came from Wenzhou and Qingtian, one came from Fuzhou, and the other three persons came from Guangdong. Among them, two knew nothing of WKWK; one often confused WKWK with another association set up in 1947 (i.e., ACV, see the next chapter); others knew more or less about WKWK and especially about its support of China in the war against Japan.

What is the potential information that can be drawn from these oral sources? After all, to remember something is to include the present, for the course of one's life modifies the memory, and some kind of link must be forged between the present and the past. With this in mind, at least two conclusions can be drawn.

First, I noted that the three interviewees who knew very little about WKWK are non-Cantonese speakers. This fact further proves that WKWK was an association that limited its activities to within the group of Cantonese-speaking immigrants, although it proclaimed itself as a community-wide association.

Second, it is clear that the most impressive contribution made by WKWK was their support of China while suffering under Japanese aggression. There is no reason to doubt the testimony, which is corroborated by written sources, that WKWK helped the Chinese to deal with day-to-day problems. Nevertheless, considering the above mentioned collective memories, it is clear that the efforts made by WKWK to help save China produced wider and stronger influences than anything else WKWK accomplished. Therefore, among the Chinese immigrants in the Netherlands, WKWK was regarded as a patriotic association rather than a mutual aid association.

In short, WKWK can be regarded as a collective representative case which portrayed the organizational efforts of the Chinese in the Netherlands before the Second World War.

C The first great uniting of the Chinese in the Netherlands

During the late 1930s, when China was under siege by Japan, the Chinese organizations in the Netherlands were quite active but not so much for mutual aid as for patriotic reasons just like the Chinese associations all over the world. In that atmosphere, through the suggestion of the Chinese Consul in Amsterdam and under the direct recommendation and management of WKWK, all Chinese associations in the Netherlands united for the first time.

Up until the early 1930s, the Chinese in the Netherlands had established various associations. According to van Heek's report of 1936, six district Chinese associations were registered at the Rotterdam Police Bureau (1936:34). According to Chen's reminiscences, at that time there were eleven Chinese associations in Rotterdam and about six in Amsterdam (1991:8-9). There are two characteristics of these associations that need to be pointed out.

First, if the associations are classified according to their membership methodology, the associations based on shared provenance were heavily represented. In the early 1930s, among the eleven Chinese associations in Rotterdam, seven were based on shared provenance. This phenomenon is due to the historical background I pointed out at the beginning of this chapter, i.e., from the early period of Chinese settlement in the Netherlands almost all of them were living in gangs that corresponded with their area of origin.

Second, the number of associations with a certain political background was rather high: there were at least three associations in Rotterdam and two in Amsterdam. In other words, nearly one-third of all Chinese associations displayed a certain political element. These were *Zhi Gong Tang* with a Rotterdam branch and an Amsterdam branch;[21] the overseas branches of the Chinese *Kuo Min Tang Party* (KMT) in both Rotterdam and Amsterdam; and the Western European Bureau of the All Chinese Seamen Union.[22] Historically, the Chinese people have been characterized as a population isolated from politics (Townsend, 1967: 10-20). Nevertheless, among the Chinese overseas, one striking characteristic is that they often take an active interest in the political fate of their motherland. The Chinese in the Netherlands are no exception. This phenomenon undoubtedly reflects the long-distance nationalism that I have mentioned in Chapter I and which will be discussed again in Chapter VII.

Returning to the general discussion, no association — except WKWK, which once proclaimed it had six hundred members — gave the number of its members.[23] It seems that from the beginning there were no clear-cut formalities to join an association. To put it differently, the distinction between members and non-members of an association was obscure.

According to the scarce documents, there was some competition among these associations in the early 1930s. The following quotations may help us to understand this situation:

We Fuzhou people were a small group. We did not know what those Guangdong people and Zhejiang people were doing. They did not want to help us, although they were much richer and more powerful.[24]

Those Guangdong people very often appeared and disappeared mysteriously [...] We Zhejiang people were afraid to get into any trouble with them. I believe that more than 90 percent of the bad guys were Guangdong people.[25]

From my father [the interviewee's father was a headman among the Guangdong Chinese in Amsterdam in the 1930s and the 1940s], I got the impression that those Zhejiang people were snobbish guys. We Guangdong people were much more generous. We always help each other, not like them. But I can not judge this by myself, because I have no contacts with Zhejiang people.[26]

I remember very clearly that before the incident of Japanese aggression against China happened, there were few direct contacts between our Zhejiang people and those Guangdong people.[27]

The feelings of estrangement between different organizations, however, were cleared up when the situation in China changed: on 7 July, 1937, the news that Japan had begun an all-out war against China shocked every Chinese, including those living in the Netherlands.[28] Soon afterwards, a coalition conference was held in the Chinese Consulate in Amsterdam to discuss how to support China. The Chinese Consul in Amsterdam suggested the conference, and the leaders of WKWK arranged it. The leaders of all the Chinese associations (including CHH) and all the influential Chinese elite were invited. At the conference, the proposal to establish a united federation to lead the Resist Japanese Aggression and Save China Movement in the Netherlands was unanimously adopted. Then, also at this conference, an official proclamation was issued that a united federation had been established, it is: *Helan Huaqiao kangRi jiuguo hui* (The Dutch Chinese Association to Resist Japanese Aggression and Save China; hereafter the Chinese Resistance Association).[29]

The aim of the Chinese Resistance Association was to unite all Chinese living in the Netherlands, regardless of political conviction, religious belief, class status, and original district differences, in order to resist the Japanese aggression. Facing this common national calamity, the Chinese did unite. Whether they were Guangdong or Zhejiang people or people from other districts, they all sat together in the association. One room in the Chinese Consulate in Amsterdam was used as the general office of the association. The Chinese Consul was the chairman. The Chinese Resistance Association set up four branches, located in Amsterdam, Rotterdam, The Hague and Utrecht. The committee members of each branch included all the influential Chinese of that area. For instance, among the 31 committee members of the Amsterdam branch, 11 were Guangdong people, 18 were from Zhejiang, and the other two were well-known Shandong businessmen (Chen, 1991:15).

From September 1937 until May 1940 (when Germany invaded the Netherlands), the Chinese Resistance Association made the following major contributions.

First, in order to focus all the Chinese people's attention on what was going on in China and to encourage contributions, a Chinese bulletin was published from September 1937 until the end of 1939. The Rotterdam branch of the Chinese Resistance Association published the first Chinese bulletin, *Rotterdam Jiuguo bao* (Rotterdam Newspaper on Saving China), in September 1937. Following this example, the other two branches in Amsterdam and The Hague also published their own Chinese bulletins. All these Chinese publications had one principal aim: to propagate the spirit of resisting Japanese aggression; thus, the contents of these publications were similar: all related to the current situation in China and asked for support for China. Although the Chinese in the Netherlands welcomed the publications, the financial burden was heavy. Therefore, in March 1938, during the sixth joint conference of the Chinese Resistance Association, the committee decided that the association should concentrate its limited financial and human resources to edit and publish one Bulletin of higher quality. From then on, a new weekly bulletin replaced all of the *Jiuguo bao* branches. This new bulletin was the *Kangzhan Yaoxun* (Bulletin on resisting Japanese aggression; hereafter KY). Every issue of KY had a print-run of about two hundred copies and was handed out free of charge. As the mouthpiece of the Chinese Resistance Association, each issue of KY kept informing the readers about the "saving China" activities promoted and organized by the Chinese Resistance Association, and encouraged more people to plunge into this patriotic movement. At the end of 1939, the bulletin stopped due to lack of money. In total, 93 issues had been published.

The second important contribution of the Chinese Resistance Association was to raise money regularly for the movement. From September 1937, the Chinese Resistance Association began asking all Chinese in the Netherlands to donate money to help China. According to an announcement published in the KY on 17 July, 1939, from September 1937 to December 1938 the Chinese in the Netherlands donated the following amount of money to China:

Dutch guilders	45,637.60
British pounds	1,863.60
Chinese yuans	152.90
American dollars	8.00

Considering that many Chinese were living in poverty, such large figures are remarkable.

Thirdly, the association played a critical role in plucking up the courage and confidence of the Chinese in the Netherlands. The Chinese Resistance Association asked Chinese pedlars all over the Netherlands to stop selling Japanese goods; asked Chinese seamen to stop working for ships that would send commodities, especially munitions, to Japan.

In October 1938, two representatives of the Chinese government, Mr. Zhu Xuefan and his secretary, came to the Netherlands to attend a conference held by the International Transportation Workers Union. The Chinese Resistance Association welcomed them with a grand reception. Through the arrangement of the association, Mr. Zhu gave a public report that revealed the savageries of the Japanese aggressors and how the Chinese in China fought bloody battles against the enemy. Then, in February 1939, another representative from China, Ms. Yang Huimin, came to the Netherlands to attend the International Scouts Assembly.[30] Upon arriving in the Netherlands, being a young heroine in the war, Ms. Yang was received like a Chinese queen by her compatriots in the Netherlands. All of these activities organized by the Chinese Resistance Association ignited patriotic feelings among the Chinese in the Netherlands.

The last important contribution of the Chinese Resistance Association was their attempts to win over the support of the Dutch people. The Chinese Resistance Association informed friendly Dutch associations about how the situation in China was going and what support was needed. To inform more Dutch people about the crimes that the Japanese army was committing, several documentary film parties were organized. All these efforts got sympathetic responses from some Dutch people. In fact, some joined in the donation movement to help the Chinese refugees of the war.

In early 1940, however, the Netherlands itself was facing the threat of invasion by Nazi Germany. Everyone worried about the coming disaster. The Chinese Resistance Association recognized how difficult it would be to

continue its activities. Then, in April 1940, a few weeks before the Netherlands was invaded, the last general meeting of the Chinese Resistance Association was held in the Chinese Consulate in Amsterdam. At that meeting, all
attendants agreed to the proposal posted by the Chinese Consul that in order
to protect all Chinese in the Netherlands and keep contacts between each
other, the Chinese Resistance Association should change its name to a neutral one. The new name was *Huaqiao huzhuhui* (Overseas Chinese Mutual Aid
Association). Since the Chinese Consulate in Amsterdam was going to be
closed, the office of *Huaqiao huzhuhui* was set up in a Chinese laundry, which
was located at Prins Hendrikstraat 124, The Hague. Maybe it was a coinci-
dence that the name of this Chinese laundry was *Huasheng*, which means
China will win.

During the first two years that Germany occupied the Netherlands, there
were five Chinese working in turns to deal with the routine affairs of the
association. For instance, through the contacts of *Huaqiao huzhuhui* with the
German authorities, the Chinese in The Hague were able to get special rice
rations for their daily food. In addition, through the repeated appeals of the
association, the Chinese who were older than sixty could be exempted from
labour service (Chen, 1991:17).

The activities of *Huaqiao huzhuhui*, however, were regarded with suspicion
by the German occupational forces. One day at the beginning of 1943, three
leaders of *Huaqiao huzhuhui* were arrested by the German army. After being
interrogated for a whole day, they were released. The German army then
confiscated all of the association's documents and closed the office. From
then on, *Huaqiao huzhuhui* could not hold any activities.

The closure of *Huaqiao huzhuhui* marked the end of this period of the
Chinese associations in the Netherlands. In fact, during the rest of the Second
World War there were no Chinese organizational activities in the Nether-
lands.

2 *Chinese associations after the Second World War*

In May 1945, the Netherlands was liberated from the German occupation.
On 13 August 1945, the Japanese surrendered. The end of the Second World
War brought a new future to the Chinese in the Netherlands.

A *Rebirth of the Chinese organizational activities*

While celebrating the liberation of the Netherlands together with the Dutch
people, the Chinese in the Netherlands were still seriously concerned about
the war against Japan in their motherland.

7 July 1945 was the date that marked the eighth year of war in China.
Under the auspices of the activists of the former *Huaqiao huzhuhui*, the Chi-
nese in the Netherlands held a commemorative meeting in *Het Verre Oosten
Restaurant* (Far East Restaurant), a Chinese restaurant owned by the former

chairman of WKWK — Kwok Shu Cheung — in The Hague.[31] This was the first public collective activity organized by a Chinese association after the war. Around two hundred Chinese from all over the Netherlands attended the meeting. At the beginning, all attendants rose and stood in silent tribute to those who had died in the war. Then, several people gave speeches. They all expressed their earnest wish for a victorious China. They also called for the Chinese in the Netherlands to continue their contributions.[32]

The defeat of Japan in August 1945 elated all Chinese and they all wanted to celebrate the great, hard-won victory. At that time, since the Netherlands had been liberated for only three months, the transportation and telecommunication networks had not yet been completely reinstated, and many materials were deficient. The victory, however, inspired the Chinese. Dozens of former leaders of Chinese associations met together to organize celebration ceremonies. Mr. Henry Liang, then a brigade commander of the Canadian army which was stationed in Utrecht, was elected as the chairman of the preparatory committee. In a very short period, the Chinese organized grand celebrations in Utrecht, The Hague, Amsterdam, Leiden and Rotterdam.

One of the organizers described the celebration parades held by the Chinese in The Hague in August 1945 as follows:

We had gala parades in five cities: Utrecht, The Hague, Amsterdam, Leiden and Rotterdam. All organizational preparations were arranged by the former leaders and activists of the Chinese Resistance Association and CHH [...] I was one member of the preparatory committee in The Hague [...] I still remember clearly what progressed on that great day in The Hague.

In the morning, we first held a memorial ceremony for all soldiers who had died in the war. Then, our parade started from Malieveld Square. The parade was formed by several hundreds of Chinese and dozens of Dutch friends. Some Chinese had organized performing groups, each with their distinctive characteristics. For instance, Guangdong people had organized a lions' dance group; Zhejiang people played a dance of gold fishes and carps; Fuzhou people played a dragon dance; and the Peranakan Chinese and Surinam Chinese came forward with their respective music performing groups. Several lovely flower vehicles riding between the performing groups increased the jubilant atmosphere. The parade, which was as long as two or three kilometers, had walked through the whole center of The Hague [...] On the way, we especially went to the Municipal hall and to the Palace to express our regards and esteem to the Dutch Queen and to the government officials. Meanwhile, we also accepted their congratulations in respect of China's victory.

The parades in the other four cities were very much the same with what had been organized in The Hague [...]

This is the first grand and successful public activity held by the Chinese in the Netherlands. (Chen, 1991:31)

After successfully organizing this parade, both the former Chinese Resistance Association and the *Huaqiao huzhuhui* had indeed finished their tasks.

In 1947, a new Chinese association was established in Amsterdam by several dozens of Zhejiang people. It was a small association based on a common district of origin and hence named *Ouhai Tongxianghui* (Ouhai District Association). In a few years, this association developed into a Chinese community-wide association and then renamed itself as *Algemene Chinese Vereniging in Nederland* (General Chinese Association in the Netherlands). The progress of this association during the past 50 years constitutes a significant part of this study, which will be elucidated in the following chapters.

B *A dormant period*

Viewed historically, the years from the early 1950s to 1975 formed a dormant period in the history of Chinese associations in the Netherlands. On the one hand, although no one declared its dissolution or termination officially, the active Chinese associations that were established before the Second World War, including the powerful WKWK, quickly became obscure in the years after the War. On the other hand, besides the *Ouhai Tongxianghui (Algemene Chinese Vereniging in Nederland)* mentioned above, few small associations were successfully able to maintain their regular activities during that period. The key reasons underlying this phenomenon, at least, can be studied from the following three perspectives. These elements shook the associations that were set up before the War to their very foundations, and consequently created a rather silent period for the Chinese association movement in the Netherlands.

First, the turbulent situations both in China and the Netherlands affected all Chinese immigrants. Being uncertain of their future, few were interested in any Chinese organization. After the Second World War, when normal communications with their families had been re-established, many Chinese in the Netherlands longed to return home. Some went back immediately, and still others took vigorous action to prepare for returning. In 1949, the Communist Party of China (CPC) came to power and the People's Republic of China was established. This changed the situation in their hometowns and made some Chinese in the Netherlands hesitate about whether to return. From the day they left home few had prepared to spend their whole life in the Western world. Yet, some did not like, or did not understand, the policy of CPC and felt uncomfortable about living in a communist country. Therefore, they took a wait-and-see attitude in this unstable period.[33]

A second key element is that the booming of the Chinese restaurant business had reshaped the structure of class status among the Chinese. As I have pointed out earlier, before the war, almost all the leaders of Chinese associations were influential persons who had acted as both boarding-house owners and shipping masters. The Chinese workers, who had to rely on the master's introduction or help to make their living, very often formed the principal members of the associations. Toward the 1950s, however, when the Chinese business boom *to associational activities* ?

catering trade in the Netherlands brought hope to every Chinese, the time when Chinese shipping masters could proudly proclaim, "I always have a large number of seamen in hand," was completely over.[34] When those leaders lost their authority, the cohesiveness of their associations was lost as well.

The third and final element of this period is the political caution the Chinese adopted immediately following the Second World War. Europe's political atmosphere following the war — exemplified by the tensions of the Cold War — made many Chinese cautious. Thus, throughout this period they attempted to distance themselves from political matters.

After 1949, the fact that there were two governments in China split the Chinese community all over the world: some were pro-Beijing, some were pro-Taiwan, while others remained neutral. In the Netherlands, the delicate relationship between the Dutch and Chinese governments made the situation even more complicated.

On 27 March 1950, the Dutch government recognized the People's Republic of China as the legal government of China. Soon after that, however, the Korean War (1950-1953) broke out, which aggravated the tension between East and West. Although in 1954 the Netherlands established diplomatic relations with the People's Republic of China at the chargé d'affaires level, the sharp ideological conflicts during the whole Cold War period impeded regular communications between the two countries. As a result, the situation became sensitive: while maintaining official diplomatic relation with the Chinese government in Beijing, the Dutch government in reality kept its political orientation much more toward the government in Taiwan. This being the case, many Chinese, whether pro-Beijing or pro-Taiwan, hesitated to speak about their views, let alone establish an ethnic association with a clearly defined political orientation. This situation helped halt the organization of new Chinese association.

During this period, one organizational activity that is worth noting is the effort to establish a guild for the Chinese restaurateurs. As the Chinese catering business began developing, some Chinese restaurateurs recognized that they should have an organization to act as their representative to protect their common interests, and, when needed, to speak with the relevant Dutch authorities; however, their efforts ended with failure before the 1980s.

The first effort was in 1948, the number of Chinese restaurants had increased to many dozens; business was flourishing. Nevertheless, because immediately after the war the level of prosperity in the Netherlands was still quite low, on 25 June 1948, a new decree was promulgated, directed toward all HORECA business in the Netherlands.[35] This new decree was highly damaging to the Chinese catering business. For example, it stated that no deep-fried food may be sold in any restaurant (Article 3:3), and that the dishes listed on the menu of any restaurant cannot be more than ten different types per day (Article 3:9).

All Chinese restaurateurs were rather disturbed by this decree. For example, *Loempia* (spring roll or egg roll), one of the best known Chinese foods in the Netherlands, and many other popular Chinese dishes would be impossible to prepare without deep-frying them in oil. In addition, it was common for Chinese restaurants to list at least twenty to thirty different dishes on the menu. The Chinese restaurants, as a special ethnic catering trade, could not survive if these prohibitions were strictly followed.

Within a few days, a new guild, the Chinese Restaurateurs Association in the Netherlands, emerged to protect their common interests. On 28 June 1948, the association sent a letter signed by 18 well-known Chinese restaurateurs to the Chinese Embassy to ask for support. According to the recollection of one signatory, through the Chinese Consul's mediation, the Dutch officials agreed not to force the Chinese restaurants to conform. Although all Chinese restaurateurs were very happy with the result and benefitted from the association's efforts, it soon sunk into obscurity after the problem was solved. One Chinese restaurateur made the following summary:

> Everyone knows very clearly that unity is strength. Being beset by difficulties made us unite together, but each went his own way as soon as the problem had been settled. No one wanted to pay more attention to maintain and develop the association (Chen, 1991:30).

It was in the 1960s that once again some Chinese restaurateurs initiated organizational efforts. At that time, when the number of Chinese restaurants in the Netherlands had risen to about four hundred, increasingly more problems needed to be solved. For instance, some Chinese restaurants were occupied with recruiting qualified Chinese cooks, while others ran into problems because they did not have enough knowledge about Dutch business regulations — such as licensing, restaurant hygiene, tax rates and administration of enterprises. Individual restaurants or their owners could not solve all of these questions. Therefore, unifying the power of the individual restaurants under an association once again became a priority.

On 1 July 1964, the guild of Chinese restaurateurs announced its establishment. Immediately, the initiators attempted to register the association with the proper authorities. After enduring nearly two years of extensive examination, the Dutch government finally accepted the registration application in June 1966.

Encouraged by this success, an executive committee was elected to replace the original preparatory committee. Then they made a public call for donations to support the association. In a few months, 254 Chinese restaurants had donated 66,775 Dutch guilders to the association. The result was better than the initiators had expected, and shortly afterwards they set up an office in The Hague.[36] A number of representatives took vigorous action to establish regular contacts with the Dutch authorities; however, all these efforts could not be sustained because so few of the executives were active. Mr. Chen expressed his regret in his reminiscences:

> In 1966, the association held its first plenary meeting in the Krasnapolsky Hotel of Amsterdam. Although at that time there were more than five

hundred Chinese restaurants all over the Netherlands, and although 254 Chinese restaurants had donated money to the association, on the day of the meeting only forty-odd restaurateurs attended the meeting. No decision could be taken [...]

It was clear that the political diversity which existed in that period had split the Chinese community in the Netherlands [...] The donation was regarded as a kind of charitable behaviour. Few donators wanted to be really involved.

For a few years, the committee members had been consecutively elected and replaced, because few really wanted to devote their energies to the association. Many just took a wait-and-see attitude [...] The association disappeared soon. (Chen, 1991:30)

One of the active committee members had this to say about the delicate position of the association at that time:[37]

Before the plenary meeting, I made uncountable phone calls to mobilize my co-villagers and friends to attend the meeting. I believe we Chinese restaurateurs need an association for mutual support and further development. Yet, few did attend the meeting, although most did not reject my suggestion at once [...]

Although we initiators stressed repeatedly that the association had no political orientation in relation to China, many Chinese restaurateurs at that time still thought we committee members were pro-Beijing. Some regarded the association as a *red* organization. Some even said it was a communist organization. Most Chinese restaurateurs felt it was too dangerous to join such an association.

Another respondent, a retired Chinese restaurateur and an amateur historian, gave me his personal analysis on the failure of the Chinese restaurateurs' organizational activity at the end of the 1960s: [38]

During the 1960s, the Guild of the Chinese restaurateurs did indeed, for a while, play an active role to help Chinese restaurants. For instance, on the initiatives of the association, a good many qualified Chinese cooks got permission to enter the Netherlands as special employees of Chinese restaurants. This greatly improved the level of the Chinese restaurants.

Nevertheless, since it was still a golden age for the Chinese restaurants, many could not see the potential difficulties for the further development of the Chinese catering business and could not recognize the necessity to have a guild either. On the other hand, among a few who did recognize that it was a must to have their own guild, the sensitive political situation also made them take a wait-and-see attitude with regard to a Chinese association. Therefore, the guild for the Chinese restaurateurs, although it had an excellent beginning, existed only for a couple of years.

This double failure lead to the conclusion that an immigrants' voluntary association can only be established and developed in a relatively lenient political environment and on the basis of the collective expectations of ordinary people. This will be further examined in Chapter V.

Nonetheless, there was a need for mutual support among the Chinese immigrants. Because the political situation was tenuous, the immigrants turned their attention to setting up Chinese religious organizations.[39]

As was mentioned in Chapter II, many Chinese immigrants who arrived in the Netherlands during the 1960s came from Hong Kong. Unlike the single sojourning men before the War, often the new Hong Kong migrants would try to emigrate as families or to fetch their family members as soon as the pioneers settled down. This being the case, many Chinese women came as dependents. Because of the sudden and passive confrontation with an alien culture, many were full of feelings of oppression and deep loneliness. In the late 1960s, a few Chinese Christians, one of them was a pastor before he emigrated from Hong Kong, began to have irregular private meetings in one of their homes or restaurants. In 1969, the first Christmas Mass was held for the Chinese in that Chinese pastor's home in Rotterdam. Subsequently, some public activities were sometimes organized that welcomed all Chinese in the Netherlands, regardless of their religious beliefs. Meanwhile, through the help of a couple of pastors sent by the Chinese evangelical missionaries in Taiwan, Chinese Christians in the Netherlands established contact with Christians in other European countries. Then, in 1973, again in that Chinese pastor's home, the first baptism was held.

When the number of people who regularly attended the Sunday Mass increased to around fifty, a room located in Brede Hilledijk of Rotterdam was rented to establish a Chinese Christian center. They organized a variety of services as well as religious services: a Chinese language class for the Chinese children, a Dutch language class for the Chinese ladies, and an interpreter service for Chinese immigrants. As the only public service centre for Chinese immigrants in the Netherlands, it attracted many Chinese.

Based on this organization, the first formal Chinese religious association was set up in Rotterdam on 14 October 1974, *Stichting Evangelische Zending onder de Chinezen in Europa* (Chinese Evangelical Mission in Europe; hereafter CEME).[40] Within a couple of years, it had organized three branches in the Netherlands: in Amsterdam, The Hague, and Utrecht.

Alongside its missionary work, CEME regulated and expanded its social services. Beginning on 1 January 1975, CEME had a full-time social worker to take care of its daily affairs. A month later, it began to publish a Chinese magazine and sent it free of charge to more than three hundred Chinese families. Then, in March, CEME bought a building located in the Katendrecht area of Rotterdam.[41] This led to the establishment of the first official Chinese Christian church in the Netherlands.

During its organizational process and in the early period after its foundation, CEME was distinguished by the way in which they integrated missionary work with social services. For some of its members, CEME was a source of practical social aid rather than a unified system of beliefs and practices. Some, at the beginning, simply wished to receive emotional support from the church. Consequently, many of the members cultivated their religious faith after joining the association.

C Developing at an unprecedented rate

From the late 1970s, the emergence of new non-religious Chinese voluntary associations broke the silence of the Chinese organizational efforts after the War. Moreover, the successive development of these associations set up an example to the potential followers and formed an indication of the coming wave of Chinese organizations.

On 18 June 1976, a new non-religious Chinese voluntary association was established in Amsterdam, *Chinese Vereniging in Nederland 'Fa Yin'* (Chinese association in the Netherlands 'Fa Yin'). This is the first district association organized by Cantonese-speaking people after the War. Despite encountering some initial objections from the Chinese community, it developed into an influential association by the 1980s. Its development will be discussed in the next chapter.

Around the 1980s, the rapid and successive emergence of Chinese sports associations was another important indication of the coming wave of Chinese organizations. This trend reflected the ever-increasing population of young Chinese and their desire to have an enriched social life.

In the 1970s, football mania spread all over the Netherlands, as the Amsterdam Football Club Ajax won the Eurocup I in 1971, 1972 and 1973;[42] the Dutch national football team lost the Worldcup finals both in 1974 and 1978. The Chinese youth in the country were no exception. Moreover, in the late 1970s and the early 1980s, as the centre forward of Ajax, Tjeu La Ling, a son of a Chinese father and a Dutch mother, scored many goals for Ajax. This fact made many Chinese in the Netherlands feel very proud of his achievements.[43] However, because of language barriers and the special working times of Chinese restaurants, few Chinese football enthusiasts joined Dutch football clubs. In 1977, the first well-organized Chinese football team named *Dong Lian* Football Team was organized in Amsterdam. Soon after that, about ten more teams were organized. Then, a couple of them united to register as an ethnic Chinese recreational association. For instance, the above mentioned *Dong Lian* team united with others and registered as H. K. 77 Sport Association in 1980. By 1983, there were at least five Chinese sports associations in the Netherlands.

There are two characteristics that were common to these associations: first, they were ethnic Chinese youth groups and organized mainly by Guangdong and Hong Kong people; second, their aim was to enrich their social life and to improve communications through sports.

In 1984, another Chinese association announced its founding in Rotterdam: *Stichting Chinese Cultuur Recreatie en Maatschappelijk Werk* (Association of Chinese Culture, Recreation and Social Work). Most of its initiators were core members of the religious association, CEME; however, this new association did not express any religious orientation in its founding declarations. Compared with other associations run by Chinese immigrants in the Netherlands, this association was the first to adopt a Western approach to organizational management. Because of its unique structure, I will examine this association in detail in the next chapter.

On 7 January 1985, a new guild for all Chinese restaurateurs in the Netherlands was founded in Amsterdam. It applied and was accepted as the Chinese section of the Dutch national association, *Koninklijk verbond van ondernemers in het HORECA – en aanverwante bedrijf* (Royal Union of Entrepreneurs in the HORECA and Related Enterprises, HCS in short). After experiencing a couple of setbacks in earlier attempts, the Chinese restaurateurs finally successfully established their own functioning guild.

From the mid-1980s onward, the Chinese immigrants consistently formed new associations. More precisely, in the Netherlands, between 1984 and 1997, on average, more than five new Chinese associations were founded per year. Thus, by the end of 1997, Chinese immigrants from all over the Netherlands had organized more than one hundred Chinese associations (cf. Appendix III).

In summary, there are three general trends associated with the development of the Chinese associations in the Netherlands during the last quarter of the 20th century:

(i)   their number keeps growing;
(ii) their variety keeps expanding;
(iii) their functions can be recognized not only from the changes in the Chinese immigrant community itself but also from their status both in Dutch society and in their community of origin.

3 *Typology of contemporary Chinese associations in the Netherlands*

To what degree or within which sphere do the Chinese associations express their various organizational motivations, social structures, and functions? This section will identify the typologies used to understand Chinese associations, which will give readers a comprehensive overview of the internal composition of the Chinese community in the Netherlands.

A *Existing models of classifying Chinese associations*

Almost all scholars who have studied Chinese associations abroad have created or used certain models to classify them. The Chinese associations have been classified in a variety of ways: from two types to more than twenty types. Some scholars' contributions are listed below. For the purpose of clarity, I reduced more than ten different models into two groups: the general classification model and the elaborate classification model.

I use the *general classification model* to identify typologies that simplify all Chinese associations into two or three types. Hereafter, I present four representative examples:

Yen Ching-Hwang's Model
In Yen Ching-Hwang's study of the social history of the Chinese in Singapore and Malaysia in 1800-1911, he divides the associations set up by the Chinese immigrants into roughly three regimes: dialect organizations, clan organizations, and secret societies (Yen, 1986).

Wu Hua's model
In 1977, Wu Hua, a historian in Singapore, published a three-volume documentary book on Chinese *huiguan* (i.e., Chinese traditional associations) in Singapore. In the book, the author puts all Chinese traditional associations into three categories: associations established based on shared provenance, on the same clan, or on shared profession. His study only focussed on traditional Chinese associations, and many recently established associations were excluded (Wu, 1977).

Edgar Wickberg's Model[44]
After examining the range of Chinese organizations in Manila and their development since the Second World War, Canadian scholar Edgar Wickberg devised a classification scheme. His model classifies all Chinese associations into one of two styles: those that have been derived from China's urban social history and norms are Chinese-style, while those that are modern Chinese adaptations of forms originating in the West are Western-style. In other words, he includes "Chinese-style bodies as surname, native-place and trade-guild associations, Hongmen bodies, brotherhoods, musical and theatrical societies, 'national arts' groups, and temples;" he includes "'Western'-derived associations as Chambers of Commerce, Lions Clubs, fire brigades, alumni associations, schools and churches" (1993:91). This is a model specially fitted to the case of Chinese associations in Manila. Nevertheless, it is a common phenomenon that many Chinese associations are, in a sense, straddling Chinese and Western styles; this is especially applicable when we study the Chinese associations in Western countries.

Bernard Wong's Model
American scholar Bernard P. Wong has studied New York City's Chinatown structure. According to him, Chinese associations there can be broken down into three categories: traditional associations, new associations, and agencies and social service providers. In short, "the organizational principles of the traditional associations were deeply rooted in the home communities, especially in the rural areas of Kwangtung";[45] and, according to Wong, the CCBA (Chinese Consolidated Benevolent Association) is at the top of all traditional associations (1982:15). The new associations are those which "have been organized recently, and are not included within the umbrella of

CCBA;" and "recruited members from different social, economic, and educational backgrounds" (1982: 23). The third kind of associations "are oriented to the larger society and have their roots in the U.S. society;" "many of
these organizations have direct connections with the government, churches,
labour unions, and the non-profit and charitable organizations, of the larger
society" (1982:23). It seems that two different standards had been used to
make this classification: the first two categories were divided by whether the
association was within the umbrella of CCBA; however, the third one was
distinguished by which society the association rooted itself in.

Because of the immense variety of Chinese associations, some scholars prefer
a detailed identification scheme, which I label *elaborate classification models*.
Hereafter, I present two examples:

Taiwan Model
The official government bureau in Taiwan has published annual statistics on
the Chinese abroad since 1950. In the *Yearbook of the Republic of China*, published by the government in Taiwan, all Chinese associations abroad were
classified into three broad groups in 1951: guilds, social associations, and
"save China" associations.[46] Since the 1960s, however, the classification system has been expanded to include 15 groups: community associations, social
associations, original district associations, surname associations, guilds, indus-
trialists and merchants associations, educational and cultural associations,
recreational associations, youth associations, women's associations, anti-
CPC/save China associations[47], welfare associations, religious associations,
non-governmental diplomatic associations, plus an "others" category.[48]

Singapore Model
According to the reference guide, *A Comprehensive Overview on Associations in
Singapore*, all associations are classified into more than 20 groups (Peng, 1983):
community associations, economic associations, labour unions, professional
associations, political associations, educational associations, sports associa-
tions, academic associations, arts associations, co-villagers associations, clan
associations, religious associations, *wu shu* associations,49 medical associa-
tions, welfare associations, friendship associations, mutual aid associations,
youth associations, women's associations, and international associations.
    The predicament of both models mentioned above is that, instead of
establishing a unified standard to classify the associations, they use multiple
classification standards. For example, community associations and international associations are classified on the basis of members' residence; youth
associations and women's associations are classified on the basis of the members' demographic group; co-villagers associations and surname associations
are classified on the basis of organizational links; and the associations of
welfare, educational, economic, and mutual help are classified on the basis of
the association's predominate function. Furthermore, they fail to account for
the fact that many current associations have multiple attributes.

The *Ouzhou Zhangshi zongqin fulihui* (The Benevolent Association for Cheung Family Members in Europe) is an example that sometimes an association is difficult to categorize simply. It was the first well-known European-wide Chinese association set up after the Second World War and does not fit neatly into any of the aforementioned classifications (Li, 1996:5). For example, if the standard of classification is based on its members' residence, this association could be classified as a transnational association; if the standard is based on its organizational link, this association should be classified as a surname association; finally, if the standard is based on its major purpose, it could also be classified as a welfare association. From this example, it is obvious that one association can be classified into various categories depending on the classification standards. To avoid this, one model should use only one measurement standard.

B *Classifying contemporary Chinese associations in the Netherlands*

The Chinese associations in the Netherlands, like in many other countries, have shown a rich variety in their way of organization. In order to give a comprehensive picture of the existing Chinese associations, I am going to classify them, first of all, on the basis of members' residence; and, secondly, according to their members' attributes.

First, based on members' residence, all Chinese associations in the Netherlands can be classified into three groups: nationwide associations, local associations and transnational associations.

Nationwide associations
This group includes those associations whose members live all over the Netherlands. For instance, since the 1970s, *Algemene Chinese Vereniging in Nederland* (General Chinese Association in the Netherlands) has successively established branches in 12 Dutch cities. The members of another nationwide association, *Stichting Landelijke Federatie van Chinese Organisaties in Nederland* (National Federation of Chinese Organizations in the Netherlands), hail from almost every well-known Dutch city: Amsterdam, Rotterdam, The Hague, Utrecht, Eindhoven, Tilburg, Maastricht, etc. Since the Netherlands is a small country, about two-thirds of existing Chinese associations are nationwide.

Local associations
This group includes those associations whose members are limited to a certain city, province or those that mainly concentrate their activities in their local district. Some Chinese associations set up on the district level can be easily identified from their names: *Vereniging Chinese bewoners in Rotterdam* (Association of Chinese Inhabitants in Rotterdam), *Vereniging Chinese ondernemers Amsterdam Chinatown*, (Association of Chinese Entrepreneurs in Amsterdam Chinatown), *Stichting Yao Yi Trefcentrum Chinezen Utrecht* (Chinese Friendship Recreational Center in Utrecht).

Nevertheless, some associations' names give them the appearance of being a nationwide association, while they actually recruit their members locally. *Fa Yin* is one example. As was mentioned earlier, the full name of *Fa Yin* is the Chinese Association in the Netherlands '*Fa Yin*.' But, most of its members are old folks that live either in Amsterdam or in small cities around Amsterdam, such as Amstelveen or Almere. The association's founders do not wish to recruit members from other areas, since it would be inconvenient and too expensive for elderly people to travel a long way to attend the association's weekly meeting.

In addition, since the 1980s, two parallel trends have emerged among nationwide associations. It seems that some nationwide associations took vigorous action to set up district branches, while some former district branches of certain nationwide associations tried to reorganize as independent associations. For example, in 1986, a group of Chinese immigrants founded *Limburgse Chinese Vereniging* (Chinese Association in Limburg). Its principal leaders and many members originally belonged to the branch of *Algemene Chinese Vereniging in Nederland* in Limburg.

Transnational associations
Some Chinese associations were originally set up in the Netherlands but recruited or planned to recruit their members from abroad as well. For instance, *Stichting Global Chinese Art* (Association of Global Chinese Art), set up in 1996, aimed to be an international association. Although its initiators are only three Chinese in the Netherlands, the association lists 12 Chinese from outside of the Netherlands as members: five live in China, two live in the United States, two live in France and one lives in Switzerland.

There are some associations that could be classified as transnational despite the fact that their name suggests otherwise. These associations appear to be limited to the Netherlands, but their members come from all over. For example, Fine Eastern Restaurant International, a Chinese restaurateurs' trade association in the Netherlands, has two allied members in England and two in Italy. Another Dutch Chinese restaurateurs' association, The Asian Restaurants, had 42 members (each representing one Chinese restaurant) in 1995. According to the introduction given by its secretary, amongst the members, two were in Belgium, two were in Spain, and one was in Italy.

On the other hand, there are also some associations that appear to be international associations based on their names, but whose membership is limited to one country. *Tai Pang Gemeenschap in Europa* (Tai Pang community in Europe) is one example. This is an association based on shared provenance, i.e., all of its members emigrated from Dapeng district of Guangdong. Although its founders planned to recruit its members from all over Europe, its membership is limited to the Netherlands.[50]

A second way to classify the relevant associations is according to their members' attributes. These attributes are their prominent distinguishing feature and, to a certain extent, act as a cement that holds together the associations.

There are seven main attributes: shared provenance, shared surname, shared dialect, shared ideology or knowledge, shared natural characteristics, shared hobby, and shared principles.

Shared provenance
It is a well-known custom that the Chinese abroad are used to establishing their association on the basis of shared provenance, i.e., all of the associations' members emigrated from the same original place. As I indicated earlier, among the Chinese voluntary associations in the Netherlands, the district-of-origin associations occupy a remarkable place both before and after the Second World War. Examples include the associations of Hong Kong, Yuan Lun, Dapeng, Qingtian, Wenzhou, Yong Ka, Taiwan, Northeast China, Indonesia and Vietnam (see Appendix III). Among these associations founded because of shared provenance, there are two characteristics.

First, the scope of shared provenance is different for different groups. Some are *Xiang*-based associations; some associations use shared original *diqu* (prefecture) as the basis for formation; and still others are groups of people who once lived or worked in the same province (or district) before emigrating abroad.[51] This is further complicated by the fact that some districts overlap. For instance, there is an association organized for all Hong Kong immigrants, but people who come from Yuan Lun, a district located in Hong Kong, have organized their own independent association. Also, Yong Ka is one county directly under the municipal government of Wenzhou Municipality, but Yong Ka people set up their own regional association soon after the Wenzhou association had been established.

Second, the traditional concept that the original district is the hometown of one's ancestors has changed pragmatically. For instance, according to the constitution of the Association for the Chinese from Northeast China in the Netherlands, all Chinese who once lived, studied or worked in Northeast China and now live in the Netherlands can be regarded as fellow provincials.[52] The membership definition for people from Taiwan and other areas of Southeast Asia is similar. That is, the Taiwan District Association defines Taiwan people as those once lived or worked in Taiwan island;[53] and the Peranakan and the Vietnamese-Chinese in the Netherlands set up their own associations on the basis of the region they inhabited in Southeast Asia.

In short, it is an understandable consequence that the significance of the place of origin consists not only of collective ties through shared dialects and habits but, even more importantly, of dramatic (and sometimes traumatic) collective experiences. Therefore, shared provenance is indeed shared personal experiences or shared sub-culture.

Shared surname
There are four associations which are organized based on a shared surname in the Netherlands, These include the associations of the Tang, Man, Pang and Choi families.[54] Among the Chinese, there is a popular belief that the people who share the same surname have a common ancestor from hundreds

or thousands of years ago. If they share the same surname and come from the same area, i.e., the same village or the same county, the relationship between them is even closer. As the descendants of a common ancestor, no matter how many generations away, they are relatives and should be eager to help one another.

Among the four surname associations in the Netherlands, the association of Choi has limited its membership not only to the people who shared the surname of Choi but also to the Choi who came from the former *Choiwuwei* village of Bo On. It is a localized lineage association. The other three surname associations do not define their locality. Nevertheless, since the three surnames are pronounced in Cantonese,[55] it is clear that their locality is the area which consists of some parts of Guangdong and Hong Kong, although the definition is not as strict as the association of Choi.

In a small country like the Netherlands, its Chinese population is rather small. Therefore, compared with their peers in Southeast Asian countries, the Chinese associations that were set up based on shared surname together with a certain locality can rarely be organized since they have sparse membership in the Netherlands.

Shared dialect

In the Netherlands, there is only one association that is based on shared dialect: *Benelux Tsung-Tsin Vereniging* (*Tsung-Tsin* association in Benelux). The Chinese who use the Hakka dialect as their principal means of communication organized this association.

Hakka is a special dialect group. The question of its origin is debatable. According to common belief, the Hakka group, as a separate category and a sub-group of Han Chinese, emerged out of the thousand-year migration process of some Han people from the Central Plains to South China. As newcomers in South China, they had to settle down in the relatively poor and distant mountain areas. Up until the 19th century, the Hakka people were distributed over the mountain area that straddles the three provinces of Guangdong, Fujian and Jiangxi. Only their common dialect differentiates them from the natives. *Hakka* in Chinese means *guest people*. This is a socially imposed identity to those migrants from North to South China. Those migrants and their descendants accepted this label to distinguish them from the natives, who they regarded as barbarians.[56]

Most Hakka people in the Netherlands also came from Guangdong Province and Hong Kong. But the Hakka dialect is different from the Cantonese dialect. Compared with the Cantonese-speaking Guangdong and Hong Kong people, the Hakka people are a rather smaller group.

Shared ideology or knowledge

The members of associations bound by ideology or knowledge share the same professional knowhow or world view. In the Netherlands, this category consists of associations organized by Chinese restaurateurs, traders, acupuncturists, writers, scholars, artists, and so on.

Holding a Chinese cuisine exhibition by one Chinese association (Photo by René de Vries).

While there are about 2,000 Chinese restaurants in the Netherlands, five associations have been established by and for Chinese restaurateurs. It is worth noting that all of these five associations are regarded as organizations for employers or owners. By contrast, no independent association for Chinese restaurant employees has been successfully organized up till the end of 1997. The reasons behind this overt phenomenon will be discussed in Chapter VI.

As mentioned earlier, many early Chinese migrants in the Netherlands were illiterate or poorly educated people. Strictly speaking, the first intellectual association set up by the Chinese immigrants in the Netherlands is the Association of Chinese Writers in Benelux, which was established in 1991 in Rotterdam. The founders were three Chinese, two female writers living in the Netherlands and one male writer in Belgium. Although there are about ten names on the association's member list, the truly active members were the core three in its initial years. Since 1994, associations of Chinese lawyers, acupuncturists and artists have been set up successfully, but their members are few.

Among this group, the *liuxuesheng* associations deserve special attention. In 1988, the *liuxuesheng* group in the Netherlands set up its first association. Since then, some associations for Chinese computer specialists, for Chinese social science scholars, and for Chinese engineers (all belong to *liuxuesheng* group) have been organized in succession. Although a gap still exists between the *liuxuesheng* and other Chinese groups, some implications have shown that the contacts between *liuxuesheng* associations and some of other existing Chinese associations are growing. For instance, the Association for Chinese Engineers in the Netherlands applied and was accepted as a member of LFCON, which is a federation being dominated by Chinese business people (cf. Chapter VI). Moreover, in May 1999, a great demonstration against NATO's bombing of the Chinese Embassy in Belgrade was initiated by *liuxuesheng* associations and joined by many other Chinese associations.

Shared natural characteristics
This category includes age- or gender-related associations. For instance, in the Netherlands today, there are more than ten associations specially organized by Chinese women, about the same amount by Chinese elderly, and three by Chinese youth.[57] Comparatively speaking, the associations organized by and for the women and elderly are among the most active ones.

Shared hobby
The number of associations based on shared hobbies has increased greatly since the 1980s. Most of them are sports clubs, and it is likely that the majority of the participants in these athletic associations are young people who grew up in the Netherlands. While watching the public activities organized by them, I noted that when they are eager to express something, many use Dutch rather than Cantonese, although they are a bilingual group.

Shared principles
Those religious associations, either Christian or Buddhist, whose members share the same faith fall into this category. There are currently about ten of these associations: two for Chinese Buddhists and the others for Chinese Christians.

As was pointed out previously, although many are titled Chinese churches or temples, they are more like ethnic friendship or mutual-help groups with an associated religious belief. Only a couple of them have a well-established religious body.

In addition, this category of associations includes three associations that have strong political orientation. Their purpose focuses on the democratic movement in mainland China. Most members of these three associations are *liuxuesheng* from mainland China. They have close links with the respective worldwide federation.

The above classification systems aside, there are still other possible ways to classify the associations. For example, the relevant associations can also be classified in terms of their professed prime beneficiary: some are mutual-aid associations, where the prime beneficiary is the membership; some are service organizations, which offer services to all Chinese immigrants or organize public activities for all Chinese. In addition, the associations can also be classified by their type of financial sources: some mainly rely on regularly collecting donations from its leaders; some mainly rely on the subsidies of the Dutch government; and some basically rely on the membership dues.

In general, the rich variety that appears in these categories is merely a preliminary picture. In the next chapter, three influential Chinese associations that have different characteristics will be selected to give a detailed demonstration of the complexity of these organizations.

CHAPTER IV

Three Case Studies

According to the written documents I have collected, more than one hundred Chinese associations established themselves in the Netherlands between 1947 and 1997 (cf. Appendix III). In addition, 41 after-school Chinese schools were set up.[1] It would be too ambitious a task to present an exhaustive study of all of these associations. Instead, in this chapter, I select three associations to provide a detailed illustration of the more general situation.

The process I followed to select these examples can be divided into roughly three steps. First, in order to become acquainted with the overall situation of Chinese voluntary associations in the Netherlands, I visited about fifty associations and Chinese schools: either to attend their public activities or to have an interview with the leaders or active members. Then, in about one year, based on my personal knowledge of these associations, I reduced my contacts to about ten of them. Finally, I selected three of the associations to be the focus of an elaborate study.

The basic standards of selection are as follows. First, the association should be one organized by Chinese immigrants who directly emigrated from China. As was described in previous chapters, there are differences between the Chinese from China and other re-migrant Chinese. Thus, in order to concentrate the study, I excluded associations organized by re-migrants from the sample selection. Second, since some associations are merely nominal or become almost invisible soon after being established, the samples I have chosen are influential associations that have existed for a longer period, i.e., for more than ten years. Third, the selected targets must be representatives of different categories with their respective outstanding characteristics.

The coming deliberations focus on the following questions: when and under what circumstances was the association set up? Are there any distinct stages in its development that can be outlined? What are the associations' characteristic roles?

1 *ACV: the oldest association facing new challenges*

The first case selected for focused study is ACV — *Algemene Chinese Vereniging in Nederland* (*Lü He Huaqiao zonghui*; General Association of Chinese in the Netherlands; hereafter ACV). Among all active Chinese associations in the Netherlands, ACV is an association with some impressive characteristics:

(i) with a history of more than half a century, it is the oldest association among the existing ones;

(ii) with a membership of more than eleven hundred, it is a large asso-
      ciation;[2]
(iii) it is the only Chinese association that has edited and published an
      association bulletin regularly for more than twenty years and con-
      tinues to distribute it free of charge;
(iv) it is also one of the most active initiators pushing the establishment of
      the European-wide Chinese association — European Federation of
      Chinese Organizations, which was set up in 1992 in Amsterdam.

A *Birth of a district-of-origin association*[3]

Established on 27 November 1947, ACV, originally named *Ou hai tongxianghui*
(Ou Sea District Association), was initially a district-of-origin association of
Wenzhou pedlars. The pedlars formed the organization to further their ef-
forts to attain a better life in the changed situation after the Second World
War.

As described in the last chapter, soon after peace returned to the world,
some Chinese in the Netherlands returned to their hometowns immediately,
while about two thousand Chinese decided to stay. With regard to their
reasons for staying, three groups can be basically outlined:

(i)   those who set up some business in the Netherlands and wanted to
      expand it;
(ii) those who married Dutch citizens;
(iii) those who lived in poverty and felt ashamed to return home with
      empty hands.

Very few people belonged to the first group. Specifically, in 1945, there were
only twelve Chinese restaurants located in big cities such as The Hague,
Amsterdam, and Rotterdam. In addition, there were a couple of small shops
run by about 15 Chinese.[4]

Shortages of daily necessities were common in the period after the war,
and circulation of commodities was needed. At that time, most Chinese continued to make their living by hawking wares in the streets. Some attempted
to do long-distance or transnational buying and selling. To obtain higher
profits, the Chinese pedlars would try to stock commodities at lower whole-
sale prices. Yet, as foreigners without access to the proper authorities, many
met innumerable difficulties in their attempts to get goods at reasonable
prices. Gradually, they decided that an association that could act as a powerful bargainer to obtain commodities for selling at a profit needed to be
established.

Another element that directly led to the establishment of the association is
related to the sharp contradictions that developed between the Chinese immigrants and some corrupt officials of the Chinese Embassy in the Netherlands at that time. The Chinese abroad always expect that the Chinese Embassy in their country of residence will be their refuge. After the Chinese

Embassy was re-established after the War, most Chinese in the Netherlands were greatly disappointed by the embassy's actions. Instead of helping the Chinese to recover from the miseries of the war, some officials of the Embassy even attempted to exploit their compatriots. One incident in 1946, as recalled by Mr. Cai Zexuan, can be taken as an example:[5]

> When the War was ended, some of us had re-established their contacts with their families in China. Then, many were eager to send money back home, not only to help their family members, but to express their emotions of love as well. Since transnational communication was not easy at that time, some Chinese went to ask the Chinese Embassy whether the Embassy could help them transferring foreign currency to their families in China. The Chinese ambassador gave a nice promise. The money earned by hard toil was then sent to the Chinese Embassy accompanied by a lot of good wishes.[6]
>
> But, as time passed, some senders knew from their families' letters that no money had been received. They found that they were cheated by the Chinese Embassy. How could we tolerate such a cheating? All of us were boiling with rage! [...]
>
> I remember very clearly: it was in 1946 that an unusual incident happened. That morning, some of my co-villagers [i.e., Zhejiang Chinese] went to the Chinese Embassy together. They wanted to get their money back. But the Chinese ambassador kept staying in his office. Only one staff member went out to meet them but with a perfunctory attitude. Those angry people rushed to the office of the ambassador and fought with the officers who tried to stop them. In chaotic confusion, Consul Zheng's head and one secretary's eye were hurt [...]
>
> Having got an urgent call from the Chinese ambassador, dozens of Dutch policemen rushed to the Embassy and arrested seven or eight of my co-villagers.
>
> A few days later, I went together with Yu Zhong and Ros, one Dutch friend of mine, to visit those arrested co-villagers in jail. We were deeply sad and unable to control our anger.
>
> After this incident, our wish became stronger and clearer that we needed an organization to protect ourselves. [7]

According to people's recollections, the preparatory work for the establishment of an association began in February 1947.[8] In that month a group of people gathered to begin the process, Mr. Yu Zhong was an active one.

Yu, born in 1910, came from Wenzhou to the Netherlands in 1936. Having studied in primary school for six years before going abroad, he was among the few who knew how to both read and write Chinese. Moreover, because of his warm-heartedness, the Chinese in the Netherlands held him in high esteem. Soon after the incident mentioned above, in order to ease the tension between the Zhejiang Chinese and the Chinese Embassy, the Chinese Consulate in Amsterdam hired Yu as a secretary. His mission was to assist the Consul in dealing with the affairs of the Chinese in the Netherlands. This career gave him a good chance to gain insights into the work of the Chinese Consulate and to raise his status in the Chinese community.[9]

During the eight months after February, Yu and some activists repeatedly discussed the most appropriate way to set up an association of their own.[10] They reached a consensus that the coming association would be easier to be set up if they simply based it on shared provenance. To have more co-villagers convinced of the necessity to set up an association, the founders proposed a simple but practical target for the organization: to acquire goods through collective bargaining. The organization, because of its collective power, would be stronger than an individual person when dealing with Dutch traders. Although most Chinese were illiterate or poorly educated, such a target was easy to understand and attractive; consequently, many responded enthusiastically to the proposal.

One day in early November 1947, about twenty activists gathered in a little restaurant located at Lange Niezel 12, Amsterdam. Yu Zhong chaired the meeting. They unanimously agreed that a district-of-origin association among the Wenzhou people should be set up. At Yu's suggestion, *Ou hai tongxianghui* (Ou Sea District Association, hereafter OSDA) became its official name. According to one explanation, *Ou* is picked up from the *Ou* river, which runs across the whole Wenzhou area. *Sea* means they had left the Ou river region and now lived overseas.[11] After the meeting, all the participants agreed to advise their relatives and friends to join the association.

A few days later, on 27 November 1947, the inaugural meeting of OSDA was held in Amsterdam.[12] A photo made at the meeting shows that nearly 90 men attended. At the meeting, Yu Zhong was elected chairman by common consent. About ten others were elected as vice-chairman, secretary, treasurer, or administrators.

To legalize its social position, OSDA sent an official report to the Chinese Consulate in Amsterdam soon after its establishment. In the report, the association asked the government of the Republic of China to acknowledge it as an official Chinese overseas association. The request was accepted.

At the same time, the association also sent its registration application to the Amsterdam Municipality, which was also accepted. This positive news encouraged the organizers. They submitted another request to the Amsterdam Municipality for an office-room for Chinese language classes. In the spring of 1948, the association was able to set up its office at Binnenkant 39, Amsterdam. It is worth pointing out that their office location has still not changed.

Many people I interviewed mentioned that the first chairman, Yu Zhong, was an extraordinary organizer. Under his leadership, the association managed to bring in stocks directly from Dutch factories at lower prices and offered some preferential treatment to its official members. For instance, the official members could get marketable commodities at lower prices and on credit. For the Chinese, who were short of capital, such preferential treatment was attractive, which explains why its membership increased to more than one-hundred and fifty within one year (Yu, 1977).[13] Consequently, OSDA established a firm foothold in the Netherlands.

B *Developing into a community-wide association*

In the 1950s, OSDA began to re-evaluate how it defined itself. This was due to two separate phenomena. First, while the Chinese catering business boom brought a new way of living to all Chinese immigrants, the original function of OSDA, i.e., to acquire commodities collectively, gradually withered away. Second, two sharply contrasting governments in China emerged, and the association adopted "love socialist new China" as a special motto. As a force at the core of the pro-Beijing Chinese in the Netherlands, OSDA could not stay as a district-of-origin association anymore; it had to open its door to all pro-Beijing Chinese.

In 1953, the association changed its name from *tongxianghui* (district-of-origin association) to *Huaqiaohui* (overseas Chinese association). In 1963, the association's committee decided that they would use the first Chinese character of *Ou Zhou*, which means Europe, to replace the original *Ou*, which was picked up from the *Ou* river.[14] Thus, the new name was *Ou Hai Huaqiaohui*, which means Association of Overseas Chinese at the Sea of Europe. Despite its awkwardness, the name reflected the organizers' desire to expand the association from a limited group based on shared provenance to a large group representing the whole Chinese community in the Netherlands.

In 1972, the first Chinese ambassador sent by the People's Republic of China arrived in the Netherlands. Recognizing that the West's perspective of the political situation was changing, the association held a significant committee meeting in 1973. After lively discussions, they decided to change the association's name to *Lü He Huaqiao zonghui* in Chinese and *Algemene Chinese Vereniging in Nederland* in Dutch.

It is interesting that in Chinese *lü* includes the meaning of the English word sojourning, but this term does not appear in its Dutch name. Therefore, if the new name would be translated from Chinese into English in detail, the English text would be something like the General Association of Overseas Chinese Sojourning in the Netherlands; however, if the translation is to be made from Dutch to English, then its name is the General Association of Chinese in the Netherlands.

Once the name change occurred, ACV began to present itself as a truly general association for all Chinese throughout the Netherlands and enjoyed a leading position among the pro-Beijing Chinese immigrants. The ACV leaders adopted two important measures to facilitate this during the 1960s and 1970s.

First, some Chinese from outside the Zhejiang group were recruited into ACV and a couple of non-Zhejiang elite were elected as committee members. At the end of the 1960s, Kwok Shu Cheung, one of the influential elite members among the Guangdong group and the former chairman of

WKWK, accepted the invitation to join ACV. Between 1968 and 1973, Cheung became one of ACV's vice-chairmen. In 1974, Cheung was named as the first honorary chairman of ACV. Cheung's visible position in ACV brought other Guangdong people to the association.[15]

Ma Wenshan is another example. Ma was a successful businessman who migrated from Shandong province. Since the 1950s, he often worked together with the ACV leaders to organize public activities. In 1968, Ma was elected as one of the vice-chairmen of ACV. In 1974, he was elected as the chairman of ACV. It is worth noting that up till now among the 12 people who have served as ACV's chairman, Ma is the only one who is a non-Wenzhou person.

Secondly, ACV revised and amplified its organizational rules to adjust the association to the new community-wide orientation. In 1977, ACV worked out its first complete, written constitution. Within it, ACV formulated its purpose as follows:

> ACV is an association for all patriotic Chinese in the Netherlands. Taking "all patriots belong to one big family, whether they rally to the common cause early or late" as its principle, ACV will unite all Chinese in the Netherlands to love socialist China. It will uphold justice. It will work for the well-being of the Chinese and promote mutual help among all compatriots in the Netherlands. It will improve the friendship between the Dutch and the Chinese in the Netherlands. It will ask the Chinese to abide by the Dutch law. It will not join any political activities of the Netherlands. It will attempt to improve the economic and cultural exchanges between China and the Netherlands.[16]

In addition, the constitution labeled *democratic centralism* as ACV's general organizational principle.[17] Correspondingly, three levels of organization were formulated: according to the constitution, the most powerful organ of ACV is the general members conference, which will be held once a year; when the general members conference is not in session, the executive committee, which will be in session once every three months, will act as the power organ; finally, a standing committee will be elected to take care of routine matters. Meanwhile, to systematize the whole organization, eight branches were set up at the Dutch provincial level.

Since then, although the constitution was revised in 1980, 1985, 1993 and 1996, the principle has been followed. Hereafter, attention will be paid to the real operational processes of ACV rather than how ACV revised its constitution.

C *Suspicion, pressure and ACV's political orientation*

As the only Chinese association that clearly proclaimed its political orientation as pro-Beijing, ACV suffered from suspicions and pressures during the period of the Cold War.

Because of the earlier mentioned incident between the Chinese immigrants and the corrupt officials of the Chinese Embassy in the Netherlands (at
that time the Chinese *Kuo Min Tang* Party was in power), most of the earliest
initiators of ACV hated the KMT Embassy. In 1949, after hearing about the
victory of the Chinese Communist Party in China, ACV as a whole immediately leaned towards the new government of Beijing. Then, in March of
1950, the Dutch government recognized the People's Republic of China as a
sovereign state. In 1954, the Netherlands established diplomatic relations
with the People's Republic of China at the chargé d'affaires level. This positive progress encouraged ACV to air its pro-Beijing opinion more publicly.
They expressed their political orientation through a series of activities.

For instance, immediately after learning about the establishment of the
People's Republic of China, ACV (then OSDA) sent a telegram to congratulate the new central government in Beijing (ACV, 1997:36).[18] In 1951, three
portraits of the leaders of the Communist Party of China (CPC for short) —
Mao Zedong, Zhu De and Zhou Enlai — and some books and magazines
about the victory of the CPC were sent to the association by the PRC's
representatives in Geneva. Then, the association held a grand ceremony to
hang the portraits on the wall and set up a reading room in the office. Also,
after receiving a documentary film called *China's War of Liberation 1945-1949*,
the association repeatedly showed the film for over a month to publicize the
victory of the CPC (Yu, 1977). Moreover, on 1 October 1950, the first
anniversary of the founding of the People's Republic of China, ACV held a
great celebration in Grand Hotel Krasnapolsky (Dam 9, Amsterdam). About
two hundred Chinese attended the party. On the roof of the hotel, a Five-
Starred Red Flag — the national flag of the People's Republic of China —
was raised for the first time in public in the Netherlands.[19] When recalling the
moving sights of that day, Mr. Hu Kelin, one of the founders of ACV, still
shows excitement:[20]

> I remember very clearly that it was on the first of October 1950 that we
> Chinese in the Netherlands held the first party to celebrate the National
> Day of the People's Republic of China. The initiators were Zhou Guoli,
> Wang Chunlin and some leaders of *Ou hai tongxianghui*. I was among the
> preparatory group. While the party was under preparation, we had re-
> ceived several blackmailing letters from the pro-Taiwan group. Although
> they were rather powerful at that time, we were not scared [...]
>
>   It was a great day. At seven o'clock in the morning, the Five-Starred
> Red Flag was raised on the roof of Krasnapolsky Hotel. Seeing our na-
> tional flag flying in the Dutch sky for the first time, you cannot imagine
> how excited we were! From that early morning till the deep of the night,
> in order to prevent sabotage by the pro-Taiwan group, we dozens of
> members of *Ou hai tongxianghui* took upon us the responsibility to guard the
> flag and to guard the meeting hall by turns [...]

When relations between the Western world and the communist East were becoming strained, however, heavy pressure was brought to bear upon this pro-Beijing association. In 1951, responding to the call of the Beijing government to resist US aggression and aid Korea, ACV requested that the Chinese in the Netherlands support China by donating money. According to Zhong Xinru, they knew little about the Korean War at that time. What pushed them to donate money for China was that the leaders of the new China had the courage to fight against the number one Western country — the USA.[21] This political action aroused serious suspicion from the Dutch authorities. Yu Zhong, Mei Zhongwei, Hu Wenqiao and some other leaders were questioned; their houses were searched, and their passports were suspended.[22]

From then on, during the whole period of the Cold War, the association, especially its leaders, was labelled as "a Communist spy in the Netherlands" and "a political organization controlled by Beijing." The *Ministerie van Binnenlandse Zaken* (the Dutch Ministry of the Interior, hereafter BiZa) watched all activities of the association.[23] Even today some elderly members of ACV who experienced that period still call the Dutch BiZa "Holland's CIA."

During the interviews I conducted, I was told that during the 1960s and the 1970s, several leaders and activists of ACV had been punished because of tax or hygiene problems, but in fact they were, to a certain degree, political victims. One informant told me the following story:

I arrived in Holland in 1936 [...] In 1961, I established my own Chinese restaurant in Amsterdam. The business was excellent [...]

Nevertheless, since the 1960s when I took the position as a major leader of ACV, my restaurant was examined very often. Finally, my restaurant was closed because I was accused of evading taxes of more than five hundred thousand Dutch guilders. It was incredible! Having got support from a Dutch lawyer and a qualified Dutch accountant, I appealed to court but lost the lawsuit. My restaurant and four private houses were put up for auction to clear the account. All property I had earned since I arrived in the Netherlands had gone. I was very sad [...]

I have one friend who had some contacts with the Dutch Ministry of the Interior, which many Chinese labeled as the Dutch CIA at that time. Some years later, this friend told me that there was no chance for me to win the court case because my name was on the blacklist of the Ministry.

I am an old man now. Thanks to the Dutch welfare system I am enjoying a comfortable life although I lost my property. While looking back, I know I did something wrong that I should not have tried to evade paying full tax. However, compared with other cases I know of, the punishment brought upon me was much harsher than upon other similar cases [...]

Although this case is too complicated to sort out in a few words, one fact cannot be ignored: this interviewee's political orientation was one factor that intensified the punishment imposed upon him.[24]

China's international position rose greatly after a series of important events: the People's Republic of China's admittance to the United Nations in 1971; the strengthened ties between the Netherlands and Beijing since 1972; the spectacular successes of the reform movement since the end of the 1970s in China. As China rose, the political pressure surrounding ACV slowly diffused.

D A thriving period for ACV

ACV flourished in the period between the mid-1970s and the mid-1980s. Three developments contributed to this part of ACV's history: (i) the expansion of their services and activities; (ii) the introduction of new leadership; and (iii) the new immigration wave from China. Below, each of these will be explored.

With the rise of their national and political dignity, ACV expanded its services and increased their social activities. For instance, ACV showed Chinese films from the People's Republic of China. Because Chinese television and videos were not yet available in the Netherlands, the presentation of Chinese films was an attractive activity. Meanwhile, it became a regular activity of ACV to organize a celebration on the Chinese National Day. ACV has invited a professional troupe of musicians and artists from China to give a performance at the party almost every year since 1983.

Since the People's Republic of China celebrates its National Day on the first of October, but the Republic of China (i.e., the government in Taiwan) celebrates its National Day on the tenth of October, which National Day party one wishes to attend is a rather sensitive issue. During the period after the Korea War untill the 1960s, only a few dozen to around one hundred Chinese dared to attend the party organized by ACV. Since the second part of the 1970s, however, the number of attendants at ACV party has often been as many as one thousand, and they come from all over the Netherlands.

Another important service they began to offer is ACV's official organ — *Huaqiao tongxun* (*Overzeese Chinezen Bulletin*; Overseas Chinese Bulletin; the ACV Bulletin for short). Because it was difficult to get information written in Chinese, the Chinese who did not read Dutch enthusiastically welcomed the ACV Bulletin.

The ACV Bulletin was first published on 17 August 1977. At the beginning, it was a monthly issue with six pages. Most of its contents were copied from the newspapers of Beijing. A couple of volunteers worked as the editors. The working conditions were very simple.[25] From 1982, one person was in charge of the editing and the publication. The reports on the Chinese in the Netherlands and the explanations about the Dutch regulations increased. In the second half of 1984, the ACV Bulletin became a semimonthly periodical.

According to Hu, the first editor of the ACV Bulletin, to decide how many copies should be printed he went to collect the addresses of all of the Chinese restaurants, which numbered about 1,800 at that time. Then, the ACV committee decided that they should print 2,000 copies of each issue of the ACV Bulletin and post one to every Chinese restaurant free of charge. When more people subscribed personally to the ACV Bulletin and when the number of Chinese restaurants increased, the copies of each issue of the ACV Bulletin rose to 6,000 in the mid-1980s. On 13 May 1996, the ACV Bulletin suddenly raised its circulation to 20,000 when a new committee took over its management. Nevertheless, due to financial difficulties, the circulation was reduced to 6,000 copies in a couple of months; then, it was again reduced to 3,000 copies in May 1997. Although occasionally there would be an advertisement in the Bulletin to ask readers to make donations, the basic rule that the ACV Bulletin is free of charge has never changed. Consequently, trying to balance the expenses of its bulletin has been a burden for ACV.

Few Chinese migrants associations abroad have been able to maintain a regularly published, freely distributed bulletin for more than twenty years. This has effectively heightened ACV's reputation. Therefore, the ACV Bulletin is more than anything else a significant symbol of ACV. Although the committee of ACV has clearly recognized that with the numerous Chinese language outlets available today the ACV Bulletin's role as an information source for Chinese immigrants has greatly decreased, nobody dares to suggest either stopping the ACV Bulletin or switching it to a commercial publication.

The second development occurred around the turn of the 1980s when a new group of people who had come to the Netherlands in the 1960s and 1970s took over the leadership of ACV. This precipitated some considerable changes in the ACV's history.

Up until the end of the 1970s, the authoritative power of ACV had been kept in the hands of those who arrived in the Netherlands before the Second World War and were advanced in years. When the Dutch authorities regarded ACV with suspicion, however, the younger newcomers, even if they were pro-Beijing in their mind, were reluctant to be activists of ACV publicly. Only when it became apparent that they need not be afraid of political persecution did more young Chinese become active members of ACV; from these new, young activists, a new nucleus emerged.

In 1980, Mr. Hu, who was born in 1941 and arrived in the Netherlands in 1962, was elected as the new chairman of ACV. Among the newly elected leading group of 12 people (one chairman, eight vice-chairmen, one general secretary and two vice-general secretaries), two-thirds of them were entering the leading circle of ACV for the first time. Moreover, in the following five terms, the chairman was elected from this group: Hu (1980-1983; 1987-1989); Mei (1984-1986); and Ye (1990-1993; 1994-1996).[26]

This group showed some new characteristics. They had a higher educational background than the first leading group. For instance, among the eight chairmen of ACV before 1979, all except Yu, who had finished his primary school education before going abroad, had merely attended primary school for two or three years. The education level of the three chairmen of ACV between 1980 and 1996 was much higher. Mei is among the few who had graduated from a Chinese university before going abroad; Ye graduated from a Chinese high school; and Hu graduated from a Chinese middle school.

Moreover, they had some practical knowledge about how to run an ethnic association in a Western country. For instance, in November 1980, Hu, as the newly elected chairman of ACV, together with four committee members paid a formal visit to the Amsterdam municipal administration. It was the first time that the leaders of a Chinese voluntary association in the Netherlands went to visit the Dutch authorities. Then, in February 1981, it was also for the first time that the Mayor of Amsterdam, accompanied by some Dutch officials, accepted the invitation of ACV to attend the Chinese New Year's party that was held by ACV in Amsterdam. On 15 May 1981, as the representative of the Chinese in the Netherlands, Hu and three leaders of ACV went to visit the Ministry of the Interior Affairs in The Hague. Drs. H.A.A. Molleman, who was in charge of minority affairs at that time, received the visitors. Their talks focussed on matters of mutual concern (the ACV Bulletin, 30 May 1981).

Through the exchange of visits, the contacts between ACV and the Dutch authorities became more direct and open, which helped to improve their understanding of one another. Since 1987, ACV has been among the few Chinese associations that have benefitted from the financial support offered by the Dutch government.

The third development from which ACV benefitted was the rich new human resources brought over by the sudden migration wave from China. As was described in Chapter II, after China opened its doors to the Western world, thousands of Zhejiang people came to the Netherlands through chain-migration. Although it claimed to be a community-wide association with members from different sub-groups of the Chinese community in the Netherlands, ACV has always been composed mainly of Zhejiang people. Therefore, as was mentioned earlier, chain-introduction, being a reasonable extension of chain-migration, played an active role in the expansion of ACV's membership. That is, many new arrivals became members simply because their relatives or co-villagers introduced them to the association.

There is another related reason for why this thriving period for ACV accompanied the rise in migration levels. In the late 1970s, the procedures for applying for a private passport in China were still rather complicated. Some claim that the relatives of the ACV activists, because of their reputation as patriotic Chinese, could go through these procedures quicker and with fewer obstacles. During the late 1970s and the early 1980s, this notion was popular among the Zhejiang immigrants, which made ACV more attractive to them.

However, almost at the same time, when the leaders of ACV were enjoying their association's social prestige both within the Chinese community in the Netherlands and in China, some new organizing activities held by the Cantonese-speaking migrants in particular were emerging. In a short period, these associations began to challenge the social position of ACV. At that time, however, few leaders of ACV recognized the potential effects of this situation.

E *Facing new challenges*

Since the 1980s, ACV's self-proclaimed position as the Number One Chinese association in the Netherlands has been challenged. These challenges mainly came from a few newly established Chinese associations, which gained popularity in a short period. For instance, the two Chinese associations *Fa Yin* and *Kah Wah* acquired a good reputation for establishing Chinese schools for Chinese children. Similarly, since 1985, the Chinese Sports Federation in the Netherlands has occupied a leading position in organizing nationwide Chinese sports meetings. In addition, another newly established Chinese association, CCRM, became popular among the Dutch authorities after it organized a series of public activities to improve the Chinese community's integration into the Dutch society (cf. the third case of this chapter). Therefore, little by little, the social position of ACV has been changed from the number one association to one among a dozen prominent Chinese associations.

Other challenges have come from within ACV itself. As an association with a long history, it was inevitable that some contradictions would arise among its members and its leadership. When outside pressure was heavy, the inner contradictions could be masked; however, when the social environment settled and the subsequent decline of group cohesion occurred, the inner contradictions became apparent. Due to differences of opinion and other issues, some members and even leaders publicly announced their withdrawal from ACV. Some simply joined other associations, and others set up their own association. In total, the resigned leaders of ACV have set up at least four new associations since the end of the 1980s.

Ultimately, the greatest challenges for ACV come from the question of how to adapt to the changed situation. Nowadays, ACV is one association among one hundred-odd other Chinese associations in the Netherlands, although it is still better known than many others are. During a rather long period, ACV had successfully used the patriotic flag to establish its position. Now, at the end of the 20th century, this is far from powerful enough to promote the cohesion and continuity of an association. It is urgent for its current leaders to find an appropriate way to maintain the ACV's viability as an organization for the Chinese rank and file.

The year 1996 marks another turning point for ACV. This was its tenth election. Before the vote, the three ex-chairmen who were regarded as the second nucleus of ACV announced that none of them would be a candidate. Moreover, none of the younger committee members enjoyed clear popular support. In other words, the third nucleus was not yet formed. Thus, the 1996 election became a competition among the younger members of ACV. It is probable that the intense competition encouraged a record voting turnout. Formerly, the number of members who came to vote was between one hundred and two hundred.[27] Unexpectedly, on 11 March 1996, more than eight hundred members went to vote at the ACV's office (the ACV Bulletin, 18 March 1996). This number of voters is the highest in the history of all Chinese associations in the Netherlands.[28]

In order to reduce the competition among the sub-groups among the ACV's members, the result was that an unprecedentedly large-scale committee of 211 members took office (cf. ACV Bulletin, 22 April 1996). On 23 May 1996, the inaugural ceremony of the 10th committee of ACV was held in Amsterdam. At the ceremony, the newly elected chairman declared that by weeding through the old to bring forth the new, the elected committee would lead ACV to face new challenges and would endeavour to energetically push its work forward.

2 *Fa Yin: for Chinese children and Chinese elders*[29]

As was described in Chapter III, the establishment of a new non-religious Chinese voluntary association marked the beginning of a new blooming period of the Chinese organizational movement in the Netherlands. This new non-religious association is *Fa Yin*, which was established in 1976.

The official name of *Fa Yin* is *Lü He Huaren Lianyihui* in Chinese; or *Chinese Vereniging in Nederland 'Fa Yin'* in Dutch. *Fa Yin* is a Bo On local dialect term meaning Chinese people (*Huaren* in standard Chinese). Like ACV, the first Chinese character of *Fa Yin*'s Chinese name is *lü*, which includes the meaning of the English word sojourning. Such a meaning, however, does not appear in its Dutch name. Therefore, if translating *Fa Yin*'s name from Chinese into English, it should be something like the Association of Chinese People Sojourning in the Netherlands.

In its early period, some officials of the Chinese Embassy and some leaders of ACV regarded the establishment of *Fa Yin* as a divisive development in the Chinese community. Sharp criticisms were heaped upon *Fa Yin*. Nevertheless, in June 1996, after 20 years, *Fa Yin* joyously celebrated the anniversary of its founding. At this grand ceremony, the Chinese Embassy in the Netherlands, some Dutch institutions and dozens of Chinese associations, including the most influential ones, sent their representatives to present their congratulations. Among the people who gave an official speech, there was the cultural attaché of the Chinese Embassy, the Dutch director of the Amsterdam Center for Foreigners (ACB), and the chairman of ACV. At the ceremony, the chairman of *Fa Yin* claimed with dignity that *Fa Yin* was one of few truly influential Chinese associations and enjoyed a good reputation among the Chinese in the Netherlands.

It is interesting to trace how *Fa Yin* has reached its current position.

A *Birth*

Fa Yin is the first voluntary association specifically organized by and for the Guangdong group in the Netherlands after the Second World War. As was mentioned earlier, during the first decades after the war, ACV was regarded as the only symbol of pro-Beijing Chinese in the Netherlands, and it tried to involve more non-Wenzhou Chinese in its affairs. Although some Guangdong people did join ACV, they often felt like outsiders. One important reason was the gap between the dialects. Since Wenzhou people formed the main body of the association, in meetings of the association, the working language was very often the Wenzhou dialect, which Guangdong people cannot understand.

After the migration wave of the 1960s, the number of Guangdong people greatly increased, and their economic power rose. Thus, some newly emerged Guangdong elite were not satisfied with the position they could hold in an association dominated by Wenzhou people; plus, they encountered some social problems distinct from the problems with the Wenzhou people.

The failure of ACV to establish a Chinese school became the direct impetus for the birth of *Fa Yin*. Recalling the characteristics of the migration trend in the 1960s from Hong Kong in Chapter II, one phenomenon was that many new immigrants in this period came with their families or fetched their families soon after the pioneers settled down. Therefore, many strongly wanted a Chinese education for their children. Between 1972 and 1975, seeing that there were no Chinese schools for Chinese children in the Netherlands, Mr. Liang, a well-known restaurateur among the Guangdong group at that time, together with several friends who were members of ACV, asked repeatedly for the establishment of a Chinese school under the auspices of ACV. After disappointing rejections, they decided to set up an association of their own.

Fa Yin was officially founded by about ten Guangdong Chinese in Amsterdam on 18 June 1976.[30] After lively discussions, the founding aim of *Fa Yin* was defined in two Chinese sentences:

> *You you suo jiao*   (Let Chinese children receive an education)
> *Lao you suo wei*   (Let Chinese elders make a contribution)

More extensively, *Fa Yin*'s founding aim was to let Chinese children in the Netherlands receive an education in Chinese language and culture; to enable Chinese elders to spend their remaining years in happiness; and to let Chinese elders make contributions toward the spreading of Chinese culture to their descendants. Mr. Liang was elected as the first chairman, and three others were elected as vice-chairmen.

B *Growth*

During the first few years after *Fa Yin* was established, ACV did not want to recognize its existence but regarded its appearance as a divisive move. Having kept his ACV membership, Liang, the first chairman of *Fa Yin*, asked ACV to accept *Fa Yin* as its branch, but ACV rejected his proposal. Moreover, ACV asked *Fa Yin* to disband itself. Seeing that there was no other solution, *Fa Yin* decided to make an effort for its further development rather than simply giving up.

Its first step was to set up an office. During the 1970s, with the blooming of the Chinese catering business in the Netherlands, the Chinatown of Amsterdam, where the Chinese grocery stores and other ethnic service-businesses were concentrated, was also flourishing. Many Chinese would go there occasionally for shopping or to enjoy the familiarity of the atmosphere. *Fa Yin* decided to set up its office near the Chinatown of Amsterdam. Some money was donated to rent an apartment and to make renovations.

On 8 July 1978, *Fa Yin* held an opening ceremony for its new office, which is still located at Rechtboomssloot 5, just next to the Chinatown of Amsterdam. In order to increase the recognition and support for the new association by more Chinese in the Netherlands, *Fa Yin* held a Chinese table-tennis game and a Chinese chess game as one part of its opening ceremony. This is the first time that a Chinese association in the Netherlands held public sports games. Several dozen Chinese took part in the games with great pleasure. This first success greatly heightened the confidence of *Fa Yin*'s organizers. They went ahead to strive for the realization of their lofty goal: the establishment of a Chinese school for Chinese children in the Netherlands.

The committee of *Fa Yin* decided to use its office as a classroom to teach Chinese children the Chinese language. This established the foundation for Chinese education. All leading members made monetary contributions towards this goal. In a few days, 23,650 guilders had been collected from 14 committee members.[31] In September 1979, the first Chinese class started in the office of *Fa Yin*. One lady who had been a primary school teacher before emigrating from Hong Kong was asked to be a volunteer teacher. The textbooks were ordered from Hong Kong. And, through *Fa Yin*'s members, around twenty Chinese children enrolled as pupils.

After nearly twenty years, the *Fa Yin* Chinese School has become one of the largest and most famous after-school Chinese schools in the Netherlands. To enable more Chinese children to follow Chinese courses in their neighbourhood, *Fa Yin* set up two branches of its school in small towns north of Amsterdam: one in Enkhuizen in 1986 and one in Den Helder in 1990.[32]

By the end of 1997, the *Fa Yin* Chinese School formed its own education system. The school has a staff of twenty teachers and has about four hundred pupils. The current director of the *Fa Yin* school is a graduate of a normal college in China, and he has attempted to conform to Chinese education standards. There are eight grades and sixteen classes. Pupils attend Chinese classes every Saturday for four teaching hours. Cantonese is the language of instruction. Only in the seventh and eighth grades are the pupils required to follow a one-hour course in *Putonghua* (i.e., standard Chinese) each week. Since 1987, when the first group finished eight years of study and graduated, the *Fa Yin* school has educated about three hundred and sixty graduates in ten years. In the autumn of 1997, at the request of some graduates, the *Fa Yin* school began to set up an advanced class for continued study. Thirty-six ex-graduates enrolled as pupils in the first year.

During its statutory term, every elected *Fa Yin* committee has to take responsibility for balancing the finances of the school. Since the establishment of *Fa Yin* in 1976 through 1998, five people have taken up the position of *Fa Yin*'s chairman. All of them have contributed generously to *Fa Yin*'s mission.

Among others, Mr. Liang has been regarded as the father of the *Fa Yin* Chinese School. Because he and his late Dutch wife do not have any children, he touchingly considers all Chinese pupils of the *Fa Yin* school as his children. As a retired person, he does not have much income. Nevertheless, he has done his best to support the school. For instance, since *Fa Yin*'s school was established, Liang had contributed 3000 Dutch guilders to the school every year until 1985 when his private savings were almost finished. In accordance with Chinese custom, when Liang turned seventy years old in 1982, all his younger relatives and friends presented gifts to him. Instead of receiving any items, he instructed all his relatives and friends to donate the gift money to the *Fa Yin* School Foundation. In 1992, when Liang's wife passed away, he let others know that whoever wanted to send flowers for the funeral should send the flower money to the *Fa Yin* School Foundation instead. From these two instances alone, the *Fa Yin* School Foundation received about twelve thousand guilders. In 1993, Liang made his will publicly known:[33]

> If one day I go to "sleep" forever, please donate all flower money to the *Fa Yin* School Foundation. Also, all of my private property will belong to the school.

The Chinese in the Netherlands understandably have great esteem for this old man and regard him as an example.

By 1998, *Fa Yin* firmly established its position as the leading Chinese school provider in the Netherlands. Founding, developing and expanding the *Fa Yin* school system are the greatest contributions of the *Fa Yin* association to the Chinese community in Amsterdam. As Liang, in an interview with me, repeatedly concluded:

> No *Fa Yin*, no Chinese school; no Chinese school, no *Fa Yin*.

Another founding purpose of *Fa Yin* was to provide welfare for Chinese elders. In view of the fact that Chinese elders are among the most isolated and vulnerable in the community, the founders hoped that *Fa Yin* could help them enjoy a happier life during their remaining years.

When they established *Fa Yin*, most of the founders were in their fifties or sixties. The Chinese elderly group played an important role during the development of the association. Thus, *Fa Yin* is popularly regarded as an association for elderly Cantonese.

Since its establishment, the *Fa Yin*'s office has been a meeting place open to all Chinese elders. They very often come to play Chinese chess, Chinese

cards or *mahjong* in groups. Some come to read Chinese newspapers or magazines, while others just come to chat with friends.

Beginning in the late 1980s and continuing today, *Fa Yin* organizes a
weekly party for its elderly members, but non-members are also welcome.
Very often, not only the elders but some younger people also come for a
good time with other Chinese. If the weather is good, around one hundred
people will gather. By the early 1990s, this weekly meeting developed into a
fixed program. From one o'clock on, people would arrive in the office hall.
At two o'clock, Mr. Hoo, a retired basketball coach from Hong Kong, would
give a special report. If a new regulation was promulgated in the Netherlands
specifically related to Chinese senior citizens, he would give an explanation.
The audience welcomed his speeches because some are poorly educated, but
some simply like the way of his talking, that is, as a man of charm and wit, he
can tell serious issues in terse and lively language. After the speech, occasionally, a professional talk on aspects of health or access to various pensions and
benefits to which they are entitled would be given. Afterwards, some kind of
public recreational activities would begin. For instance, someone would teach
all participants to sing a Chinese song or someone would organize karaoke.
While some preferred singing folk songs, some enjoyed performing traditional dances. This period is usually very lively. Around half past three, some
pastries bought from a Chinese shop nearby would be distributed to each
participant. After eating the light refreshments, some would leave, some
would chat with friends for a while, and some might sit together to play cards
or *mahjong*. The whole meeting would officially end at four o'clock but sometimes would last much longer.

Fa Yin has also set up a foundation for its elderly members. The money
was collected from Chinese businessmen in Amsterdam. The foundation
funds have usually been used to subsidize some activities. For instance, during the Chinese New Year, the Chinese Dragon Boat Festival, the Chinese
Mid-Autumn Festival, and on the Western Christmas Day, *Fa Yin* will not
only have a public festival but will also invite all of its elderly members to
have dinner together in a Chinese restaurant. Because the association subsi-
dizes these activities, all participants only have to pay a small fee.[34] In appreciation of these activities, some elderly members of *Fa Yin* make positive
contributions to the Chinese community. For example, they often act as
active volunteers and assistants in various public activities organized by the
Chinese associations in Amsterdam.

Throughout the 1990s, *Fa Yin* has maintained a friendly relationship with
ACV. The unfriendly attitude of ACV towards *Fa Yin* changed in the early
1980s for two reasons. On the one hand, the leaders of ACV recognized that
it was impossible to stop the emergence of new Chinese associations; on the
other hand, the *Fa Yin* Chinese School was highly appreciated. Moreover,
their common pro-Beijing orientation brought them even closer. One telling
phenomenon is that since the fifth committee of ACV (1980-1984), before
every election, a couple of positions on the ACV's standing committee would
be reserved for the representatives of *Fa Yin*. Within the tenth committee of

ACV (1996-1999), the chairman of *Fa Yin* was invited to be a vice-chairman of ACV, and one vice-chairman of *Fa Yin* was invited to take a position as ACV's standing committee member.

C *New Pursuits*

After celebrating its twentieth anniversary of its founding, the leaders of *Fa Yin*, on the basis of its highly improved social position, proposed two new projects to pursue in the future. One is to buy a building for its school, and the other is to have a *home* for its elderly members.

Since the mid-1980s, when the number of classes in the *Fa Yin* school increased to more than a dozen, finding a suitable place to conduct classes has puzzled the leaders of *Fa Yin*. Very often, a couple of months before another term begins, they have to worry about how to rent a suitable building for the next school year: the rent cannot be too high; the location should be somewhere in the centre of Amsterdam; and the building should have more than twenty classrooms. Fulfilling all of these requirements has not been easy. In 1995, when the owner of the school building that had been rented by *Fa Yin* for a couple of years suddenly wanted to raise the rent and they could not bargain for a reasonable price, it was almost impossible for the *Fa Yin* school to begin a new term. Because of this, how to collect money to buy a building for the school is constantly under discussion in *Fa Yin*'s committee.

A class of Fa Yin *Chinese school* (Photo by Li Minghuan).

Fa Yin is among the few Chinese voluntary associations that is not only able to balance their revenue and expenditure but make some surplus each year. There are at least two reasons for this. First, during its history of more than twenty years, *Fa Yin* has often called for and received donations to improve education in Chinese language and culture. Second, the *Fa Yin* school is among the few Chinese schools that are more or less subsidized by the Dutch authorities concerned.[35] Through careful calculation and strict budgeting, the *Fa Yin* School Foundation has accumulated some capital. Nevertheless, it is far from enough to purchase a building for the school. Besides, there are many complications that accompany a major capital investment. For example, if it was possible to get a bank loan to buy a building, how could they guarantee they can collect enough money to repay the loan? How can they balance the daily expenses and the maintenance costs of the building? Although issues like this remain unresolved, the committee of Fa Yin still wants to propose the project of buying a building for the *Fa Yin* school as a long-term target.

The project of having a common home for its elderly members in Amsterdam has made some progress after it was put forward in 1996.

The Netherlands is well known for its social welfare system. Amongst others, the establishment of an elders' home to jointly take care of elders is highly appreciated. However, few Chinese elders can benefit from it because of language barriers and different living habits and customs. In order to help the Chinese elders to professional help and keep them from isolation and feelings of abandonment, a Chinese elderly home was established in The Hague in 1994 and in Rotterdam in 1995. Since then, the Chinese elders in Amsterdam have been even more eager to have such a home for themselves. *Fa Yin*, as an association with many elderly members, is working for this goal enthusiastically.

The New Chinatown Project has brought new hope for them. Mr. But, the current chairman of *Fa Yin*, is among the major initiators of the project.[36] In 1996, the Amsterdam Center for Foreigners (ACB) agreed to be involved in the project as the general coordinator, and then in 1998 to hold the secretariat. The house-building association of Amsterdam, *Het Oosten* (The East), is responsible for the treasury and will be the real estate investor of the project. In addition to the founders of the New Chinatown Foundation, Rabo Vastgoed BV (one of the largest real estate companies in the Netherlands) joined the Foundation in June 1998. Moreover, being responsible for the development of the entire IJ-bank area, of which the New Chinatown Project is a part, the Municipality of Amsterdam has established a coordinating committee to guide the development of the whole project. Based on all this support and cooperation, the proposed New Chinatown Project is developing into a feasible plan. A group of influential Chinese founded the New Chinatown Foundation. Because But chairs this group,[37] *Fa Yin* is a partner of the foundation.[38]

In accordance with the project, the new Chinatown will be constructed on the southern IJ-bank in Amsterdam. It will cover an area of at least 50,000m^2

(not counting public space) and include a trade convention center, a shopping plaza, some office buildings, and a Chinese cultural and recreational centre. Yet, what has attracted the attention of many of *Fa Yin*'s elderly members is that within the planned 25,000m^2 of residential buildings, about 12,000m^2 will be specially designed as social housing including housing for Chinese elderly people.[39] Thus, many elderly members of *Fa Yin* cherish the idea that in the near future they will be able to live in a culturally familiar atmosphere and will be able to find support among each other.

3 CCRM: "We have nearly finished our tasks!"

CCRM, *Stichting Chinese Cultuur Recreatie en Maatschappelijk Werk* (Foundation for Chinese Culture, Recreation and Social Work), was established on 2 March 1984.[40] A few days later, on 14 March, CCRM held a grand inaugural meeting in Rotterdam. The background of its founding is rather different from many other Chinese associations in the Netherlands. In more concrete terms, as a Chinese association with an obvious Christian background and a close affiliation with the Dutch political party the *Christen Democratisch Appèl* (Christian Democratic Appeal; hereafter CDA), CCRM is a marginal association among all Chinese associations in the Netherlands. The CCRM's structure, along with important founding elements, requires special attention.

A *CEME: the basis of CCRM*

As was described in Chapter III, CEME, the first official Chinese Christians Association, was set up in Rotterdam in 1974. A few months after its establishment, CEME managed to buy a building and, moreover, to have a full-time social worker to take care of its daily affairs. Progressing quite rapidly, CEME attracted the sympathy and approval of a considerable number of Chinese immigrants. By the early 1980s, CEME had also established Chinese evangelical missions in Amsterdam, The Hague, and Utrecht. Although CEME had combined the missionary work with practical social services, its influences were limited because most Chinese immigrants are not Christians. During the early 1980s, some activists at CEME deliberated on a new plan to organize a non-religious, voluntary association. Mrs. Chan played a key role in this development.

Mrs. Chan's hometown is in Hunan, an inland province of China. At the end of the 1940s, she, as a little girl, went together with her parents to Hong Kong when it appeared that the Chinese Communist Party would soon gain control of the country. In Hong Kong, she finished her middle school education in a Christian school and became a devout Christian. She married a Chinese pastor. In view of Hong Kong's unstable situation, the couple left for Europe in 1968. After arriving in Europe, Mrs. Chan first spent some years in Belgium, and then went to the Netherlands to study Dutch and sociology at Leiden University.

These experiences shaped Mrs. Chan's personality and her future career. Firstly, born into a family that is antagonistic to the Communist Party, Mrs. Chan is loyal to the Republic of China. Her political orientation, which she has never tried to hide, has provided her with important financial resources and social backing after she became a Chinese association leader in the Netherlands. Secondly, having grown up in Hong Kong and able to speak Cantonese fluently, she often identifies herself as a Hong Kong Chinese and is accepted as such by others. Such a we-group link has offered Mrs. Chan much help from like-minded fellow Chinese for her organizational efforts. Thirdly, thanks to her studies in universities in Belgium and the Netherlands, Mrs. Chan has not only mastered the Dutch language but gained wider knowledge about the Western world. This, to a certain degree, has paved the way for her to overcome the language and cultural barriers. Therefore, she is much better than many other Chinese association leaders in maintaining proper contacts with the relevant Dutch institutions. Finally, since her husband is a well-known Chinese pastor among the Chinese Christians in the Netherlands, the Chinese Christian Brothers and Sisters respect her as Mother Priestess.[41] While Mrs. Chan was preparing for the establishment of CCRM, this *religious* loyalty was transformed into a kind of *organizational* loyalty. For example, one room in the church established by CEME was used as the office of CCRM until 1987 when CCRM was able to buy its own office. Moreover, many active volunteers of the Chinese Church also assisted Mrs. Chan with her work for CCRM.

Among the current Chinese association leaders in the Netherlands, few possess so many valuable assets. Being devoted to the Chinese church and CEME for years, Mrs. Chan became the most important initiator of CCRM. When asked about the reasons, she said:[42]

> Between 1974 and 1983, I had dedicated myself completely to the Chinese church for nine years. I liked the work very much. However, in order to strive further for the legitimate rights and interests of our Chinese in the Netherlands, I could not confine myself within the four walls of the church. Having discussed this with my husband, he agreed to let me be *borrowed* from the church for a while.

> [Who wanted to borrow you?]

> The Chinese community. My Chinese brothers and sisters.

Thus, it was in 1983 that Mrs. Chan looked for an opportunity to open a new field of action.

B *CDA: the Dutch guidance of CCRM*

In the early 1980s, the new Dutch Minorities Policy was put into effect. Before 1980, similar to many other Western European countries, the official policy of the Dutch government with regard to immigrant groups was characterized by the assumption that the Netherlands was not a country of immigration, and thus many immigrants would return home sooner or later. However, later, after facing the clear reality of a substantial permanent immigrant community, the idea that immigration was temporary had to be abandoned. Then, the government formulated a new Minorities Policy that aimed to overcome social deprivation by improving the economic and social position of the minorities. This change in policy became a hot topic and provoked a lively debate in the Netherlands.

In the country's Chinese community, many just ignored the discussion. Although according to the newly defined concept of a minority the Chinese would not belong to the protected group, few Chinese cared about it.[43]

Such being the case, Mrs. Chan began to organize her compatriots under the support of the Dutch political party, CDA, which was in government at that time. Through the introduction of Ms. Evenhuis, a CDA member of Parliament, Mrs. Chan joined CDA in 1983, and soon after also joined the *Interculturele Beraad* (Inter-cultural Deliberation Committee; hereafter, IB), a subsidiary of CDA. While recalling her personal experiences in that period, Mrs. Chan told me:[44]

> Having attended the training courses of CDA and followed the discussions organized once a month by IB, I came to know some well-known Dutch politicians. They had not only encouraged me to participate in the socio-political movement of Holland, but these discussions also made me look at our own Chinese community with fresh eyes [...]
>
> Then, I thought we Chinese have encountered uncountable difficulties in this country, but we are used to being an invisible group. We always try to settle difficulties by ourselves. Is this a permanent solution? Why don't we let our voice be heard by the Dutch authorities concerned? We Chinese are a minority in the Netherlands, why can't we benefit from the New Minorities Policy?
>
> Only if we have a well organized association to represent all Chinese can we Chinese have a voice in the matter!

The organizational work started under the full guidance of CDA. In Mrs. Chan's words:

> Ms. Evenhuis was so kind as to take us by the hand and teach us how to organize an ethnic voluntary association effectively in the Netherlands. We shall never forget her heart-warming support.[45]

Besides Ms. Evenhuis, some names of the active politicians of CDA can be found now and then in the relevant reports of CCRM as well: Mr. J. G. H. Kraijenbrink and Drs. M. Smits, CDA members of Parliament; Dr. K. Sieteram, Mr. Jos Marey, and Mr. S. Rambocus, the leading members of IB. Moreover, in the first few years after CCRM was established, it was normal that some high-ranking Dutch public officers would appear as distinguished guests at CCRM's significant meetings. Most were CDA members: Drs. W. J. Deetman, then Minister of Education, Arts and Sciences; Drs. C. A. van Dijk, then Minister for the Interior; and Mr. E. Brinkman, then Minister of Welfare, Public Health and Culture.

C *A marginal association*

The leaders of CCRM were very proud that they enjoyed full support from so many high-ranking Dutch officials in a very short period. However, from the perspective of the Chinese rank and file, many were confused with its social image: is CCRM a Chinese association or a Dutch institution? Such a doubt, in fact, is a reflection of a unique feature of CCRM: it struck a root in the Chinese community; grew up from a Christian base; and was guided by a Dutch political party. The following discussion will elaborate this point.

Firstly, CCRM's Dutch and Chinese names reveal a great deal about the organization; after all, the name of an association is its public flag. CCRM has a very Dutch-style Dutch name and a very Chinese-style Chinese name.[46] In short, its Dutch name was an imitation. At that time, the name of the Dutch ministry that took care of all social affairs was *Ministerie van Cultuur, Recreatie en Maatschappelijk Werk* (Ministry of Culture, Recreation and Social Work; CRM for short).[47] CCRM is the combination of Chinese and CRM. By naming a Chinese association after a Dutch ministry, the founders clearly wanted to attract more attention from the Dutch officials. This seems to have achieved its desired effect. At the same time, the initiators could not completely ignore the Chinese tradition. If one should make a word-to-word translation of CCRM, the association would have a strange and complicated Chinese name. Thus, the founders chose another independent Chinese name for the association, that is, *Zhonghua huzhuhui* (Chinese Mutual Aid Association), which is clear and memorable.[48] Among the Dutch officials, the Dutch name is well known; but among the Chinese, almost everyone only knows its Chinese name.

Secondly, how CCRM defined its aims is also revealing. The first aim proposed by the initiators of CCRM was:

Mingque shenfen (To clearly define the identity of our Chinese)
Zhengqu quanli   (To strive for our legitimate rights and interests)

More precisely, the foremost aim of CCRM was to have the Chinese immigrant community recognized by the Dutch government as an official minority under the New Minorities Policy. According to Mrs. Chan:[49]

At that time, many Chinese did not understand why we wanted the Chinese community to be recognized as an official minority in the Netherlands. Some even asked me: Are you too poor to feed yourself? Don't you feel ashamed to beg money from the Dutch government? I had to tell them: the recognition as an official minority has nothing to do with being individually rich or poor. I am not embarrassed since we want to strive for our legal rights and interests! The establishment of CCRM is to change the old social image that we Chinese are an invisible group. We Chinese have to speak out.

Such an opinion has clearly been influenced by the Dutch political culture. Among the Chinese, however, such a concept does not fit into the popular group ideology. Moreover, since it was established, CCRM has often been in a dilemma because of its wish to please both the Chinese and the Dutch sides.

Finally, let us see how CCRM settled its finances. Among the Chinese abroad (not only in the Netherlands), it is almost accepted through common practice that the major leaders of a Chinese association should be the major sponsors or main subsidy providers of the association. However, this was not the situation at CCRM. CCRM gets financial help from three sources: the Dutch authorities, Taiwan authorities, and donations by Chinese immigrants in the Netherlands. Concerning these sources, every Chinese association commonly taps the third one; the second source of funding is also a normal method used by pro-Taiwan associations. Yet, before CCRM successfully obtained some subsidies from the Dutch authorities in 1985, this financial source was uncommon to the Chinese in the Netherlands and was regarded as a violation of the Chinese tradition of self-reliance.

In 1985, just the second year after CCRM was established, while formulating the *Rijksprogramma Welzijn Minderheden* (State Program for the Welfare of Minorities), the government planned for the first time to use 250,000 guilders for the Chinese immigrant community. In the bilingual information newspaper of CCRM, it was stressed repeatedly that it was Mr. E. Brinkman, a CDA politician and the Minister of Welfare, Public Health and Culture at that time, who made this decision. CCRM is the first Chinese association to benefit from this new policy.

Gradually, after receiving more funding from various sources, CCRM created some salaried posts. These salaried positions were taken up by some of its leaders and assistants. Although it is normal in Dutch society for the leaders of an association to be paid for their work, such a state of affairs caused suspicion and gossip about CCRM in the Chinese community (cf. Chapter VI).

D *An influential association*

During the dozen years after its establishment, CCRM organized a series of significant activities. Some were first-ever events in the history of the Chinese in the Netherlands. Many of its early activities were organized to realize its aim to clearly define the identity of Chinese and to strive for their legitimate rights and interests.

For example, on 22 December 1984, CCRM launched a drive to organize A Public Petition Day for all Chinese in the Netherlands. In total, 12 Chinese associations accepted CCRM's invitation to sign their names to the petition. The petition requested the Dutch government to pay more attention to the difficulties that Chinese immigrants were encountering. On Petition Day, not only did more than 1,300 Chinese attend the meeting, but five representatives from the relevant Dutch departments also came to receive the petition.[50] Since this is the first time that the Chinese in the Netherlands presented a petition to the Dutch government publicly, CCRM created a name for themselves.

A few months after Petition Day, CCRM once more played a leading role in a Chinese protest movement provoked by two incidents. An article in a Dutch newspaper was the first incident. As described in Chapter II, the Chinese catering business is the pillar of the Chinese economy in the Netherlands. Among the Chinese dishes served in the Netherlands, *babi-panggang* (roast pork) is widely known. On 14 September 1985, two Dutch culinary experts published an article in the Dutch newspaper *Algemeen Dagblad* (Universal Daily; hereafter AD). In the article, using the case of some *serious* mistakes made by Chinese cooks when preparing *babi-panggang*, the authors aimed their sharp criticism at the preparation of all Chinese dishes. Because of their sarcastic remarks in the article, and especially due to its title, namely *Afhaalchinees maakt er een potje van* (Take-away Chinese food shops prepare their food sloppily), it provoked the wrath of many Chinese restaurateurs. Several protest letters were sent to AD and the authors. Some suggested that all Chinese restaurateurs stop their subscription to AD.

Then, before the AD incident was resolved, a second incident happened. In 1986, a McDonald's poster was pasted along the streets in the Netherlands. In the poster, there was one striking sentence: "*Nee, niet weer de Chinees.*" ("No, not Chinese [food] again"). It is clear that this poster violated the advertisement convention that any advertisement may not assault or belittle other products or groups.

In view of the above facts, CCRM published a series of articles in its newsletter — the INFO Krant — in order to kindle the Chinese community's sense of obligation and responsibility to protect their own rights.[51] Some of these articles gave detailed analyses on how the incidents would endanger the Chinese catering business, while others tried to persuade the Chinese to ignore any concessions offered. CCRM also once attempted to organize a nationwide protest movement but failed. Nevertheless, because the INFO Krant was a bilingual newspaper, the protesting voice of the Chinese has, to a certain degree, also been heard by the Dutch authorities.

Meer begrip, minder misverstand (more comprehension, less misunderstanding) is another resounding slogan advanced by CCRM. On 12 February 1986, CCRM organized a large-scale activity in The Hague, namely, Friendly Meeting Day: the Netherlands and Her Chinese Inhabitants. CCRM clearly and publicly propagated this new slogan for the first time at this gathering. Sixty groups gave performances of Chinese and Dutch arts. More than six thousand Chinese and Dutch came to visit this meeting. Mr. Dijkhuizen, alderman for economic affairs of The Hague, and Mr. Halleen, alderman for education and culture of The Hague, came to host the opening ceremony.[52] Mr. Brinkman, then the Minister of Welfare, Public Health and Culture, attended the meeting and gave a speech. In the speech, he told his audience that his Ministry had decided to subsidize this public activity.

On 10 March 1989, CCRM held an unprecedented ceremony to celebrate the fifth anniversary of its founding. The ceremony was held in the *Efteling*, a famous Dutch recreational park. There were a record number of participants: around 11,000 Chinese and Dutch friends attended the ceremony. Mr. De Koning, then the Minister of Social Affairs, accepted the invitation to host the opening ceremony and gave a friendly speech.

As early as 1986, CCRM was able to buy a building as its office and named it the *Chinese Trefcentrum in Rotterdam* (Chinese Activity Centre in Rotterdam). In the autumn of that year, after being funded by *the authorities*[53] and collecting donations from the readers of its newsletter, CCRM was able to spend 132,000 Dutch guilders to buy a three-storey building in Rotterdam.[54] On 14 March 1987, CCRM invited the Dutch Minister of Education to host a great opening ceremony for the Centre. In the building, a couple of rooms were used as the office of CCRM. In the basement, a Chinese Culture Corner had been accurately positioned: the Chinese four treasures for study, calligraphy and painting (i.e., writing brush, ink stick, ink slab and paper); Chinese tea sets; some Chinese music instruments; some facial makeup used in Peking operas; and so on. In addition, a Chinese library and a free telephone information service were also set up. The establishment of the Centre was widely appreciated by the Chinese in Rotterdam.

CCRM has also contributed to the information services available for Chinese who are facing language barriers by publishing a newspaper in Chinese and setting up Chinese information services.

On 14 April 1984, only a few weeks after its establishment, CCRM began to publish a Chinese information newspaper: *De Chinese half-maandelijke INFO Krant* (The Chinese Half-Monthly INFO Newspaper; INFO Krant for short). To a certain extent, the INFO Krant was based on a newsletter issue published by CEME. It is interesting to point out that after CCRM was established, the issuing of CEME's newsletter stopped, and the whole editing and printing group was transferred to work for CCRM. However, instead of only focussing on explaining Christian doctrines like CEME's newsletter did, the INFO Krant announced its working intention as follows:[55]

> The INFO Krant will be distributed to all Chinese who live in the Netherlands and to our Dutch friends who have regular contacts with the Chinese. The INFO Krant has two important functions: to offer information to the Chinese and to the Dutch; to improve the contacts among the Chinese and the contacts between the Chinese and the Dutch.

The INFO Krant was first designed as a Chinese-language information newspaper. At the suggestions of CCRM's Dutch advisers, the INFO Krant changed to a bilingual newspaper in its fortieth issue: about two-thirds of the articles are written in Chinese and one-third in Dutch. Then, for the Dutch officials and authorities, the INFO Krant became an important informative source about the Chinese community in the Netherlands. INFO Krant reached its peak circulation of about 9,000 at the end of the 1980s.

It was a heavy burden for CCRM to balance the INFO Krant budget. There were three sources of funding for the INFO Krant: subsidies from the Dutch authorities, income from advertisements, and the donations of its Chinese readers. From the eleventh issue of the INFO Krant, when the funding from the Dutch authorities was relatively substantial, CCRM created some salaried posts for editors and typists. Nevertheless, since 1990, in response to a decline in funding from the Dutch government and rising printing costs, the INFO Krant has had to make some adjustments. Its format was changed: the literary supplement was cut and the number of pages decreased from eight to four.[56] Between 1994 and early 1996, the INFO Krant was affiliated as an Information Supplement to two Chinese advertising newspapers in succession. Still, the cost far outweighed CCRM's budget. Finally, on 1 May 1996, CCRM stopped publishing the INFO Krant.

While the INFO Krant was on the decline, some more delicate changes were happened to the working program of CCRM.

E *A sponsor of new associations*

The major changes in CCRM's working program were a response towards the updated minorities policies of the Dutch authorities. In the early 1990s, the Dutch government once more redefined its minorities policies. In 1992, aimed at the improvement of integration into Dutch society, the government put a new policy into effect. According to this new policy, instead of encouraging the minorities to organize themselves to perfect their social status, the government requires all minorities and foreign immigrants to turn to the existing governmental agencies when they need care and assistance (Vermeulen, 1997: 146-147). The existing Dutch institutions/agencies are divided by social sections, e.g., for elders, for women, for youth, for disabled and so on. Recognizing this fact, CCRM quickly formulated its working program that focussed on setting up new associations for Chinese elders, for Chinese women, and for Chinese youth; and then to contact the relevant Dutch institutions for support.

The first nationwide Chinese association initiated and sponsored by CCRM is the *Chinese Landelijke Ouderen Vereniging 'Chun Pah' in Nederland* (Chinese Nationwide Old Folks' Association *Chun Pah* in the Netherlands; hereafter *Chun Pah*).[57] In October 1989, CCRM held a public meeting to celebrate the *1e Landelijke Chinese Ouderendag* (First Nationwide Day for Elderly Chinese). Several dozens of elderly Chinese were invited. At the meeting, the proposal to organize an association for elderly Chinese was put forward. The program of the proposed association as worked out by the leaders of CCRM focussed on two points:

(i) to help the elderly enjoy the welfare services available in Dutch society;
(ii) to arrange consultations with the relevant Dutch welfare departments and ask them to pay more appropriate attention to the Chinese elderly.

This proposal received sufficient support. Then on 21 December 1989, *Chun Pah* proclaimed its establishment in CCRM's office. Besides having a Liaison Group organized in *Chun Pah*'s name, all of this new associations' administration and activities were taken care of by CCRM's executive committee (Chun Pah, 1998: 7-13). For instance, the general secretary who was in charge of *Chun Pah*'s daily affairs is Mr. Cheung, one of the active leaders of CCRM. *Chun Pah*'s funding from the Dutch authorities was also set up and secured by CCRM.

Following the model of setting up *Chun Pah*, CCRM had initiated other three nationwide Chinese associations from 1991 to 1996. They are:

(i)   *Chinese Landelijke Vrouwen Vereniging 'Wai Wun' in Nederland* (Chinese Nationwide Women's Association *Wai Wun* in the Netherlands; hereafter *Wai Wun*) in 1991;[58]
(ii) *Chinese Jongeren Organisatie* (Chinese Youth Organization, hereafter CJO) in 1994;
(iii) *Netwerk Chinese Vrijwilligers* (Network of Chinese Volunteers, hereafter NCV) in 1996.

The common features of the above-mentioned associations at their early period can be concluded as follows. At first, their initiators and first leading group were composed of active leaders of CCRM; CCRM also secured their funding from the authorities concerned. Secondly, taking the relevant Dutch institutions as the model, *Chun Pah*, *Wai Wun* and NCV have set up seven local branches at the Dutch province level. Thirdly, according to the initiating purpose of CCRM, all of them were targetted to set up formal and regular contacts with the relevant Dutch institutions. For instance, the local branches of *Wai Wun* have had close contacts with the local Dutch Women's Center. And NCV applied to and was accepted as a branch of the Dutch Network of Volunteers. With the latter's support, several training courses for Chinese social workers have been held; and two Chinese women are employed as general coordinators of NCV.

Nowadays, the above-mentioned four associations are amongst the best organized and active Chinese associations in the Netherlands. Thus, they represent a contribution made by CCRM to the Chinese community. However, with the emergence of a new leading core in each of these associations, they are not under CCRM's supervision any longer. For example, by 1993, when *Chun Pah* had set up six branches[59] with more than 1,600 members throughout the Netherlands and its contacts with the relevant Dutch authorities had been properly secured, *Chun Pah* started to redefine its social image as an independent association rather than a branch of CCRM. According to the current leaders of *Chun Pah*, "It is after 1993 that we really started to deal with all daily affairs by ourselves and become an independent association" (Chun Pah, 1998:13).

In general, within a couple of years after their establishment, all of these associations have asserted their autonomy, or they have started to keep the initiative in their own hands. To put it differently, the development of these new associations has, from their respective perspectives, taken over the social functions of CCRM and, systematically, finished their initiator's career. The CCRM was facing an unexpected result from its own creations.

F *"We have nearly finished our task!"*

In the spring of 1996, when ACV was looking forward to its 50th anniversary and *Fa Yin* was busy celebrating its 20th anniversary, the chairwoman of CCRM publicly issued an announcement: "CCRM has nearly finished its task! It is not necessary for CCRM to exist any more. In the near future, we will officially declare the disbandment of CCRM."

On 13 December 1996, after the founding ceremony of NCV, I interviewed Mrs. Chan for the third time. When asked about the reasons for the disbandment of CCRM, she said:

> Some dozen years ago, no Chinese in the Netherlands knew how to organize themselves or how to strive for their legitimate rights and interests. Then, we set up CCRM with a clear purpose. We have done our best to organize and guide the Chinese rank and file in the Netherlands step by step [...] By now, no one can ignore the fact that we have been quite successful in promoting and organizing services and activities in response to the special needs of the Chinese and, moreover, to improve the friendship between the Chinese and the Dutch.
>
> Now, you see, the associations of Chinese women, elderly Chinese and Chinese youth have come into being. Furthermore, the neighbourhood committee for Chinese inhabitants in Rotterdam was established and is running very well. Today, the Network of Chinese Volunteers has become constituted and is self-managing. Why should CCRM still exist? Our task is almost finished. Or, in other words, the original task of CCRM has now been transferred to these newly established associations. I believe this is the best option for our Chinese community.
>
> About myself. Ten-odd years ago, I said to my husband and myself that I would leave the church to work for the Chinese community for a period of ten years. By now, more than ten years have passed. It is time for me to return to my church that I love so much!

In fact, in the mid-1990s, CCRM changed its social image and started to maintain a rather low profile. The building that CCRM bought in 1985 was sold in 1995, when a Chinese Old Folks' Home was set up in Rotterdam. It is a five-storey building. The ground floor has been arranged as a Chinese

Activity Centre. There is one library, one reading-room and one meeting hall. In addition, some rooms are used as the offices for the above-mentioned associations.

After keeping a low profile for quite a long period, however, in February 1998, a new booklet titled *Oud Doel – Nieuw Beleid* (Old Objective – New Policy) was issued to "all supporters of CCRM" by the newly organized board of CCRM. In the booklet, after briefly reviewing the achievements of CCRM in its first 14 years (1984 - 1997), the new policy that will be implemented by CCRM is announced. The major points of its new policy are as follows:

First, instead of disbanding the organization, CCRM will continue to try to reach its objectives but with a new approach. The original tasks set out by CCRM have been successfully transferred to some newly established associations. Thus, from now on, in principle, CCRM itself will not be directly engaged in executing social work any more. Instead, it will concentrate its efforts towards supporting other existing Chinese associations, specifically to advise and give guidance, and if deemed appropriate, to offer financial support for social activities organized by those friendly associations.

Second, the board made a public announcement that at the beginning of 1998 CCRM has set up a Reserve Fund. The purpose of this fund is to support projects aimed at improving the integration of the Chinese into Dutch society. This fund is open to applicants not only from all existing Chinese associations, but from Dutch associations as well. This Reserve Fund starts with an amount of 150,000 Dutch guilders, which came from the sale of the CCRM building. As was mentioned earlier, one part of the budget of buying the building was a donation from the Chinese people all over the Netherlands.[60]

Third, the re-organized CCRM is asking for new support and donations. The board is asking for: (i) volunteers; (ii) donators/friends of CCRM (donating 25 guilders or more); (iii) sponsors (donating 500 guilders or more); and (iv) donations from co-operating associations.

In short, CCRM has played an important role in the history of the Chinese associations in the Netherlands, especially from its establishment to the early years of the 1990s. Its strong aim to become a leading Chinese institution in the Netherlands was expressed clearly as soon as it was set up; and indeed, it had successfully realized its goal within a very short period. Nevertheless, just like its quick rise had surprised many people, the fact that it has promptly stepped down from the social stage has also surprised all outsiders. Its developing process, as well as its working strategies in particular, have stimulated many of the ideas that will be discussed in the following chapters. Moreover, will its new policy bring about a new social image of CCRM amongst the Chinese associations? Will its new function as a consultant or a financial supporter be recognized, or accepted, by other associations? If not, what are the reasons? If yes, to what extent and in which way? The new path of CCRM requires continued study.

CHAPTER V

To Have Dreams Come True: Organizational Motivations

The preceding three chapters have attempted to present a general picture of the Chinese immigration process and Chinese associations in the Netherlands. In the next three chapters, the study will focus on the following three topics: the initial founding motives behind the birth of the associations; the organizational structure of the associations; and the social roles played by the associations.

What are the major motives to push the Chinese immigrants to organize their own ethnic associations? What factors have shaped their motives? Have their organizational motives been affected by the influences of mainstream society or their original society? These questions form the basis of the current chapter.

It is a normal phenomenon that the original aims can differ from the actual functions of a certain association. In this section, however, the study will concentrate on the initial founding motives. The real social roles played by these associations will be the topic of Chapter VII.

1 *Practical considerations*

Primarily, the birth of Chinese associations in the Netherlands was the early Chinese newcomers' instinctive way of coping with the harsh realities of immigration. Or, to put it differently, because they were a group of outsiders coming from a distant Eastern world, the formal or informal establishment of ethnic associations was a way to survive in the Western world. Thus, in the beginning, the urge to organize associations among the Chinese themselves arose from some practical considerations.

A *The harsh reality*

As was illustrated in Chapter II, the initial Chinese settlers in the Netherlands were ex-sailors or former peasants who came as pedlars. These early Chinese immigrants had three common characteristics.

First, their motivation for going abroad was economic. Most Chinese arrived in Europe with nothing but their dream of economic betterment. Their common wish was to get rich as soon as possible and then return home. Therefore, they were individual male emigrants who had left their families behind, irrespective of whether they were married or not. As soon as they arrived in the Netherlands, however, many experienced the gap between their expectations and their opportunities. Their own survival was not easy, to say nothing of fulfilling their family's expectations.

Second, most of them lacked basic knowledge about the receiving society. They faced language barriers, and they knew nothing about the immigration regulations that were operating in Europe. Since many were born to peasant families or were former peasants themselves, they were accustomed to ordering their lives within the boundaries of family customs and traditions in small villages. In their hometowns, families — usually extended families — not only provided moral support but were sources of economic security and mutual aid as well. This familiar state of affairs, however, did not exist in the receiving country. Consequently, many of these new immigrants experienced loneliness and isolation in the Western world. They had to learn about the society through their own experiences.

The third common characteristic is that, as an ethnic immigrant group, they were highly visible in the Western world. They could not hide themselves, even if they kept silent. They faced formidable obstacles that derived from cultural and national differences, including the deep-seated social and racial prejudice of the Western world.

One harsh reality encountered by these early Chinese immigrants was the search for an immediate means of subsistence. The existing network available to these early immigrants consisted of their relatives, fellow villagers, or people with the same ethnic background. Because of chain-migration, newcomers were often brought over by someone they knew. Then, through the acquaintance's introduction, a Chinese Master would accept the newcomer: to provide a place to stay and a means of subsistence. This process usually led the early Chinese immigrants to live together in shared accommodation where they found themselves bound to duties of mutual support, which often resulted in the formation of gangs. This situation was not necessarily desirable but was clearly a requirement for the early Chinese immigrants.

The element of cohesion among those early Chinese gangs in the Netherlands was usually shared provenance. Gangs based on common clan links, a normal occurrence among the Chinese organizations in Southeast Asia (cf. Wu, 1977), did not appear in the Netherlands because of the limited immigration scale.

Customarily, within a gang, one person would act or would be acknowledged as Number One. These individuals would normally possess the following characteristics: they arrived in the Netherlands earlier than most of others; they understood some English or Dutch; and, of much greater importance, they were the Chinese Master (or Chinese agent) of a Dutch company. Each gang's Number One was responsible for the accommodations and job placement of its members. Gang formation was a common phenomenon among early Chinese immigrants and formed a basis for the subsequent development of official ethnic associations.

The support given to members of a certain gang, however, was not always reliable. For instance, finding a job very often depended on the personal contacts between the Number One and a Dutch company. Disturbance or disruption of this contact might very well deprive all the members of their means of subsistence. Moreover, the limited job market for the Chinese led to stiff competition among the Chinese heads to win or strengthen their position as an agent for a Dutch company. During the early 1920s, such competition even led to bloody fights: the so-called "Chinese gang wars" reported in Dutch newspapers. The fighting not only resulted in casualties among the Chinese but also lessened the image of the Chinese as a whole, which affected their social position in the Netherlands (cf. Wubben, 1986: 57-79).

The early Chinese immigrants needed support beyond job placement. For instance, someone who became ill needed to know how to get the necessary treatment; someone who was deeply depressed because of failures in the new country needed help returning home; someone dying in poverty expected someone else to arrange his funeral. None of the Chinese heads by themselves could promise that they would be able to offer all these forms of assistance to their fellow immigrants. Thus, to share the responsibility for the day-to-day relief of the Chinese immigrants, some Chinese masters began forming organizations, which launched the first organizing wave in the Netherlands.

B *Handling day-to-day problems*

The first organizing wave among the Chinese in the Netherlands appeared in the 1920s. The associations aspired to handle the day-to-day problems of immigrants and to pursue dependable security through collective strength. In other words, through associations, the leaders hoped to shift the sense of aid from an accidental personal deed to a collective sense of obligation.

WKWK, one of the Chinese association mentioned earlier, can be regarded as an example. As the first community-wide Chinese association successfully established in the Netherlands, WKWK's founders designed the association to formalize mutual assistance within the Chinese community. This was accomplished by collecting money from two sources: the donations of all the heads of the organizations and the membership dues of those who had some income. Obviously, only a formal and powerful association could impose these compulsory contributions. Because WKWK was able to offer such strong primary support to the poor Chinese in the Netherlands — e.g., subsidize seriously ill patients, arrange funerals, help those who failed to return home, and so on — it attracted about six hundred members from amongst the one-thousand odd Chinese who had settled in the Netherlands up to that point (see Chapter III).

ACV's predecessor, OSDA, is also an example of the early associations in the Netherlands. As was described in Chapter IV, after the Second World War, there was a shortage of daily necessities in the whole of the Netherlands; as a result, some Chinese tried to earn a living by selling goods for daily use. This, however, required obtaining supplies from Dutch companies.

The establishment of OSDA was motivated by a practical desire for an organization that could obtain stocks directly from factories or companies at lower prices. Because many Chinese were short of capital, under the arrangement of the association, its registered members could expect cheaper commodities from the association; moreover, they could get them on credit as well. During those difficult years, this association helped a number of Chinese find a means of livelihood. A few were even able to accumulate enough primary capital for future business developments (Cf. Chapter IV).

It is necessary to understand how these early Chinese associations ran their administration. The following interviews can give us a general picture.

My interview with Mr. LT offers some insights into the early organizational background of one association. Mr. LT was born in 1926 to a Chinese father and a Dutch mother. His father, Mr. LS (1882-1956), was head of the Chinese Club in Amsterdam from the late 1920s through the 1940s. According to LT's reminiscences, the Club often helped sick Chinese with medical aid, Chinese medicines, and arranged funerals. LT said:[1]

I remember vividly that my father was highly respected by other Chinese. We lived in Binnen Bantammerstraat[2] at that time. Whenever he walked along that street with his stick, he was greeted by the Chinese who worked there, or lived there, or who just happened to pass along that street [...]

When asked why his father enjoyed such high respect from his countrymen, LT told me with a sense of pride that his father not only ran his business very well but also acted as head of the Chinese Club:

My father was the head of the Chinese Club in Amsterdam. The Club was located in one room on the ground floor of our house. Everyday some Chinese came to play Mahjong in the Club. I think they were happy that my father offered them a free and nice place to meet and to have fun together. Sometimes, they also got free food in the Club. Moreover, my father had a Chinese *apotheek* [i.e., drugstore]. He helped many sick Chinese with medical aid. If the patients were poor, both treatment and medicine were free. All costs were paid by my father simply because he was the Number One.

Did his father cover all the costs of helping the members of the Club as LT said? Some other Chinese elders also remembered the Club among the well-known Chinese organizations in Amsterdam that existed before the Second World War. No one could give me further information about the sponsor(s) of the Club. However, I noted an important point from LT's elaboration. He talked about there being a place for Chinese to play Mahjong in the Club. Thus, it is very possible that the tips collected from the Mahjong players would cover the costs of running the Club.

Another early Chinese club organized by LK in Amsterdam shows a similar picture. This interviewee told me:[3]

It was in the middle of the 1950s, I became a Chinese restaurant owner [...] I felt pity for the newcomers who arrived with empty hands. Then, together with some friends, we set up a *Hualian julebu* (Chinese cooperative club) for our countrymen. The Club was set up in my restaurant, which was located in Zeedijk[4] of Amsterdam.

In the restaurant, a couple of Mahjong tables and two game machines were especially put in readiness for the members of our Club. During spare time, some members would come to play Mahjong together. Or, if there were not enough people to play Mahjong,[5] one could gamble with a game machine. If sometimes, someone had no money for food, he could simply come to the club to have free food. Many elderly Chinese know this Club and said it was a Chinese Commune in the Netherlands [laughing].

I wanted to know who covered the expenses of the Commune. Then this interviewee told me that he had paid for everything. He explained that his restaurant was always full of people. Most members of the club were his co-villagers. The older members brought over newcomers. They came to this interviewee's restaurant to play Mahjong or game machines and then enjoyed free food together. When asked whether the interviewee felt that offering free food for all members of the club was a heavy burden, he said:

At the beginning, not! Among the dozens of people who came to play Mahjong or game machines in my restaurant, only a few were without a job. I could easily introduce them to work in one of the Chinese restaurants since it was a golden period of our Chinese catering business. But, later on, some bad guys also came to our club to have free food and even asked for money. This situation worsened quickly, which finished the club.

According to this interviewee, since the turn of the 1960s, the area around Zeedijk has become infested with junkies and hard drug dealers. The public security of the area turned sharply worse. As a result, this interviewee had to sell his restaurant and close his club.

To clarify a few things, I will say a few more words about playing Mahjong, as this is the most popular entertainment among the Chinese. Actually, playing Mahjong is something between entertainment and gambling. According to the rules, the winner of each set will collect money from other players. It would be real gambling if the loser of each set had to pay several hundreds of guilders, but it remains entertainment if the payments at each set are limited to only a few guilders. It is normal for the person who offers a public place for people to play Mahjong to collect a tip from the total amount of money circulated among the players. If an association owns the place, the tip will be collected in the name of the association. This is an easy way for an association to collect funds. It works well because even those people who lose consider the tip a donation to the association. This is one important reason why many Chinese associations, from the very beginning up till today, have arranged a place for its members to play Mahjong.

In sum, these early Chinese associations shared some features. As the newly arrived Chinese immigrants coped with the discrepancies between their dreams and the social reality, the first Chinese associations were formed to create a safer environment for the immigrants, which could help them realize their expectations of economic betterment. The founding motivations of these early associations were very practical: to have immediate security through the collective strength of an ethnic organization.

2 *Creating a positive social image*

As was demonstrated earlier, however, since the 1970s the changing situation both in China and in the Netherlands have reshaped the Chinese immigrant community in the Netherlands. Therefore, the organizational patterns of Chinese associations have also changed. The second organizational wave among the Chinese in the Netherlands appeared in the 1980s, after more than two decades of dormancy. The organizational pattern of this period displayed some new characteristics that were reactions to the new features of the Chinese immigrant community as a whole.

A *Features of the current Chinese immigrant community*

The Chinese immigrant community in the Netherlands currently displays at least three features. First, it is dominated by first-generation immigrants; thus, their organizational motivations cannot be appraised without starting from this demographic feature.

From the three immigration phases outlined in Chapter II, it is clear that the majority of the present Chinese immigrants in the Netherlands arrived during the last quarter of the twentieth century.[6] Moreover, many arrived as inexperienced youths. As first-generation immigrants, they carry a heavy burden to fulfill the great expectations cherished not only by their direct family members but also by all of their relatives and friends. Their outsider's feeling cannot be erased, even among those who have become naturalized Dutch citizens. For instance, one barrier was, and continues to be, the language. Many Chinese immigrants start learning Dutch from reading menus in the Chinese restaurants where they worked, and they often stay at a level that would only allow them to make minimum contact with the Dutch customers. Few read Dutch newspapers. For another thing, few Dutch officials feel inclined to communicate with the Chinese immigrants directly, whose language they rarely understand. Due to this lack of communication, needless misunderstandings and friction have occurred. All of these in turn have deepened the outsider's feeling of many Chinese and have affected their organizational activities directly.

A second feature of the current Chinese community is that they are a group that strongly depends on their ethnic catering business. The close interconnectedness and sharp competition that exist within this limited ethnic

If you haven't been to sea palace, you haven't been to Amsterdam

Advertisement of a Chinese restaurant in Amsterdam

economic enclave are worth noting because they have greatly affected the organizational activities.

The following tables show the growth trend of Chinese restaurants in the Netherlands. In the 1950s, the average yearly increase in the number of Chinese restaurants was as high as 67 per cent; in the 1960s and the 1970s, it remained around 17 per cent. Since the early 1980s, however, the number of Chinese restaurants has stayed at around 2,000. It seems that this is the saturation point. Since 1982, the proportion of Chinese restaurants among all restaurants and cafés has hovered around 30 per cent. There are about 14 Chinese restaurants per every 100,000 residents, and this has not changed since 1982 (see Table 5).

Table 4 *Chinese Restaurants in the Netherlands (1947-1996)*

Year	*Chinese restaurants*		*All restaurants*	*Chinese restaurants:*
	Number	*Change*	*& cafés*	*All restaurants & cafés*
1947	23			
1960	225	+ 202	1,925	12 %
1970	618	+ 393	2,859	22 %
1982	1,916	+ 1298	5,981	32 %
1989	2,040	+ 98		
1991	1,988	− 52	6,829	29 %
1992	1,843	− 145		
1996	2,170	+ 327	7,630	27 %

Sources: 1947 quoted from Chen, 1991:29; others from HORECA Nederland, 1997:15; 16.

Table 5 *The number of Chinese restaurants per every 100,000 residents*

District	1982	1991	1996
North Holland	10.7	10.1	12.8
East Holland	11.2	12.1	12.3
West Holland	15.0	14.6	14.7
South Holland	14.1	13.4	14.7
Whole Holland	*14*	*13.2*	*14*

Sources: HORECA Nederland, 1997:19.

The social position of the Chinese immigrants in the Netherlands has been clearly affected by the fact that the Chinese catering business is its economic pillar. For instance, in order to have an optimal number of customers for each Chinese restaurant, the Chinese have scattered throughout the Netherlands and, therefore, have become "the most geographically dispersed ethnic community in the Netherlands" (Penninx et al. 1993:204). As a result, in the Netherlands, there are no big ethnic Chinese living quarters, i.e., there are no Chinatowns like those located in Southeast Asia or in North America.[7]

Because the ethnic economy, or career structure, of the Chinese in the Netherlands is rather unilateral, the competition lying ahead of them is intense. This has affected the group's solidarity and aggravated the differences among the Chinese. The sharp competition encountered by Chinese restaurateurs comes from two sides: the competition among Chinese restaurants themselves and the pressure coming from the establishment of other ethnic restaurants — e.g., restaurants set up by Indians, Italians, Turks, Greeks, and so on. In order to survive, all Chinese restaurateurs have to find solutions, such as improving the quality of their dishes, lowering their prices, or uniting together to compete with other groups. While some have used legitimate methods, others have resorted to crooked ways. Still others, who recognized the threat to the catering business, have tried to fit themselves into other economic sectors. Nonetheless, few restaurateurs have succeeded in expanding their business into areas such as grocery, trading companies, and certain ethnic services.[8]

The catering business is a service trade that runs concurrently with the main economic stream of the host society. In dealing with Dutch customers everyday, the Chinese have to learn, more or less, how to respect Dutch habits and how to update their dishes to Dutch people's taste. A popular saying among Chinese restaurateurs is "the client is King," and "the Dutch government is the Ruler of all Chinese restaurateurs." Therefore, the Chinese associations' founders or leaders (many are restaurateurs) are very sensitive about the attitude assumed by the Dutch authorities towards the Chinese, and this attitude has always been taken seriously in planning their organizational activities.

Analyzing the relationship between Chinese bosses (most commonly Chinese restaurateurs) and workers can elucidate the third feature of the current Chinese immigrant community. During my interviews with Chinese workers, they often said to me: "Exploitation of Chinese workers by Chinese bosses has no mercy!" It is normal for Chinese restaurant workers to work about sixty hours per week. Some wives told me that their husbands do not have time to talk to their children: the fathers are still sleeping when the children get up in the morning, and the children have already fallen asleep when the fathers come back from work deep in the night. No weekends, fewer paid holidays than the Dutch official regulations, little compensation for extra working hours — these are not unusual conditions for Chinese restaurant workers.

Although many Chinese immigrants know that the working conditions of a "Dutch job"[9] are better, it is impossible for most of them to find a Dutch job because of language barriers, lack of necessary skills and access. In addition, since some immigrants came from poor rural areas and were used to living in a harsh environment, they do not regard the working conditions in Chinese restaurants as unacceptable.

For some Dutch, the working conditions of many Chinese restaurants are unbelievable. There are laws to protect the rights of workers, so why do the Chinese workers in the Netherlands not ask for protection? According to Marxist theory of social class, one class, because it takes the surplus produced by another class, exploits and oppresses that class; therefore, conflict is an inevitable product of class relationships and will transform the society. However, up to this point, the class differences within the Chinese immigrant community have not yet caused serious public conflicts. The reasons underlying this phenomenon are related to the following characteristics of class structure within the Chinese community.

First, the boundary defined between a boss and a worker is far from fixed. On the one hand, social mobility within Chinese immigrants is rather high. Most present Chinese restaurateurs were once Chinese restaurant workers; conversely, some present workers were once Chinese restaurateurs. Many Chinese restaurateurs achieved a higher socio-economic status simply by working long and hard and judiciously investing their savings. This has set an example for other Chinese restaurant workers: to realize their dream, they must accept hard working conditions.

On the other hand, since many Chinese restaurateurs in the Netherlands are first-generation immigrants, they retain their hard working tradition. Moreover, many Chinese businessmen are small-scale operators; they have to work hard themselves to decrease expenses. Several Chinese restaurateurs mentioned during my interviews: "My workers work six days a week, but I have to work seven days a week." A well-known female Chinese restaurant owner, who is often seen in full dress in public meetings, once said to me, "as an honoured guest, I get dressed for a dinner party in the Chinese Embassy. As soon as I arrive in my restaurant, I take off my formal attire and go to clean the toilet immediately. This is my life."

The second characteristic of the class structure of the Chinese is that class conflict to a certain degree has been concealed by the collective ethnic identity. On the bosses' side, they often stress to the workers a sense of unity:

No matter if I am a boss and you are a worker, we are one, like fingers on a hand.

We are in the same boat. If my business is running well, you workers in my restaurant have your livelihood assured.

In other words, both the Chinese bosses and Chinese workers are closely tied together with one "rope": the common status of being an ethnic immigrant group.

On the workers' side, because of chain-migration, many have to accept hard working conditions arranged by his or her sponsor. Meanwhile, taking their co-villagers who reached entrepreneurship through hard work as their reference group, many of today's workers expect to realize their own dreams through hard work. On this point, there might not be an appreciable difference with other immigrant entrepreneurs in Western countries; the ethnic networks based on chain-migration serve as a source of cheap labour for entrepreneurs, while causing little class conflicts (cf. Waldinger, 1990).

Third, *class* is a very sensitive term among the Chinese immigrants. In mainland China, during Mao's reign, class struggle as a political action to fight against all non-proletarian elements was heavily stressed for decades. Whoever was identified as a bourgeois element or had a bourgeois ideology would be the target of public criticism. Many suffered greatly from the various political movements that drew on this artificial class distinction. For many, the concept of class is closely related to an autocratic period or non-democratic state. Immigrants regard the Western world as societies of success. Consequently, those who reach their dreams of upward mobility are highly respected, but those who are workers all of their life are regarded as failures. Acknowledging this makes it easier to understand why many Chinese migrants, although living abroad for years, still do not want to use or hear any talk of class or class struggle, let alone any argument of uniting on the basis of working class.

The final feature of the current Chinese community is that their organizational motives cannot be studied without considering that they are bound to an affluent welfare state. Welfare services are something completely new for most Chinese newcomers. As was described earlier, many Chinese immigrants simply wanted to convert their dreams of economic prosperity into reality through migration. Based on such a motive, many of them simply work, work, work.

After settling in the Netherlands and learning more about the society, it seems that the general attitude assumed by Chinese immigrants towards the Dutch welfare system becomes rather vague and ambivalent. The Dutch welfare system is sustained by high taxes. Nevertheless, in the eyes of many

Chinese, from successful entrepreneurs to workers, the tax policy of the Netherlands is one of the worst laws in the Netherlands. Many Chinese in the Netherlands came from mainland China where a tax system did not exist until the 1980s; others came from Hong Kong where the tax rate is much lower than in most Western countries. These immigrants understandably need time to accept the progressive taxation system of Holland. As immigrants, they work hard because they want to earn more money. However, after finding that the more they earn the higher the tax they have to pay, most are terribly upset by this "deprivation" of their interests. Many Chinese people regard the Dutch welfare system as a way to support lazy people. Of course, there are many reasons for the Chinese to evade taxes. Nevertheless, deep down in their minds, one motive comes from the belief that they do not have a duty to pay taxes to support those who do not work.

On the other hand, how to benefit from the Dutch welfare services has also become a hot topic among the settled Chinese. As was mentioned earlier, before the war, a major motive for establishing a Chinese association was to handle their day-to-day problems. Even after the war and before the 1980s, the Chinese in the Netherlands were still accustomed to solving all difficulties by themselves. They collected money to set up Chinese schools for their children, to organize charitable activities, to help their elders, and to help those who encountered difficulties. With the assistance of Dutch social workers and Dutch officials, some Chinese began to learn that it is their legitimate right to ask for subsidies from the Dutch welfare institutions. In the mid-1980s, when a Chinese association for the first time obtained funding from the Dutch authorities, many Chinese were surprised and excited: "Oh? We never dared to expect funding from the Dutch government!" Then, by the mid-1990s some Chinese association leaders publicly proclaimed that they would disband their association if the Dutch authorities stopped funding it; such an attitude in turn surprised the Dutch officials.[10]

In short, the current Chinese immigrant community in the Netherlands has some outstanding features: demographically, they are dominated by first-generation immigrants; economically, they are heavily skewed towards the Chinese catering business; socially, they are characterized by a higher mobility within their ethnic economic enclave; and generally, they hold an ambivalent attitude towards the Dutch welfare system. Acknowledging these will help clarify the new patterns in the Chinese associations that have emerged since the 1980s.

B *Maintaining ethnic cohesion and continuity*

In a pluralistic society like the Netherlands, immigrants with an unique background may cultivate their cultural tradition and re-establish their self-esteem and identity in their new environment. Out of this situation, ethnic associations allow for the restoration and maintenance of their identity. Hereinafter, some examples will be given to show how this purpose has precipitated the birth of a new pattern for their associations.

Continuing the ethnic culture by establishing Chinese schools
Language is the foremost element to help sustain ethnic cohesion and continuity in an alien environment. Because many Chinese descendants who are
born and bred in the Netherlands speak Dutch by preference, the preservation and encouragement of Chineseness in the next generation has become
an increasingly important objective among the parents. Started from the
consensus that Chinese language schools can be virtual islands of Chinese
culture in the larger Dutch society, the establishment of such schools for
Chinese children has become a collective initiating pursuit.

   According to the data I have collected, nowadays, Chinese have established in total 41 after-school Chinese schools in the Netherlands. Often, the
development of Chinese associations and the establishment of Chinese
schools are two interrelated phenomena: sometimes a special association was
organized in order to take responsibility for running an existing school; sometimes an existing association becomes the backer for the founding of a school.

   Besides the case illustrated in Chapter IV on the relationship between *Fa
Yin* and *Fa Yin* school, another interesting case that provides an example of
this relationship between associations and schools is the interaction between
the following four associations: the Association of Chinese Entrepreneurs
Rotterdam, *Dam Wah* Foundation, the Chinese Voluntary Trustees Committee of *Dam Wah* Middle School, and *Dam Wah* Friendship Association.

   Aimed at providing mutual support for Chinese entrepreneurs in Rotterdam, *Vereniging Chinese ondernemers Rotterdam en omgeving* (Association of Chinese
Entrepreneurs Rotterdam; hereafter CER) was set up in 1983. As an ethnic
employers' association, CER enjoys support from Chinese restaurateurs and
other businessmen in Rotterdam.

   In 1991, when the Municipality of Rotterdam and its residents planned to
celebrate the 650th anniversary of the founding of the city of Rotterdam, the
CER decided to call upon all Chinese residents in the Netherlands to donate
a traditional-style Chinese pavilion, designed to be located in Rotterdam
harbour. About one hundred Chinese responded to the call. The pavilion
was named *Dam Wah* Pavilion: *Dam* comes from Rotterdam: the Chinese
character picked to represent this Dutch word means both red and loyal;[11]
Wah comes from a Chinese character that can mean Chinese or China,
magnificent or prosperous. The pavilion is a symbol of the friendship between the Dutch (especially of Rotterdam) and the Chinese.

   When the pavilion was finished, there were more than 10,000 Dutch
guilders left over from the donations. After repeatedly discussing what to do
with the remaining money, the CER committee decided to use it as the starting
fund to set up a scholarship foundation. The foundation's aim would be to
improve Chinese education among the Chinese children in the Netherlands.

   In 1995, after four years had passed, I asked one of the foundation's
founders, Mr. HY, about the original motive to set up the foundation:[12]

   As Chinese businessmen in Rotterdam, we are often asked to make donations for the Chinese schools. It is an honour for us to do so. We cannot

accept a potential future that one day our descendants cannot read and write Chinese. If our children lose their knowledge of Chinese culture, it means we Chinese lose our future.

Therefore, we think we should do something more to improve the Chinese education for the Chinese children in this Western country. I think it is a great pity that some Chinese children do not want to study Chinese. They go to Chinese school because they are forced to by their parents. We should not only support the management of the Chinese schools, but, more importantly, we must find an effective way to heighten the Chinese children's interests in studying Chinese. So, we decided to set up a foundation. We decided to give awards to those students who have done exceedingly well in their Chinese studies. This is the primary motive to set up *Dam Wah* Foundation for the Chinese children of Chinese schools.

His response was very quick and smooth, as if he were giving a speech. Afterwards I found out that he has repeated the same thing to many people in his attempts to get more people to support the foundation.

According to the regulations drawn up by the CER committee for the *Dam Wah* Foundation, every Chinese school in the Netherlands, regardless of how many pupils it has, will be invited to select a couple of its best students to be awarded a *Dam Wah* prize at the end of every study year. The prize will include one *Dam Wah Zhuangyuan* Cup[13] and a scholarship that usually covers one year's tuition.

All members of the CER committee have contributed to the *Dam Wah* Foundation. In addition, dozens of Chinese have also contributed. In a couple of months, the foundation collected about 60,000 guilders. In 1992, the *Dam Wah* Foundation was officially established, and its first committee members all came from CER. In August 1993, the foundation awarded 16 students from eight Chinese schools the first *Dam Wah* prize.[14] By the summer of 1999, in total, the *Dam Wah* Foundation has given 40,000 guilders as awards to about two hundred pupils from 22 after-school Chinese schools in the Netherlands.[15]

In order to give the Chinese pupils who have passed through Chinese primary school an opportunity to continue their Chinese studies, the committee members of the *Dam Wah* Foundation decided to start an after-school Chinese middle school in Rotterdam. In the spring of 1996, the Preparatory Committee for *Dam Wah* Middle School was set up. On 1 September 1996 *Dam Wah* Middle School held its opening ceremony. About twenty Chinese youth, all with a diploma from one of the Chinese schools in the Netherlands, enrolled as its first pupils. All committee members of the *Dam Wah* Foundation acted as the voluntary trustees of the newly established middle school. Then, the Chinese Voluntary Trustees Committee of *Dam Wah* Middle School was officially registered. According to the founding aim of the *Dam Wah* Middle School, it will not only continue to teach the students Chinese language, but it will also give them some practical training on translation,

trade, public relations and so on. It is expected that the graduates will be able
to find a better future by using their knowledge of the Chinese language and
Chinese culture for professional communications between the Netherlands
and China.

More recently, the establishment of a *Dam Wah* Friendship Association has
been proposed. This association would help all *Dam Wah* prize-winners and
the students of *Dam Wah* Middle School to keep contact with each other; in
addition, it would strive to increase Chinese studies among Holland-born
Chinese.

In general, preservation and encouragement of their own culture is a
shared emotional need among first-generation Chinese immigrants. To teach
Chinese language and culture to the Holland-born Chinese is regarded as a
prerequisite to maintaining their culture and their ethnic cohesion. Therefore, many Chinese associations are motivated to contribute to Chinese education; furthermore, the appeal of organizing a new association to improve
Chinese education attracts support from Chinese immigrants of all ranks.

Highlight the Chinese presence by organizing Chinese sports associations
Currently, most forms of sport are regarded as independent of language,
nationality, or cultural boundaries. Yet, interestingly, many immigrants' have
established ethnic associations based on their favourite sports. Some studies
on migrants' associations have illustrated this phenomenon. For instance, a
study on immigrant organizations in the Netherlands points out that "socio-
cultural and sports associations come in second in the case of Turks and
Moroccans, but they form the largest category of local organizations for most
of the other immigrant groups" (Penninx et al., 1993:178).[16] Another study
on immigrants in Germany also mentioned that "in the early 1980s there
were about 200 Italian associations, of which one-fifth were sporting clubs"
(Fijalkowski, 1994:127). On the motivations of organizing sports associations
among immigrants, some stated simply: they have limited goals such as offering a meeting place and organizing sporting events. Their form of organization is loose, small-scale and dependent on the input of a few volunteers
(Penninx et al., 1993:178).

I have somewhat different arguments on this phenomenon. Sports associations are equally popular among the Chinese in the Netherlands. As was
mentioned in Chapter III, around the beginning of the 1980s, the successive
emergence of youth sports associations indicated the coming organizational
wave among the Chinese in the Netherlands. By the 1990s, of the one hundred-odd Chinese associations about one-tenth were mid- or large-scale
sports associations, and almost all of them were quite active.[17]

In 1985, a nationwide Chinese sports federation was established, *Stichting
Chinese Sport Federatie in Nederland* (Chinese Sport Federation in the Netherlands in English; hereafter CSFN). By the autumn of 1997, CSFN had successfully organized 13 consecutive nationwide sports meetings for the Chinese in the Netherlands. Concerning their organizational motives, it seems
that the problem is not as simple as the explanation mentioned above. In my

opinion, the motives cannot be studied independently of the group's feelings of national self-consciousness. In other words, looking below the surface of things, organizing ethnic sports associations is a reflection of the immigrants' emotional needs: a reflection of their longing for group cohesion and continuity. One of CSFN's leader's comments shows this deeper feeling:[18]

> Holding Chinese sports meetings is a tool; our real target is to unify all Chinese. It is our purpose to show our culture to the Dutch people and to the whole Western world.

Why does organizing ethnic sports associations appeal to so many immigrants? On the surface, as a popular, existing, productive organizational style, sports associations are widely welcomed by many people; an immigrant group is not an exception to this. However, among immigrants, sports associations have their own characteristics. It is worth noting that not all sports are without cultural boundaries; some sports do have clear national characteristics, which logically become a ready-made link to bind the immigrants together. For instance, among the ten-odd ethnic Chinese sports associations in the Netherlands, about half of them are centered around distinctive Chinese sports, such as *wu shu*,[19] dragon-boat rowing and lion-dance. I once asked one founder of a Chinese lion-dance association for his personal motive for organizing the association; his answer impressed me:[20]

> Whenever I hear the special sound of gongs and drums for the lion-dancing, I feel as if I were in my hometown; moreover, I will be immediately filled with energy [...]

Of course, only a first-generation immigrant can feel this. When the same question was posed to Holland-born Chinese youth, a common answer was: "I am joining the lion-dance association just for fun."

The lion-dance and some other Chinese national sports are vivid Chinese cultural symbols. Therefore, regardless of whether the players recognize the implication or not, the fact that these Chinese national sports are performed in an alien environment and are winning appreciation from the host society is important. These sports have become a means to highlight their ethnic identity.

In addition, because most sports are independent of ideology, they may be easily used as a popularly accepted link to bind the immigrants together. As was mentioned in Chapter II, Chinese immigrants in the Netherlands are often divided by their various dialects, provenance, or political beliefs. Yet, by tracing the initiating process of CSFN, it is clear that people from different groups are working together in this association.

CSFN was organized in 1985.[21] In studying its history, I interviewed several people. Their responses about the initiators of the association drew my attention.[22] When asked about the original initiator of CSFN, G. told me:

It's me, together with X. and L., who first raised the suggestion of setting up a Chinese sports federation. I believe it is an effective way to unite all Chinese in the Netherlands together [...]

I remember very clearly that it was in October 1984, when the Vietnam-Chinese association held its sports meet in a gymnasium, that the three of us met there together. I mentioned that it was great that now more and more Chinese came to attend sports meetings. However, it would cost too much money and energy if various Chinese associations organize their sports meetings separately. They all agreed with me. Then, we reached a consensus that we should set up a Chinese sports federation with the intention of, first of all, to hold a joint Chinese sports meet once a year; for another thing, to try to unite all Chinese. Since then we have worked together to push the project from words to reality [...]

The response from another informant on the same question was as follows:

We [i.e., the speaker Z. and C.] are the real initiators of many Chinese associations in the Netherlands. For instance, we are initiators of CSFN, which is very well-known today. We are the first ones to put forward such an idea that we should organize an association to unite Chinese youth by holding sports meets. Moreover, it is due to our endeavours that from 1986 on CSFN had obtained some funding from the Dutch authorities concerned for a couple of years [...] We are the initiators. Absolutely!

The answer from a third person gave another name for the initiator:

About that "playing ball association,"[23] I remember very clearly that my late friend Q. was its initiator. Yes, now many people work for that association, but about ten years ago it was established as a result of Q's initiative. Because of his special contribution, Q. was elected as a lifelong chairman of that association. Everyone knows it [...]

The three interviewees told me three different initiating backgrounds of CSFN and in total named six different initiators. As was mentioned in Chapter I, since there are rarely original documents to detail the early period of an association, it is impossible to bring the real initiator(s) to light. This shows a shortcoming of the oral sources: they cannot completely get rid of the subjectivity of the informants. Yet, at least two other constructive meanings can be drawn from the superficially contradicting oral sources.

First, CSFN has enjoyed great prestige in the Chinese community, so much so, that people regard it as an honour to be its initiator. Second, based on the relevant oral sources, I conclude that CSFN is an united association that really opens its door to all Chinese immigrants in the Netherlands, because among the six possible initiators, one emigrated from Wenzhou, two from Guangdong, two from Hong Kong and one is an ethnic Chinese who re-emigrated from Vietnam. At that time, they were leaders of four existing

Chinese associations. Moreover, there are some differences between their political orientations towards Beijing and Taiwan. Nevertheless, all of them have contributed to the establishment of CSFN.

The creation of Chinese women's associations

The creation of associations organized by and for Chinese women became a new phenomenon after the 1980s. Its potential social significance is worth noting. Generally, the establishment of Chinese associations is, among other things, motivated by a desire to form a socio-psychological defense against the feeling of isolation or depression experienced in the wider society. The contemporary development of Chinese women's associations exemplifies this point.

Some scholars have claimed that in general women of ethnic minorities suffer from multiple disadvantages: inferior class, gender, nation, colour, race and/or ethnicity (for example, Drury 1994; Anthias, 1992). The Chinese immigrant women are no exception. Moreover, the influences of traditional Chinese culture on its people living abroad should be noted. In traditional Chinese society, Confucianism underlies people's daily behaviour; it has been accepted as the legitimate ethical code of conduct and has provided a unified culture over many centuries. Unfortunately, Confucianism has never promoted equality between the sexes. For instance, according to Confucianism, the dictum *san cong si de* should be adhered to by all Chinese women. It means "the three obediences and the four virtues." *San cong* means that a woman of good behaviour must obey her father before marriage, obey her husband during her marriage, and obey her son(s) in widowhood. The four virtues are fidelity, physical charm, propriety in speech, and skillfulness in needlework and household work. In general, this code implies that leadership is in the hands of men and that women should obey men. Since 1919, *san cong si de* as a moral concept has been criticized and rejected by educated people and is, to a certain degree, regarded as a spiritual fetter imposed on Chinese women. Furthermore, in the constitution of the People's Republic of China, it is repeatedly mentioned that men and women have equal rights and duties. Nevertheless, the latent influence of this Confucian concept on the behaviour of Chinese people can still be noticed everywhere, including the Netherlands.

For instance, the earliest organized Chinese associations, from WKWK before the Second World War to ACV and *Fa Yin* before the 1980s, have all shown a male orientation. No woman has been elected as the major leader of *Fa Yin* in its twenty-year history. In addition, although the current standing committee of ACV (formed in March 1996) is composed of as many as 221 members, only 13 are women.

One Chinese woman's experience related to ACV is quite typical. This lady's personal background compared with the other members of ACV is rather unusual. She is among the few who had finished a university education before migration. Her late father-in-law was a founder and key leader of ACV and very active within the Chinese community in the Netherlands from the 1940s until he passed away in 1986. Her husband is also a well-known

person who has held the position of vice-chairman, chairman, and honorary
chairman for life of ACV. She joined ACV in the early 1970s. When ACV
needed an educated person to be its secretary, she was elected. Although she
successfully handled a great deal of ACV's public activities over nearly twenty years, she has been treated as nothing more than an assistant or as the wife
of a Chinese association's leader. I remember clearly that once, a few days
before the Chinese National Day of 1988, the lady showed me an invitation
letter sent by the Chinese Embassy in the Netherlands. The letter was to
invite honorary guests to attend the coming Chinese National Day Party held
by the Embassy. The letter only mentioned her husband's name. She said to
me rather unhappily:

> Of course, my husband has done a lot for the Chinese community, but I
> am making my own contribution as well [...] I have done quite a lot of
> things independently. But it seems that nobody cares about that. In their
> opinion, I am only the wife of my husband. I am invited only because I
> am his wife. If I were a *man*, I believe I would have been invited simply
> because of my own contribution.

Other interviewees corroborated her account. Many mentioned in private
conversations that this lady enjoys a better reputation than her husband,
although he always has a higher position in the public sphere than she.
Moreover, this lady joined ACV's organizing activities much earlier than her
husband did, since he had to manage their restaurant during the 1960s and
1970s. When asked why her husband enjoys the honour while she contributed equally, the responses of the informants were often alike: "because she is
a female"; "her husband is a leader, that is an honour for her as well." Her
husband told me directly:

> I believe that she would have become one of ACV's prominent leaders
> much earlier and that she would have held a much more important social
> position among the Chinese community if she had been a *man*.

If a capable woman with a supportive family background like this lady is
encountering so many prejudices because of her gender, what about the
position of other women?

The following phenomena are not exceptional. During the meetings held
by ACV, very few women attended meetings independently. When asked
why there were so few women at the meetings, I was told: "one representative of each family is more than enough." I asked several respondents "why a
man, but not a woman as the representative of a family?" No one gave me a
direct answer. Some even questioned me in return: "why not?" I know it
should be taken for granted (and one should not harbour any doubts about it)
that only a man can be the representative of a family, if Chinese tradition —
such as *san cong si de* — is taken into consideration.

In the mid-1980s, because they were disappointed that men dominated the associations, a number of Chinese women established Chinese women's associations. *Wa Lai* is one of them. This association's name in full is *Stichting Centrum 'Wa Lai'* (Foundation *'Wa Lai'* Centre). *Wa Lai* is a Cantonese term that means "encourage Chinese people" or "arouse the Chinese."[24] Both Chinese and Dutch who have some contacts with the centre are used to calling the association simply *Wa Lai.*

Wa Lai was founded on 21 January 1987. According to its initiator, Ms. Mai, the history of *Wa Lai*'s establishment is as follows:[25]

> I came from Hong Kong to the Netherlands in 1966, soon after I married my husband. He is a Dutch man.
> Without difficulties, I was able to find a job teaching English and French in one Dutch primary school, because I know four languages. I can speak Chinese, Dutch, English, and French. I like my job [...][26]
> In November 1979, I initiated the setting up of an after-school Chinese class in Amsterdam. Since more and more parents were willing to have their children educated in Chinese language and culture, I initiated the establishment of the *Kah Wah* School in 1983.[27] My purpose is to give Chinese children a chance to meet with each other and to learn some reading and writing in Chinese. I expect that they will keep coming and stay on, that would be good enough [...]
> As the head of *Kah Wah* School, I have come to know many Chinese mothers. I found that many of them were living in depression. Most cannot speak Dutch. Their lives are limited to serving within the home and the restaurant. They do not know where to find the help they need. I was often asked to settle things for them.
>
> [Which kind of things?]
>
> Some little problems such as receiving a letter in Dutch but cannot read it, or getting a call from the school where her child is studying but does not know what the call is about. Yet, there are serious problems as well. For instance, one Chinese woman was beaten black and blue by her husband but did not know where to find help; one husband disappeared and left his wife at home without any money and the wife could not speak even one Dutch word; one Chinese woman was in prison but could not make any communications with the police; and so on.
> At that time, although there were some Chinese associations in Amsterdam, none took care of Chinese women. Therefore, I decided to organize an association to help our sisters. Which is *Wa Lai.* It was successfully established and is running very well.

After *Wa Lai*, some local and nationwide Chinese women's associations have been established. As was mentioned in Chapter IV, CCRM hastened the birth of *Wai Wun* in the early 1990s. By the end of 1997, there were over ten Chinese women's associations all over the Netherlands. They have been a rather active group. Many members are satisfied with having a kind of "separate women's world" where they can have contacts with each other freely and in an unrestrained atmosphere. [28]

It is important to point out that the aim of the Chinese women's associations is different from modern Western feminist associations. Most Chinese women's associations seek to value the traditional Chinese cultural heritage (despite there being a clear tradition of discrimination against women). For instance, few women's associations have put forward clearly that they are endeavouring to unite Chinese women together to struggle for male-female equality or to abolish the present inferior status of their members both in private and public spheres. Instead, their aim mainly focusses on how to guide Chinese women in maintaining the so-called Chinese woman's virtues: gentleness, tactfulness, and meticulousness. Or, they aim to guide every Chinese woman to become, as the typical Chinese saying expresses it, an admirable *xian qi liang mu* (sweet wife and virtuous mother).

Consequently, any activity that moves away from the conservative Chinese tradition will still meet with strong opposition from the Chinese community. For instance, although Ms. Mai, the head of *Wa Lai*, mentioned several times during my interviews that *Wa Lai* was running successfully, I knew it had encountered some difficulties. From my interviews with some Chinese men, especially elders, I was told several times that *Wa Lai* was a bad organization because it has tried to encourage several Chinese wives to divorce their husbands. This caused some Chinese women's husbands or parents to prevent them from joining *Wa Lai*'s activities.

Wa Lai's role in these divorces was more legitimate than their critics' claim. Through the support of a Dutch association for sheltering assaulted women, the '*Blijf van mijn lijf*' *Stichting* ('Hands off my body' Foundation), *Wa Lai* did help some injured Chinese wives to escape from the control of their husbands and strove to protect the rights and interests of these women throughout the divorce procedures. As an association for women, its actions were reasonable. Nevertheless, when asked about how *Wa Lai* helped the assaulted Chinese women, Ms. Mai said:[29]

> Yes, I helped some women to get a divorce, but you must know that I only helped them when they had problems, when I really could not get the couple to live together any more. I will support the wife, only when she was beaten terribly by her husband; only when the husband left home and did not care about his wife and children [...]
>
> Once I helped a woman in court for divorce [...] That husband was so angry that he insulted me in Chinese, in very bad words, as if I was a very bad woman. I kept silent. But the judge could see his anger from his face and had to ask him to shut up!
>
> [How many of such cases have happened during the last ten years after *Wa Lai* was established?]

No, not many, not many. There have been only ten to twelve cases [...] If a wife comes to me and says she wants a divorce, first of all I would ask for the reasons and then I always suggest her to go back, to think again, at least to think for three months. I always try to get the couple together again. I often tell the lady in trouble that you have to think twice which will be stronger: the hurt from your husband or to be completely isolated? If you are divorced, you will lose everything. You will be alone. The Chinese will look down upon you. You have to think whether you are a strong woman. In fact, many returned to their home and never came back to ask our help for a divorce.

From how Ms. Mai reacted to my questions, her ambivalent situation is obvious. On the one hand, she understands that she, being a leader of a Chinese women's association, should protect Chinese women from injury. After all, she knows how to navigate the Dutch system and ensure the protection of assaulted women's rights; she has contacts with Dutch shelters for assaulted women; and she is able to take her party into court and win the case. On the other hand, however, even as a rather Westernized Chinese woman, she cannot shake off the spiritual shackles of Chinese tradition.[30] She knows how much the activities of Chinese women's associations have been restricted by the traditional Chinese cultural pattern. So much so, she stressed repeatedly that she very often has advised assaulted women to go back home instead of suing for divorce.

In general, despite that the Chinese associations based on gender are a relatively separate group among the Chinese organizations in the Netherlands, their purposes are also related to cohesion and continuity of the ethnic community. They are women's associations but not feminist associations in the Western sense. By establishing an individual little world for Chinese women, these women's associations are motivated to unite the Chinese women together and to enrich their life. At the same time, all of these associations have carefully defined their functions within the restrictions of the traditional cultural pattern.

3 *Acting as a unified representative*

Striving to create a positive social image of the Chinese immigrant community is another popular motive for setting up a new Chinese association. Chinese associations as a whole are trying to act as a unified representative towards the Dutch society or the society of their origin. Heightening the profile of the Chinese through their organizational activities has many practical implications, which will be studied below.

A *To speak to the Dutch society*

Immigrant associations first are closely bound to their host society. Any changes of that environment will directly shape and reshape the association. Specifically, the general attitude and policies of the Dutch government concerning immigrant associations have guided the Chinese association movement.

Compared with other ethnic groups, like Turks, Moroccans and Surinamese, Chinese immigrants in the Netherlands are a very small ethnic group. Among the 2.2 million foreign-born inhabitants and their immediate descendants in the whole of the Netherlands, only about four percent belong to the ethnic Chinese group.[31] Moreover, until the mid-1980s, Chinese immigrants were regarded as a self-reliant group with few problems. Therefore, when the Dutch government announced its new minority policy, expressed in a set of documents — the Overall Ethnic Minorities Policy (1980), the Draft Minorities Bill (1981), and the Final Minorities Bill (1983) — the Chinese immigrants were excluded. As a part of its welfare objectives, the Dutch government deemed it necessary to improve the social status of the ethnic minorities, but it was limited to officially recognized minorities only. The particular help includes occupational training, bilingual education, interpreting and translation services, social work, subsidies for ethnic cultural activities, and so on.

Whether the Chinese in the Netherlands should be considered an official ethnic minority is a delicate problem. In the Netherlands, the original selection of the target minorities for the relevant welfare policies utilized two criteria: "The first criterion was that a 'special responsibility' for the presence of these minorities was accepted by the Dutch government. This applied to people from (former) Dutch colonies, migrant labourers from the Mediterranean, and political refugees. The second was that the social position of these groups had to be clearly underprivileged, especially in housing, education, and employment" (Pieke, 1988:12).

The second criterion, i.e., underprivileged, confused the Chinese for a long time. In the 1980s, when the golden period of the Chinese catering business was over, it became clear that the period when all social cares and needs of the Chinese could be provided by themselves was also over. Thus, the advantages of being an ethnic minority attracted the attention of some Chinese leaders. In the mid-1980s, a few Chinese leaders submitted a request that the Chinese should be given official ethnic minority status. This argument immediately met with strong opposition from other Chinese leaders. They were afraid that such a title would bring new discrimination to the Chinese in the Netherlands and, furthermore, could be disadvantageous to their economic undertakings.

After discussing this for several years, most Chinese leaders reached a consensus that included two basic points. First, the Chinese as a group is not a minority of consistently low social position like in the definition of ethnic minority, although they do encounter some difficulties. Second, the Chinese hope that the Dutch government will offer the necessary help to improve the social position of the Chinese, regardless of whether they do belong to an ethnic minority or not. The Dutch government, after a prolonged period of surveys and inquiries between 1984 and 1988, declined to grant minority status to the Chinese. Nevertheless, it allowed local governments to subsidize services and organizations catering to the local Chinese population (Pieke & Benton, 1998:158).

Since then, the relationship between the Chinese associations, especially their leaders, and the Dutch authorities has entered a much more delicate stage. The principal attitude of the Chinese leaders is prompted by two influences. On the one hand, their attitude is influenced by Confucian culture. Briefly speaking, Confucian culture implies respect for authority. Strident individualism or rebelliousness is considered a serious offense. Therefore, to most Chinese immigrants, any instruction from the Dutch government should be highly respected. Western pressure group politics are completely strange to most of them. More precisely, becoming a pressure group for Chinese immigrants is never a factor among the motives for organizing Chinese associations in the Netherlands. Although some newly established Chinese associations have stressed that they will strive to serve the collective interests of the Chinese in the Netherlands, that is all they wish to do. Further, they still clearly define respect for Dutch authorities as an essential prerequisite. One example is ACV in the 1950s and the 1960s. When suspicions from the Dutch government put heavy pressure on the ACV's leaders, their defense was to passively add a clause to their constitution: ACV "will not be involved in any political activities in the Netherlands" (cf. Chapter IV).[32]

On the other hand, their attitude is defined by the structure of the Chinese economic means, which is heavily inclined towards catering. As was mentioned earlier, the dependence on their catering business often makes Chinese immigrants feel insecure. It is apparent that most Chinese in the Netherlands have accepted the consensus that they should obey the instructions of the Dutch government, at least nominally, and should be friendly with the Dutch society. The associations have often overstressed this loyalty to the host society not only because of the newly arrived immigrants' inferiority complex but also because of the belief that compliance with the regulations is practical and beneficial.

To be a friend or a supporter of the government in power is a common orientation of the Chinese immigrant associations in the Netherlands. Therefore, the relevant policies formulated by the Dutch government affect the development of the Chinese association movement.

For instance, the proliferation of Chinese associations after the 1980s is a direct response to the new minorities policy formulated at that time. A key point of the new ethnic minorities policies formulated by successive legislation in the early- and mid-1980s was to develop the cultural identity of immigrants and promote contact between immigrants and the Dutch majority; to this end, the strengthening of immigrant or ethnic organizations is encouraged. Such being the case, the Chinese organizational efforts experienced an unprecedented explosion: about ninety per cent of the existing Chinese associations were set up after 1980. Just like Mrs. Chan told me:[33]

> CCRM is the first Chinese association being fairly subsidized by the Dutch government, because we have done excellent work to promote contacts between the Chinese and the Dutch [...] However, after having seen that the immigrants' organizational activities could be subsidized by the Dutch government, many Chinese vie with each other in establishing several forms of associations [...] It seems as if dozens of Chinese associations have appeared overnight.

As was mentioned in Chapter IV, from the early 1980s, ACV, *Fa Yin* and CCRM all established some contacts with the Dutch authorities. In addition, CSFN, *Wa Lai* and some other newly established associations also tried to ask for subsidies either from the local municipal authorities or from CRM. After finding it too complicated to deal with so many different Chinese associations, around the beginning of 1987, the representative of CRM put forward a suggestion to all Chinese association leaders. He indicated that all Chinese associations in the Netherlands should unite together to organize one federation; the Ministry will only accept that future federation as the representative of all Chinese in the Netherlands; and only the requests presented by that federation will come under consideration. Although it seems superficially reasonable, this suggestion in fact posed a difficult question to Chinese leaders.

As was already mentioned, the Chinese associations in the Netherlands are divided on the basis of various districts of origin, differing dialects and religions, and differing political beliefs. These divisions hamper harmonious cooperation within the community. The Chinese leaders knew that none of the existing leaders could speak for the Chinese community as a whole nor could any of them be accepted as the central figure to organize a united federation for all Chinese. However, none of them dared to say "no" to that Dutch official directly, since he was regarded as the enforcing officer of the Dutch authorities whose *suggestion* was a sort of *instruction*. The Dutch official asked ACV and CCRM — the two most influential Chinese associations at that time but with sharply contrasting political orientations — to be in charge of the unification process. Due to the push of the Dutch official, the two associations, despite the differences between them, reached a consensus that they both wanted to please the Dutch authorities. Besides, as a face-saving device, the internal divisions should not be presented to the Dutch; the impression that the Chinese in the Netherlands are a cohesive community should not be spoiled. At the same time, however, a latent competition started between the leaders of the two associations, as both were eager to become the chairman of the new federation.

Over the six months between the spring and autumn of 1987, several meetings on how to organize the federation were held in the name of the

CRM and under the direction of ACV and CCRM. Finally, LFCON, the federation of Chinese associations in the Netherlands, was founded in Amsterdam on 26 October, 1987. The establishment of LFCON offers some noteworthy points.[34]

First, its foundation was the product of Dutch policies and Dutch officials rather than an initiative of the Chinese themselves. For instance, from the first meeting focussed on the federation, instead of discussing whether it was possible, or necessary, to have the federation, the only subject matter discussed in detail was how to execute the Dutch authority's *instruction.* "To organize a united federation is the instruction of the Dutch authorities to us Chinese, we should implement this instruction." This assertion was stressed repeatedly by the organizers in all meetings. Moreover, unlike other Chinese associations, the continuity of LFCON relies on the support provided by the Dutch government. In 1998, when LFCON was in a state of financial crisis due to new government funding regulations,[35] one of its leaders told me, "we shall disband LFCON if the Dutch government stops funding it. LFCON is needed by the Dutch government more than we need LFCON."

Second, from the very beginning, some Chinese associations have kept their attitude as an outsider, although they dared not to fight against the federation due to its government backing. This negatively affects LFCON's function as a unified representative of the entire Chinese community. When LFCON was being organized, the leaders of all existing Chinese associations, which numbered around forty at that time, were invited, but fewer than twenty sent representatives. When LFCON declared its foundation, only 17 associations agreed to be members.

Third, some Chinese associations never stopped their efforts to organize another federation as the umbrella organization of the Chinese. CCRM is one representative case. As was mentioned earlier, during the 1980s, CCRM was one of the most influential Chinese associations in the Netherlands and had close contacts with the Dutch authorities. CCRM quit in the middle of the organizing process when its representatives thought that ACV arrogated all powers of the federation to itself and its few like-minded associations. Because of this resentment against LFCON, CCRM attempted to organize another federation several times. Its efforts failed because the Dutch authorities insisted on accepting LFCON as the only Chinese federation.

In October 1997, when LFCON celebrated the tenth anniversary of its founding, 45 Chinese associations were registered as its members.[36] However, some nationwide associations, such as *Chun Pah* and *Wai Wun*, and some active associations, such as BLIH and *Wah Fook Wui*, were still outside LFCON. Moreover, when initiating an activity among the Chinese, LFCON was very often on the same footing as other Chinese associations.

In sum, over ten years after LFCON was established, it is still unable to speak as the sole legitimate representative of all Chinese associations either within the Chinese community or towards the Dutch government.

B *Towards China*

For first-generation immigrants, it is not easy to give up their nostalgia for their original country. An aphorism says, "exile is the nursery of nationality" (Anderson, 1992:2). Migration is generally different from exile: immigrants move voluntarily, while those in exile are forced to go. Within a certain sphere, however, voluntary migrants and refugees face similar situations: both have to find a new way to live in a strange country; both have to learn to understand a strange culture; and both have to deal with strange neighbours. The distance from where they were born-and-bred and the feeling of nostalgia for a period that can never return have understandably been the nursery of nationalism for migrants and refugees.

Moreover, especially after the 1980s, developments in China have offered an unprecedented economic opportunity for Western entrepreneurs, which has attracted the attention of the Western world. Many of the Chinese migrants or ethnic Chinese abroad want to avail themselves of these opportunities. Among others, influences from China have sometimes underpinned the creation of Chinese associations.

There are two governments in China: one of the People's Republic of China and one of the "Republic of China" in Taiwan. It will be clearer to describe the influences from each side separately.

Influences from Taiwan

Since 1949, when Chiang Kai-shek lost the civil war and retreated to Taiwan, the KMT government has put great emphasis on influencing overseas Chinese. In the opinion of the late Chiang Kai-shek and his government, overseas Chinese can be used as a powerful force to help re-conquer mainland China. The Overseas Chinese Affairs Commission (hereafter OCAC), a unit under the National Executive Yuan in Taiwan, is the principal organization that deals with overseas Chinese affairs.[37] From the 1970s up to the end of 1986, OCAC sponsored 61 working seminars on overseas Chinese affairs, attended by 1,552 overseas Chinese from around the world. According to one account, the seminars have cultivated a new elite to act as leaders in Chinese immigrant communities (Government Information Office, 1988: 395). OCAC has initiated many Chinese associations abroad.

In the Netherlands, CCRM, the Association of Taiwan Entrepreneurs in the Netherlands, the Overseas Chinese Association in the Netherlands, and a few other associations have accepted, directly or indirectly, OCAC's guidance in their founding. Especially among some transnational associations, the strength of OCAC was quite significant.

The Union of Chinese Associations in Europe, of which several dozens of the Chinese in the Netherlands are active members, is a typical case. The hand of OCAC is clearly discernible in the history of its founding and the arrangement of its annual meetings. However, other factors have also shaped this union.

On April 5 1975, when Chiang Kai-shek died, OCAC suggested that large-scale mourning ceremonies to honour the late president should be organized wherever there are Chinese communities. With the support of OCAC, pro-Taiwan Chinese in Germany invited the leaders of pro-Taiwan associations in Europe to a "commemorative meeting." The meeting was held on April 16 in Hamburg, with about forty participants from various European countries. At the meeting, someone suggested that to support "free China" more effectively, an integrated union of all of the Chinese in Europe should be established. Through such a union, pro-Taiwan Chinese in Europe could discuss and meet with one another. The proposal was accepted. The meeting also decided to try to hold a meeting at least once a year; to influence and attract more overseas Chinese, this meeting was to be held successively in all the Western European capitals.

In 1976, the annual meeting was held as scheduled in Brussels. More than 160 people from a dozen European countries attended. The meeting officially proclaimed the founding of the Union of Chinese Associations in Europe.[38]

From the very start, the Director or Deputy Director of OCAC and representatives in Europe of the Taiwan government, especially those in the country where the annual meeting was to be held in any given year, have always dominated such gatherings. The government of the People's Republic of China have sharply criticized these gatherings. When the annual meeting of the union is to be held in a country that has diplomatic relations with Beijing, a diplomatic protest is lodged by the embassy. In some cases, the governments of such countries have refused applications for such annual meetings. In 1978, for instance, when the fourth annual meeting was to be held in Spain, the Spanish government declared its presence unwelcome, and thus the meeting had to be held in a Chinese restaurant. Dozens of Chinese from European countries other than Spain were simply refused entry visas. Thereafter, to prevent the recurrence of such an incident, the union decided to adopt a new name, *Lü Ou Huaqiao lüyou guanguang lianyihui* (Friendly Association for the Overseas Chinese Tourist Business in Europe), designed to sound like an organization for tourism and travel business cooperation. When the country where they intend to hold their meeting is sensitive about its diplomatic relations with China, the new name is used and the business of the meeting is nominally confined to the theme of "tourism for overseas Chinese."[39]

Since the 1990s, uniting the Taiwanese entrepreneurs abroad has become a major objective of OCAC.[40] In view of European integration, many powerful Taiwanese companies attempted to set up a daughter-company inside Europe before the continent closed its borders. For instance, by the mid-1990s, more than ninety Taiwanese companies set up their offices in the Netherlands. Then, for business purposes, around five hundred people from Taiwan settled down in the Netherlands. In 1994, the Association of Taiwan Entrepreneurs in the Netherlands was set up. In 1995, the Federation of Taiwan Entrepreneurs Associations in Europe was established. In a working report, OCAC's chairman clearly lists the establishment of the above-mentioned associations as a significant achievement.[41]

Influences from mainland China
The influences from the authorities of mainland China are also visible. One example is the founding of the European Federation of Chinese Organizations (hereafter EFCO). EFCO was officially set up in May 1992 in Amsterdam. The idea for founding such a European-wide association for all pro-Beijing Chinese associations was first proposed in 1983. In that year, the *LüFa Huaqiao julebu* (Overseas Chinese Club in France) purchased a new office building in Paris with money collected from its members. The Ambassador of China to France, an official delegation from Beijing, and more than ten fellow-associations in other Western European countries were invited to attend the inauguration of the building. Most of these leaders were pro-Beijing and did not attend the pro-Taiwan annual meetings organized by the Union of Chinese Associations in Europe. During the meeting, an informal proposal arose from discussions about the need for improved mutual communications between fellow associations and for the establishment of a unified voice: it was necessary to set up their own European-wide federation.

The proposal was not put into effect until high-ranking officials of the People's Republic of China clearly expressed their positive attitude towards the establishment of a federation. During those years after 1983, the topic of how to organize a federation had been discussed now and then among the active initiators, who are Chinese immigrants living in the Netherlands, France, United Kingdom, Spain and Austria. Nevertheless, they made no obvious progress. Because the responses from the authorities in Beijing on the issue were rather equivocal, they could not completely justify their efforts. The turning point happened in 1990. Then, the Asian Games were held in Beijing for the first time. Many leaders of the pro-Beijing Chinese associations from Europe went to Beijing to watch the Games. When they were received by the chairman of the Overseas Affairs Office of the State Council and some other high-ranking officials, the topic of organizing a federation was put forward. This time the response were clear: Beijing would be happy to see a united federation of Chinese associations in Europe.

The attitude of Beijing was significant to all pro-Beijing Chinese associations in Europe. To the initiators, their organizational activity was now under the patronage of the Chinese government; to others, Beijing's approval changed the federation from an association fed by the ambitions of a few persons to a semi-official organization. Finally, in May 1992, the inaugural conference of EFCO was held in Amsterdam. A delegation headed by a vice-chairman of the standing committee of the Chinese National People's Congress made a special trip from Beijing to Amsterdam to congratulate the establishment of EFCO.

Large-scale associations like EFCO are not the only ones who appreciate support from Beijing; some small-scale associations also cherish the acknowledgment from the relevant local authorities in China, especially associations that are based upon shared provenance.

In January 1997, while doing fieldwork in Dapeng, I came upon an interesting case that is meaningful to the issue I am discussing here, although it is only partly related to the Chinese associations in the Netherlands. One day, while sitting in the office of the Dapeng Returned Overseas Chinese Association, I saw LQ coming in. LQ was born in Dapeng in 1926, emigrated to Germany in 1965 and just came back to pay a visit to his hometown. He made a request to the local officials:

> Since more than one year ago, I have been requested by some co-villagers to be one of the initiators to make preparations for setting up a Dapeng association in Germany. You know, there are several hundreds of Dapeng people in Germany but they have little contact with each other. We believe that if we want some greater development, we should unite together. Nevertheless, it is not easy if there are only a few of us working for this purpose. Before I came back here, some active initiators asked me to have a discussion with you. As the representatives of the native government of our original hometown, could you write an open letter to all Dapeng residents in Germany? In the letter, we hope you will express clearly that you support the organization and appeal to all Dapeng people over there to join, to support the association. I believe such a letter will produce a greater effect.

The two officials agreed. In a couple of days, I saw a draft of the letter on the desk. The main contents of the letter is as follows:

> We are very glad to know that all of our fellow-villagers in Germany are going to organize a regional association. As the representatives of the local government and the people of your original hometown, we sincerely hope that you will unite together as soon as possible and make your contributions.

A few days later, while sitting in his new house to be interviewed, LQ started his talk with the following saying: "Falling leaves settle on their roots. I will finally return to my hometown. Therefore, I build this house for my potential resettlement, although I still don't know when I will be back." When asked why he thought a letter from the Dapeng Returned Overseas Chinese Association will be helpful to push the birth of a Dapeng regional association in Gernmany, LQ said:[42]

> Although we live abroad, there is a general consensus among us that the support from the hometown government will legitimate and strengthen our position to organize a regional association. We have houses here. We have relatives here. Our roots are here. We come back for visiting now and then. We have many contacts with our hometown.

From the cases mentioned above, one phenomenon is clear: the first generation of Chinese immigrants, no matter how long or how far away they have been, have never completely departed from their native country. Therefore, before they organize a new association, many hope to win the support of the government of their region of origin to legitimate their position. Moreover, the higher the level of the government that supports or recognizes them, the higher the position that the association will enjoy among their fellow immigrants.

C *Transnational links*

It is also a noteworthy phenomenon that some Chinese associations are motivated by transnational links. The association called *Tai Pang Gemeenschap in Europa* (Tai Pang Community in Europe; hereafter TPGE) is a case in point. The impetus for its founding came from the Association of Tai Pang Community in Hong Kong.

Tai Pang is the Cantonese pronunciation of Dapeng. As was mentioned in Chapter II, Dapeng, an area under the jurisdiction of former Bo On, is a major *qiaoxiang* of Chinese immigrants in the Netherlands. According to the statistics presented by the Dapeng government, in 1995, the permanent residents of Dapeng itself numbered 6,679, but the Dapeng emigrants in Hong Kong and abroad with their descendants numbered over 25,000. Among the emigrants, about 20,000 are living in Hong Kong.[43] Because of their emigration process, which was described in Chapter II, the contact between the Dapeng emigrants in Hong Kong and in the Netherlands is very close. Before emigrating to the Netherlands, almost all these Dapeng people once stayed in Hong Kong, whether for a few months or a few years. After settling in the Netherlands, whenever they pay a visit to their hometown, they will go through Hong Kong. Moreover, transnational families, i.e., part of the family lives in the Netherlands and another part lives in Hong Kong or Dapeng, are a common phenomenon.

In 1976, Dapeng people in Hong Kong set up their own association, named Hong Kong Tai Pang Residents Association. When the news was sent to their co-villagers in the Netherlands, some active Dapeng businessmen in the Netherlands initiated a contribution drive for this Hong Kong association. In a short period, a sum of money amounting to 200,000 Hong Kong dollars was collected and sent to the Hong Kong association as a special gift to congratulate them on the establishment of the association.[44] When asked why Dapeng people in the Netherlands were willing to contribute to an association in Hong Kong, the current chairman of TPGE said:[45]

> Because we belong to one Dapeng family. We know each other. When we go home, we are often received by our co-villagers in Hong Kong, very warmly.[46] We are always willing to support each other, although there is a great geographical distance between us.

At the beginning of the 1980s, after seeing the success of the Tai Pang association in Hong Kong and, moreover, the esteem the association enjoyed in their hometown, some successful Dapeng immigrants in the Netherlands decided to found their own association. The proposal to organize a Tai Pang association among the Dapeng people in the Netherlands, in turn, received full support from the Tai Pang association in Hong Kong. The leading committee of the Hong Kong Tai Pang Residents Association immediately decided that 200,000 Hong Kong dollars would be donated as a gift to the Tai Pang association in Holland as soon as it was founded. Moreover, when TPGE held its founding ceremony on 5 February 1984, the representative of the Hong Kong Tai Pang association promised that TPGE's plan to buy an office would be supported by its fellow association in Hong Kong.

Other similar cases clearly exemplify the transnational origins of many associations. For instance, the Tang family is a big clan in the New Territories of Hong Kong.[47] Many members of this clan emigrated to Europe during the 1960s and 1970s. In 1984, the Tang clan members in the United Kingdom set up a surname association called the Association of the Tang Family in Europe. Then, under its influence, Tang clan members in the Netherlands also set up the Association of the Tang Family in the Netherlands. Its chairman told me:

> The Tang Family is a clan with a long history. In our hometown, we still keep the genealogical register of our clan which shows that we are the offspring of a princess of the imperial family.
>
> We, Tang people, now have our surname associations in the United Kingdom, Thailand, Hong Kong, Taiwan and elsewhere. We help and support each other when in need, although each association in each country is an independent association.

The invisible transnational network that exists among Chinese immigrants all over the world is a matter that has attracted increasing attention. In Chapter VII, this issue will be studied again from the perspective of the social functions of the Chinese associations.

D A synthesis case study

To show a clearer coherence, I have attempted to analyze the organizational patterns from different perspectives. Although one or two factors may play the principal role in their motivation, few associations were mobilized by a single cause. Rather, in most cases, the syncretism of internal and external dynamics is the source of organization. Thus, for a comprehensive understanding, a synthesis study is necessary.

I will take EFCO as a case study. As was mentioned, a new turning point for EFCO's establishment came when its initiators won support from esteemed and high-placed leaders of the People's Republic of China. Other factors, however, have shaped the birth of EFCO as well.

One of these is the remarkable characteristics shared by all of its initiators. Between 7 and 9 December 1996, the fifth annual meeting of EFCO was held in Amsterdam. During breaks in the meetings, I interviewed five active initiators (among the first initiators, three have passed away). From the interviews, I found that the initiators (as well as the three who have passed away) have three characteristics in common:

(i)   they are (were) first-generation immigrants from China (six from Wenzhou and two from Hong Kong);
(ii) they are regarded as successful Chinese businessmen;
(iii) they are (were) active leaders of existing and well-known Chinese associations in their respective countries.

From how they talked about the motives behind organizing EFCO, the implication is that they were the right people to accomplish the task of uniting the Chinese immigrants all over Europe, and they were indeed very successful. The following expressions are representative of their general beliefs:

> United we stand, divided we fall. If we want to improve our position both in Europe and in China, we should have a powerful union to be our collective representative. We initiators are active leaders of the Chinese community in the respective countries. We feel we are responsible in the striving to unite the Chinese. It is our duty to act as the organizers. We are very glad to see our dream has come true.[48]

> Now you see more than one hundred people sitting here and many have fired off speeches vehemently. But among them, how many really contributed to the establishment of EFCO? Five years ago, few people believed that we could set up such a European-wide federation. But we worked for it. We have reached our goal. In order to let more people understand our project, I cannot remember how many times I traveled between the European countries; I cannot calculate how much money I have spent on long-distance phone calls [...] If we didn't persevere in our strivings, a Chinese union in Europe would still be a dream now.[49]

> In England, my association is an umbrella association to which more than fifty Chinese associations are affiliated. Thus, I dare to say that I may be regarded as an acceptable person to initiate organizing a European-wide federation [...] Someone said EFCO has too few association members.[50] No, this is not true. In fact, I am the representative of more than fifty Chinese associations in Britain.[51]

These initiators, all of whom are successful Chinese businessmen and association leaders in their respective host countries, have been actively searching for respect at a transnational level. Their efforts to organize EFCO were partly inspired by their potential for self-actualization. They wanted all European Chinese to recognize them as their collective representative.

Furthermore, the process of European integration has also influenced the organization of EFCO. EFCO was established when the integration of

Europe was at the center of attention of leading politicians. There was a new motive at work. When the initiators met again in Beijing in 1990, they saw that the future Chinese federation could become a distinct channel of communication with the European Commission. Those behind the proposal continue to hope that the European Commission will accept their association as the formal representative of the European Chinese community. To this end, the initiators have sought publicity on a European scale by, among other things, charging one of the vice-chairmen to look after relations with the Commission of the European Union.

In short, several factors have shaped the organizational pattern of EFCO. As the initiators were eagerly attempting to solidify their role as the Chinese representative on a European level, European integration created an opportunity for them to explore this position; then, the official support from their original motherland legitimized their efforts. As an outcome of these factors, EFCO firmly established itself as a force on the European stage.

Undoubtedly, as a long-distance migrant group, the Chinese in the Netherlands have cherished dreams of a better future through migration. The proliferation of the Chinese associations resulted from their efforts to have their dreams come true. Comparing their organizational motivations at the present day with those before the war, it is clear that their motives have been updated from passively dealing with day-to-day problems to much broader goals. More precisely, the motivations involved in organizing ethnic associations can be summarized as follows: to cultivate their own cultural tradition; to re-establish self-esteem; to highlight their presence in both the original and adopted societies; to create a positive social image; to act as intermediaries with the authorities and even try to become participants in policy-making. These motivations are still at work today and evidenced by the fact that these associations are still striving toward their goals. However, regarding these goals and expectations, the Chinese association initiators and leaders have a clearer vision than most of their followers, which is the focus of the next chapter.

CHAPTER VI

Leadership and Membership: Organizational Structure

Chinese associations are readily observable entities that demonstrate some striking characteristics of the Chinese community. Every association has an official constitution, and most associations pursue a visible social position through various public activities. A variety of Chinese associations exist in the Netherlands. Neither the internal structure nor the external networks of each individual association are easily identified from the outside.

How can you identify a leader of a Chinese association? Are there any common socio-cultural characteristics of the leaders? Who is willing to join a Chinese association and why? What are the decision-making procedures within an association? Here I shall analyze these questions.

1 *Leadership*

Leaders are the core of an association. While studying the Chinese associations in Southeast Asia and the United States, some scholars have pointed out that the Chinese organizations actually depend more on their leaders than on their members for survival and expansion (cf. Skinner, 1958; Wong, 1977; See, 1988; Wickberg, 1988); some even regard Chinese communities abroad as "plutocracies" (Crissman, 1967). Concerning the Chinese associations in the Netherlands, a successful association generally depends on their leaders' attributes. This includes the leaders' ability to organize, to articulate an ideology, and, most importantly, to relate to both ordinary people and the authorities in the Netherlands and China.

A *The social status of Chinese association leaders*

While studying the roles played by the elite in New York City's Chinatown, Wong divided the Chinese elite into two groups. One is *Kiu Ling*, i.e., the traditional leaders; the other is *Chuen Ka*, i.e., supervisors of, or social workers in, the social service agencies. Wong clearly identified the two groups not only in terms of age, birthplace, lifestyle, occupation, dialect, and language ability but also in terms of the differences between their ethnic identities, values, interaction patterns, etc. (1977). His distinctions, however, cannot simply be transferred to identify the elite of the Chinese community in the Netherlands.

The Chinese associations in the Netherlands that I have studied are voluntary entities. Officially, their leaders neither receive payment from the association nor run a business in the name of the association. Moreover, many
leaders have to contribute money, time, and energy to the association. Therefore, for many leaders of Chinese associations, it is a voluntary and self-
imposed task to take up a post in an association. They have to run their
business or maintain other work to make their living. Reviewing the personal
status of current Chinese association leaders, most can be included in one of
the following three groups:

(i)   successful business persons;
(ii)   social workers;
(iii) politicians and professionals.

Successful business persons take up many leading positions in the Chinese
associations.[1] After visiting and studying fifty associations, I have formulated
two standards to define an association as headed by Chinese business persons: (i) two-thirds of the committee posts are taken up by business persons;
or (ii) the major leading posts (chairman and vice-chairmen) are taken up by
business persons.

The result of my analysis is that Chinese business persons dominate the
committees of 25 of the associations I chose. Among them, eight associations
are organized by and for the Chinese restaurateurs or Chinese business persons, which are headed by business persons for obvious reasons. Ten associations are based on clan or shared provenance. It is worth noting that successful clan members or co-villagers head all the associations organized by
traditional links. The other seven associations are communal associations,
such as ACV and LFCON. In the standing committee of ACV, more than
eighty per cent are Chinese business persons, and most leading positions of
LFCON have been taken by successful Chinese business persons. Crissman
stresses that leadership of the Chinese associations is based on wealth and its
concomitant prestige (1967:199). To a certain degree, this is true. However,
the point to ponder is why and how have these persons, consciously or
unconsciously, converted their economic capital into social and symbolic
power? This question will be the major topic of the next chapter.

The second group of Chinese association leaders comprises qualified social workers. For instance, the major leaders of CCRM, *Wa Lai*, *Chinese Brug*,
NCV and some other ten-odd Chinese associations are social workers. This
group has three observable characteristics.

First, most of them are women. As was mentioned in Chapter IV, NCV,
the first Chinese volunteers' association in the Netherlands, was established
on 13 September 1996 in Rotterdam. Its aim is twofold: to become a community-wide organization with an expanded social work role and to improve
the abilities of Chinese social workers while protecting their rights. Its two
general coordinators and the heads of seven regional groups are all women.

Second, Christians are heavily represented in this group. In mainland

China, either "social work" or "social worker" is a new concept that has only recently gained some acceptance. In the Netherlands, it is still a strange concept for many Chinese immigrants. The appearance of Chinese social workers is an outcome of the adjustment of some progressive Chinese immigrants to Dutch society. Since the leading social workers such as Mrs. Chan, the head of CCRM, and Ms. Mai, the head of *Wa Lai*, are Christians, the concept of social work was first spread among Chinese Christians. The idea of offering services to people in need is easily combined with the Christian paradigm.

The third characteristic of this group is that many social workers prefer to regard themselves, and sometimes prefer to be regarded, as "employees of the Dutch government" rather than merely as "volunteers." In a developed state like the Netherlands, social work is one component of its welfare system and has consequently become professionalized. While volunteers take up most social work positions, some qualified professional social workers can be salaried or subsidized by the government. Since the late 1980s, some Chinese volunteers have become professional social workers and were subsidized by the government.

This position has a dual effect among the average Chinese immigrants. On the one hand, the social prestige of officials working for the Dutch authorities is much higher than social workers, which may help the social workers win respect from their compatriots. On the other hand, it is difficult for others to accept these people as leaders. According to tradition, a Chinese leader should play a leading role in donating financial contributions for the Chinese community. However, instead of contributing, these social workers receive wages. During my interviews, sometimes I heard my interviewees complain that the subsidies from the Dutch government to the Chinese community had been transferred to personal purses. The examples they mentioned often related to the salaried social workers employed by the government.

The professional social workers are a new group among the Chinese immigrants and their roles and social status are rising. Many of them are active in establishing or managing Chinese associations. Some of them even interact with the Dutch government on behalf of the Chinese community. I, therefore, define these people as a special group among the Chinese leaders, although many Chinese regard them as "office bearers" rather than "leaders."

The third group of Chinese association leaders is composed of politicians and professionals. As was mentioned in Chapter I, the Peranakan Chinese in the Netherlands are generally a highly educated group. Professionals such as doctors, professors and scientists normally head their voluntary associations. Besides the Peranakan associations, some associations organized by and for Chinese professionals who came directly from China have been established since the beginning of the 1990s. For instance, there are currently five associations for Chinese artists, three for Chinese acupuncturists, one for Chinese writers, and some for Chinese *liuxuesheng*. Some leaders of these associations are capable professionals in their respective spheres. There are, however, some exceptions.

Unlike the Chinese community in the United States, which has included some famous Chinese professionals, the Chinese in the Netherlands are a relatively poorly educated community. Moreover, as noted in Chapter II, a few Chinese scholars who came as *liuxuesheng* but now work in the Netherlands are usually reluctant to join any existing Chinese associations. Consequently, some self-styled "professional associations" are formed by amateurs. For instance, one chairman of a Chinese acupuncturists' association was a businessman rather than a qualified acupuncturist.

In 1994, the *Stichting China Law* was set up and aimed to offer special legal protection and advice to ordinary Chinese immigrants. Its Chinese name can be translated as Consultative Association of Dutch and Chinese Lawyers, which sounds as if it is a professional association. Its committee is composed of four Dutch and four Chinese. It is interesting that among the four Dutch there are two lawyers, one accountant and one catering business adviser, while among the four Chinese there are three restaurateurs and one businessman.

Few Chinese in the Netherlands have been identified as a politician by profession. One special example is Mr. Ho Ten Soeng. Ho is a Chinese descendant who was born in Surinam. After finishing his middle school education in Surinam, Ho came to the Netherlands for his university education. From the beginning of the 1990s, Ho began to throw himself into Dutch political affairs. In 1994, as the representative of CDA, Ho became the *Wethouder* (Alderman) of Alkmaar. Although Ho cannot speak Chinese, he identifies himself as Chinese. Since he became the first well-known Dutch politician with Chinese blood, he has often been invited to be the leader of Chinese associations. For example, he was invited to be the chairman of NCV; his name appears among the honorary advisers of the Federation of *Wu Shu*, Dragon- and Lion-dance Associations in the Netherlands; among the members of a leading group on Chinese education in the Netherlands; and a couple of other organizations.

In sum, among the three groups of Chinese association leaders, the first enjoys a dominating position; the second is a new group that is developing quickly; and the third is a limited group still in its infancy.

B *Types of leadership*

The professions or occupations of the Chinese association leaders were described above. In this section, the study will focus on the differences of their actual position within their respective associations.

One common feature of the Chinese association is that they usually create many leading posts for their members. For instance, one Chinese dragon-dance association has elected a committee of as many as fifty persons, which gives almost all of its members a title. As was mentioned earlier, in 1996, ACV elected an enormous leading committee: besides one chairman, it has created up to 18 vice-chairmen, 84 posts for its standing committee, ten honorary chair positions, five honorary vice-chairman posts, 18 senior consultants, twenty-five honorary consultants, and as many as 211 committee members (ACV, 1997: 27-28).

It is obvious that the committee members in an association do not share equal power with the leadership positions, regarding either their interests or the decision-making process. In view of the leading posts within one association, they can be roughly divided into three groups: powerful, nominal, or honorary leaders.

Chairman, vice-chairman, treasurer, and secretary usually form the powerful posts in an association's committee. The people who have taken these posts form the nucleus of the association. Normally, they are the people who will be involved in the decision-making process. At the same time, they must be the principal contributors to the association. Consequently, their desires, capabilities, and even personal characteristics will directly affect the respective association.

Chinese associations abroad generally have a relatively stable nucleus.[2] In the Netherlands today, for example, in well-known associations such as CCRM, *Wa Lai*, Chinese Brug and HYXSH, the major leaders have taken leading positions ever since the organizations were established.

Nevertheless, in some associations, the people who have held the highest posts have changed, but a few powerful persons still form the core of the association, regardless of which post they actually hold. For instance, as was described in Chapter IV, in the fifty-year history ACV, three leading nuclei have been composed. The first two that appeared in the 1950s and 1970s in succession have left the social stage; but the third one is still growing. The case of *Fa Yin* shows some differences. Mr. Liang's contributions to *Fa Yin* was introduced in Chapter IV. In 1989, when the third board was organized, Liang resigned from the chairman's post because of his age. Since then, five other persons have been elected as the chairman of *Fa Yin*. Nevertheless, Liang maintains the continuity of the leadership. Despite his resignation, Liang's suggestions have always been taken seriously. Someone told me that *Fa Yin* is Liang's real home and he is the head of the *Fa Yin* family.[3]

Besides the leaders with real power in an association, there are some nominal leaders. As was just mentioned, the tenth committee of ACV has as many as 221 members. It is clearly over-staffed, and most of them are leaders on paper only. From the interviews and from my observations, ACV can never hold its real plenary committee meetings, which should be attended by at least one-third of the total 221 committee members. Only a few of the plenary sessions of its standing committee are attended by more than half of its 84 members. At the ten plenary meetings of ACV's standing committee that I visited, only around twenty standing members regularly attended the meeting. Similar phenomena can be observed in some other associations.

Why did these associations keep leadership posts for nominal members? Were those nominal leaders concerned with their position being a mere formality? If they accepted the position, what is the reason behind their decision? In order to find the answer to the first question, we should first look at the social position of the relevant associations.

The Chinese association leaders generally have to donate contributions to the association, although some have used the association for their own ambitions. Thus, to many associations, creating more leading positions or titles is an acceptable measure to attract more supporters and followers. Not surprisingly, some smaller associations have assigned leading posts to all of their members. In addition, some associations that have claimed to be community-wide — such as ACV, CSFN, FWDLO — *need* to organize a rather large committee.

Of the many reasons for maintaining a nominal position, three are important to this discussion. First, they maintain their image as a nationwide association by having committee members from various groups. For instance, as noted in Chapter IV, ACV grew out of an association based on a common district of origin. Since ACV chose its present name in 1968 and attempted to present itself as a community-wide association, each new committee had to have some non-Zhejiang Chinese as members. In the tenth term of the standing committee, about one-tenth of the posts were specially created for Guangdong Chinese. These people are invited rather than elected, since most ACV's members are Zhejiang Chinese, and few non-Zhejiang Chinese are well enough known to the Zhejiang members to be voted onto its leading committee.

The second reason that many Chinese associations have an over-staffed committee is the balance of *guanxi* relations. The typical Chinese concept, *gei mianzi*, means "to give face" (i.e., to show due respect) to a certain person if he or she is given a post in a well-known association. Powerful leaders have their respective *guanxi* relations. Then, if a post is given to one, the other two or three cannot be ignored in order to save face. Since there is no limitation on the number of committee members, why not "give face" to all *guanxi* members?

The following is a typical example. I once visited an association's committee meeting. The topic for discussion was the candidates for the coming election. The present chairman presented a list of candidates and asked for comments. I noted that what he asked was: "Is there anyone else that should be added?" One long-time committee member pointed to a name and asked, "Who is this person?" The chairman said, "Oh, he is a very capable man, a good friend of mine. Although he arrived in the Netherlands only a couple of months ago, we should put his name as a candidate for our committee." There were no more objections: the nominee was accepted. Afterwards, in the list of this association's new committee members, I found this man had been appointed as a consultant. This man left the Netherlands soon after, but his name still stays among the committee members of that association.

The third reason is due to practical considerations. That is, although some persons with titles may not contribute to the association, because they are committee members they are officially committed to certain responsibilities. Therefore, the association can request their contributions when seriously needed.

It is interesting to study the reactions of these nominal leaders to their positions. The following quotes are from my interviews with some of them.

The late Mr. KU was Cantonese. He was a vice-chairman of the ninth committee of ACV before he died. He had been active in the activities organized by ACV and attended all committee meetings but hardly said a word. During my interview, he complained several times that he had never been treated as a vice-chairman. He said:[4]

> I am an outsider to them [i.e., the real powerful leaders of the association]. Yes, I am a vice-chairman, but that is a beautiful title only. Besides me, there are ten-odd vice-chairmen. I know most of us are only a committee member in name [...]

> [Why did you accept to be a vice-chairman of ACV, which you think belongs to the Zhejiang people?]

> Because it is the oldest and biggest association in the Netherlands. Moreover, the Chinese Embassy regards it as the most important Chinese association in the Netherlands. It has a very good name in China. Many want to get a leading position in ACV. [Then, he mentioned some names.] But they could not succeed. I am selected. It is a great honour.

Mr. LW is about sixty years old. He is a standing committee member of two well-known Chinese associations but rarely attends the relevant committee meetings. When asked about the reasons, he told me:[5]

> It is useless to attend the meetings. The decisions have already been made before the meeting among a few powerful persons.

> [Such being the case, why did you accept the position in name?]

> I have the title because I cannot be ignored. Formerly, I was included in that little circle that manages the association. I quit since I could not get along with one person [he mentioned the name and complained very much about him]. Now I am busy with my own restaurant. To keep my own business running well is much more important.

Then, this man told me some of his thinking on how to give more scope to the collective force of Chinese associations. Regardless of whether his suggestions could be put into practice or not, I found that he is a person with a keen and discerning mind. Since his position at the moment is in name only, however, his suggestions are considered just idle talk.

Ms. LX's father was one of the founders of ACV. Having heard about my research, she came to see me and asked to be interviewed. She talked about her personal opinion about ACV:[6]

> I am glad that at last they elected one of my sons to be a standing member of the tenth committee, although I know they have not cared about us since my father died [in 1979]. It is very possible that my son is a committee member only in name. Nevertheless, this fact at least means that they have recognized my father's contributions to the association because they have given a position to my son.

> [You mentioned several times about "they." Could you please tell me who they are?]

> You know who they are of course. They are the real power-holders. [Then she mentioned five names.]

The reactions of Mr. ZS, Mr. YC and some other interviewees have shown some similarities; that is, they do not care about their nominal position in a certain association.

> I don't care about it. I do not want to be a committee member. They put my name on the list. They wanted me to support them. But I told them very clearly that I have no time. [7]

> I don't want to be involved in any Chinese associations. I am a doctor. I work. I have my patients. I enjoy my life here. That is all. I told them clearly that I can do nothing for the association. But they still wanted to add my name on the list. OK, I can only be a member in name. [8]

In view of the reactions of the nominal leaders quoted above to their respective positions, three types of attitudes should be noted. The first basic attitude is dissatisfaction with the position. These people complained about it; they wanted to change their position but could not succeed. The second type is enjoyment. They print the title(s) on their name cards. They are satisfied that they can show the card to others as a sign of their social status, regardless of whether their position is real or nominal. Moreover, it is clear that a nominal position in the Netherlands may become a symbolic honour somewhere else, especially to improve someone's social status in a home community (this point will be studied further in Chapter VII). Finally, the third type of attitude is indifference. Some people have no interest in the association's affairs and do not care about their title(s) or the honours it carries.

Nevertheless, nothing is immutable. During the years that I have followed the development of the Chinese associations in the Netherlands, I saw some people change from being a powerful leader to holding a nominal position or even completely withdrawing from social affairs. Other people moved in the opposite direction. I will return to study this phenomenon when I discuss the qualifications of being a leader of a Chinese association.

Another interesting feature of Chinese associations in the Netherlands is that about seventy per cent of the existing associations have created certain honorary posts. These include honorary advisers, honorary consultants, honorary chairmen, life chairmen, life committee members, and so on.

For instance, ACV created its first honorary post in 1977. Between 1977 and 1986, only one person had the "honorary chairman" title. In 1987, the number of honorary posts in ACV increased to five, and the number of all honorary posts rose to as many as forty between 1987 and 1996. CSFN is another example. It has three life-long honorary chairmen, three honorary chairmen (two live in Hong Kong and one lives in the United Kingdom), and eight honorary advisers. Another example is an association for Chinese professionals, which only has about ten members but has created up to 72 posts for honorary advisers. One Chinese association founded in June 1997 created three posts for honorary chairmen, eight posts for honorary advisers, five posts for foreign honorary advisers (who live in Germany, France, the United Kingdom, Norway and Sweden), and five posts for advisers.

To explain this phenomenon, we must study it from at least three perspectives. First, the voluntary association is a non-profit organization. The only reward that it can present to the people who have contributed to its establishment and development is moral encouragement. The best moral encouragement is to give them an honorary title. Some associations, like ACV, have clearly incorporated a clause in their articles of association that all retired ex-chairman will get an honorary title. In addition, other associations — like *Dam Wah* — have announced from their beginning that whoever donated more than a certain amount of money (it is five hundred Dutch guilders in the case of *Dam Wah*) to their foundation would be granted an honorary title.

Second, to heighten the social position and expand the effect of the association concerned, it is a popularly adopted approach of many associations to invite well-known people to be their honorary leaders. The more successful people that a certain association is able to involve in its affairs, the higher social prestige the association will enjoy. For instance, as I mentioned above, at least five Chinese associations invited Mr. Ho Ten Soeng to accept an honorary post after he became the Alderman of the Dutch city Alkmaar.

Third, it is undeniable that some leaders have set up honorary posts for the benefit or interest of the association. For example, a new Chinese association was set up in 1996. Before it was formally established, the founders tried to get leaders of other well-known Chinese associations to be its honorary advisers. As many as 14 leaders accepted this invitation. All advisers were invited to the inaugural meeting and nine of them attended. At the meeting, the chairman of the association gave the first speech. After explaining the aim of the association, the chairman mentioned the name of one adviser and said that this adviser had donated five hundred guilders to the association. Then he expressed the association's gratitude to the advisers in advance for their generous contributions. Because the Chinese, especially the Chinese leaders, are concerned about face-saving at public occasions, all the advisers who attended the meeting made donations on the spot. Altogether 3,950 guilders were collected from the advisers. Afterwards, one adviser said angrily, "He [the chairman] asked too much! He has gone too far!" It is common to ask honorary leaders to contribute, but the way this chairman behaved was too straightforward to be accepted by the advisers.

I have compared the characteristics of the persons who have been invited to accept a kind of honorary post in Chinese associations. Three interesting facts are worth noting.

First, there are some Dutch names among the honorary leaders of some Chinese associations. For instance, a Dutch official, the director of ACB, has been invited to be an honorary adviser for *Fa Yin*, ACV, LFCON and some other Chinese associations. An association for Chinese acupuncturists has invited three Dutch doctors and officials to be its advisers. These associations' invitations to Dutch people reflect their general desire to build ties of friendship with the Dutch society, and to obtain necessary support from the mainstream society when it is in need.

The second item is that some associations have invited Chinese from other European countries or even from China to be their honorary leaders. For instance, CSFN has honorary chairmen from the United Kingdom and from Hong Kong. FWDLO has honorary advisers from Germany, France, the United Kingdom, Norway and Sweden. Meanwhile, I also noted that some well-known Chinese in the Netherlands have been invited by Chinese associations in other European countries to be their honorary leaders. For example, the Federation of Chinese Sports Organizations in the United Kingdom has invited two well-known Chinese from the Netherlands to be its honorary chairmen. This reflects the people's desire to maintain the transnational links among the Chinese immigrants in Europe.

Finally, the third fact I have noted is that some associations have invited Chinese professionals to be advisers. For instance, the Board of *Fa Yin* Chinese School invited five Chinese scholars and journalists to be its advisers. Some associations have elected Chinese doctors to be health adviser or medical adviser, because their elder members have increased in number and asked for such help. An association for Chinese cooks has invited a couple of famous Chinese cooks in Beijing to be its advisers. In addition, *Gong Fu* associations usually ask some *Gong Fu* masters to be their honorary advisers. It is a new trend that more Chinese associations are beginning to recognize the importance of professional knowledge.

It is an honour to be invited to accept one of these posts, especially if it is a well-known association. The honorary leaders, if they want, can give suggestions or criticisms to the association, but in most cases they enjoy the title rather than involve themselves in the affairs of the association. For instance, one well-known Chinese in the Netherlands cannot even count exactly how many invitations he has accepted from Chinese associations to be their honorary leader. When asked about his titles in Chinese associations, he told me:

> At present, I am the chairman of EFCO and LFCON, and the honorary chairman of ACV and two other associations. But, about the number of posts of being an honorary adviser or consultant, I cannot remember exactly for how many of these posts I have been asked. Many, quite many.

I was very often asked to be an honorary committee member, adviser or consultant of a certain association. Sometimes, the association is well organized and active, but sometimes the association may disappear soon after it proclaimed its establishment. Thus, I cannot tell you exactly which kind of honorary posts I have accepted for how many associations.

[Did you accept all invitations?]

Normally, I will not reject the invitations. They invited me because they respect me. We are after all Chinese immigrants living in this Western world. We should support each other. I always think it is a very good tradition among the Chinese associations in the Netherlands that the leader of one association is invited to be as an adviser or an honorary chairman of another association.

[Why?]

Yeah, of course, then it will be easier for us to establish contacts, to exchange information, to organize collective activities, if necessary.

What this man said expresses the role of honorary posts from a formal perspective. It is true that the interlocking relationships between the Chinese associations very often have been established due to the customary approach that a leader of one association will be invited to accept an honorary post in another association. This collective characteristic of Chinese leadership among the Chinese communities abroad has been well documented (cf. Skinner, 1958; Li, 1970).

C How to become a leader?

What will qualify a certain person to become a leader of an ethnic Chinese voluntary association? How can someone come forward and be accepted as a Chinese association leader?

Obviously, some requirements concerning being a leader of a Chinese association are similar to those for normal leaders. For instance, they should enjoy prestige and command universal respect; they should have strong organizational abilities and leadership skills, and so on; none of these normal requirements will be discussed here. What I am going to study is what qualifies a person to become a leader of a *Chinese voluntary* association.

To become a leader of a *Chinese* association, the first and most important requirement is that he or she should be able to discern a clear Chinese identity and should represent the interests of the Chinese community.

The following case shows how important it is for a leader to show clear loyalty to the Chinese community. Ng Ri Ming was a powerful Number One of the Bo On gang in the Netherlands during the early 20th century. He acted as the Chinese shipping master of a big Dutch shipping company,

Stoomvaart Maatschappij Nederland, for years. In the 1930s, more than seven hundred Chinese sailors worked for this company. In 1937, Chinese all over the world reacted to Japan's invasion of China. Then, Ng, as a powerful person, was elected as the chairman of the Amsterdam branch of the Chinese Resistance Association.[9] In the first years, he played a leading role in collecting donations for China. In the spring of 1939, however, some Chinese sailors found out that a freighter of the *Stoomvaart Maatschappij Nederland* in Rotterdam harbour was planning to ship arms and ammunition to Japan. They went to see Ng at once and asked him to cancel his contract with the company and to persuade all Chinese sailors to stop working for them. Keeping his own personal economic interests in mind, Ng rejected the request. This event immediately blackened his name among the Chinese. Ng was labelled a traitor and was dismissed from his chairman's position. Afterwards, he never regained his reputation among the Chinese in the Netherlands.

Nowadays, it is not surprising that some ethnic Chinese abroad have adopted flexible identities (Wang, 1988; Ong, 1999). From my studies, however, for those who are a leader of a Chinese association, they have, in the end, identified themselves first of all as Chinese. The case of Mr. Ho, which was mentioned above, is an example of this. He is regarded as a Chinese leader because he identifies himself as Chinese, despite the fact that he cannot speak Chinese. On the other hand, there are some social activists in the Dutch society who have Chinese blood, but they have never involved themselves in any Chinese association because they identify themselves as Dutch rather than Chinese.

Secondly, as the leaders of *voluntary* associations, they should have a certain economic foundation that will allow them to contribute money, energy, and time to their association. As was illustrated at the beginning of this chapter, many Chinese association leaders are successful or wealthy people. As leaders of voluntary associations, they often must donate money to balance the associations' expenses. For instance, in October 1994, CSFN, a Chinese sports association, held the tenth Sports Invitational Tournament in Amsterdam. In order to organize this game, which attracted 1,200 athletes, players, and sport enthusiasts from Europe, Asia, and America, the chairman and committee members of CSFN donated nearly 400,000 guilders.[10] As another example, during one week around 18 September 1997, ACV held a great party and unfolded a set of activities (exhibitions and performances) to celebrate the fiftieth anniversary of its foundation. The total expense was nearly 500,000 guilders. Besides one thousand guilders provided by the Amsterdam Municipality as a subsidy and some income from advertisements, about two-thirds of the expenses were collected from its chairman, vice chairmen, standing committee members, and committee members.[11]

It is said that a chairman of one of the well-known Chinese associations in the Netherlands should be prepared to donate several tens of thousands of guilders per year to his (it is rarely "her") association. In 1996, a few weeks before the election of its committee for a new term, one association made an unwritten regulation to lay down the desired donations they expected from their new leader. Specifically, whoever is voted in as the new chairman should donate ten thousand guilders to the association, while each new vice chairman should donate five thousand guilders and each new standing committee member should donate three thousand guilders. In another case, on the voting date, in order to have more "members" vote for him, one candidate rented two buses to bring all of his supporters from several cities to Amsterdam for voting. In addition, he paid several thousand guilders as "membership dues" in the name of all these supporters to let them become "members," which gave them the right to vote (for him).

If this is always the case, who besides the well-to-do can afford to be a candidate? Thus, there is a popular saying among the Chinese abroad: "money is the basis of the Chinese association leaders." On the other hand, while only well-to-do people are able to take up leading positions in such associations, not all wealthy people want to be leaders. Some very successful Chinese business persons prefer to remain invisible among the Chinese organizational activities. In the end, all of these facts are a reflection of personal considerations on conventions concerning economic, political, cultural, social and symbolic capital. This is the topic of the next chapter.

In the first segment of this chapter, I identified some leaders who are Chinese social workers. Most of these people are not very rich and cannot donate thousands of guilders at once to their respective associations. However, most of them are not financially responsible for their family's livelihood either. This is an important element underlying the phenomenon that many of these social workers are women.

Meanwhile, in a welfare state like the Netherlands, some people are living off aid from the welfare support system. Among them, a few are active in Chinese associations. A couple of leaders of Chinese associations belong to this group. Sometimes they have been appointed as vice-chairman, standing committee member, and so on. I found that they have two common characteristics.

The first one is that they are willing to contribute their time and energy to the public cause. One man, whom I have known for years, is often out of work. He has joined several Chinese associations. Whenever there is a great activity organized by Chinese associations in Amsterdam, he will be very active among the organizers or volunteers. He is a person, as he said about himself and is so regarded by others, who always takes a great interest in doing something that can liven things up and be enjoyed. Although he rarely contributes money to the associations he has joined, some powerful leaders have regarded him as indispensable. In 1997, through the nomination of the chairman (who is the most powerful leader of this particular association), he became one of the vice-chairmen of that association.

The second common characteristic of these "leaders" is that they usually can only take the position of a deputy to the chief of the association. Although they have held some sort of leading position and have done practical work for the association, they have to rely on the chief's support and obey the latter's instructions. For example, the man I just mentioned, although he is often in the office of that association to deal with its daily affairs and to be in charge of some meetings or activities, cannot make any important decision for the association without getting the consent of the chairman in advance.

The procedure for electing association leaders is another process that is worth noting. During the 19th century and the early years of the 20th century, in Southeast Asia and North America, some traditional procedures existed for electing or choosing the Chinese association leaders. For instance, having been directly appointed by the Chinese government, the relevant Chinese association leaders became quasi-officials abroad. In some cases, to heighten the social position of the association, well-known officials or scholars from China were invited to be the leaders (Liu, 1981: 209-210). Moreover, in some earlier clan or dialect associations, to prevent leadership from being monopolized by certain unscrupulous persons for selfish gains, some associations selected their leaders by the will of a deity or spirit.[12] Such selection procedures, however, never happened in the history of the Chinese associations in the Netherlands.

In view of how the Chinese associations in the Netherlands elect their leaders, the following phenomena should be noted. First, for the Chinese associations that I have studied, it is normal to hold regular elections. For instance, ACV holds its election every three years; a few smaller associations such as the Association for Chinese Acupuncturists hold their election once a year; and most associations, such as LFCON, *Fa Yin*, and CSFN, hold their elections every two years. Some associations, like ACV and *Fa Yin*, ask all of their members to come for the election. However, the committee members of LFCON are elected by the vote of representatives of its association-members, i.e., each association-member will send one person as its representative to vote.

Some of these elections are serious affairs. For example, LFCON's first election of its committee members was very tense. As was noted earlier, LFCON is an association set up at the suggestion of the Dutch government, and the rivalry between a few influential Chinese associations was great. In one of the preliminary preparatory meetings, some participants proposed holding a vote immediately. Altogether, there were about thirty participants who were the representatives of about twenty associations. Among them, the representatives of 17 associations decided to attend the voting, which meant that they became the first association members of LFCON. Each association was asked to send one name as a candidate and send one representative to vote. According to an oral agreement, the one who got the most ballots among the 17 candidates would become the first chairman of LFCON, and the next six would be its first committee members. Since the decision of voting was made on the spot and the voters came from different associations, each with their respective orientations, the results were unpredictable. When the result was announced, I saw that the winners and their comrades were visibly pleased.[13]

Nevertheless, such an emphatic voting procedure is not common. Very often, the voting is something symbolic — merely going through the motions without any opposition — which is the second characteristic phenomenon that should be pointed out. Sometimes the leading positions have already been distributed between a few powerful people before the public voting is held. Sometimes the poll will not be formally made known until the results of the public voting has been modified by some "discussions" among the leaders or founders.

For instance, due to the historical reasons noted in Chapter IV, Zhejiang members dominate ACV. Because of a tradition based on a narrow co-villager ideology, most Zhejiang members will only cast their votes for the candidates who are their co-villagers. Since the 1970s, however, to present ACV as a community-wide association, before each election, the key leaders would invite well-known Chinese whose original hometown is outside Zhejiang to share the ACV's leading positions. In 1996, the preparatory committee of the tenth election of ACV added four Guangdong Chinese among its 17 vice-chairmen, although the votes these non-Zhejiang people polled would not even have placed them on the standing committee.[14] For similar reasons, more Cantonese-speaking people (who come from either Guangdong province or Hong Kong) have been added to the list of ACV's standing committee.

The third phenomenon is that many leaders are eager to get their leading positions approved by the Chinese government, either by Beijing or by Taiwan. Very often when a newly organized association holds its founding ceremony or when an existing association inducts newly elected members to another term of a committee, officials from the Chinese Embassy will be invited. The pro-Taiwan associations will also invite officials from the relevant Taiwan representative offices in the Netherlands. It is regarded as a symbol of legitimacy if a Chinese official, the higher the better, attends the ceremony and gives a congratulatory speech. The following example may help to demonstrate how important it is for Chinese association leaders to obtain their "legitimacy."

One week after an association was established, another association with a similar organizational purpose also announced its establishment. People who disagreed with the initiators of the first organization organized the second. A few weeks later, I went to interview the chairman of the first association. When asked his opinion about the second association, he said with feeling:[15]

> You know, the official of the Chinese Embassy attended the founding ceremony of my association, and his congratulatory speech has clearly legitimized our social position. We are grateful. But later on I heard that the same official attended the other association's founding ceremony, too, and gave a similar congratulatory speech as well. How can he handle things in this way? I really cannot understand.
>
> [Don't you think the people have rights to set up their own voluntary associations?]

Yes, I know. But our two associations are conflicting with each other. Only one should have a legitimate position. If my association could not get the official of the Chinese Embassy to attend our ceremony, I would have admitted my failure. Similarly, if their association could not get their social position recognized by the Chinese Embassy, I believe they would have given up. Now, however, both associations have their legitimate positions recognized. Undoubtedly, competitions will develop. It is too bad. I had to send a letter to the Chinese Embassy to lodge my protest.

What this man said may put undue emphasis on the influence of the Chinese Embassy on the Chinese associations in the Netherlands. Nevertheless, it is a common reaction of most Chinese association leaders in the Netherlands. The implication of this phenomenon and the factors pushing this trend of China-orientation will be studied further in the next chapter.

Since at present there are more than one hundred Chinese associations in the Netherlands, there are as many as several hundred Chinese association leaders even if we induced only each association's chairman and vice-chairmen. Among them, however, few have been recognized and accepted by the Chinese community, more or less, as their representatives or leaders.

An appropriate Chinese proverb says: "Better be the head of a group of chicken than a follower in a group of bulls." There are many instances in which the losers in the election, or competitions, of one existing association simply went on to head a new one. In other words, in a democratic society like the Netherlands, if someone has the ambition and ability to organize a new voluntary association, he or she may go ahead and give full play to his or her talent. When a new association proclaims its founding, one or a couple of new association leaders emerge.

For instance, it was in early 1995 that I first met one middle-aged Chinese man. At that time, he had just immigrated into the Netherlands and attempted to set up his business. Two years later, when I met him again, I found from his name card that he had already become the chairman of four associations: two associations are European-wide and the other two are worldwide. Although one cannot know what significance these associations have, at some public occasions such as a joint meeting of Chinese associations, this man just stood up and gave a speech as a Chinese association leader.

Nevertheless, being a leader of an association (especially of new and small ones) is far from becoming an accepted leader of the Chinese community. More precisely, only those who have made contributions to the development of the Chinese community for years may be accepted as leaders. During the last 12 years in which I have followed the development of the Chinese associations in the Netherlands, I have observed that, alongside the proliferation of Chinese associations, new association leaders have kept coming forward. However, only a limited number of them are able to maintain their position and thus be rightfully recognized as a true leader.

2 *Membership*

Leaders and individual members of an association may cherish a variety of different and contrasting goals. Although some scholars stress that one characteristic of the Chinese associations is that the leaders decide everything for their respective associations (cf. See, 1988; Wickberg, 1988; Wong, 1977; Crissman, 1967), whether the common individual members are indeed completely unaware of what their leaders are doing or of what is going on is uncertain. Therefore, this section will focus on the general responses and reflections of the ordinary Chinese immigrants towards the Chinese associations in the Netherlands.

A *The rights and duties of members*

As ethnic associations, its members usually come from one ethnic group and interact based on common language, culture and tradition, similar experiences in an alien environment, and shared identity. Moreover, nowadays, the principle of *voluntariness* has been adhered to as the basic organizational principle by all contemporary Chinese associations in the Netherlands.[16]

In accordance with the relevant laws of the Netherlands, the voluntary associations can be registered as two types of organizations: *Stichting* or *Vereniging*. It would be too complicated to explain the concrete differences between these two types of associations. Basically, while a *Vereniging* should have some members, a *Stichting* is not required to have any members. To put it differently, everyone is allowed to register a *Stichting* simply in his or her personal name but without any partners or followers. Among the well-known Chinese associations in the Netherlands, CSFN, CCRM and *Wa Lai* are *Stichtingen*; but ACV, *Fa Yin*, and most women's and elder people's associations are *Verenigingen*.

Verenigingen should draft clear regulations to define the rights and duties of their formal members. The relevant regulations stipulated by *Fa Yin* can be taken as one example. These regulations define the rights and duties of its members as follows:[17]

1. *Membership*: All Chinese and their descendants who agree with the purpose of *Fa Yin* can apply to become a member;
2. *Joining procedures*: The applicant should be introduced by one formal member; fill in an application form and submit it to the committee. When the application is approved by the committee, the applicant is accepted as a formal member;
3. *Membership dues*: The new member should pay 25 guilders to the association's foundation when accepted by the association. The membership dues is 25 guilders per year. A member who is older than 65 years need not pay membership dues.
4. *Rights*: All members have the right to vote and to stand for election; to have a say and make suggestions in all of the association's affairs.

5. *Resigning*: Any member who wants to resign from the association should send a formal letter to the committee two months in advance. Having been approved by the committee, the person is officially removed from membership. All fees that have already been paid will not be returned to the person concerned.

I have compared *Fa Yin*'s constitution with some other constitutions of Chinese associations in the Netherlands. I found that the basic requirements of those associations are similar, although certain differences exist. For instance, *Fa Yin* requests that any new applicant should have one introducer, but some associations ask for "two introducers," and some do not have any such request. Also, many associations have fixed their membership dues between 25 and 50 guilders per year. The exception is one small association for the "first class" Chinese restaurateurs that has membership dues as high as 3,000 guilders per year.

Whether the relevant regulations can be truly carried out is another question. Some common conclusions can be drawn from my studies. First, chain-introduction is the most popular approach for Chinese associations to attract new members, and for Chinese people to learn of and join a certain association. Whenever I have interviewed people who are members of a Chinese association, one question I would pose to them was how they came to know about this association and why they decided to join it. All of the answers I got were similar: it was through the introduction or suggestion of a friend or a relative. Thus, whether the constitution of an association requires that new applicants have an introducer or not, few members of associations do not have introducers. Moreover, because many associations expanded through chain introduction, special *guanxi* networks within an association have developed. The effects of these *guanxi* networks on the decision-making procedures will be discussed in the last section of this chapter.

A second phenomenon is that the emphasis on paying annual membership dues is the only way in which an association's membership can be officially recognized. Yet, many associations cannot regularly collect their membership fees. For example, one association set up in 1995 had about thirty people registered as its first members, 15 of which were elected as its first committee members. According to its constitution, every member must pay annually membership dues of one hundred guilders. At the end of 1996, in a committee meeting I observed, the secretary reported that only nine persons paid their membership dues in the first year and none in the second year. I found from the list of payments that not even all the committee members had paid their dues. When the secretary asked whether those who did not pay their dues could still be listed as formal members, none of the attendants answered. After a while, the topic was changed. No one returned to the question of membership dues. In August 1997, I met the secretary again and asked him whether some more membership dues had been received in the third year. He smiled and said, "I am afraid you are the only one who still remembers it."

The above-mentioned case to a certain degree exemplifies the situation of many Chinese associations. ACV is another illustrative case. Since the 1970s, when the Chinese in the Netherlands accepted the Chinese National Day (on the first of October) as a regular public activity, it has become a custom that a few months before the festival, ACV will send some volunteers to collect donations for the celebration and ask its members to pay their membership dues at the same time. Beginning in the late 1980s, the names of donators and the amount of their donations are then published in the ACV Bulletin. From the lists, I found the number of donators is between two and three hundred, but the number of people who paid their annual membership dues is only between sixty and seventy. As was noted in Chapter IV, the election of the tenth term of the committee of ACV has special implications. Thus, in a committee meeting held by ACV soon before its tenth election, the question of how to check the formal membership was raised since it relates to who would have the right to vote. After an animated discussion, the committee made a special compulsory rule: on the polling day, everyone had to pay 25 guilders as an annual membership fee for the present year before receiving their formal ballot. This decision was carried out, and more than twenty thousand guilders were collected from more than eight hundred voters. This feat — an association collecting such a large amount of money as membership dues in one day — was unprecedented in the history of the Chinese associations in the Netherlands. Afterwards, in a meeting held by the tenth committee, one vice-chairman who was elected to the position for the first time said: "when holding the next election three years later, we should ask all members to pay 75 guilders for three year's annual fee altogether before they vote." Then, another vice chairman immediately responded: "Don't be so silly! Do you think they need ACV or ACV needs them?" Although it seems that they only said it for fun, I believe that the implications are worth thinking about.

Briefly speaking, whether members fulfil their duties for the association very much depends on whether their expectations can be realized by the association. This is the topic of the following section.

B *Expectations of members*

Why do Chinese immigrants join an association? How do they select the association to join? What do they expect from the associations? From my interviews and observations, it can be inferred that nowadays the expectations held by most members are driven by different interests that can be roughly divided into two categories: those with personal business interests and those looking for pleasant leisure-time.

Some people choose to join a certain association for their business interests. Although the voluntary association itself cannot seek profits directly, some people may seek or expect indirect dividends from their membership in a certain association. The following is one representative example.

The Asian Restaurants is a Chinese restaurateurs' association set up in

1994. It has individual Chinese restaurants as its members. That is to say, regardless of how many owners one restaurant has, these owners can only register one membership in the name of the restaurant. On the other hand, if one Chinese restaurateur owns three restaurants, he has the right to register three memberships in the name of the three restaurants. The principal purpose of The Asian Restaurants is to improve the social status of Chinese restaurants. More concretely, in order to heighten the social status of the first-class Chinese restaurants, it attempts to inform Dutch customers about the differences between *real* Chinese restaurants and the other, less genuine ones. The association expects that one day the first-class Chinese restaurants will be able to enjoy an equal footing with first-rate French restaurants. In the founders' eyes, although nowadays there are about two thousand Chinese restaurants throughout the Netherlands, most of them can hardly make "excellent Chinese dishes according to the standard of Chinese cuisine." "Many Chinese restaurants in the Netherlands have discredited and are continuing to discredit Chinese cuisine," one initiator said to me.

The initiators of this association are owners of some elegant Chinese restaurants in the Netherlands. The association not only charges annual membership dues of as high as three thousand guilders, but also requires that any new applicant will not be approved until the association's committee has examined the quality of the restaurant. In spite of these unusually strict rules, the association attracted 37 members in its first year. In an interview with one of its members, I asked what his motive was to join the association. He told me:[18]

> I believe that it is a great honour to be its member. We are all among the first-class Chinese restaurants in the Netherlands. All activities the association has organized are focussed on improving the social status of our members.

Clearly, this association charges much higher membership fees than most other Chinese associations. When asked whether the members are willing to pay their annual dues, this interviewee said:

> No problem. Because it is worth paying. For instance, the association has printed fifty thousand excellent brochures to make propaganda for us members. Having listed the names and addresses of all members complete with very nice photos, the brochure stresses the differences between *real* Chinese cuisine and the sham. All members can distribute the brochures in their respective restaurants [...]
>
> In February of 1995, the association organized a great party to celebrate the Chinese New Year. Most of the honoured guests were Dutch. They were high-ranking Dutch officials, well-known Dutch entrepreneurs, and distinguished persons. Their knowledge of the high quality Chinese cuisine will bring a bright future for the first-rate Chinese catering business in the Netherlands.

When asked about whether he or his restaurant has benefited from the association, this man paused for a while then said:

> Maybe yes, maybe not. I don't know exactly. But I believe I will benefit from it sooner or later. Moreover, since the competition among the Chinese restaurants is very intense, it is important to get support from a strong organization.

HORECA Chinese Section (hereafter HCS) is an association for all Chinese restaurant owners and has become the Chinese section of a Dutch nation-wide association for all restaurateurs (cf. Chapter III). Since it was set up in 1985, the overall number of its members now amounts to more than seven hundred Chinese restaurant owners.[19] Among my interviewees, 28 are members of HCS. From their comments, it is easy to infer that collectively they expect the association to lend support to their catering business.

At an annual meeting of HCS in 1996, I met a middle-aged Chinese lady whom I have known for years. She has to manage her restaurant herself since her husband died a couple of years ago. I was surprised to meet her there since I had never met her in any Chinese associations' meetings or public activities. When asked why she attended the meeting, she said:[20]

> This is the first time I attend a meeting of HCS. You know I am always busy with my own restaurant. Since it is very expensive to employ a worker, I have to work as a waitress, a cleaner, and sometimes as a cook as well in my restaurant. It is my fate.
>
> My friends and relatives sometimes suggested to me to join this or that Chinese association, because they feel that my life is pitiful. But I had neither interests nor time. Even this HCS, I had no interest in it until a couple of months ago. I changed my mind because what one of my friends said impressed me deeply. He said, nowadays, the competition among restaurants has become much sharper than anytime before. No restaurant can easily survive without finding a strong backing [...] It seems HCS has some power, since it is the Chinese section of an official Dutch institution. I wish that HCS will be able to do something to support us [...]
>
> I attend this meeting because we were informed that after the annual work-report by one leader, an important lecture will follow. The lecture is on the revised hygiene regulations that all Chinese restaurants have to comply with. I was told the lecture will be given by a Dutch official, and someone will translate it into Chinese for us. Moreover, the Dutch official will answer our questions then and there.

Similar expectations cropped up in my interviews with other members of HCS. Also, I found that the expectations related to practical business interests are clear and urgent among the members of all the associations for Chinese business persons and professionals. Therefore, an important challenge for the management of all Chinese associations is how to cater for their members' requirements and expectations. This will be discussed in the next chapter.

Nevertheless, not all Chinese immigrants are purposefully trying to advance their business interests through associations. Many people, such as elderly people and housewives, join a certain association only to look for a place for pleasant engagements.

Between March and December 1995, I followed several major programs organized by one of Amsterdam's Chinese women's associations. Then, between June and December 1996, I attended almost every weekly meeting organized by *Fa Yin*. These activities provided me with ample opportunities to interview ordinary members.

Unlike the associations for Chinese business persons or professionals, these two associations have different aims: the members' welfare and friendship. Both associations often attract from dozens to hundreds of people to their activities. When asked about their motives for becoming a member of the Chinese association concerned, the popular answers are as follows: for fun; to meet friends and have some conversation; to escape from a boring life in an alien environment. Most members of these associations are retired people or housewives who have physically settled down in the Netherlands but not mentally. They have kept a certain distance from the Dutch society, regardless of how many years they have lived in the Netherlands. Thus, they are glad that the Chinese associations have created a familiar world for them and organized some activities to enrich their life.

One of my informant's comments about her motivation to join a Chinese women's association may, to a certain degree, represent the collective desire of many Chinese housewives in the Netherlands: [21]

In 1980 I arrived in the Netherlands soon after I married my husband, he works in one Chinese restaurant in Amsterdam [...] I found I had suddenly been thrown into a strange and cold world. My husband works day and night in the restaurant. I always felt lonely, restless, and frightened.

A couple of years ago, through the introduction of my cousin, I joined this Chinese women's association. Since then, my life has changed. I am glad to know that there are so many Chinese sisters, same as me, living in this country. We meet regularly and have chats together. We help each other. We attend courses organized by our association, to learn Dutch, to learn dancing, singing, sewing and home-cooking. We enjoy ourselves very much. Moreover, through the arrangement of this association, I also joined the social works section to help the elderly Chinese who are sick, weak, or disabled. I feel my life is rich now, although I even feel I am too busy, and sometimes exhausted.

In Amsterdam, due to some disagreements among the initiators, the Chinese women's association set up in 1991 divided into two in 1993, and the Chinese elders' association set up in 1991 also divided into two in 1993 and then into three in 1996. Nevertheless, many members do not know or do not care about the differences between these associations. Some members just pick up and follow the programs in which they are interested, regardless of which association is the organizer. One lady I met very often at the activities organized by both women's associations is a housewife, i.e., a wife of a Chinese restaurant owner. During an interview with her, she casually mentioned the differences between the two Chinese women's associations:[22]

I heard some stories about the disagreement between the leaders of the two associations. But I don't care. Why should I care? I have joined both of them. The membership fee is very cheap, only 25 guilders for one year. It means nothing to spend 50 guilders a year for being a member of the two associations. I do so. Therefore, I receive programs distributed by both associations regularly. It is not bad, isn't it? Of course I do not take part in all programs. I simply select the interesting programs to attend.

[Do you go to the general meetings for voting?]

No, no, no, never. I don't care about who will take the chair. I only like to enjoy all the interesting programs that they organize for us.

One interviewee, a divorcee in her sixties, told me:[23]

I cannot tell you exactly how many associations I have joined.

[Did you register as a formal member and pay membership dues?]

No, it is not necessary. Too much trouble. I am an old lady, usually the association will not charge a person like me for membership dues. Anyhow, it is too boring to stay at home. My children all have grown up and have their own life [...]
  You know that there are three Chinese associations for elders in Amsterdam. It is good. One has its weekly meeting on every Tuesday afternoon, however, the other two on every Thursday afternoon. This is bad. Why should these two associations arrange the weekly meeting on the same day? I tried to convince the leaders that they had better select different days for meetings, but no one listened to me.[24] I am disappointed. I wish the different associations will arrange their respective activities on different days. I wish I could have a jolly time together with other Chinese every day, EVERY DAY!

The responses of the two interviewees are significant. Their reason for joining Chinese associations is to find a familiar and harmonious environment in their spare time. They want somebody to organize activities for them, but they themselves do not want or have no ability to contribute to the organization of such affairs. They simply enjoy their position as ordinary members.
  This type of member shares two characteristics. First, many of them are

poorly educated and especially lack knowledge about the receiving society. Some male retirees spent their lives within the four walls of the Chinese kitchens, where little knowledge of Dutch society can be learned. And some women are housewives who have little motivation to know the receiving society. Hence, as long as a Chinese association creates opportunities that may more or less enrich their lives, they are easily satisfied.

And the second characteristic of this group is that most of them lead a normal life without any clear ambition for their future. Among them, some were restaurant owners who are now retired and just enjoy their easy life-style; some are housewives dependent on their husbands; and some just live on welfare support. They have no ambition, or, to put it in other terms, they have no interests in ascending to a position of power. One man of about seventy is always active in one association, but rejects any nomination to be a candidate for committee membership. When asked about his reasons, he told me:[25]

> It is too much trouble to be a committee member. Whoever wants the position, he may take it. I don't care, and I don't like it. I help to organize the activities because I enjoy doing it. It is simply for fun! For fun! (He repeated the last words several times.)

Regardless of whether there is any other reason behind it, this kind of member, active but without ambition, is always welcomed by all association leaders.

With the significant increase in the number of Chinese associations and with the similarities of many of them, how to attract more members for their associations has become a great challenge for many leaders.

C *Responses from outsiders to associations*

At the very beginning of this book, it was pointed out that since the 1980s the general organizational trend of Chinese immigrants in the Netherlands has shown an increase in the total number of Chinese associations. However, the percentage of the rank and file Chinese immigrants that bother to register as formal association members remains low. This situation is in need of exploration.

During my research, I attempted to find out detailed information about the membership of the associations I studied; however, it often turned out to be a futile effort. Among the mid- or large-scale associations, few have an available list of their members. Moreover, even with regard to the few that are able to produce a membership list, further studies have to be made before their figures can be accepted. The following is an representative example.

I once went to visit the head of an association that has been proclaimed by its leaders as the most active and one of the largest Chinese associations in the Netherlands. When asked about how many members there are in the association, this head said: [26]

We have one notebook to let all new members register. Every new member will have his or her name written down in the book with a registering number. According to the record of the notebook, there are more than five hundred persons registered in our association by now. Therefore, I can tell you clearly that we have *more than five hundred members* by now.

[Do these five hundred members pay their membership dues and attend the activities regularly?]

Of course not all of them. There are always some new members joining and some old members stop coming to the activities.

[Do you strike out the names of the members who stop coming from your membership list?]

No. We never cross out any names from the list. It is not a few of them who come back to pay the membership dues again after they stop coming for one or two years. They are always welcomed.

[How many members have come to pay their membership dues of the present year?]

By the end of last month there are *one hundred and ninety-eight*. Since we do not have a fixed period for registration, the number of registered members of the present year may still increase because more people may come to pay their membership dues in the coming months.

From the description quoted above, it can be seen that this association has two membership figures: less than two hundred and more than five hundred. The former one is the number who have paid their membership dues for the current year, and the higher figure is cumulative. The leaders of this association prefer to use the *cumulative name list* as the membership list of the association.

Comparatively speaking, the statistics of membership as handled by this association is clearer. Many others, especially the large-scale associations, can only produce an indeterminate estimate of the number of their members. Moreover, since a larger membership is regarded as an evidence of the higher social position of the association, the number of members proclaimed by some association leaders is often greater than what the figure is in reality. The following are the numbers of members proclaimed by the relevant association leaders or secretaries:

Chun Pah with branches: 1,491 members by June 1998 (Chun Pah, 1998:14);
ACV: more than eleven hundred members (ACV, 1997:3);
Wai Wun with branches: more than one thousand.[27]

HCS: more than seven hundred Chinese restaurant owners;[28]
Fa Yin: more than two hundred members.[29]

It should also be noted that the associations based upon shared provenance normally proclaim that all their co-villagers or co-provincials are members, even if they have not actually registered. In addition, there are some smaller associations whose members vary in number from a few to dozens.

Regardless of whether the numbers given above match the facts, if all the quotable numbers of the relevant Chinese association members are put together, there are about five or six thousand Chinese who have at one time officially registered as formal members of a Chinese association. This is a very low number considering there are up to one hundred thousand Chinese immigrants and their descendants residing throughout the Netherlands.

What reasons underlie the fact that many Chinese immigrants do not bother to become formal association member? Some extracts from my interviews may help provide the answer.

Having spent eight years in the Netherlands as an undocumented worker in several Chinese restaurants, Mr. ZJ returned to his hometown of Rui'an in 1992. Now, living with his wife and two sons in a recently bought five-storey house, he enjoys a life of plenty on the basis of the money he earned and saved in those eight years. When asked whether he had been involved in any Chinese associations while he was in the Netherlands, he shook his head and said:[30]

No, never. I heard about the names of those associations. But I saw nothing of what they could have done for us common people. Can they help me to get a resident permit? No! Why should I contact them? [...] Yeah, once a year there would be a party around the first of October to celebrate the Chinese National Day. Also, every year several parties were held in Amsterdam, Rotterdam, and some other big cities to celebrate the Chinese New Year.

[Did you go to enjoy the parties?]

Yes, of course. Usually, the boss would close the restaurant early when there was a party. Then we were able to go together. It was great fun, not only to watch the performances but to meet co-villagers and friends as well [...] I saw some famous Chinese movie stars during those years. They were invited to give performances in Holland. That was great! In my hometown, in such an unknown and little city, I can only watch those movie stars on TV.

Obviously, this interviewee's reaction to Chinese associations is self-contradictory: he did not like any Chinese associations in the Netherlands, and yet he did enjoy the activities held by the Chinese associations. As we will see in other examples, this is representative of many Chinese people's reaction to Chinese associations.

The case of Mr. LT represents the outsiders' reaction from another perspective. Mr. LT's father was a well-known leader of several Chinese associations in the Netherlands before the Second World War. During the 1960s, Mr. LT himself once actively joined the efforts to organize an association for the Chinese restaurateurs. During the 1980s, however, he kept a distance from all Chinese associations. When asked for the reasons, he gave some explanations in general terms: he personally has lost interest in any association activities; there are many differences of opinions between the newcomers and elders like himself;[31] the new leaders paid no attention to him because "they do not know the history." Among these and others, he stressed one reason repeatedly:[32]

> I don't like those so-called leaders. They are just a certain kind of rich Chinese restaurateur. You see, they are everywhere. One day, you see them hold Buddhist rites. Another day, you will see them attending a meeting held by a Chinese Christian association. Moreover, they always sit in front of the platform. But, in fact, what have they done for the rank and file Chinese? Nothing! They are making a show for themselves. Why should I join their associations just to be a stone to build up the position of a handful of leaders?

I got similar responses from other interviewees. The following answers are quoted from my interviews with people who have different backgrounds:[33]

> Only the Chinese millionaires are interested in organizing associations. It is a good place for them to show themselves off. (The interviewee is a middle-aged man and works for a Dutch company.)

> For the big Chinese bosses, organizing an association is one part of their business. We are workers. We don't have our own business. Therefore, we don't care about any associations. If I have time and energy, I prefer to find extra work to earn some more money. Why should I spend time to join those associations just to please those big bosses? (The interviewee is a waitress in her late thirties.)

> I heard that there are several Chinese associations in Amsterdam. I think, however, all these associations are places where only old people and those who can eat the rice of idleness meet with each other and while away their time. Now and then I also see some more Chinese associations organized by and for those Chinese bosses that make a show in Amsterdam. I am not interested in any of them. (The interviewee is a self-employed man around forty.)

> Of course I know ACV. I come from Wenzhou, and some of my relatives are active in that association. I myself however am not an official member of ACV. Simply because I have no time. I am busy with my business. I

have three children in school. I have to earn money not only to support my family but also to support my parents in Wenzhou. (The interviewee is an owner of a small Chinese restaurant and a widow.)

If there is an interesting program, I'll go with my friends to enjoy it [...] I never think of joining any Chinese association. Why should I do that? It is not necessary. The activities organized by those associations, such as China week, and performances in Chinese festivals are open to everyone. (The interviewee is a teenager born in the Netherlands.)

They said that their association is to be the voice of all Chinese in the Netherlands. Rather, I only see a few big bosses, so-called leaders, represent the Chinese insofar as when they receive high-ranking delegations from China at the dinner table. (The interviewee is a Chinese lady who had been active in one nationwide Chinese association but quit the association in 1996.)

Since I became unemployed, I tried to find a Chinese association that is worth joining. During the last six months, I have gone to several associations to follow their activities, and sometimes to help them organize affairs. However, I am greatly disappointed about the education level and qualities of either leaders or members. I can have no sympathetic contacts with them, and they do not accept me either. Therefore, I decided to quit from all such stupid activities. (The interviewee is a female engineer in her fifties who emigrated to the Netherlands in the mid-1980s.)

As we can see, different people have different reasons that hold them back from registering as a member of a Chinese association. Although their personal differences are significant, their attitude towards Chinese associations as a whole cannot be completely separated from their socio-economic status. Basically, all outsiders or non-members can be classified into three groups: business persons, those who work for Chinese employers, and those who work for Dutch employers.

Concerning the first group, because they regard it as a heavy burden to be involved in any Chinese association, some business persons simply have no desire to join or to head any Chinese association and even try to keep a certain distance from them. After all, as was mentioned earlier, the activities held by many voluntary associations depend on the donations of well-to-do business persons among their members. Thus, some business persons are afraid that the association will abuse their wealth.

The second group is a big collective that includes those who work for Chinese employers. In their minds, joining an association is something that requires owning a personal business. From their remarks quoted above, many workers have defined the organizers of most Chinese associations as a they-group, i.e., the boss group. Some simply call well-known Chinese associations — such as ACV, HCS, COCA, or COR — *lao ban hui* (bosses' associations). Many have no interest in joining an association because it is a ladder for the bosses to climb, and in no way does the association allow the ordinary members to be vocal. They have no interest in serving as a foil to a few leaders. It should be noted that until the mid-1990s, there was no Chinese labour union specifically set up to protect the interests of Chinese workers. This issue will be discussed further in the following chapter on the social functions of the Chinese associations.

Finally, among the people who are employed by the Dutch, few have an interest in Chinese associations. The people of this group usually have fewer obstacles — such as language — preventing them from integrating into the Dutch society. Many have more contacts with their Dutch colleagues, neighbours, or friends than with their fellow country people. One reason why they are not interested in the existing Chinese associations is that most Chinese associations are organized for people with a rather low education who cannot integrate into Dutch society properly. In addition, there are also some very practical reasons. Since most organizers of Chinese associations are related to the Chinese catering business, the relevant meetings or activities are arranged in accordance with their time schedule. For example, the weekend is the best and busiest time for the catering business, so no meetings of the Chinese associations will be held during the weekend. Consequently, many Chinese associations will organize their meetings or activities either on Monday or late at night (after 23:00 hours) when many restaurants are closed. This arrangement is inconvenient for the people who are outside the Chinese catering business.

Returning to the main discussion, is the limited membership a reflection that most Chinese immigrants adopt an indifferent attitude towards the Chinese associations? To put it differently, while admitting that the actual membership of the Chinese associations is currently at a relatively low level, it should not be ignored that the proper figure of Chinese immigrants who have more or less been involved in the Chinese associations' activities is much higher.

First, as was pointed out in Chapter V, it is a normal phenomenon that one family will have only one representative (in most cases the male head of the family) join the association. If we take this point into consideration, the total number of Chinese association members will be thousands of Chinese immigrant *families* instead of individuals; in other words, the total number of members would more than double.

Secondly, a low level of official membership is also due to the organizational system itself. On the one hand, as was noted earlier, all those associations registered as *stichting* do not solicit members; on the other hand, many of the associations that have some members do not clearly define different treatments or attitudes towards the members and non-members. Hence, some Chinese consciously or unconsciously benefit from the functions of the associations even if they remain outsiders. For example, many Chinese parents have benefitted from the Chinese schools for their children, but very few of them bother to register as a formal member of the relevant Chinese associations. In addition, some people keep claiming that the associations "have done nothing for us common people" while they enjoy the associations' activities (e.g., public parties and performances at Chinese festivals).

Moreover, among the Chinese business persons who do not join Chinese associations, some have also been, directly or indirectly, involved in the Chinese associations at some point. For example, when a large-scale China Week was held by LFCON, COCA and some other Chinese associations in Amsterdam in September 1997, some Chinese business persons who are outsiders of these associations became sponsors because they regarded it as an opportunity to advertise and highlight their names. Thus, in this sense and others, they have benefitted from the associations.

In the end, the relationship between the Chinese associations and the Chinese immigrants who are non-members can be illustrated as follows: these non-members have heard of certain Chinese associations; many have more or less benefitted from their activities; however, they have almost no more contact with the associations than simply enjoying the activities organized publicly. Many remain unaware of and do not care about the respective aims and activities of these Chinese associations.

3 *Organizational arrangement*

When studying the general characteristics of the organizational structure of Chinese associations, it is important to consider how *informal* organizational arrangements can work within *formal* associations. To put it differently, it is safe to say that although apparent varieties exist among Chinese associations, such as varying sizes, aims, functions, and levels of participation by its members, similarities exist in that their organizational structure and adaptation to the environment depend very much on informal and unseen links.

A *The decision-making process*

Among the contemporary Chinese associations in the Netherlands, it is normal to read from their constitutions that the final decision-making power of the association belongs to the general members. Often, the members' democratic participation is clearly defined as well. In practice, however, this article is hardly more than just words on paper. This contradiction can be explained from two major angles.

On the one hand, the democratic process is a significant model for all Chinese associations in the Netherlands. Democracy is the basis on which the Chinese voluntary associations have grown up. For a very long time, the paternalistic-authoritarian political culture has dominated Chinese society. Partly because of this historical background, the Chinese abroad are more sensitive about their freedom than many other nationalities. Therefore, regardless of how the decision-making process is to take place, most organizers of the Chinese associations will clearly stress that the association will be ruled by its members. Otherwise, the association can have no appeal to Chinese immigrants.

On the other hand, however, few Chinese associations seriously pursue a mode of democracy for some pragmatic reasons. For example, for the middle-scale and large-scale associations, it is difficult to find a right time and sufficient funding to hold a general meeting for all of its members. Moreover, when nothing of importance has suddenly arisen that could affect their daily life, most members will not think it is necessary that they should put aside the work in hand in order to attend a regular members' meeting.

We can take the annual members' meeting of HCS as one example. Among the Chinese associations in the Netherlands, HCS is among the few that are able to hold its annual members' meeting regularly. However, being an association that claims to have more than seven hundred members, its annual meetings are often only attended by fewer than one hundred members. For example, for its annual meeting in 1996, the organizers had sent out an announcement more than two months earlier. All members were informed that an election for committee members would be held on that date and a lecture on the new rules of restaurant hygiene would be given afterwards. In addition, before the meeting, a dinner would be served to all attending members, and each member could bring along one of their family members. Despite all the publicity, the number of attendants was less than twenty per cent of the total registered members. Yet, the organizers expressed their satisfaction with this number of attendants.[34]

Most leaders of Chinese associations have recognized the difficulties of holding a general meeting for its members. Some appropriate adaptations have been made in light of actual conditions. Some associations do have a regulation to define the quorum for its members' meeting, but no one takes this regulation seriously. For instance, *Fa Yin* has decided that its general members' meeting will have the power to make decisions only if more than one-third of its members are present. However, neither its leaders nor its members follow this regulation. No objections to the decisions made by all previous members' meetings have been raised, although most of the meetings were far from reaching the quorum.

Taking such facts into account, some associations simply avoid the relevant regulations. A regulation of how many people will constitute a quorum for the annual general meeting usually cannot be found in an association's constitution. For example, on 18 September 1997, EFCO held a meeting of its standing members in The Hague. While discussing a new draft of its constitution, the chairman asked the attendants to put forward suggestions on how many participants should form a quorum for its members' meeting to have the final say. The common response was that a quorum should comprise at least one-third of all members. If such a quorum is seriously required, however, then in practice, there would never be a general meeting of members with the power to make decisions. At the end, all participants agreed that it is not necessary to insert a regulation about a quorum in the constitution.

Because the power of a general members' meeting to make decisions is usually nothing but an empty shell, to my knowledge, the real power to make decisions lies in the hands of a few key leaders of each association and their invisible links. Therefore, a common structure of a Chinese association is that it has a closed core and a certain number of loosely organized members.

B *Interlocking leadership and loosely organized members*

Some small associations are organized around a few close friends, and some associations registered as *stichting* have no members. These two kinds of associations will not be included in the current discussion. Hereafter, the discussion will focus on middle-scale and large-scale associations (i.e., the Dutch *vereniging*).

Usually, the closed core of these associations is composed of a few powerful leaders, and all important decisions are made among them. Quite often, it seems that during a meeting of the standing committee or a meeting of the board members, an important decision was taken after some elaborate discussions. Sometimes, however, this is only superficially so. Actually, before the public meeting takes place, the real discussions had already been carried on among the core members. More precisely, the real decisions have been made through phone calls among the core members or have been made at the dinners attended by the core members. I will not say that all discussions held in meetings are mere formalities, but it is justifiable to say that meetings frequently will not be held before a consensus has been reached among the core members. In the meetings, some amendments may be added to the original draft, but the basic resolutions usually will not be changed. Saying that the function of many of these meetings is nothing more than formalizing a decision that was already made is not too far from the truth.

There are usually some major supporters or members of the association active around the core decision-makers. Normally, because of chain-introduction, they are good friends or close relatives of the people at the core. Moreover, since there is no limitation to the number of leading posts of a certain association, many of these enthusiasts will eventually be accommodated with a title.

Then, at the periphery of an association, there may be dozens or a few hundred members: some pay their membership dues regularly, others irregularly, and some never do. They registered as members of a certain association for various reasons: a friend suggested it and they felt uneasy to say no; for personal companionship; to get experience; and so on. They may well enjoy the programs in which they are interested but ignore the activities they do not like. Meanwhile, some may keep complaining about the lack of well-organized programs. Nevertheless, few will actually bother about such affairs as how to perfect the association.

In the course of my study, I have found a result that contains a peculiar tension: the Chinese associations as a whole are the product of a democratic system, but there is no democracy within the association. More precisely, among the Chinese in the Netherlands, establishing one's own association has been accepted as a democratic right; however, an authoritarian style of leadership is accepted as normal within the associations. Generally, the members' participation rate in the association's affairs is low. Moreover, if a couple of leaders or some members are not satisfied with the decisions made by a few core leaders, the result is that the losers will quit the existing association and, if they want, simply try to organize a new association by themselves. The case of *Chun Pah* is an example of this.

As was mentioned in Chapter IV, *Chun Pah* was set up in 1989 as an association for elderly Chinese. It organized parties, tours and lectures for Chinese elders and created a good image for itself in the Chinese community. In about three years, it was said that the number of its members had increased from nine initiators to more than seven hundred. The association received subsidies of more than twenty thousand guilders per year from the Dutch authorities. Meanwhile, as the first Chinese association organized for and by the Chinese elderly, it also received plenty of donations from Chinese business persons. In 1992, however, some sharp conflicts arose among the committee members. Some complained that the accounts of the association were not in order, and a certain group had taken more than its share. Some even accused a couple of leaders of taking the association's money. Some members therefore argued that a democratic supervisor system should be established to square and publish all accounts. Yet the people who were in charge of the financial affairs insisted that it was not necessary to make the accounts open for public inspection because this might cause further misunderstanding. Since their opinions were ignored, the members who nursed a grievance simply quit *Chun Pah* and organized a new Chinese elders' association, named *Tung Lok*, in 1993. Two years later, however, disagreements rose among some activists of *Tung Lok*. One group complained that the chairwoman was autocratic and criticized her for having done something too foolish and thus asked for a new election. The chairwoman and her supporters, however, simply brushed all criticisms aside. As a result, another new Chinese elders' association was established by the opposition faction.

This being the case, no truly democratic atmosphere can be found within such an association. Moreover, the association often becomes more and more firmly ruled by a peer group. Given all of this, what is the future of the Chinese associations if they are developing in such a way? How do hundreds of Chinese association leaders today in the Netherlands cope with innovation and with rapidly changing environments?

Let us turn to the next chapter for this discussion.

CHAPTER VII

A Bridge and A Wall between the Two Worlds: Organizational Functions

In the preceding chapters, we have studied why and how the Chinese associations are organized. What is the social consequence of the existence of these associations in the Netherlands today? Moreover, what are the social roles or functions, either manifest or latent, that constitute the social reason for their existence and development? This chapter searches for answers to these questions.

1 Social activities organized by associations

Associations derive their significance from organizing various social activities. It is quite common that an association will be distinguished more by its social functions than by its membership. Before going into a theoretical study, it is necessary to give some examples of the concrete activities that Chinese associations have organized. Which kinds of activities have been organized and how have they been organized? What are the major targets which the organizers intend to influence?

Generally, an association organizes an activity with particular emphasis on a definite purpose. To give a clearer picture, the examples are grouped according to the major targets on which the organizers intended to exercise their influence. In other words, the relevant activities have been sorted into three categories: those organized among the Chinese immigrants in the Netherlands; those organized with regard to China; and those organized with regard to the Dutch society.

A Activities organized within an ethnic environment

The Chinese immigrants are the social basis of the Chinese associations. Thus, it is understandable that a great part of the activities organized by the Chinese associations are focussed on the Chinese immigrants themselves.

In Chapters III and V, I described how important it was that the Chinese associations handled day-to-day problems for their members before the Second World War. Also, I explained the compulsory measures imposed by some Chinese associations to fulfill their aim of mutual welfare at that time. This situation, however, has gone forever. Nowadays, the principal public activities organized by the Chinese associations within the Chinese community are basically related to the following targets: cultivation of the Chinese

cultural heritage; leisure-time programs; and, to a certain degree, protection
of common interests for either the whole Chinese immigrant community or a
certain group among them.

Cultivation of cultural heritage

The first important part of the activities organized by the Chinese associations is focussed on the cultivation of the Chinese cultural heritage. Significant activities are, amongst others: running after-school Chinese schools
for Chinese children; publishing Chinese newspapers; setting up Chinese
libraries; organizing Chinese theatrical performances; arranging special Chinese arts exhibitions, and so on.

Cultural continuity is treasured by the Chinese. Examples in Chapters IV
and V showed how closely interlocked Chinese schools and Chinese associations are. When considering the general situation of Chinese education held
by the Chinese themselves, the role played by Chinese associations can be
differentiated into three levels.

First, some Chinese schools are sponsored by Chinese associations. At the
beginning of 1998, of the 41 Chinese schools in the Netherlands, only 11 of
them were more or less subsidized by the local Dutch authorities.[1] According
to an investigation by LFCON, every year up to 500,000 guilders must be
collected by the respective Chinese associations to run the Chinese schools.[2]
It is a challenge to find the right ways to collect this kind of money. For
instance, among the Chinese in the Netherlands, it has become a custom to
use the money collected from various parties organized during the Chinese
festivals to support the local Chinese schools. Very often, when such a party
is held, the organizers will try to sell a kind of "lottery tickets"; the more, the
better. Because all awards are donated by Chinese business people or by
companies, a part of the money received from selling tickets can be donated
to the Chinese schools. Another occasion to collect money for the school is
the closing ceremony held at the end of each school year. While holding the
closing ceremony, many schools will invite the leaders of the relevant associations. Then, the participants will donate some money to cover the budget for
the next year.

Teachers are the mainstay of every school. Due to the limited financial
resources, the teachers working in Chinese schools (there are about three
hundred of them throughout the Netherlands) cannot be salaried according
to the Dutch regulations.[3] Thus, in order to appreciate the teachers' voluntary contributions, at the end of each school year, it has become an unwritten
rule that the Chinese associations will organize a Thank-You Banquet for the
teachers working in the relevant schools.

The second role played by some Chinese associations relates to their attempts to match the requests of the Dutch Department of Education by
improving the level of education at Chinese schools. Specifically, this role is
related to the 1996 Teaching Foreigners Modern Languages Policy, which
was promulgated by the Dutch Ministry of Education, Culture and Sciences.[4]
According to this new policy, as soon as some essential prerequisites concern-

ing the quality of the mother tongue school are fulfilled, it may expect full funding from the local Dutch government.

In the beginning, it was not clear whether the Chinese mother tongue education could be included in the funding target designed by the above-mentioned new policy. Thus, to have the Dutch authorities recognize that Chinese children need to be educated in their mother tongue, on 1 April 1996, a special group named Improving Chinese Language Education in the Netherlands was set up with the support of existing Chinese associations such as LFCON, ACV, *Fa Yin* and some others. Between April and August 1996, the group conducted a survey on the general situation of Chinese schools. In all, 131 teachers were involved during this inquiry. The survey report, entitled "We hope to be supported and recognized by the government so that the Chinese education can become even better," was subsequently published in September and sent to the Dutch authorities. They hoped it would be a basis to stimulate special attention for culturally sensitive services for Chinese schools.[5]

According to the prerequisites defined by the new policy, among others, all teachers who are to teach an ethnic mother tongue should have acquired a diploma to teach this language, and at the same time their Dutch language level should at least be CITO-2 level.[6] More than four-fifths of the teachers working in Chinese schools, however, are not yet up to this standard.[7] Many teachers are housewives who had a Chinese education before emigration and are making earnest efforts to teach the Chinese language to pupils. To heighten the teachers' quality, some training courses have been planned and sponsored by LFCON and some other nationwide Chinese associations. For instance, between 25 October and 13 December 1996, a seven-week training course was held in Zwolle and Utrecht for Chinese teachers from all over the Netherlands. Some qualified teachers, three Chinese and one Dutch, were invited to give training courses on Chinese grammar, teaching methods, child psychology, and school management. At the end of the course, 42 participants received a diploma presented by the chairman of LFCON.

Meanwhile, on 8 and 9 October 1996, a symposium on "Chinese language education in European Chinese schools" was held in Zandvoort, sponsored by EFCO, LFCON, ACV, *Fa Yin* and some other associations. About one hundred and twenty Chinese school teachers and Chinese association leaders who are enthusiastic in promoting Chinese education came from 11 European countries to attend the symposium. At the meeting, representatives from other European countries explained how the policy on teaching their mother tongue to Chinese children has been carried out in their respective countries. The representatives also elucidated how they have made efforts to develop Chinese education. All agreed that the Chinese schools all over Europe should strengthen mutual cooperation.

In November 1997, finally, Chinese language education was recognized as an official mother tongue education by the Dutch Parliament. Still, the Chinese associations as well as the Chinese schools continue working on upgrading their teachers.

The third important level that Chinese associations work on is related to organizing meaningful activities for pupils studying the Chinese language. For instance, since the mid-1980s, *Fa Yin* and ACV have organized a "supervised summer tour to China" for pupils of Chinese schools. The associations have not only sent functionaries as organizers and guides to China, but also used their special contacts with the administrations in China to make the tours more attractive and productive. In China, as well as visiting the places which are famous for their scenery or historical significance, the participants would follow some Chinese courses. Moreover, some parties would be specially organized to let the Chinese youth from abroad get together with their peers in China.

Some cultural activities for Holland-born Chinese descendants have been held in the Netherlands as well. For instance, since 1987, CCRM and *Wah Fook Wui* have funded supervised summer holidays named Chinese Culture Camp for Chinese youngsters. The duration of this camp is about one week. In the camp, a couple of qualified teachers sent by OCAC from Taiwan will give professional courses on Chinese calligraphy, Chinese painting, Chinese national dances, Chinese musical instruments, Chinese traditional folk handwork, and Chinese *Gong Fu*. Further, some attractive entertainment such as a one-day tour, picnic, dancing party, or sports meeting will be held as well.[8] In July 1997, one Chinese Buddhist association (Buddha's Light International, Holland section — also held a Chinese Culture Camp in Paris for Chinese descendants from the Netherlands.

Besides the Chinese mother tongue education, other activities aimed at the cultivation of Chinese culture can be listed. One well-known example is the organization of Chinese performances during traditional Chinese festivals. Since the mid-1980s, it has become a custom for several Chinese associations to work together to invite a troupe from China to give performances in the Netherlands around the Chinese National Day and the Chinese Spring Festival. Such an activity demands considerable human and financial resources. First, a proper troupe should be carefully selected. The troupe should enjoy a good reputation among the Chinese, and it should be distinct from other troupes that have already visited the Netherlands. Then, the relevant administrations in China should be contacted, and sometimes it is necessary or advisable to bargain with them about the costs. All costs needed for travelling, accommodation and performances have to be borne by the host associations. I was told by a leader who has been active in organizing performances for years that, on average, about 50,000 guilders are needed to cover the expenses of one troupe from China for two or three performances in the Netherlands. He said to me repeatedly: "although this is a heavy burden, it is a major contribution of our Chinese associations to the Chinese community in the Netherlands." Some other interviewees also spoke similar words to me. It is not easy to see a Chinese theatrical performance in a Western country, which makes this kind of cultural activity attractive. However, it can only be put on collectively by associations with sufficient financial resources.

Establishing Chinese libraries for Chinese immigrants in the Netherlands is another objective already realized by some Chinese associations. By the mid-1990s, there were three small Chinese libraries in the Netherlands run by Chinese associations. The first was set up in Rotterdam: first run by CCRM, and some years later transferred to *Wah Fook Wui* and *Vereniging Chinese Bewoners in Rotterdam* (Association of Chinese Inhabitants in Rotterdam). *Wa Lai* set up the second in Amsterdam, and *Stichting Yao Yi Trefcentrum Chinezen Utrecht* (Foundation *Yao Yi* Friendship Center of Chinese in Utrecht) set up the third in Utrecht.[9] Each library has its own characteristics.

The Chinese library in Rotterdam is the first and the largest one. It has subscriptions to about thirty Chinese newspapers and periodicals published in Taiwan and Hong Kong. It also has as many as seven thousand Chinese books, two thousand Chinese magazines, and about two hundred Chinese videos in its collection. There is a reading room in the library, and there are book and video lending services. According to the library's registration book, in the whole year of 1997, admissions to the library totaled more than six thousand.

The *Wa Lai* library is mainly for Chinese children. Its collection is mostly children's books in Chinese or books especially published for parents to help their children. Aside from purchasing new books with its limited funding, a great part of its collection has come from two sources: books donated by its members and material temporarily borrowed from its members. More precisely, the members lend their books to the library for a certain period and get them back whenever they want them.

The Utrecht library has a collection of more than six thousand books and magazines. All books are gifts presented by authorities or associations in Zhejiang and Guangdong provinces, that is, sent from the major hometowns of the Chinese immigrants in the Netherlands.

The third public cultural service rendered by certain influential Chinese associations is to publish a Chinese information newsletter or newspaper. By the end of 1997, there were five well-known information newspapers published by Chinese associations in the Netherlands:

(i) ACV Bulletin has been published fortnightly (sometimes every three weeks) by ACV since 1977 (cf. Chapter IV:1);

(ii) the *Chinees HORECA Nieuws* (Chinese HORECA News) is published quarterly by HCS and is distributed to its registered members;

(iii) the *Brug Nieuws* (Bridge News) is published quarterly by a local Chinese association *Chinese Brug* in The Hague and is distributed to its registered members;

(iv) the INFO Krant, published by CCRM, began in 1984 and stopped in May 1996 (cf. Chapter IV:3).

(v) LFCON *Nieuwsbrief* (LFCON Newsletter) published quarterly by LFCON between 1990 and 1997 and distributed to its association members and the Dutch authorities concerned; but stopped in 1998 without any public announcement.

Among all of these, the ACV Bulletin is the only Chinese bulletin, although now and then there will be a page in Dutch specially edited by DaCy, a Chinese youth association. Others are bilingual bulletins pursuing two aims: to keep their members informed of relevant news and to create an image of the Chinese immigrants for the Dutch authorities and the Dutch society.

However, nowadays, the position of Chinese-language information distribution, which has formed an important part of the Chinese associations' publications, has been occupied by new and more convenient and powerful approaches, e.g., the mainland China-, Hong Kong- or Taiwan-based newspapers; Chinese broadcasting; and more recently, the Chinese TV channels. This point will be reviewed again when the future of the Chinese associations is to be studied.

Leisure-time programs

The discussion in Chapter V explained how some Chinese associations were initiated to create a form of socio-psychological defense against the feeling of isolation experienced in the wider society. These associations are active in organizing leisure-time programs for their members.

Programs that seek to enrich the life of the elderly and to help them attend pleasant social activities are among the meaningful ones offered by some Chinese associations. There is a popular saying among the Chinese: "Staying in front of a stove the whole day long; staying only with a pillow the whole night long," which implies that their lives are isolated within a Chinese restaurant kitchen and a bedroom. Many elderly Chinese immigrants did live in this way after their arrival in the Netherlands when they were young. Nowadays, thanks to the welfare system in the Netherlands, many have retired with a pension and are looking for ways to enjoy their remaining years. They often have received support from the Chinese associations.

Stichting Chen Hui[10] is a Chinese association aimed at offering help to the elderly Chinese in Amsterdam. Because the Amsterdam authorities concerned have sponsored it, it has been able to employ two social workers; in addition, it gets help from some Chinese volunteers. It has not only brought elderly Chinese together to have collective activities, but its volunteers regularly go to visit needy Chinese elders.

The associations organized by the elderly Chinese themselves are also active. The regular activity organized by these associations is a weekly or fortnightly get-together meeting. The centers or halls for these meetings all have some recreational facilities. On the dates of Chinese festivals, these associations will take part in the celebrations. Now and then, medical specialists will be invited to give talks on aspects of geriatric health. Occasionally, day trips are organized. At any rate, the greatest benefit for the participants is simply the opportunity created by the relevant associations to meet their peers and thus not feel so alone.

Some of the activities organized by Chinese women's associations have similar functions. For example, in 1995 and 1996, when I personally followed the programs presented by an association named the *Chinese Vrouwen Vereniging*

Amsterdam en Noord Holland (Chinese Women Association in Amsterdam and North Holland), I found that, on average, it had four programs each month (more in spring and autumn but fewer in summer and winter). The programs can be grouped as follows:

(i) Lectures on aspects of the prevention and cure of some diseases, and lectures on welfare services (about 27%);

(ii) Recreational activities, such as learning singing or dancing or lessons in *Taijiquan* (about 45%);[11]

(iii) Get-together meetings (about 21%);[12]

(iv) Day trips in the Netherlands or to neighbouring countries (about 7%).

When compared with the programs arranged by other Chinese women's associations, I found that this pattern is more or less the same everywhere.[13]

Organizing sports or games for and by the Chinese forms another important part of the public activities held by Chinese associations. For example, CSFN was set up in 1985 as a nationwide sports umbrella association to which some thirty smaller sports teams or clubs are affiliated. Since then, a large-scale Chinese sports exhibition has been held yearly. CSFN is the general organizer, while about twenty other Chinese associations will be co-organizers or co-sponsors. Table 6 shows the development of the Tournament held from 1985 to 1997. Amongst others, it is worth noting the Worldwide Overseas Chinese Sports Invitational Tournament held in 1994,

Chinese chess games have attracted both Chinese and Dutch players (Photo by René de Vries).

which has been regarded as a great achievement. News and reports of this Tournament appeared in almost all influential Chinese newspapers all over the world.

Table 6 *Chinese sports exhibitions in the Netherlands (1985-1997)*

Date	Event	Players + audiences	Sports teams from outside of the Netherlands
14 Oct. 1985	indoor football; basketball; volleyball; badminton; table-tennis; Chinese chess	200 +300	None
16 Oct. 1986	Ibid.	200 +300	None
19 Oct. 1987	Ibid.	300 +300	None
17-18 Oct. 1988	Ibid.	300 +500	Britain; France; Belgium
17 Oct. 1989	Ibid.	200 +300	Britain; Belgium
16 Oct. 1990	Ibid.	200 +300	Britain; Belgium
16 Oct. 1991	Ibid.	200 +300	Britain; Belgium
21 Oct. 1992	Ibid.	1,000 + 1,000	Britain; France; Belgium; United States; Canada
27 Oct. 1993	Ibid. + bowling	300 +300	None
24-27 Oct. 1994	football (outdoor); indoor football; basketball; volleyball; badminton; Chinese chess; table-tennis; bowling; tennis; *wu shu*	1,200 + 5,000	mainland China; Hong Kong; Taiwan; Britain; France; Belgium; Spain; Austria; Italy; Portugal; Sweden; Norway; Hungary; Thailand; Singapore; Canada; United States
16 Oct. 1995	indoor football; basketball; volleyball; table-tennis; badminton; Chinese chess; tennis; bowling	300+300	Britain; Belgium
15 Oct. 1996	Ibid. + *Taijiquan*; *wu shu*	300+300	Ibid.
13 Oct. 1997	Ibid.	300+200	None

Sources: Special issues on Nationwide Chinese Sports Meeting, published yearly by CSFN.

Negotiations and protection

Chinese associations fulfill another important function: they unite the Chinese to campaign for their legitimate rights and interests on social and welfare benefits, housing, medical care, and legal rights. Some examples are worth mentioning.

The first example is the establishment of Chinese elderly homes. At the beginning of the 1990s, the *Chinese Brug* in The Hague and CCRM and *Chun Pah* in Rotterdam began consultations with the relevant Dutch authorities about the possibility of setting up a Chinese elderly home. It was a difficult project to actualize. On the one hand, to get the project funded, the relevant Dutch officials had to be convinced that the Chinese elderly tended to miss social benefits because there was no social institution taking care of their unique needs. On the other hand, a lot of patience was also needed to convince the Chinese elderly to support the project. They had to be convinced that the planned Chinese elderly home would meet their specific needs. Moreover, they also had to be convinced to give up the traditional opinion that only poor and pitiful persons would live in such a "home." The associations mentioned above carried out all of these efforts. In 1994, the first Chinese Elderly Home was established in The Hague; the next year the second one was set up in Rotterdam. The facilities that the Home provides include day-care, cleaning, cooking, as well as the services of interpreters and accompanying people for medical treatments. Some elderly people who were previously isolated by language and culture have found a new *home* where they feel themselves safer and more comfortable. Chinese associations understandably take pride in these success stories.

A second example of associations fighting for the rights and welfare of the Chinese is the achievements of HCS in their campaign for legitimate rights and interests. As a nationwide trade association of Chinese restaurateurs since 1985, HCS has striven to respond to the needs and aspirations expressed by its members.

For instance, in January 1986, soon after the association was officially set up, in order to improve the quality of their cuisine and to strengthen the competitiveness of the Chinese catering business, the Training School for Chinese Cooks in the Netherlands was set up in Utrecht. Four cooks of a special classification were invited from China to be the teachers. Over about two years, alongside many lectures and demonstrations, four terms of systematic training courses were held and about two thousand Chinese cooks received a diploma. The school ended in 1988 when the primary aims had been realized. Afterwards, several short-term training courses for Chinese cooks were organized now and then. Normally, the courses related to matters of how to prepare proper Chinese cuisine.[14]

HCS has also tried to keep its members informed of recent developments related to the HORECA business through a regular quarterly newsletter. For example, in 1997, the major contents of four issues covered the following topics: an investigation of the current situation of the HORECA market in the Netherlands; an article written by a Dutch specialist elucidating the current eating-out habits of the Dutch people; some discussions related to potential influences on the HORECA business caused by supermarkets prolonging their opening hours; a review of the regulations on hygiene.

Moreover, networking with others to study potential possibilities of promotion in the Chinese catering business has continued to be a focus of HCS. In early 1997, through the initiative of HCS, a group organized by the students of the *Hoge Hotelschool Maastricht* (Hotel Academy of Maastricht) conducted research on the current situation of Chinese-Indonesian restaurants in the Netherlands. The research report, The Image of the Chinese-Indonesian Restaurant Business, was presented in October 1997.[15] The report was subsequently translated into Chinese and widely disseminated among HCS's members. In the annual meeting of HCS held on 7 November 1997, the report was stressed to raise awareness of the weaknesses of the Chinese catering business. The leaders of HCS strongly recommended reading the report and considering both the criticisms and the constructive suggestions.

According to its assertions, HCS is also prepared to lobby for its members' interests. For instance, their negotiations with companies and institutions have secured their members some preferential treatment. These include a tax reduction for playing music in their restaurants, a ten per cent reduction when engaging the services of Van Beuningen Lawyer Firm, and a certain discount when dealing with several insurance companies or banks.

Concerning the protection of their members' profits, the associations are, however, far from all-powerful. This limitation, among others, will be studied in the last section of this chapter.

Promoting positive integration
The progressive association leaders understand that their immigrant community must develop an integrated relationship with the host society. Some Chinese associations have played an important role in promoting the positive integration of the Chinese immigrants into Dutch society. For instance, through the arrangements first by CCRM then by *Wah Fook Wui*, many important regulations operating in the Netherlands have been translated from Dutch into Chinese and published in dozens of brochures and folders. Major topics are as follows: opportunities to learn the Dutch language; the relevant policies towards services for the elderly; existing health services; training and employment opportunities; brief introductions to the important Dutch systems of immigration, taxation, welfare, education, and so on. These publications are available in the Chinese library of Rotterdam.

Chinese associations sometimes invite specialists to give lectures on current issues. For example, on 27 January 1992, after the Dutch government made some improvements in its general minorities policies, CCRM, together with some other associations, held a symposium to adapt the thinking and activities of the Chinese immigrants to the updated minorities policies. Five Dutch political parties accepted invitation to send a representative to the symposium. After answering the questions posed by the Chinese audience, the Dutch politicians all encouraged the Chinese to communicate more with the Dutch society and to try to improve the process of integration. It is the first time that so many Dutch politicians came together for a face to face discussion with the Chinese.

The Chinese associations also play an important role in helping Chinese immigrants get access to the social services. At present, three Chinese associations, *Wa Lai* in Amsterdam, *Wah Fook Wui* in Rotterdam, and *Chinese Brug* in The Hague, have set up free telephone information services for Chinese immigrants who need information about the social services offered by the Dutch state. This service was begun in the late 1980s by CCRM. During the first couple of years, through the help of some Chinese volunteers, the free service provided operated less than ten hours per week. In 1990, after receiving some funding from the Municipality of Rotterdam and from the Ministry of Welfare, Public Health and Culture, CCRM was able to set up a couple of salaried positions. After that, one or two social workers worked for the telephone services on every working day. While CCRM ran the system, there was an average of 3,500 to 4,000 telephone requests per year from callers living all over the Netherlands. Most questions reflected a lack of knowledge about the Dutch society. Interestingly, about 65 per cent of telephone callers were Chinese women wanting to know how to get a proper education for their children or asking about help for family violence. Other callers asked for help in finding a job. In 1993, about 25 per cent of the callers were newcomers, and their questions all related to how to get residence permits in the Netherlands (cf. CCRM, 1994:17-18). Since the mid-1990s, after CCRM stopped with their public activities, the telephone service has been operated by another local Chinese association in Rotterdam, *Wah Fook Wui.*

In short, from the descriptions above, three relative aspects can be concluded from this comparative perspective: there are more activities organized by the Chinese associations among the Chinese themselves in big cities like Amsterdam and Rotterdam, fewer in small cities; more for elders and housewives, fewer for middle-aged workers; more for poorly educated persons, fewer for the middle-class, relatively educated professionals. The reasons underlying these phenomena will be discussed in the last section. Nevertheless, nowadays, no Chinese in the Netherlands will completely ignore the existence of the Chinese associations.

B *Activities directed towards China*

Chinese people often say: "Chinese overseas are just like 'married daughters,' no matter where they live, China is their parents' home." Given this, it is reasonable to expect that they would be willing to help their parents' home whenever it is in need. Asides from the personal ties, Chinese associations arrange a number of activities designed to connect the Chinese abroad with China. The principal activities conducted by the current Chinese associations for the reinforcement or establishment of contacts with China can be differentiated into the following three types: receiving visiting officials from China, making donations to one's hometown, and visiting China.

Receiving visiting officials from China

During my interviews, I was often told that most activities organized by some well-known Chinese associations are related to receiving visiting officials from China. To a certain degree, it is true that, for instance, according to reports published in ACV Bulletin, ACV and some other Chinese associations received 28 delegations from China in 1995 and forty delegations in 1996.

Between 1995 and 1997, I was invited several times to be a guest at dinner parties held by Chinese associations for delegations from China. These were opportunities for me to gain insight into these events. Normally, when a delegation is planning to visit the Netherlands, the leaders of the relevant Chinese associations will be informed. On the arrival date, someone will go to meet the delegation at the airport. Then, accommodation, meetings, dinners, and sightseeing will be arranged and more or less funded by the host association(s). Because all expenses have to be borne by the hosts, it is important to have many people come forward to entertain the guests. The number of people who are willing to act as hosts, however, depends on how important the delegation is.[16] For example, it is easier to get more people involved when the delegation is sent directly by the governments of Zhejiang or Guangdong, where many Chinese in the Netherlands come from, or when the delegation has some power to deal with overseas Chinese affairs.

From the point of view of some official visitors from China, they are happy to be received by Chinese associations. There are no language barriers and no differences in cultural habits; moreover, the hospitality extended to them always gives them a certain feeling of being at home. From the point of view of the hosts, although some keep complaining that it is a burden to be a host, they are active in organizing or joining reception activities. Different people may cherish different motivations; however, an ex-chairman of ACV vividly expressed a common motive:[17]

> I know there are many complaints about us [i.e., Chinese association leaders]. One sharp criticism is that we spent too much time and money receiving official delegations from China. Someone even said that you leaders insofar only enjoy having banquets with the Chinese officials. It is unfair. Of course we do not just simply have a dinner together. This is to set up *guanxi*.[18] When there are persons who reject helping to entertain the guests from China, I often said to them: as a common individual, is it possible for you to invite a high-ranking office-holder, let alone the mayor of a city or the secretary of a municipal Party Committee, to have dinner with you? Now, through the efforts of our association, we have created such a chance for you! I have to say you are too stupid if you don't know how to use this opportunity.

From these talks, receiving official guests from China in the name of associations is clearly seen as a practical approach to social status advancement. This is particularly interesting and will be touched upon again in the coming discussion.

Making donations to one's hometown
In the special issue published by ACV to celebrate its 50th anniversary, the important donations to China between 1976 and 1994 from the Chinese in the Netherlands are listed as follows (ACV, 1997:43):

1976: donations for earthquake victims in Tangshan (no amount is mentioned);

1978: donated 260,000 guilders to the administration of Guangdong province to help Chinese refugees from Vietnam;

1986: donated money to build a lecture and study building for Wenzhou University;

1987: donated 70,000 guilders to help the fire victims in Northeast China;

1991: donated 750,000 guilders to help the flood victims in eastern China, which was collected by ACV and 22 other Chinese associations in the Netherlands;

1994: the donation sent to the Hope Foundation in China was used to subsidize 1,100 Chinese children from impoverished families and establish two primary schools in areas of Zhejiang province.

A bridge in Wenzhou mountain areas is a donation of Wenzhou emigrants in the Netherlands (Photo by Li Minghuan).

Most of these donation drives were initiated in the name of ACV, working together with some other Chinese associations. The money was collected from the Chinese all over the Netherlands, although many were not official members of ACV.

Since all emigrants want to fulfill the expectations of their own home community, contradictory goals are bound to arise. For instance, as mentioned above, the donation sent to the Hope Foundation in China was used to build two primary schools in Zhejiang province. This drew criticism from the Chinese donators whose original hometown is located in Guangdong province. As one interviewee told me:

> The donation made by our Guangdong people should be donated to our hometown in Guangdong. How can they [the leaders of ACV who are Zhejiang people] simply use our donation to build schools in their hometown? It is using our donation to build up their reputation! This is completely unfair. They can never expect us to make donations together with them again.

This interviewee makes two noteworthy points: donations are regarded as an approach to building up a reputation; however, on the other hand, it is worthwhile only if the donation is destined for their own hometown.

Visiting China

LFCON, ACV, *Fa Yin*, CSFN, HCS, and all associations based on a common district of origin have, sooner or later, formed delegations under the auspices of the relevant association to visit China. For instance, in April and May 1996, a delegation formed by LFCON went to visit China. The aim of the visit as proclaimed by the delegation was to improve the cooperation between Chinese associations in the Netherlands and the relevant administrations in China. The delegation visited Beijing, Wenzhou, Shenzhen, and four other well-known cities. As a delegation comprising eight *important* Chinese association leaders from the Netherlands, they were received as state guests. At the airport, they were guided through the passageway for distinguished guests. In every city, they stayed in the state guest-house. They were received by several state leaders of the People's Congress and the State Council as well as by the highest-ranking officials from the local governments they visited. In addition, two cadres were designated to accompany the delegation during the whole visit in China. Such a case, of course, is unique. Although few delegations would be received at the state level, it is normal that a delegation organized in the name of an association in the Netherlands would be received as the honoured guests of the local government. For instance, having visited China as a member of one delegation in the name of ACV, a lady said to one of her friends, "now I know how great it is to be a member of ACV."

Another related story is that of Mr. KH, an owner of several Chinese restaurants in the Netherlands. Formerly, he was not interested in any Chinese association. In the spring of 1995, when one district-based association was choosing a delegation to visit his hometown, he was invited to join the delegation, although he had not yet become a member of that association. After coming back from the trip, he said to me:

> The trip was much better than I had expected. At first I thought I would join the delegation simply for personal fun, also, to see whether there is a possibility for investment. As a delegation coming from abroad, we were very warmly received. Many opportunities and preferential rights kept being presented to us [...]
>
> I was deeply touched [...] I have worked in the Netherlands for more than twenty years. I cannot calculate how much money I have already paid for taxes. I can say very proudly that I have contributed my youth to the Netherlands. However, who cares? Up till now, who of the high rank-ing Dutch office-holders has even taken notice of me? In contrast, in my hometown, we were received as guests of honour. We were treated so friendly. Wherever we went, we were received by the highest local leaders and were invited for banquets [...]

Since then, this man has been active in Chinese associations and has become one of the well-known association leaders in the Netherlands.

In short, looking forward to having a backing from their original home com-munity is a normal phenomenon among the migrants abroad. However, it is also worth pointing out that they are psychologically motivated activities rather than politically motivated ones.

C *Activities directed towards the Dutch society*

For the Chinese associations in the Netherlands, looking to the Dutch society to attain certain social influences started no earlier than the 1980s. In Chap-ter V, an interpretation was given of the reasons that Chinese associations entered into a dialogue with the Dutch society. What have the relevant associations actually done to make themselves a socially visible group in the Dutch society? The following cases, especially selected from the events that happened in the 1990s, illustrate answers to this question.

Donating money to Dutch flood victims
In February 1995, Chinese associations for the first time appealed to all Chinese immigrants for a donation to the Dutch. In that January, large areas in the southeastern and central parts of the Netherlands suffered from exten-sive flooding. Thousands of families living in the flooded districts had to be evacuated, together with their livestock. At the end of the month, about twenty Chinese associations collectively launched a campaign to help the affected Dutch people by appealing to the Chinese community for contribu-tions. In a few days, the Chinese Committee for Helping the Dutch Victims

Amsterdam Chinatown Festival 1997 (Photo by Li Minghuan).

of the Flood was organized, and various charity activities among the Chinese
were initiated.

On 1 February, when some Chinese associations held the Chinese New
Year's Party in the Sea Palace Restaurant in Amsterdam, the organizers went
to every table to collect donations. Nearly three thousand guilders were collected on the spot.

On 9 February, I attended the weekly meeting of one Chinese elders
association, *Tung Lok*. Before any other business, a speech was given to invite
all participants to contribute for the affected Dutch people. After the speech,
an old lady stood and sang a familiar Chinese folk song that her husband had
re-composed to express sympathy for the flood victims. By the end of the
meeting, nearly twenty people had signed their names on a piece of red
paper pledging their donation. Each donation was between ten and twenty-
five guilders.

On 14 February, on the night of the Chinese Lantern Festival,[19] a great
charity party was held in Utrecht and was attended by around five hundred
people. The slogan of this charity party was "Live in the Netherlands, Love
the Netherlands." At the end of the party, the organizers collected 108,888
guilders.

It is necessary to elaborate on the special meaning of this donation. It has
become a modern Chinese myth that *eight* is a "lucky figure" suggesting
richness and wealth. This myth was first prevalent among the people in Hong
Kong and then quickly spread to the whole of China and to the Chinese
abroad. When asking for a number for a private telephone or car, some
Chinese owners are willing to spend a large amount of money to buy a
number containing *eight*. Moreover, the more figures of *eight* there are in the

number, the higher the price they are willing to spend. Not surprisingly, if the price of a car number contains six *eights*, it may be higher than the price of the car itself. Only by acknowledging this custom can the latent meaning of 108,888 guilders, the amount of the donation mentioned above, be properly understood; it is a symbol of the good faith of the organizers.

Chinatown-Amsterdam Festival
As an association for the Chinese business people in Chinatown-Amsterdam, the *Vereniging van Chinese Ondernemers in Chinatown Amsterdam* (Association of Chinese Business People in Chinatown Amsterdam; hereafter COCA) has worked towards the target of economic prosperity in the area. COCA was founded in August 1988. Since 1989, as one part of its campaign to attract more customers to Chinatown-Amsterdam, COCA organized some public activities with Chinese cultural characteristics during both the Western New Year and the Chinese New Year; for example, having lion-dance performances during the day time and a Chinese fireworks display during the night. To attract attention, three great Chinese New Year's festivals were held in Chinatown-Amsterdam in 1994, 1995 and 1996.

In 1997, however, instead of having a Chinese New Year's festival, COCA, together with six other Chinese associations and several Dutch associations, held a great Chinatown Festival from 19 to 21 September in Amsterdam. For this festival, a troupe was invited from China to give performances. The relevant programs also included: a lion-dance demonstration, Chinese *Taijiquan* and *wu shu* demonstrations, a Chinese karaoke competition, and a few Chinese cultural exhibitions. Reportedly, more than ten thousand people came to visit the festival each day. After the success of this festival, COCA decided that the Chinatown Festival will be held every year in September to replace the festival at Chinese New Year. When asked about the motivation of this decision, one of the major leading persons of COCA simply explained it as follows:[20]

> We are business people. Although many Chinese prefer to have an exciting festival at Chinese New Year, we should first of all consider which arrangements will be more profitable for our business.
>
> The weather in September is much better than in the winter at the time of Chinese New Year. A Festival held at Chinese New Year may please more Chinese; however, a Festival in summer will attract much more Dutch people as well as many tourists from other countries. Therefore, we prefer the latter. Formerly, we spent seventy thousand guilders to arrange a festival especially for the Chinese at Chinese New Year, which only attracted a few thousand people. In September 1997, the same amount of money was spent but the audiences who came were in the tens of thousands. Thus, we have no doubt that the festival should be organized in summer.
>
> Of course, our aim is to promote the prosperity of Chinatown-Amsterdam by showing Chinese culture to Dutch people.

From this conversation, among others, COCA has clearly targeted the Dutch society for their activities. This new focus has brought changes in the Chinese associations in the Netherlands, which will be elaborated further in the ensuing discussions.

Showing respect to Dutch officials
At the beginning of 1997, the leaders of LFCON asked to have a meeting with the high-ranking officials of the Amsterdam municipal government. As a response to the request, Mr. Schelto Patijn, the mayor of Amsterdam, decided to have a meeting with the representatives of LFCON on 12 August 1997.

According to the Dutch officials who were asked to arrange this visit, it would be a meeting to discuss some important but concrete problems. For the Chinese associations in Amsterdam, especially for those associations located in the centre of Amsterdam, however, the visit of the mayor was first of all an honorary event rather than an occasion for practical discussions.

On the day of the meeting, many Chinese, mostly women and elderly people, were asked to wait in the offices of ACV, *Fa Yin* or BLIH.[21] Moreover, some were formally dressed, although it was an unusually hot day in the Netherlands. In the office of *Fa Yin*, I interviewed several persons who were waiting there. When asked about why they have come to welcome the mayor, some answers were as follows:

Why do I come? I was asked to come to welcome the mayor. It is an important and great event. It is said that we will have a chance to put forward our requests to the mayor directly.

It is a great honour to be visited by a high-ranking Dutch official such as the mayor of Amsterdam.

The mayor did come to visit the Chinese associations but went to have a meeting with the leaders of LFCON first. No one who was waiting to welcome the mayor was informed about his time schedule.

It was not until half past four that one of the committee members of *Fa Yin* rushed to the office and said to everybody, "Attention! The mayor is coming! Give a warm applause when he arrives." (Afterwards I was told that this man had to wait outside the office of LFCON for a long time in order to know when the mayor was leaving for *Fa Yin*.)

Finally, the mayor arrived in the office of *Fa Yin*. Everyone stood and applauded. The lady who stood next to me was one of my interviewees. Seeing the mayor walking into the hall together with some Chinese association leaders, she asked me in a surprised whisper:

Is this the mayor of Amsterdam?
["Yes," I answered.]
No bodyguard? How can a mayor go out without having bodyguards?

Before I could help this lady understand why a Dutch mayor need not have bodyguards around him, another applause burst forth after the mayor finished a brief and formal speech. Then, in order to express their thanks for the mayor's visit, the chairman of *Fa Yin* presented the mayor with some souvenirs. All people stood up and applauded again when the mayor left. In less than ten minutes, the visit was finished. No one complained that they had had to wait for more than three hours for this ten minutes. Moreover, after the mayor left *Fa Yin*, some people were asked to take a short cut to the office of ACV to welcome the mayor there. They were told that this was to give the mayor an impression that we Chinese are very enthusiastic to welcome him.

Applause, brief speech, souvenirs — a similar sequence took place in the offices of both BLIH and ACV. Finally, in the office of ACV, when some more souvenirs were presented, the mayor said:

> I wish I had prepared some transport facilities to carry the souvenirs I have received today [laughing].

The mayor was of course making a joke; however, it can be regarded as a reflection of his feeling that the response of the Chinese to his visit was strange to him.

As was described earlier, it has become customary for an association to invite high-ranking Dutch to be guests of honour whenever there is a large-scale public activity. However, it is seldom that a high-ranking Dutch official comes to a regular meeting place to visit the ordinary Chinese people. Therefore, the visit by the mayor was a unique event, which was a topic of conversation for weeks afterward. In the newsletter of LFCON, and in ACV Bulletin, it was stressed that the Amsterdam Mayor's visit to Chinese associations was a significant achievement. At the same time, the associations that are also located near the centre of Amsterdam but were not visited by the mayor kept complaining about having been ignored. One leader said to me angrily:

> We are an influential Chinese association as well. There is no reason why the mayor went through this area but did not visit us. It is a game played by a few leaders of LFCON! They look down upon us. They just tried to keep the mayor for themselves.

In general, regardless of whether there are concrete results of such a visit, the fact that a high-ranking Dutch official came to pay a visit was a symbol of official recognition of the associations and their leaders.

2 *Social significance of the Chinese associations*

Regarding the major activities undertaken by the current Chinese associations as outlined above, what is the social significance they have engendered? Do they have any actual effects on the relevant societies — the Chinese immigrant community, their original society, or the host society? If so, how and to what degree?

On this point, Merton's discussions of manifest functions and latent functions are relevant. Through the activities organized by the Chinese associations, the following can be concluded about their social functions: their manifest function is that, on the one hand, they have formed an invisible *wall* by accentuating the we-group feeling and differentiating their members from outsiders; on the other hand, they have built a *bridge* to the wider society by acting as a representative agent and as an intermediary between the authorities, the general population, and their community. Meanwhile, a latent function of the associations has been the construction of an ethnic *niche*; that is, a cultural and social space that is distinct from both the receiving and sending societies. Moreover, those who are familiar with both new and old worlds have developed a sense of superiority, because they are able to benefit from their position of straddling two worlds: the achievement in one would become capital for upward mobility in the other. Below, further arguments are presented.

A *A wall to protect the Chinese immigrants*

The social significance of the Chinese associations, first of all, should be studied not only from its direct and evident functions but also in regard to its circuitous influences.

On this point, the theoretical framework related to *symbolic capital* or *symbolic power*, which was proposed by Pierre Bourdieu, offers a helpful way to explore the social functions of the Chinese associations as a whole. Starting from a common understanding that capital is accumulated labour, Bourdieu's original views are as follows: there are immaterial forms of capital, i.e., cultural, symbolic and social, as well as a material or economic form of capital. Moreover, with varying levels of difficulty, it is possible to convert one of these forms into the other (cf. Bourdieu, 1986, 1990; Calboun et al., 1993). Thus, a principal point to understand the social significance of the Chinese associations as a whole is the *symbolic power* they have created and have been using.[22] Nowadays, this symbolic power is becoming increasingly needed by the Chinese immigrant community, their original society and the host society.

Superficially, it seems that the Chinese associations are something dispensable for the majority of the Chinese. As mentioned above, at the present time many Chinese associations are simply focussing their work on leisure-time programs since the Dutch welfare state has already taken over the basic practical functions that Chinese voluntary associations had assumed before the Second World War. Using vivid Chinese expressions, the current role played by many Chinese associations is more like "adding flowers to beautiful brocade" rather than "providing coal in snowy winter weather" or, to put it differently, to "make perfection still more perfect" rather than "provide timely help." Thus, the Chinese association has been regarded by some people as a public arena prepared by and for those who are established in business or who need to use their ethnic background to climb up the social ladder. For those who have to work day and night in Chinese restaurants, few are interested in registering as a formal member of the Chinese association.

However, as was noted earlier, a limited number of actual members does not mean that the majority of the Chinese immigrants have not beneffited from the activities undertaken by Chinese associations. Given the fact that either their children are studying in the Chinese schools or they themselves do not miss the festival performances organized by the Chinese associations, they resemble non-paying and non-participating beneficiaries of the work done by the dues-paying members of the relevant associations. However, on the other hand, it is worth noting that some non-members are volunteers for the public activities organized by the Chinese associations or generous donators of various charities initiated by the Chinese associations.

Taking these facts into account, a better conception of the latent significance of the Chinese associations for the individual can be developed. First of all, the existence and the development of the Chinese associations are in themselves a symbol. This expresses that the Chinese are organized and are represented to outsiders. This expresses an effort to integrate individual motivations into a coherent and ordered institution. Moreover, the social activities undertaken by the associations — whether they are just colourful festival celebrations or serious negotiations with the authorities — have continued to reinforce the national feeling and promote the cultivation of Chinese culture, language and traditions. In the long run, all of these activities form a cohesive power to attract the Chinese on the basis of shared cultural and ethnic identity. Furthermore, on special occasions when something extraordinary happens, the Chinese rank and file can be mobilized in the name of the Chinese associations. The consequences, which are too extensive to cover completely in this study, are far-reaching.

Ultimately, the function ethnic associations serve is like a symbolic wall to give all Chinese a we-group socio-psychological defense against the feelings of marginality or isolation experienced in the wider society and to have their differences, culturally or economically, noticed by outsiders. As an immigrant group, they need to develop a symbolic power by using their ethnicity as a resource. To a certain degree, the existence of Chinese immigrant associations — and the vivid activities freely organized by them in a society dominated by the Western culture — is no longer simply a means; it may be considered as an end in itself. Moreover, what has attracted my special attention as well is how this symbolic capital has been converted into personal practical benefits. To put it differently, in the long run, some association leaders who have an established powerbase will strive for direct political participation in their receiving country for either collective or individual purposes. Further examination of this topic is presented in the third section of this chapter.

B *A bridge to the Chinese immigrant community*

Symbolically speaking, Chinese associations have been functioning as a kind of a *grade separation bridge*: at different levels, it connects the Chinese immigrant community with the Dutch society; it improves the links between the Chinese migrants and their home community; and it sets up or expands an organizational network on a transnational level.

An intermediary between the Dutch authorities and the Chinese community
The Dutch authorities need Chinese associations to bring all Chinese immigrants into the society's orbit. Before the 1980s, the Chinese had few contacts with the Dutch authorities. Since then, however, the situation has changed when the policies worked out by the Dutch government shaped and reshaped the orientations of the Chinese associations.

From 1980 onwards, the concept of multiculturalism received rather extensive attention in Dutch policy documents. In 1983, a government memorandum foresaw an essential role for the minority organizations themselves (Vermeulen, 1997:134; 142). In 1987, for the first time an amount of up to 250,000 guilders was granted to support Chinese associations. This subsidy increased to 500,000 guilders per year in the next few years. This development became a turning point in the relationship between the Dutch government and the Chinese associations.

Since the funding targets were determined by the Dutch authorities, these authorities were for the first time in the history of the Chinese associations in the Netherlands respected as *sponsors* of the Chinese community. Moreover, it was also for the first time in history that a Dutch authority initiated a Chinese association, i.e., LFCON (cf. Chapter V). In addition, as was mentioned above, a visit by a high-ranking Dutch official is regarded as an honour for an association. It is telling that the Chinese associations that have been selected as eligible for subsidies are now very proud of their special position.[23] Taking these associations as an example, many existing Chinese associations now, more than anything else, look toward official governmental regulations when making and stating their working programs.

In this way, certain Dutch authorities have specifically brought the Chinese associations under their jurisdiction. The circle has been closed to shape the Chinese associations: in order to get government funds, the relevant associations may have to, at least nominally, put their own ambitions aside to follow the instructions of the Dutch authorities; then, once they are subsidized, they are no longer able to ignore the Dutch authorities' requests. Thus, two entangled aims have become the major focus of some associations: the struggle for subsidies and the efforts to convince the benefactors that the way the funds are used will properly meet their expectations.

Some scholars regard the relevant state funding of ethnic organizations as a form of manipulation and control. Others take the view that it should be possible in a democratic multicultural society to see state funding as a part of the total democratic process through which organizations play an effective

The Dutch officials are invited as guests of honour to an activity organized by a Chinese association (Photo by Li Minghuan).

political role (cf. Rex, 1994:9-10). Then, what is the consequence when the Chinese associations in the Netherlands have more or less been brought into the Dutch organizational channels? The problem can be studied from at least two respects.

In one respect, as a response to the support they have received from the Dutch authorities, many Chinese associations are willing to function as a bridge between the Dutch society and the Chinese community. Moreover, as time passes, when such a response has been encouraged repeatedly, the relevant associations would subsequently take the bridge function as a matter of routine or see themselves as bound to this duty.

The granting of state funds has been highly appreciated, particularly by the Chinese association leaders. The allocation of these funds has been taken as a token of the rising social status of the Chinese in the Netherlands.[24] Moreover, fulfilling the requests of the Dutch government has been accepted as paying a debt of gratitude by the associations. For instance, whenever there is a need to consult or to study the Chinese community, the relevant Chinese associations are willing to function as an intermediary. The authorities get the information they need through certain Chinese associations. The relevant regulations can be transferred to the Chinese immigrants through the network of Chinese associations. Besides, as a respected sponsor of the Chinese associations, whenever there is an activity organized by the Chinese associations, the Dutch officials will be invited as guests of honour. Through the cooperation of the Chinese associations and the Dutch authorities, more high-ranking Dutch officials, who are regarded as the embodiment of the

Dutch state, have been requested to meet the Chinese populace more closely than ever before. Because of this contact, the Chinese immigrants in the Netherlands are no longer seen as a scattered and invisible group.

Nevertheless, from the other viewpoint, when an immigrant association can only function if it presents itself in the way that the state wants, it has partly erased its own characteristics. For instance, it will be very difficult for an association to pursue its particular aims — let alone to proclaim itself as a pressure group — when it receives subsidies from the government. Sometimes, not only its functions but also its existence has to be subjected to the relevant policies of the government. On this point, CCRM is a good example. CCRM has heavily depended on the Dutch governments' funding since it was established. In the late 1980s CCRM was very active and influential while it had ample state funds. However, after Dutch funding policies changed in 1992, CCRM had to reduce its social activities, and since 1997 it has become almost invisible (cf. Chapter IV:3).

An agent to bind Chinese emigrants to their home communities
The bond that links the individual Chinese emigrant to his or her village of origin is usually strong. Some Chinese associations started from a common sense of nostalgia for their now distant homeland. The focus here, however, will not be the individual motives and the consequences of links between individuals. It will be the connections through institutional mechanisms, and its social effect.

The Chinese associations, symbol of the Chinese immigrants in their respective receiving countries, sometimes also play significant roles in the local development of their original areas.

When I did my research in Wenzhou, I found a consensus among the local administrators: the Wenzhou people in Europe are a vital force behind the development of their home region. For instance, I often heard talk like "having close links with Western Europe is the special opportunity of our Wenzhou qiaoxiang. We should grasp this opportunity to advance ourselves." A similar notion appears now and then in the local newspapers as well. How is Wenzhou to be developed by grasping this opportunity? The local officials gave me different answers: some told me about magnificent goals for the whole area; others talked about concrete plans of their own. In my experience, however, none of the interviewed administrators have ignored the significance of the Chinese associations in Europe, including those of the Netherlands. For example, whenever they were talking about the contributions of Wenzhou emigrants, the name of the relevant associations would be mentioned. If the interviewee had been in the Netherlands as a member of one government delegation, he would mention the warm reception he was given by the relevant associations. Moreover, some documents related to the emigrants abroad could not be made and distributed to the people in need without the help of the network formed by the relevant associations. The following is a telling case.

Since 1990, a yearly Get-together Meeting of Prominent Zhejiang Migrants Abroad has been held in several international cities.[25] The major sponsor is the provincial government of Zhejiang. Its aim is to improve the cooperation between Zhejiang province and its migrants abroad, between Zhejiang migrants in different areas, and between Zhejiang province and the countries where some Zhejiang migrants have settled down.[26] An invitation to attend this meeting has been regarded as an honour. In the eyes of the invited participants, it is more than anything else a proper opportunity to show their improved social position and to establish *guanxi* with the government circles of their hometown and their peers all over the world. From the point of view of the Zhejiang authorities, this yearly meeting informs Zhejiang migrants of the social and political developments in their home country and encourages contributions to their hometown. Yet such a meeting cannot be held without the support of Chinese associations abroad. Whenever the meeting is held outside of China, the local associations set up by Zhejiang migrants will prepare for the meeting. In addition, the invitations have always been sent out through the network of associations. As a response, all leaders and activists of the relevant associations will be invited to the meeting as "well-known Zhejiang migrants abroad."

In short, the label "Chinese association abroad" is applied here to a group whose members interact based on a collective experience of emigrating from a common area. It is a convenient way in which group members can be recognized and contacted by the administration in the emigrants' country (or area) of origin.

Transnational networks of Chinese associations
Although the practical benefits of using an associations' network in a small country like the Netherlands are not clear, some can still be observed. For instance, the establishment of EFCO (cf. Chapter V) and the yearly meeting of prominent Zhejiang Chinese abroad just mentioned are specific examples of setting up an associations' network.

One of my own experiences will also provide an example to show how an associations' network can play a practical role. In December 1997, the current chairman of EFCO, who lives in the Netherlands, sent me to Italy to collect information for the EFCO committee. Before I left, I was given a list of Chinese associations with their leaders in the cities that I was instructed to visit. I could not predict how I would be received since I knew none of them. In about two weeks, I travelled from the north to the south of the Italian peninsula to visit seven cities. The whole trip was arranged within the Chinese association's network. Milan was the first city I visited. Before I arrived in Milan, the chairman of one local Chinese association had been informed about my visit by a telephone call from Amsterdam. Someone was sent to pick me up from the airport. Then, I was driven to a forum specially organized by the association at the suggestion of the EFCO chairman. After the forum, during dinner, the chairman of the association in Milan made a telephone call to the chairman of an association in Torino to inform him about my plan, and to stress that I was sent by the chairman of EFCO. The next day, when I arrived in Torino, the same arrangement was followed. In this way — that is, being sent by one association in one city to an association in the next city — I finished my visits and collected the required data.

However, nowadays, alongside the fast development of globalization, transnational networks of Chinese associations have in particular functioned in economic spheres (Liu, 1998). An associations' network gives all those involved an organizational background to know each other. Since all participants are supposed to have a shared heritage, it is easier to know a certain person's status; that is, to gain a kind of association credit which can be used, recognized, and accepted. At some transnational meetings or activities held by the relevant association(s), a few may find a likely business partner immediately; however, the much more important consequences are for the future. In more concrete terms, the primary contacts and information exchanges that are carried out will become a cornerstone for future business dealings or mutual social support.

C A niche to program a new dignity

As they are forming a wall as well as a bridge, the basic functions of the Chinese associations have resulted in a series of social consequences from straddling the two worlds of the host country and the country of origin. Specifically, the social significance of the Chinese associations is multiple and paradoxical: to let the Chinese immigrant community remain detached while trying to be connected; to improve their integration while being a force retarding assimilation; to adapt their thinking to the new conditions while keeping their independence; and so forth. Based on this, a kind of social *niche* is appearing through the following conversions of the social status of Chinese immigrant people:

    (i)   from invisible to visible;
    (ii) from marginality to assertion;
    (iii) from their achievements in the Netherlands to higher reputation in China.

From invisible to visible

As was mentioned in Chapter III, the Chinese immigrants in the Netherlands were a silent group before the 1980s. Such a state of affairs, however, has changed forever. The group has become visible through collective action. As was described in the first section of this chapter, by organizing various public activities, the Chinese immigrant community has greatly increased its social visibility. Moreover, it seems that the percentage of Chinese immigrants who are willing to stand up and speak out is rising. Some activities were organized with the clear target to attract more social attention. The following incidents are representative.

In the summer of 1997, the chairman of LFCON was elected as the chairman of the European-wide association EFCO, and some Chinese association leaders in the Netherlands formed a preparatory group to host the fifth annual meeting of EFCO. In December 1997, at the request of the preparatory group and supported by some Dutch politicians, EFCO held its fifth annual meeting in the Dutch Parliament Mansion in The Hague. One year later, in December 1998, EFCO held its standing committee's meeting in the EU Mansion in Brussels. Among other things, these two arrangements clearly reflected the organizers' wish of pursuing higher social visibility for the Chinese.

With respect to the Dutch authorities, the Chinese immigrants are more visible in their working projects than at any time before. For example, when ACV celebrated its 50th anniversary, some high-ranking Dutch officials, such as the state secretary of Public Health, Ms. Terpstra, and the mayor of Amsterdam, Mr. Patijn, sent their enthusiastic letters of congratulations. Anything like this was completely unimaginable several decades ago when ACV was still looked upon with suspicion. In addition, as was mentioned earlier, Dutch politicians or institutions have played an important role in the establishment of certain Chinese associations such as CCRM and LFCON. Then, more recently, in a short period of three months, i.e., between April and June 1999, three reports concerning the Chinese in the Netherlands had been published in succession under the sponsorship of the relevant Dutch authorities and institutions. The first one is about how to enrich the life of the Chinese immigrants in their spare time in order to protect them from gambling addiction; the second one is a general overview of the Chinese community in Europe; and the last one is the achievement of a two-year project that, on the basis of an extensive investigation of the social status of the Chinese throughout the Netherlands, has worked out some principal suggestions in order to help the Dutch government redefine its policies towards the Chinese immigrants.

The Chinese immigrants, both their contributions and problems, cannot be ignored any longer.

From marginality to assertion
The conversion from marginality to assertion, which is an important facet of the Chinese associations in the Netherlands, can be examined from three perspectives.

First, with the aid of the symbolic power embodied in the association, the association leaders can realize their dreams to move up to a leading nucleus within the Chinese immigrant community. To a certain degree, the ethnic association has provided a social space within which the social status of the participants can be recognized. Some are willing to be esteemed by others for their achievements, no matter their size. Especially among migrants, their original dream was to struggle for betterment. Their success should not be limited to their own circle; they also deem it important to have this fact recognized by others. In other words, the significance of the formal organization is not determined by the affairs that it has discussed or settled. "With regard to its psychological effects, its most important part is the actual, direct social connection which is established between the members by the very fact of their being together and discussing" (Thomas & Znaniecki, 1984: 255).

Second, the public activities organized by the associations — such as the Chinatown festival and the Chinese New Year's party — where the Chinese are hosts and the Dutch are attentive customers, have helped to quell their outsider feelings. This is accomplished because the Chinese immigrants are recognized by the dominant society as a social force with its own distinct culture.

Third, to the society in their region of origin, many emigrants also want to become a new force at the core and believe they should be respected as such. This is because, individually, they have contributed to their respective families or clans through remittances or by having brought over someone else to their new world; moreover, collectively, they have contributed generously to their hometown. Furthermore, they believe that their experiences in a developed Western country have given them a wiser and advanced view on their country of origin. They have to take into account the distance between themselves and their native people created by their emigration; however, many regard this more as a basis for building up their dignity than a weakness.

From their achievements in the Netherlands to a higher reputation in China
In the early 1970s, while studying the Chinese associations in Britain, one researcher argued that one reason for the inherent weakness of Chinese associations in Britain is that any efforts expended to build up a formal leadership position in a certain Chinese association in Britain will contribute nothing to raising his or her position in the home community (Watson, 1977: 200).

My study, however, has found contrary indications. It cannot be overemphasized how important an effect the Chinese associations abroad have made upon their original home community and, at the same time, how great a positive consequence they have been fed back.

It is necessary to point out that for a long historical period only government-supported associations could exist in mainland China. Thus, from my interviews, I found that in some rural areas of Wenzhou, the native people still clearly regarded the "Chinese association in the Netherlands" as a kind of government administration. One old man told me very proudly, "My son is a cadre in Holland." In fact, I know his son is a Chinese restaurant owner and a committee member of ACV. As was mentioned earlier, ACV and some other associations often receive government delegations from China. Then, these association leaders have some group photos taken with the high-ranking Chinese officials. Such photos are highly appreciated by the people in their hometown. One local official in Wenzhou told me:[27]

> Our co-villagers in the Netherlands are very successful. They are enjoying very high social status. Many Chinese national leaders have their photos taken together with them. From the photos they have sent us, we can see

they have been photographed together with the highest Chinese national leaders Jiang Zemin, Zhu Rongji, Qian Qichen and many others.[28] We are proud of them!

Besides enhancing reputation, an affiliation with an association can also yield some practical benefits, which come from the preferential treatment rendered by the relevant governments in their home country. As was listed earlier, occasionally donations to China (very often to their home community) have been initiated and collected by some Chinese associations. Then, logically, because these contributions are made in the name of the association, as a response, the representatives of these associations will be given a kind of association credit, which, more than anything else, can be used to gain some preferential treatments proffered by the local government. The following is an example of the kind of special courtesy that has been shown to whoever possesses an association credit.

In China, there is a tradition to regard a *tomb* as an eternal *home* for all human beings. Moreover, some believe that the location of the ancestral family tomb has implications for the fortune of all descendants, regardless of where they are. Still, for some Chinese abroad, as part of their desire to keep their roots, they wish to have a family tomb in or near their hometown.

In Wenzhou, since the 1980s, along with the economic development, a new trend has evolved: many families want to have their family tomb built in a conspicuous place, even if it would occupy a large piece of farmland. Some affluent families have also tried every means imaginable to ornament the tombs: marble archways, private gardens, well-decorated pavilions, and so forth. This "tomb building mania" was carried further still: not only have tombs for the deceased ancestors or for the elderly family members been built but also some for still active middle-aged family members and even for the children. Because Wenzhou people have spent too much money and used too much land to build tombs, the central government of China has sharply criticized this "tomb problem." Then, in 1996, the local government of Wenzhou enacted some decrees and systematically put them into effect. First, all newly planned family tombs may not be built on farmland and may not occupy an area of more than one *mu*.[29] Second, all tombs that have been built on farmland should be moved. This second step is too difficult to enforce, because few of the family members could accept the instruction of having their family tombs moved. Sometimes the local police had to be mobilized when a tomb had to be moved.[30] Nevertheless, to pay sensible attention to the feelings of the Wenzhou migrants abroad, the family tombs that ran counter to the relevant policies but belong to "Wenzhou leaders abroad" would be treated by the authorities in an exceptional way. Eventually, it was proposed that a solution could be reached through discussion. This often led to a "provisional regulation" that the status of the tombs would be "temporally" maintained with the provision that a certain amount of money had to be paid as a fine.[31]

When asked who can be regarded as "a Wenzhou leader abroad," one high-ranking official of Wenzhou municipality clearly gave me the following answer:[32]

> The committee members of the Chinese associations in their country of residence can be regarded as "Wenzhou leaders abroad."
>
> [Do you take into account the significance of the association?]
>
> No. All association leaders will get this preferential treatment. It is very difficult to judge which association is significant and which is not. The standard adopted by us is that whoever can prove he is a committee member of one existing Chinese association, can be treated as a "Wenzhou leader abroad."

Such being the case, one can understand how important an association affiliation can be. Therefore, I was not surprised that some Chinese who are not actively engaged in Chinese associations in the Netherlands are willing to present themselves as important members or even as active committee members of certain Chinese associations when visiting their original hometown.

For instance, one day in Shenzhen, when paying a visit to a local government administration, I ran into a man who was introduced by a local official as a "well-known Chinese association leader who had just come back from the Netherlands to pay a visit to his hometown." The name card this man gave to me claimed that the holder was the vice-chairman of *Fa Yin*. Yet, I had never met this person in the two years that I had followed the activities of *Fa Yin*. In addition, once in Wenzhou, when I was introduced to a "Chinese association leader" from the Netherlands, I found that the association he claimed to lead did not exist.

In short, because of the physical distance and cultural difference between the Netherlands and China, it is not strange that some migrants simply expect to get access to some practical benefits in their original country from the potentiality embodied in the associations in the Western world (although this may not always be true). The active maintenance of a collective symbol (an ethnic association is one possibility) compensates to some extent for the ungrounded feeling of homelessness that comes along with migration. Then, a new dignity develops.

3 Who is benefitting the most?

Who is benefitting the most from these organizational efforts? The answer will be given through an analysis starting from three vantage points: the Chinese association leaders, the governments in the sending and receiving countries, and the ordinary Chinese immigrants.

A *The Chinese association leaders*

As was mentioned earlier, the expenses for the festival activities of the relevant associations are often underwritten by their leaders. While acknowledging that most Chinese immigrants, especially most business people, are working single-mindedly towards their economic advancement and material betterment, why are they willing to commit their time, financial resources, and energy to initiate and develop the Chinese associations in the Netherlands? Do they simply gain satisfaction from the honour brought forth by the association? The answer cannot be simply "yes" or "no." In the end, the associations set up by and for the Chinese abroad have both symbolic and instrumental significance. Although the voluntary associations themselves are nonprofit institutions, the symbolic power they embody can be converted to practical benefits under given conditions.

Some scholars who have studied the Chinese associations in Southeast Asia or North America have noted that one of their important functions is to form an "opportunity structure" (Wong, 1982; Wickberg, 1993, 1994). In more concrete terms, a name card that indicates officer status in several important associations is a door-opener in several ways. Thus, the ambition of founding new associations is good business sense rather than personal vanity (Wickberg, 1993). I will accept these arguments as a starting point to develop further hypotheses, taking Chinese associations in the Netherlands as direct examples. I prefer, as was pointed out earlier, to describe it as *association credits*.

Like their peers in either Southeast Asia or North America, the Chinese association leaders in the Netherlands are also eager to use the symbolic power created by the association to build up an association credit for economic capital accumulation.

The New Chinatown Project is one example of how an association credit is used for a business purpose. The project of having an Asia Trade Centre established in Amsterdam was first proposed in 1995. Obviously, this program is, primarily, for economic purposes. A well-known Chinese businessmen, Mr. But, heads the project. As the manager of the biggest Chinese restaurant in the Netherlands, he is also an active association leader. He is the chairman of *Fa Yin* and LFCON, the vice-chairman of ACV, as well as the major leader of several other Chinese associations. Because of his association leadership background, many relevant associations — LFCON, *Fa Yin*, ACV — have been included in the project. Moreover, in the plan, not only has an Asia Trade Centre been designed, but some elderly accommodation and a building for cultural activities including Chinese cooking classes, sports and a Chinese library are also planned. Thus, the whole project becomes a "community plan," which undoubtedly has strengthened the competitive power of the project.

In addition, there are some instances of association leaders or initiators using the establishment of a voluntary association as a means to realize certain hidden purposes. For instance, the Dutch term *stichting* has several meanings: foundation, institution, organization, and so on. Originally, a *stichting* could be either a nonprofit association or a profit-seeking entity, if the profits are reinvested in the objectives of the given *stichting*. The usual translation of *stichting* into Chinese is *jijinhui*, however, which would give people an image that the given entity is a nonprofit association or even a philanthropic association. Some people have made use of this difference between the two cultures.

For example, one Chinese *wu shu* master has set up a Chinese *wu shu* *stichting* in the Netherlands. According to its statutory articles, the association is to propagate Chinese traditional culture in the Netherlands. Then the initiator, acting as chairman as well as director of his *stichting*, attended the relevant meetings as a Chinese association leader. Whenever his *stichting* is going to hold a public cultural activity, it will stress that it is a cultural association and ask donations from the community for support. When someone is planning to join the *stichting* as a member and learn *wu shu* from the master, he or she is asked to pay a tuition fee. Moreover, when this *stichting* is expected by other Chinese associations to give a performance, the chairman will charge a fee and stress that he, as well as his family, has to live on his trade.

Sometimes the card of *stichting* can be played from another angle. For instance, one person has set up a travel agency in the Netherlands to arrange European trips for tourists from China. Having experienced sharp competition, this person found a new approach to reach his purpose. He contrived another name for his agency using the title of *stichting* and translated this newly registered entity as something like Foundation for Economic Cooperation in Chinese. Meanwhile, he named himself a representative of the *stichting* instead of a manager. This normally will give his potential Chinese customers the latent suggestion that they are dealing with a non-profit-seeking association. This new image, to a certain degree, has helped him gain more customers.

In Chapter VI, another example was mentioned: in less than three years a Chinese immigrant has set up four *stichtingen*, of which two are European-wide and the other two are worldwide. This initiator and chairman has been received by some Dutch administrators and politicians as a representative of the Chinese community. He has also used these advantages to build up his business reputation. For instance, the names of the Dutch officials whom he has met are listed in his business advertisements to prove that he is an internationally prominent figure. In September 1997, in the name of one of his *stichtingen*, this chairman organized an art exhibition. In the Chinese version of the bilingual advertisement, it was stressed that this exhibition was supported by the Dutch government by word of its high-ranking officials, was recommended by Dutch parliament members, and so on. In the English version, however, it was stressed that the chairman had "the full cooperation of Chinese art organizations from all over the world."

Thus, certain persons clearly contributed to their economic achievements by creating such entities based on their ability to grasp the differences between the Dutch and Chinese cultures.

In addition, it is also worth noting that there are clear internal differences between the Chinese association leaders. As was pointed out in Chapter VI, Chinese association leaders can be divided into three groups: successful business people; social workers; politicians and professionals.

For the first group, as a response to their underwriting the expenses for the festival activities of the relevant association(s), the symbolic capital that they have accumulated from the Chinese associations has, more or less, improved their economic and social status. To put it differently, what they have done for their respective associations and what they have been repaid can be regarded as a process of conversion between symbolic and socio-economic capital.

Concerning the second group, social workers are the go-between people whose aim is to help their own ethnic group to participate in the social programs of the Dutch society. As a response, some of them are now employed by state institutions or are dependent on government departments, while some are looking for similar possibilities. They are a clearly visible group that has gained some practical benefits from state facilities.

Among the third group, some artists and sports masters are among those who have played their association card for practical profits. Some aspiring politicians may find a career if they can successfully realize the transformation of the Chinese immigrants from an ethnic group in itself to an interest group for itself.

In short, a basic feature of the Chinese associations as a whole is that they are much more concerned with their elite than with their ordinary members.

B *The sending and receiving countries*

The Chinese associations are rooted in their receiving country and have kept various links with their country of origin. Both the Dutch and the Chinese states, from various perspectives and to a certain degree, have definitely taken advantage of the establishment and the progress of the Chinese associations.

The Dutch state

Seen from a social point of view, the relevant Chinese associations still serve a mutual-aid function. More and more Chinese immigrants, including the elderly, women, and the young, are advised and guided by the associations about how to arrange and adjust their lives in the Netherlands. In a sense, this has not only had a homogenizing effect on the Chinese immigrant community but has also decreased the social burden of the Dutch state.

Economically, some Dutch officials and companies have recognized the potential of the Chinese immigrant associations as a non-governmental midpoint between the two countries: some Chinese associations in the Netherlands maintain special contacts with government agencies and with the political elite in China (including mainland China, Taiwan, Hong Kong and Macao). Through the appropriate Chinese associations, there is easy access to business and policy information in China.

Culturally, some Chinese associations have financed performances and exhibitions of Chinese artists in the Netherlands, which have been attended by Dutch audiences. Moreover, the Chinese associations are running dozens of after-school Chinese schools. In a sense, the Chinese associations are using their own resources to train a new generation: a generation that has mastered the Dutch language, knows Dutch society, and is now mastering the Chinese language and culture. They will be most useful when it comes to bridging the cultural, social and economic differences between the two countries.

In the end, all of these have resulted in positive mutual contact and understanding between the Chinese and the Dutch. This is the first and one of the most important steps for the establishment of an ethnically harmonious society.

The Chinese state

How China has gained advantages from their emigrants in the Netherlands through their associations can be briefly stated as follows.

The first advantage is philanthropic aid. A popular Chinese saying is: "Blood is thicker than water." A great many cases have shown that the Chinese associations perform a variety of functions, but most importantly they mobilize and collect donations to help the victims of natural disasters whenever there is such a need in their home country.

Economically, the Chinese state may expect the Chinese associations to act as go-between. For instance, some Chinese associations have organized visits to China for some Dutch entrepreneurs, which may result in direct investments in the future. In some cases, through the introduction of an association, some state-owned enterprises in China have found a reliable go-between to facilitate trade with Dutch companies. In addition, many times when a Chinese commodities fair was to be held in the Netherlands, the Chinese associations would be asked to offer help.

Culturally, the Chinese associations as a whole have been a long-existing Chinese cultural window in the Netherlands. They have organized a variety of activities to present Chinese culture to the mainstream society. By highlighting Chinese culture, they have helped the local people gain insight into China, and thus they have improved the understanding between the Dutch and the Chinese.

The last and the most sensitive problem is related to the political loyalty of the Chinese immigrants. In Southeast Asia, the political loyalty of Chinese immigrants is a very sensitive problem. In the Netherlands, this question has not yet attracted serious social attention. The first and the most important reason is that the dominant society has a strong political and cultural confidence. The second reason is that although some current Chinese associations in the Netherlands claim that they are a patriotic overseas Chinese association, this is not more than in an imaginary sense. Their so-called political loyalty to their far-distant motherland is just "a politics without responsibility or accountability"(Anderson, 1992). In reality, the members of these associations prefer to live in the Netherlands rather than in China. The political situation in the Netherlands involves them and their families much more directly, regardless of whether they are committed to it. Undoubtedly, their wish for the prosperity of China is stronger than that cherished by most Dutch people, and their happiness about the progress made by China is indeed greater. Nevertheless, it is important to recognize the potential meaning of this phenomenon: what they want to gain from the strength and prosperity of China, to a certain degree, is primarily improvement of their social position in the Netherlands.

In short, as has been repeatedly stressed, the desire cherished by the progressive Chinese immigrants is to have their own objectives realized through their efforts to benefit from their social position of straddling the two worlds, but not to simply be used as a tool either by the Dutch or the Chinese authorities.

C The ordinary Chinese immigrants

The ordinary or the non-elite Chinese immigrants have formed the social basis of Chinese associations. How much of their life has been involved in Chinese organizational activities?

I have pointed out earlier that many Chinese immigrants who are eligible to become members continue to remain outside of Chinese associations. At the present time, no Chinese association in the Netherlands has achieved what sociologists describe as "completeness," meaning that all those eligible for membership actually are members (Merton, 1968: 338-354; 368-370). Nevertheless, many of them have, directly or indirectly, benefitted from the Chinese organizations. Therefore, to a certain degree, they can be regarded as non-participating or non-paying beneficiaries, although they do not see themselves as such.

One fact already pointed out is that many activities rendered by the Chinese associations can be enjoyed by all members of the Chinese immigrant community rather than by only the members of the association: the Chinese schools, Chinese libraries, Chinese publications, Chinese elderly or women's centres, and so on. Moreover, all ordinary Chinese immigrants have also benefitted from the rising visibility of the Chinese immigrant group in either their host or original societies, which has been realized by the collective efforts made by Chinese associations.

The relevant associations differ in their attitudes toward non-members. Some aspire after more members, and some associations are indifferent towards the total number of their members.

The Chinese associations in the Netherlands as a whole are a voluntary institution that is far from all-powerful. Sometimes the gap between their pretensions and the actual outcome can be quite great. In fact, the functions performed by the associations cannot always meet the needs of the immigrants. A variety of phenomena and the reasons underlying them are worth studying.

First, along with the development of mass communication media, the function performed by certain Chinese associations to keep the Chinese immigrants regularly informed has been more or less replaced or reduced. As has been mentioned, an important contribution made by certain Chinese associations was to keep Chinese immigrants informed about current affairs through their publications. Nevertheless, since the 1990s, this function has been more or less replaced by mass media. Many varied information sources in the Chinese language are now available. For instance, since 1990, a radio program in Chinese (Cantonese) sponsored by the *Nederlandse Programma Stichting* (Dutch Program Foundation; NPS for short)[33] broadcasts news and relevant information every workday.[34] Among the more poorly educated immigrants, this Chinese radio program has become the most popular information source since it reports news promptly and is easy to receive. Another approach to transmitting information in Chinese are the Chinese television channels. Three Chinese cable and satellite channels are now available that mainly import programs from Hong Kong or Beijing and televise some European-Chinese community news. In addition, four issues of a Chinese-language daily, edited and published in Europe but sponsored by powerful news agencies located outside Europe, offer a conventional information medium. Besides these, a couple of Chinese commercial companies in the Netherlands have also published their advertisement newspapers, which have a few pages focussed on Chinese community news in the Netherlands.

Second, up to now the Chinese associations have had scant success in realizing the unity of the Chinese community, which almost every Chinese association has emphasized as greatly needed. For instance, as was mentioned earlier, HCS is a rather influential association with hundreds of Chinese restaurateurs as members. Nevertheless, its aim to regulate competition among the Chinese restaurateurs themselves has not been so successful. Since the beginning of the 1990s, serious problems have arisen for many HCS members: some restaurants have played unfair tricks in their competition — e.g., reducing their prices to an unreasonable level, employing some non-eligible workers to lower their costs, discrediting certain restaurants, and so on. Thus, it has been repeatedly suggested that HCS should try to regulate competition. After attempting to deal with these problems for years, however, HCS has realized few substantial achievements.

The failure of LFCON to become a community umbrella association is another case. To be able to speak effectively for all Chinese immigrants, LFCON, designed as the collective representative of Chinese associations, must unite as many members of the community as possible. The number of LFCON member associations has increased from 17 to 45 between 1987 and 1997; however, its membership has never numbered more than half of the existing Chinese associations. Some influential associations still refrain from becoming a member of LFCON.

A new and considerable challenge to the Chinese associations came from the initiating activities of a Dutch labour union for the Chinese restaurant workers. In Chapter V, an analysis was done on why the class differences within the Chinese immigrant community have not yet caused serious public conflicts. It should be noted that recently (i.e., the end of the 1990s) a few

Chinese restaurant workers who are not satisfied with their working conditions have begun to look for support from the Dutch labour union. Meanwhile, some activists of the Dutch labour union are also attempting to get involved with the Chinese restaurant workers and attract union members among them. Although its influence is limited at the present, the implications and development of this movement need to be followed in the future.

To sum up, ethnic migrants in alien surroundings, like the Chinese in the Netherlands, often forge a sense of collectivity. Despite individual differences in training and experiences before and after their arrival, they have identified themselves, and are always identified by non-Chinese people, at the aggregate level by their shared ethnic background. To ensure a better future and to realize the potential from their ability to straddle two worlds, their associations are functioning as an important collective symbol and, therefore, are indispensable not only to the immigrants themselves but also to the sending and receiving states.

The Chinese associations in the Netherlands are still developing. They have been and continue to be important to Chinese in the Netherlands, to their receiving and sending societies. Their potential functions are far-reaching.

CHAPTER VIII

What is the future?

The Chinese immigrants' organizational history in the Netherlands and their general characteristics have been discussed. In this last section, an outlook on its foreseeable future development will be presented.

1 *Looking at Chinese associations in Europe from a global perspective*

Chinese voluntary associations can be found wherever Chinese immigrant communities exist. From a global perspective, the ethnic Chinese associations first emerged in Southeast Asia and then spread to other continents. The Chinese associations in Europe are among the newly established associations but have quickly increased in number. A brief comparison between the Chinese associations in Europe and Southeast Asia or North America will help put their roles and dynamics in a wider context.

The proliferation of Chinese immigrant associations has become an attractive phenomenon in Chinese communities during the last decades of the twentieth century. It has been felt in countries around the world, with the notable exception of a few, such as Indonesia and Indo-China, where organizational activities among the ethnic Chinese have been curtailed.[1] Furthermore, the growing number of Chinese associations in Europe is more impressive than on any other continent.

The only regularly published statistics with respect to Chinese associations abroad are issued by OCAC of Taiwan. Although some figures are questionable, I will quote them here for the sake of comparison. Taking all of the Chinese associations outside of China into consideration, in 1946 there were 3,957 Chinese associations; by 1965, this number had risen to 7,687 and had increased to 9,255 by December 1995.[2] Based on these statistics, I have made the following three charts to give a relatively interesting comparison among the development of the Chinese associations on the five continents.[3]

In short, if we compare the number of Chinese associations in Europe with that of the whole world, in absolute percentage they still form the smallest part, but their relative rate of increase has been the highest. This is one of their striking characteristics.

2 *Looking at Chinese associations in the Netherlands from an European perspective*

If we compare the Chinese associations in the Netherlands with that in other European countries, two characteristics are noteworthy.

Chart 5 *The percentages of the*
Chinese associations on the
five continents in 1950

Chart 6 *The percentages of the*
Chinese associations on the
five continents in 1991

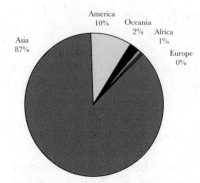

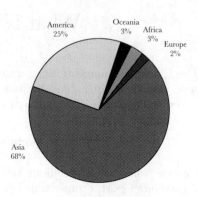

Chart 7 *The percentage of increase of the Chinese associations*
abroad from 1950 to 1991

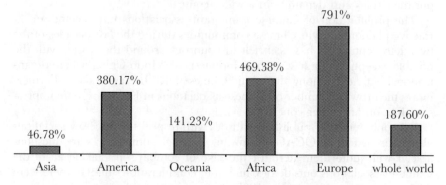

First, the fact that there are more than one hundred associations among 100,000 Chinese immigrants indicates that the organizing rate among the Chinese in the Netherlands is high.

According to Wickberg, the Filipino-Chinese are among the most highly organized of all overseas Chinese societies since approximately 1,000 Chinese associations serve a Chinese population of 1,000,000. If taking his claim as a standard, the organizing rate of the Chinese in the Netherlands is as high as that of the Chinese in the Philippines.

In Europe, the three countries with a notable Chinese community are France, Britain, and the Netherlands. In Britain, the total number of Chinese associations is more than two hundred, double the number of that in the

Netherlands; but the Chinese population in Britain is more than double that in the Netherlands.[4] In contrast, although it has a Chinese community as large as that of Britain, there are fewer than fifty Chinese associations in France (Live, 1998).

Moreover, among the Chinese communities in Europe, only the one in the Netherlands has successfully established a nationwide association federation, LFCON. The Dutch authorities accept it as the representative of the entire Chinese community. Comparatively speaking, the cooperation among the influential Chinese associations in the Netherlands is better than in other neighbouring countries. For instance, in economic and human resources, no individual association of the Netherlands can compete with the Association of French Residents of Indochinese Origin, set up in 1982,[5] or the Friendly Society of Teochew in France, set up in 1986.[6] Nevertheless, the sharp competition between these associations in France, and in the whole of Europe, has severely limited their impact. By contrast, the cooperation between ACV, *Fa Yin*, CSFN, HCS, and some other associations of the Netherlands have helped them to successfully rise to a leading position in the Chinese communities at the European level. The next point further substantiates this.

The second characteristic of the Chinese associations in the Netherlands is that they are active at the European level. The yearly Chinese sports meeting held by the Chinese associations in the Netherlands exemplifies this orientation. As I have outlined in Chapter VII, from 1988 onwards, almost every year several sports teams of Chinese immigrants from other European countries were invited to join the games in Amsterdam. In 1994, a Worldwide Overseas Chinese Sports Invitational Tournament was held, and more than one thousand contestants and supporters came from Europe, Asia, and America to attend.

The active roles played by some Chinese associations in the Netherlands to push the establishment of EFCO and to support its development serves as another example. As was outlined before, ACV is among the few key initiators of EFCO. Its official opening ceremony as well as several preparatory meetings were held in Amsterdam and sponsored by the Chinese association leaders in the Netherlands. In addition, one of the Chinese association leaders became the first chairman of EFCO. According to the constitution of EFCO, its annual meeting will be held in every European country where it has member associations; the association(s) that hold(s) the annual meeting should take care of the financial arrangements and, as a response, one representative elected by the host associations will take the position as EFCO chairman until the next annual meeting. Since few Chinese associations in Europe have steady financial income and most rely on the contributions of their leaders, it is a heavy burden to hold an annual meeting that may be attended by several hundred people. In 1996, due to a shortage of financial resources and some internal contradictions, no association wanted to hold the fifth annual meeting of EFCO. Then, to maintain the integrity of EFCO, its member associations in the Netherlands took over the responsibility for a second time.[7]

In addition, during 1997 and 1998, when the Chinese association leaders in the Netherlands not only took over the position of chairman but also formed the fifth core of EFCO committee, EFCO successfully established contacts with the European Commission for the first time. On 6 July 1998, the representatives of the European Commission received a delegation headed by the current chairman of EFCO and comprising seven other leaders, four of whom were from the Netherlands. At the meeting, the delegation presented an official letter together with "A Report on the Chinese Community in Europe" to the vice-president of the European Commission. Their purpose was multifold: to present a general picture of the Chinese who live in the European Union; to call for proper attention to their presence; and particularly to highlight their human and economic potential for the European Union and the obstacles in the way of its full realization. At the end of the meeting, the representative of the European Commission said:[8]

> From now on, the relationship between the Chinese community in Europe and the European Commission has opened a new page. We hope one book will be written.

Although the above quoted speech is more than anything else a diplomatic expression, the relevant Chinese association leaders, particularly the leaders coming from the Netherlands, were very pleased and very proud of their achievement. They moreover regard this meeting as a symbol that EFCO has, finally, been recognized by the European Commission as the general representative of the Chinese immigrant community in Europe. EFCO chairman said to me afterwards:

> Now, no matter whether others [i.e., the Chinese association leaders in other European countries] agree or not, we Chinese associations in the Netherlands have in fact formed the most important pillar of EFCO. Without our contributions, EFCO could not exist, let alone be accepted by the European Commission.

Their ambitions, as well as their efforts, to become the representatives and leaders of all of the Chinese in Europe are obvious.

3 Power structures and the differences between the generations

It is a common trend among Chinese associations all over the world that their organizational approaches have become more diverse. Meanwhile, the internal power structures within certain Chinese immigrant communities, which are reflected in the leadership compositions and decision-making processes of the associations, have also undergone changes, although very often these changes are subtle and not very apparent.

In Chapter VI, I reported on the power structures of the Chinese associations in the Netherlands. When compared with the structures of the Chinese associations in Southeast Asia or North America, some similarities and differences can be observed.

About the *similarities*, no matter where the Chinese associations are, it is clear that the Chinese elites, or the successful Chinese business people, have acted as the principal leaders as well as the financial supporters of most of them. To put it differently, the leadership in an influential association is allied with the success or failure of the person in question, and the associations are also ranked in prestige terms by type and size. It is normal for the ability of a general meeting to make decisions to be an empty shell; the real power lies in the hands of a few key leaders of each association. In addition, although most voluntary associations regularly hold elections for its committee members, some are merely a formality. The phenomenon I have described in Chapter VI can be observed among the ethnic Chinese communities in many other countries, that is, establishing one's own association has been accepted as a democratic right; however, an authoritarian style of leadership is accepted as normal within the associations (cf. Crissman 1967; See, 1988; Wong, 1977, 1982; Wickberg, 1988, 1992, 1994).

About some *differences*, Wong's study on the social structure of the Chinese in Chinatown-New York has shown contradictions between the leading groups formed by different generations. In this case, a newly emerging leading group is formed by the supervisors or social workers in the social service agencies. They are second-generation Chinese who were raised and educated in the United States. Many of them realized that they could use their positions as lawyers, businessmen, or social workers to tap resources from the city, state, and federal governments for the betterment of their ethnic group. Some radical young Chinese-Americans even returned from the suburbs to Chinatown to organize their people to fight against "oppression." They wanted to be the principal intermediaries and lobbyists for the community, and they have made numerous attacks on the traditional leaders (Wong, 1982: 23-25).

Another study has shown similar findings. Having made a study of the large Chinatowns in the United States and Canada during the 1970s, Thompson also stressed the transition of leading powers. He clearly points out: "the majority of new and vigorous voluntary associations are composed of students and young professionals who occupy key roles in the ethnic communities"; moreover, "college students, young professionals, and social service workers constitute the 'new leadership' that is successfully challenging the old merchants for control of community decision making" (Thompson, 1980: 284).

In the case of Chinese associations in the Philippines, Wickberg noted the appearance of certain Western-derived associations. They are school alumni associations, Lions clubs, Chinatown fire brigades in Manila, and others.[9] Some are the outcome of the efforts of the second- and third-generation residents to seek new forms of associations. Being middle-class associations, they are useful for organizing social life and for business networking. Moreover, there are also Chinese human rights associations, for example, the *Kaisa para sa Kaunlaran* in Manila. Such being the case, "a political activist may find that an alumni association or Lions Club with enough members is equally useful as a political base." Hence, the leaders of these non-Chinese-type associations have become a new active leading group of the Chinese societies in the Philippines (Wickberg, 1994).

The above-described phenomena have not yet clearly emerged among the Chinese immigrants in the Netherlands. As was mentioned repeatedly, the Chinese community in the Netherlands is still dominated by first-generation immigrants. The voice of the second or third generation has not yet become strong enough. Up till now the existing nationwide associations organized by and for the Holland-born or Holland-educated generation have, to a great degree, kept organizing activities within their own circle. It is true that some of them are active in attending the yearly Chinese sports meetings that are organized by CSFN; some are willing to be volunteers to help the elderly Chinese; they have, however, formed a rather small group among the Holland-born Chinese youth. It has not yet become clear whether there are already younger persons who have aspirations to try to occupy a leading position in one of the well-known Chinese associations in the Netherlands. It is obvious that the expectations held and behaviours expressed by this new generation are rather different from their parents. While some may prefer to depart from the old organizing fashion of their parents, others may stick to their ethnic roots and try to reshape the existing Chinese associations. All of these potentials are in themselves an interesting topic but need a separate study. Nevertheless, the only thing I would like to point out herewith is that it will be some time before the Holland-born or Holland-educated Chinese will become a visible independent component among the Chinese leading group.

4 *Trans-ethnic integration in the association development*

Reviewing the recent trend of the Chinese association development all over the world, one interesting phenomenon is the tendency of trans-ethnic integration. This tendency can be observed from three orientations:

(i)   some Chinese associations have included non-ethnic Chinese people as the recipient of their services;

(ii) some Chinese have joined existing non-Chinese associations in the host society and have even become activists or leaders;

(iii) some local associations are organized by Chinese and local people together and sometimes with the people of other ethnic origins.

Relevant cases can be cited from the development of the Chinese associations in many different countries.

In Thailand, the *Hua Kiaw Poh Teak Tung Foundation*, a charity association set up by Chinese immigrants in 1897, has become the best known charity institution since the 1950s. It offers services to whoever is in need regardless of their ethnic origin. When a natural calamity has occurred in Thailand, it helps to provide relief to the people in the disaster area. Because there are children who are unable to go to school, a special foundation has been set up for granting funds to cover the cost of education. Paid for by the donations of its members and followers, it has established a 22-storey charity hospital in Bangkok; all destitute people can benefit from its services, although the hospital is still named "*Hua Kiaw*" (i.e., overseas Chinese).

In the Philippines, one of the major tasks taken up by some local Chinese associations has been helping destitute Filipinos. The project "To contribute school buildings for the rural Filipinos" is an example. From the end of the 1970s to the early 1990s, under the auspices of the biggest nationwide Chinese association, Federation of Filipino-Chinese Chambers of Commerce and Industry, the Chinese business people have altogether established 1,240 school buildings in rural areas throughout the Philippines. Another popularly welcomed activity taken up by the Chinese associations is to set up charity medical centres. By the early 1990s, local Chinese associations had established more than ten charity medical centres in Manila. In addition to normal medical services during workdays, these charity medical centers offer free medical services for the poor during weekends or holidays. The Chinese associations cover all costs of these special treatments.

The establishment of the Chinese sections of the International Association of Lions Clubs (Lions Clubs for short) is an example with worldwide significance. According to the relevant reports, the Chinese Lions Clubs are rather active in some cosmopolitan cities, such as Vancouver, Toronto, San Francisco, London and Manila. Most members of the Chinese Lions Clubs are professionals or middle-class people. They have initiated or joined various charity activities to serve the needy.

Comparatively speaking, the Chinese associations in the Netherlands still have their charity activities mainly aimed at either the needy among the Chinese in the Netherlands or in their home country. In their perception, the Netherlands is a prosperous welfare state. The Dutch government has set up comprehensive institutions to take care of all poor and needy people. In Chapter VII, I gave an example of a charity donation campaign organized by some Chinese associations in the Netherlands to help the Dutch victims of the flood in the spring of 1995. Nevertheless, it should also be regarded as a symbolic gesture. In other words, what they wanted was to express to the Dutch society their feelings of friendship and sympathy. By comparing the charity donations they made to their hometown with that to the Netherlands, the difference becomes obvious (cf. Chapter VII).

Among the Chinese associations in the Netherlands, two have affiliated themselves with Dutch associations. The first is HCS, a nationwide association of Chinese restaurateurs set up in 1985. HCS has become the Chinese section of the Dutch HORECA association. The second one is Network Chinese Volunteers, which affiliated itself to the Dutch Network Volunteer immediately after its establishment. It is worth noting that in addition to their initial purpose of integration, their potential of finding Dutch backing and proper funding sources has also functioned in choosing the affiliation target.

In the Netherlands today, associations founded by both Chinese and Dutch persons in collaporation can be found as well. One example is the *Vereniging voor Traditionele Chinese Geneeskunst in Nederland* (Association for Traditional Chinese Medical Science in the Netherlands), which was set up in 1995. The majority of its members are Chinese acupuncturists, but some Dutch acupuncturists are accepted as members as well. All leaders are Chinese acupuncturists, and most of the Dutch members were their students who learned the Chinese medical traditions from them.

The cases of individual Chinese immigrants (from mainland China, Taiwan, or Hong Kong) joining Dutch associations are few. Among my interviewees, only a couple of them clearly told me that they were members of certain Dutch associations or parties. For instance, among the initiators of CCRM, two are members of the Dutch political party CDA. One Dutch association for physicians has accepted some Chinese medical doctors.[10] Besides these, one businessman, who is also an active leader of one surname association in the Netherlands, told me that, except for the Chinese members who have re-emigrated from Southeast Asian countries, he is the first and only Chinese member of a local Lions Club in the Netherlands who has directly emigrated from China. In recent years he has twice made donations to help blind people and children suffering from cancer in the name of the Lions Club of the Netherlands. "You can never say 'no' to any requests made by the Lions Club if you have become its official member. Few Chinese dare to make such a promise," this interviewee said.[11] It seems that by now the trans-ethnic charity associations like the Lions Club have not yet been recognized or accepted by the Chinese in the Netherlands. Such a situation is quite different with that in Southeast Asian and North American countries.

In short, to organize voluntary associations based on trans-ethnic membership and targetted at their shared objectives has not yet become a visible trend among the Chinese in the Netherlands.

5 *Conjectures regarding the future*

From the brief comparisons illustrated above, I will try to present an outlook on the future development of the Chinese associations in the Netherlands. Hereinafter, I present a variety of reasonable conjectures.

(a) The Chinese associations in the Netherlands will still keep developing; more precisely, new associations will keep being founded, and the existing associations will keep reshaping themselves to meet the changing needs of the Chinese immigrants themselves and of the receiving and sending societies. There is a popular saying among the Chinese that "old bottles can be endowed with new wine." The model of establishing a voluntary association based on blood bond brought over from their original country is a kind of "old bottle." Through flexible adaptations, this model was adjusted to the changing environments, and it has catered to the changing requests of the immigrant community. In other words, a single association may be fragile and may be gone soon after its birth, but the general model of the Chinese associations is flexible and resilient. Because of this, various Chinese associations have maintained an active social image in Europe for about one hundred years and in Southeast Asia for more than two hundred years.

(b) The Chinese association leaders in the Netherlands will continue to struggle for a leading position at the European level. Because Europe is becoming increasingly united, the forward-looking Chinese association leaders have repeatedly stressed the need to participate in the decision-making process on migration and minority policies at the European level in order to help serve the interests of the Chinese immigrants. Some Chinese association leaders in the Netherlands are among this active group. In terms of their collective quality — e.g., their education, language fluency, knowledge and organizing ability, etc. — however, many cannot yet be qualified as fully competent to be European Chinese leaders. They are challenged by the developments of the Chinese associations at the European level, which is asking for qualified leaders with broader knowledge and vision.

(c) As time passes, the new locally-born or locally educated generation will become more active, and their visibility will be heightened among the Chinese associations in the Netherlands. Because the second generation is socialized, educated and trained in the receiving country, their organizational orientations show clear differences from that of their parents. Nevertheless, while some may prefer to depart from the old organizing fashion of their parents, others may stick to their ethnic roots and try to reshape the existing Chinese associations. Moreover, some will try to become the new representatives, or new intermediaries, of the entire Chinese community. This reality has appeared in both Southeast Asia and North America today. It will undoubtedly become a reality among the Chinese immigrant community in the Netherlands soon.

(d) The potential that China may become a global power in the next century will increasingly affect the development of the Chinese associations in the future. On the China side, its traditional focus on its emigrants abroad will be continued, such as preserving ethnic ties with the Chinese abroad by maintaining contacts, providing education to new generations born overseas, establishing economic cooperation with overseas Chinese entrepreneurs and business people, and encouraging investment in China. Furthermore, China will step up its contacts with overseas Chinese around the world and strengthen its efforts to adjust its relevant policies to meet the new demands arising among the Chinese overseas. This is evidenced

by the fact that more Chinese elites abroad have been chosen to serve as
a bridge between the Chinese governments and the Chinese residing
abroad. In 1996, 176 Chinese abroad were selected to be Overseas Delegates of the Overseas Chinese Affairs Commission of Taiwan. Meanwhile, in the *qiaoxiang* areas of mainland China, a few of the delegates of
the Chinese People's Political Consultative Conference at various levels
(from province to county) have been chosen from the villagers residing
abroad.[12] Almost all of these delegates are selected from Chinese association leaders. Among the Chinese association leaders in the Netherlands, at
least five of them have been chosen at some time as such delegates at the
country or provincial level either in mainland China or in Taiwan. It is
understandable that the social prestige of the Chinese associations abroad
would be heightened when their "association credit" has been further
legitimized in their country of origin.

(e) Finally, the Chinese associations in the Netherlands clearly will continue
to move within both their own ethnic environment and the wider society
and will benefit from their special position of straddling the two worlds.
Meanwhile, at the moment, more and more Chinese association leaders
are talking about integration of the Chinese into the Dutch society, but at
the same time they try to keep their ethnic community insulated to promote their own interests. The ethnic and cultural syncretism is a source of
strength. When Chinese associations as a collective institution are cultivat-
ing their shared ethnic culture and trying to highlight their potential for
both their sending and receiving countries, the ordinary Chinese people
will benefit from these efforts. Alongside the peaceful development of globalization, this orientation will become more popular and clearer to all
ethnic immigrants.

In sum, the development of the Chinese associations will not cease in the
near future and requires continued study. I hope the arguments presented in
this study can serve as some basis for further exploration of the topic. It is
obvious that a deeper insight into the social significance of the Chinese associations abroad can only be achieved from broader comparative research in
both practice and theory. I cherish this wish as a deeper ambition and will
take this study as a new starting point toward the future.

Abbreviations

ACB	*Amsterdam Centrum Buitenlanders* Amsterdam Centre for Foreigners 阿姆斯特丹外侨中心
ACV	*Algemene Chinese Vereniging in Nederland* General Association of Chinese in the Netherlands 旅荷华侨总会
AD	*Algemeen Dagblad* Universal Daily 大众日报
BiZa	*Ministerie van Binnenlandse Zaken* Ministry of the Interior 内政部
BLIH	*Stichting Buddha's Light International — Holland* International Association of Buddha's Light, Holland section 国际佛光会荷兰协会
CCRM	*Stichting Chinese Cultuur Recreatie en Maatschappelijk Werk* Foundation for Chinese Culture, Recreation and Social Work 荷兰中华互助会
CDA	*Christen Democratisch Appèl* Christian Democratic Appeal 基督教民主党
CER	*Vereniging Chinese ondernemers Rotterdam en omgeving* Association of Chinese entrepreneurs Rotterdam and environs 鹿特丹区华商会
CEME	*Stichting Evangelische Zending onder de Chinezen in Europa* The Chinese Evangelical Mission in Europe 旅欧华侨福音布道会
CHH	*Chung Hwa Hui* Chinese Association 中华会
Chinese Brug	*Stichting de Chinese Brug* Association of the Chinese Bridge 中侨社会服务中心

Chun Pah	*Chinese Landelijke Ouderen Vereniging 'Chun Pah' in Nederland* Chinese nationwide elders' association '*Chun Pah*' in the Netherlands 荷兰松柏联合总会
CIA	Central Intelligence Agency 中央情报局
CJO	*Chinese Jongeren Organisatie* Chinese Youth Organization 华裔青年会
COCA	*Vereniging van Chinese Ondernemers in Chinatown Amsterdam* Association of Chinese business people in Chinatown Amsterdam 阿姆斯特丹唐人街华商会
CPC	The Communist Party of China 中国共产党
CRM	*Ministerie van Cultuur, Recreatie en Maatschappelijk Werk* Ministry of Culture, Recreation and Social Work 文化康乐社会工作部
CSFN	*Stichting Chinese Sport Federatie in Nederland* Chinese Sports Federation in the Netherlands 全荷华人体育运动联合总会
EFCO	The European Federation of Chinese Organizations 欧洲华侨华人社团联合会
Fa Yin	*Chinese Vereniging in Nederland 'Fa Yin'* Chinese Association in the Netherlands 'Fa Yin' 旅荷华人联谊会
FWDLO	The Federation of Chinese Wushu, Dragon- and Lion-Dance Organizations in the Netherlands 荷兰武术龙狮总会
HCS	*Koninklijk verbond van ondernemers in het HORECA - en aanverwante bedrijf, sectie Chinees Indische bedrijven* Royal union of entrepreneurs in the Horeca and related businesses, Chinese-Indonesian business section 荷兰皇家中国饮食业公会
HORECA	hotel, restaurant and cafe 旅馆餐饮业
HYXSH	*Hua Yi Xie Shang Hui* Consultative Association of Chinese Descendants 华裔协商会

IB	*Intercultureel Beraad* Inter-cultural Deliberation Committee 跨文化研究会
KMT	Chinese *Kuo Min Tang* Party 中国国民党
KY	*Kangzhan yaoxun* Bulletin on resisting Japanese aggression 抗战要讯
LFCON	*Landelijke Federatie van Chinese Organisaties in Nederland* Nationwide Federation of Chinese Organizations in the Netherlands 全荷华人社团联合会
NCV	*Netwerk Chinese Vrijwilligers* Network Chinese Volunteers 华人义工网
NPC	The National People's Congress 中国全国人民代表大会
OCAC	The Overseas Chinese Affairs Commission, ROC 中华民国侨务委员会
OCW	*Ministerie van Onderwijs, Cultuur en Wetenschappen* Ministry of Education, Culture and Sciences 教育文化科学部
OKW	*Ministerie van Onderwijs, Kunsten en Wetenschappen* Ministry of Education, Arts and Sciences 教育艺术科学部
OSDA	Ou Sea District Association 瓯海同乡会
PRC	People's Republic of China 中华人民共和国
ROC	Republic of China 中华民国
THHK	*Tiong Hoa Hwee Koan* Chinese Association in Indonesia 中华会馆
TPGE	*Tai Pang Gemeenschap in Europa* Tai Pang Community in Europe 旅欧大鹏同乡会

Tung Lok	*Chinese Ouderen Vereniging 'Tung Lok'* Chinese Elders' Association '*Tung Lok*' 阿姆斯特丹老人同乐社
VWS	*Ministerie van Volkgezondheid, Welzijn en Sport* Ministry of Public Health, Welfare and Sports 民众健康福利体育部
Wa Lai	*Stichting Centrum 'Wa Lai'* Foundation Center 'Wa Lai' 华励中心
Wah Fook Wui	*Stichting Welzijnsbehartiging Chinezen Rotterdam Wah Fook Wui* Foundation for Welfare Promotion for the Chinese in Rotterdam 鹿特丹华人福利促进会
Wai Wun	*Chinese Landelijke Vrouwen Vereniging 'Wai Wun' in Nederland* Chinese nationwide women's association '*Wai Wun*' in the Netherlands 荷兰慧嫒会
WKWK	*Wah Kiu Wei Kun, Chineesche Vereeniging in Holland* *Wah Kiu Wei Kun,* Chinese association in Holland 荷兰华侨会馆
WVC	*Ministerie van Welzijn, Volkgezondheid en Cultuur* Ministry of Welfare, Public Health and Culture 福利健康文化部

Glossary

Chun Pah [松柏] Two evergreen trees, i.e., pine and cypress, which are often used to signify "good health and long life."

diqu [地区] prefecture

gei mianzi [给面子] Give face, meaning to show due respect to someone.

gong fu [功夫] A form of Chinese traditional physical culture

guanxi [关系] A popular Chinese term which means having special approaches and connections in order to attain one's objective.

guiqiao [归侨] Returned-emigrants from abroad.

haiwai guanxi [海外关系] Overseas relations, i.e., have relatives or contacts abroad.

Hakka [客家] Guest people. Han Chinese people, living in the mountainous region straddling the provinces of Fujian, Guangdong and Jiangxi, and speaking their own dialect. They have migrated from the Central Plains of China. Hence, their name "Guest people."

HORECA [旅馆及餐饮业] A Dutch abbreviation meaning hotel, restaurant and cafe.

Huaqiao [华侨] Overseas Chinese or Chinese overseas. Originally, it meant those Chinese who sojourn abroad, but does not include settlers. Contemporarily, it simply refers to Chinese who have the permanent right to reside in their adopted country but retain their Chinese citizenship, including the citizenship of the People's Republic of China, Republic of China (Taiwan), and the Hong Kong Special Administration Region.

Huaren [华人] It refers to the Chinese who have settled down somewhere outside of China and have also obtained foreign citizenship.

Huaqiao-Huaren [华侨华人] A general term to combine the above-mentioned two groups of people together.

Huaqiao huzhuhui [华侨互助会] Overseas Chinese mutual aid association.

Huayi [华裔]	Chinese descendants who were born and have grown up outside of China or have been educated and socialized in the country that their parents or ancestors have adopted.
huiguan [会馆]	A generic name of Chinese traditional voluntary associations which are normally organized on the basis of shared provenance, clan, or similar occupation.
liuxuesheng group [留学生群体]	Originally, this term meant Chinese students studying abroad. Nowadays, this term includes not only those Chinese students who are studying abroad, but also those who finished their studies and now are working there. This term very often even includes their family members. Instead of a simple label indicating someone's temporary and transitional status, *liuxuesheng* has come to denote a fixed social identity. Once labeled *liuxuesheng*, they are willing to keep this social identity.
Putonghua [普通话]	standard Chinese language
qiaojuan [侨眷]	Overseas Chinese dependant[s] and relatives
qiaowu [侨务]	affairs related to *Huaqiao* and *qiaojuan*
qiaowu ganbu [侨务干部]	officials who are in charge of *qiaowu*
qiaoxiang [侨乡]	Chinese regions of large-scale outmigration to abroad.
qin peng hao you [亲朋好友]	A popular Chinese term meaning "relatives and good friends."
san cong si de [三从四德]	The three obediences and the four virtues. *San cong* means that a woman of good behaviour must obey her father before marriage, obey her husband during her marriage, and obey her son(s) in widowhood. The four virtues are fidelity, physical charm, propriety in speech, and skillfulness in needlework and household work.
Taijiquan [太极拳]	A kind of traditional Chinese fitness exercise to achieve harmony of body and mind.
tongxianghui [同乡会]	An association set up on the basis of shared provenance. Or, in other words, a district-of-origin-related association.
tung lok [同乐]	It is a Cantonese term meaning to share happiness together.
wu shu [武术]	A kind of martial arts such as shadowboxing, swordplay, etc., formerly cultivated for self-defense, now a form of physical culture.

xiang [乡]	The Chinese government is organized in five hierarchical levels: country [*guojia*, 国家], province [*sheng*, 省], prefecture [*diqu*, 地区], county [*xian*, 县] in rural areas or urban districts [*qu*, 区] in urban areas, and lastly township [*xiang*, 乡] in rural areas or street [*jiedao*, 街道] in urban areas. One *xiang* usually consists of several villages [*cun*, 村] with one town as its center.
xianqi liangmu [贤妻良母]	sweet wife and virtuous mother
Zhuangyuan [状元]	The best one. In ancient China, under the traditional imperial examination system, "*Zhuangyuan*" is the title conferred on the examinee who came first in the highest imperial examination. In modern China, "*Zhuangyuan*" has been converted to name the best one in any field.

Chinese associations in
the Netherlands (1947-1997)
(Founding years and names)[1]

1947
Algemene Chinese Vereniging in Nederland   旅荷华侨总会

1960s
Algemene Overzee Chinese Vereniging in Nederland[2]

       荷兰华侨总会

1964
Vereniging van Chinese Restaurants in Holland[3]   中国餐馆同业公会

1974
Stichting Evangelische Zending onder de Chinezen
    in Europa

       旅欧华侨福音布道会

1975
Chinese Christelijke Contact Groep   荷兰华人基督徒联络社

1976
Chinese Vereniging in Nederland "Fa Yin"   旅荷华人联谊会
Chinese Sportclub "On Hang"   安恒体育会

1977
Vereniging "Inisiatip"   海牙印尼华人联谊会
Helan Huaqiao Xiehui   荷兰华侨协会

1980
Chinese Sportclub Lun Fat   联发体育会
H.K.77 Sport Vereniging   东联体育会
Stichting Evangelische Zending onder de
    Utrechtse Kerk

       旅欧华侨福音布道会
       Utrecht 教会
De Veiendenkring Lian Yi Hui   印尼华人联谊会

1981
Eindhoven Chinese Christian Church   华人基督教会
                                                      (Eindhoven)

1982
Peranakan Vriendenkring   印尼华人联友社
Chinese Kung-fu Vereniging   中华体育会
Gemeenschap van Chinese-Vietnamese
Vluchtelingen in Nederland   荷兰越南华裔联谊会

1983
Chinese Jongeren Sportclub in Amsterdam   阿姆斯特丹青年体育会
Amsterdam Lutherse Jeugd Club voor Chinezen   阿姆斯特丹青年团契
Vereniging Chinese Ondernemers Rotterdam
    en Omgeving   鹿特丹区华商会

1984
Stichting Fine Eastern Restaurants   东方美食协会 [4]
Tai Pang Gemeenschap in Europa   旅欧大鹏同乡会
Yung Kwang Association in Holland   荷兰荣光联谊会
Stichting Chinese Cultuur Recreatie en Maat-
    schappelijkwerk   荷兰中华互助会
Stichting Chinese Cultuur en Maatschappelijk
    werk Waterland-Zaanstreek   荷兰华特兰华侨会
H.K.Y.L.T.M. Association[5]   元屯区旅荷华人协会
Stichting Chinese Gemeenschap in Tilburg   堤堡华人基金会

1985
Koninklijk verbond van ondernemers in het
    HORECA – en aanverwante bedrijf, sectie
    Chinees Indische bedrijven   荷兰皇家饮食业公会中印饮食业分会
Stichting Family Tang in Nederland   旅荷华侨邓氏宗亲会
Stichting Chinese Sport Federatie in Nederland [6]   全荷华人体育运动总会
Chinese Cooking Arts Club   中荷食雕协会
Stichting Chinese Samenleving Eindhoven   安多芬华人协会
Stichting Familie Man   荷兰华侨文氏宗亲会

1986
Chinese Buddhist Center Amsterdam   阿姆斯特丹观音堂佛教中心
Breda Lutherse Jeugd Club voor Chinezen   路德宗青年团契
                                                     (Breda)
Chinese Stichting Gemeenschap Eindhoven   华人基金会
                                                     Eindhoven 分会
Algemene Chekiang Chinese Vereniging in
    Nederland   旅荷浙江青田同乡会

Algemene Chinese Wu Shu Federatie in Nederland 旅荷华侨武术协会
The Hong Kong Civic Association in the
    Netherlands 荷兰香港公民协会
Vereniging van Gediplomeerde Chinese Koks 荷兰中厨协会
Vereniging Oriental Cuisine Holland 荷兰东方厨艺协进会
Limburgse Chinese Vereniging 旅荷林堡华侨总会
Familie Pang Vereniging in Nederland 旅欧荷兰彭氏宗亲会

1987
Stichting Chinese Belangen 华人协会
Stichting Centrum "Wa Lai" 华励中心
Chinese Coordination Centre of World
Evangelism in Europe, Promotion Centre in
    the Netherlands 关怀欧洲区华福工作荷兰小组
Stichting de Chinese Brug 中桥社会服务中心
Hua Yi Xie Shang Hui[7] 华裔协商会
Chinese Vrouwen Vereniging in Eindhoven 安多芬旅荷华侨妇女会
Stichting Landelijke Federatie van Chinese
Organisaties in Nederland 全荷华人社团联合会

1988
Vereniging van Chinese Ondernemers in
    Chinatown Amsterdam 阿姆斯特丹唐人街华商会
Stichting Promotie Drakenbootraces Nederland 荷兰龙舟推广协会
Association of Chinese Students in the Netherlands 中国留荷同学会
Rotterdamse Chinese Vrouwen Vereniging 鹿特丹华人妇女会
Regionale Chinezen Werkgroep Noordoost Brabant
    Brabant 地区华人活动中心
Fuyin Chuanbo Xiehui 福音传播协会

1989
Chinese Landelijke Ouderen Vereniging "Chun Pah"
    in Nederland 荷兰松柏联合总会
Stichting Holland Hua Shia 荷兰华夏文康策进会
Stichting "Taiwan Shian-Chin" in the Netherlands 荷兰台湾乡亲联谊会
Alliance for a Democratie China in Nederland
    中国民主联合阵线荷兰分部
Minzhen Minlian Helan Fenbu 民阵民联荷兰分部
Ouzhou Zhongguo Minyun Gongzuozhe Xiehui
    欧洲中国民运工作者协会

1990
Benelux "Tsung-Tsin" Vereniging 荷比卢崇正总会
Netherlands Xiangqi association 荷兰中国象棋协会
Stichting Chen Hui 晨曦会

1991
Chinese Landelijke Vrouwen Vereniging "Wai
  Wun" in Nederland 荷兰慧媛会
Den Haagse Chinese Vrouwen Vereniging 海牙华人妇女会
Stichting Lai Yin voor Chinese Vrouwen in
  Provincie Utrecht 乌特勒支励妍妇女会
The Association of Chinese Writers in Benelux 荷比卢写作人协会
Vereniging Chinese Bewoners in Rotterdam 鹿特丹华裔居民协会
Canguan Dongzhu Zhanwang Hui 餐馆东主展望会

1992
Vereniging Familie Choi in Benelux

　　　　　　　　　　　旅荷比卢深圳市蔡屋围同乡会
Dam Wah Studiefonds 丹华奖学基金会

1993
Chinese Vrouwen Vereniging Maastricht 荷兰马城雅贤妇女会
Arnhemse Chinese Vrouwen Vereniging 安恒华人妇女会
Stichting Yao Yi Trefcentrum Chinezen Utrecht 乌特勒支华人友谊中心
Chinese Ouderen Vereniging "Tung Lok" 阿姆斯特丹老人同乐社
Stichting Leeuwendans Rotterdam 鹿特丹华人醒狮会
Chinese Vrouwen Vereniging Amsterdam en
  Noord Holland 阿姆斯特丹暨北荷兰省华人妇女会

1994
Chinese Jongeren Organisatie 新一代
The Asian Restaurants[8] 荷兰亚洲美食协会
Stichting China law 荷华法律顾问协会
Chinese Ouderen Vereniging "Kie Ling" 鹿特丹耆年会
Internationale Vereniging voor Oosterse kunst
  Onderzoek 国际东方美术研究会欧洲总会
Vereniging vor Noord-Chinezen in Holland 旅荷东北华人同乡会
Stichting Buddha's Light International — Holland[9] 国际佛光会荷兰协会
Dutch association for Chinese Youth 荷青总会
Stichting Chinese Cultuur, Muziek en Kunst
  Nederland 中华文化音乐艺术协会

1995
Vereniging van Wen Chow Chinezen in Nederland 荷兰温州同乡会
Fonds of Chekiang Chinese Vereniging in
  Nederland 荷兰青田同乡会基金会
Vereniging voor Traditionele Chinese Geneeskunst
  in Nederland 荷兰中医药学会
Stichting Caihong 彩虹中西文化交流活动中心
Stichting Chinese Kunst in Holland 荷兰中国艺术家协会
Ouzhou Zhongguo Shuhua Yuan 欧洲中国书画院

Helan Zhongyi Xuehui	荷兰中医学会
Stichting China Link	中荷纽带基金会
Stichting Chinese Muziek	比荷音乐社
Vereniging van Yong Ka Chinezen in Nederland	旅荷浙江永嘉同乡会

1996

Stichting Europese Bijzondere Leerstoel TCM	欧洲中医疑难病研究学会
Yau Luen Vereniging	荷兰北部友联会
Stichting Welzijnsbehartiging Chinezen Rotterdam Wah Fook Wui	鹿特丹华人福利促进会
Quan He Zhongwen Jiaoyu Jijinhui	全荷中文教育基金会
Helan Huaren Bao Diao Tongmeng	荷兰华人保钓同盟
Stichting Global Chinese Art	荷兰环球中国艺术家协会
Vereniging Wu Shu in Noord Holland	北荷兰省武术龙狮协会
Netwerk Chinese Vrijwilligers	荷兰华人义工网

1997

Chinese Vrouwen Vereniging Tiburg	Tilburg 华人妇女会
Federation of Chinese Wu Shu, Dragon- and Lion-Dance Organizations in the Netherlands	荷兰武术龙狮总会
Lü He Rui'an Jiaoyu Jijinhui	旅荷瑞安教育基金会
Fine Eastern Restaurants in the Netherlands[10]	荷兰东方美食集团
Association for Chinese Engineers and Scholars in the Netherlands	荷兰华人学者工程师协会
Lü He Fujian Tongxiang Lianhe Zonghui[11]	旅荷福建同乡联合总会

APPENDIX IV

Bibliography

ACB & LFCON
1994 *Karakters in Het Laagland, De positie van Chinezen in Nederland: Situatieschets, Knelpunten en Aanbevelingen* [Characters in the Lowland, the position of Chinese in the Netherlands: Situation Sketch, Bottle-necks and Recommendations]. Printed in Amsterdam.

ACV Bulletin [华侨通讯]
1977-1998 "华侨通讯" [Overseas Chinese Bulletin]. A Chinese bulletin published by ACV in Amsterdam.

ACV [旅荷华侨总会]
1997 "旅荷华侨总会五十周年纪念特刊"[Special issue to celebrate ACV's 50th anniversary (1947-1997)]. Printed in Amsterdam.

Alund, Aleksandra
1994 'Ethnicity and modernity: on "tradition" in modern cultural studies'. In Rex & Drury, ed., pp. 57-68.

Anderson, Benedict R. O'G.
1991 *Imagined Communities, Reflection on the Origin and Spread of Nationalism*. Revised edition. London: Verso.
1992 *Long-distance Nationalism, World Capitalism and the Rise of Identity Politics*, Amsterdam: CASA – Centre for Asian Studies Amsterdam.

Ang, Ine
1993 'To be or not to be Chinese: diaspora, culture and postmodern ethnicity'. *Southeast Asian Journal of Social Science*. V. 21, No. 1, pp. 1-17.

Bastenier, Albert
1994 'Immigration and the ethnic differentiation of social relations in Europe'. In Rex & Drury, ed., pp. 48-56.

Baviera, Aileen, S. P. & Teresita Ang See, eds.
1992 *China across the Seas: the Chinese as Filipinos*. Quezon City: Philippine Association for Chinese Studies.

Bedrijfschap HORECA [Business branch HORECA]
1992 *Chinees-Indische restaurants: Onderzoeksresultaten* [Chinese-Indonesian restaurants: research results]. The Hague: Bedrijfschap HORECA.

Benmayor, Rina & Andor Skotnes
1994 'Some reflections on migration and identity'. In Benmayor & Skotnes, eds., pp. 1-18.

Benmayor, Rina & Andor Skotnes (special editors)
1994 *Migration and Identity*. New York: Oxford University Press.

Benton, Gregor & Frank N. Pieke, eds.
1998 *The Chinese in Europe*. Houndmills: Macmillan Press Ltd.

Benton, Gregor & Hans Vermeulen, eds.

1987 *De Chinezen: Migranten in de Nederlandse Samenleving* [The Chinese: Migrants in the Dutch Society]. Muiderberg: Coutinho.

Blussé, Leonard (Translated from Dutch into Chinese by Zhuang Guotu & Cheng Shaogang

1989 "中荷交往史"[A History of the Relationship between China and Holland]. Printed by Lukoudian chubanshe (no city name is mentioned).

Blythe, W. L.

1969 *The Impact of Chinese Secret Societies in Malaya: A Historical Study*. Oxford: Oxford University Press.

Bonacich, Edna

1973 'A theory of middleman minorities'. *American Sociological Review*. Vol. 38, pp. 583-594.

Bottomley, Linda Basch, Nina Glick Schiller & Christina Szanton Blanc

1994 *Nations Unbound: Transnational Projects, Postcolonial Predicaments and Deterritorialized Nation-States*. Langhorne, PA: Gordon and Breach.

Bourdieu, Pierre (translated by Richard Nice)

1986 'The forms of capital'. In Richardson ed., pp. 241-258.

1990 *The Logic of Practice*. Cambridge: Polity Press.

Brown, Judith M. & Rosemary Foot, eds.

1994 *Migration: The Asian Experience*. Oxford: St. Martin's Press.

Calboun, Craig & Edward Lipuma & Moishe Postone, eds.

1993 *Bourdieu: Critical Perspectives*. Cambridge: Polity Press.

Calboun, Craig

1993 'Habitus, field, and capital: the question of historical specificity'. In Calboun et al., pp. 61-88.

Campani, Giovanna

1994 'Ethnic networks and associations, Italian mobilisation and immigration issues in Italy'. In Rex & Drury, ed., pp. 143-147.

Carchedi, Francesco & Marica Ferri

1998 'The Chinese presence in Italy: dimensions and structural characteristics'. In Benton & Pieke eds., pp. 261-277.

Castles, Stephen & Mark J. Miller

1993 *The Age of Migration, International Population Movements in the Modern World*. Houndmills: the MacMillan Press.

Cator, Writser Jans

1936 *The Economic Position of the Chinese in the Netherlands Indies*. Oxford: Kemp Hall Press Ltd.

CCRM (Stichting Chinese Cultuur Recreatie en Maatschappelijk Werk)

1994 *Integratie is mogelijk door Goede Samenwerking, speciale uitgave ter gelegenheid van het tienjarig bestaan van de Stichting CCRM* [Integration is possible through Good Cooperation, special issue on the occasion of the CCRM's tenth anniversary of founding]. Printed by CCRM in Rotterdam.

Chen, Bin [陈彬]

1991 "荷兰华侨简史"[A brief history of the Chinese in the Netherlands].

Personal reminiscences. Printed by Helan songbai lianhe zonghui in Rotterdam.

Chen, Murong [陈慕榕] ed.

1990 "青田县志"[Qingtian county chronicles]. Hangzhou: Zhejiang renmin chubanshe.

Chen, Wanfa [陈万发]

1989 "受英文教育者眼中的宗乡总会" [Chinese clan and regional associations in the eyes of the English-educated]. In 总会三年 [Three years of the Singapore Federation of Chinese clan and regional associations], pp. 50-52. Printed in Singapore by the Federation.

Chen, Xuewen [陈学文] ed.

1991 "浙江省华侨研究历史论丛"[Selected papers on the history of Zhejiang migrants abroad]. No publishing house.

Chineesche Zeeliedenbond [Association of Chinese Seamen]
(Edited and published by Het West-Europeesch Bureau van het All-Chineesch-Zeemans-Verbond)

1934 *Menschenhandel in Europa* [Human-trade in Europe]. No publishing house.

Christiansen, Flemming

1998 'Chinese identity in Europe'. In Benton & Pieke, eds., pp. 42-63.

Chun Pah [荷兰松柏联合总会]

1998 "我心安处就家乡"[Waar ik me prettig voel, noem ik mijn thuis; Where I feel comfortable, there is my home]. Printed by Helan songbai lianhe zonghui in Rotterdam.

Comber, L.

1959 *Chinese Secret Societies in Malaya: A survey of the Triad Society from 1800-1900*. Singapore: Donald Moore.

Cornelius, Wayne A., Philip L. Martin & James F. Hollifield

1994 *Controlling Immigration, A Global Perspective*. Stanford: Stanford University Press.

Coser, Lewis A. ed.

1976 *The Idea of Social Structure, Papers in Honor of Robert K. Merton*. New York: Harcourt Brace Jovanovich.

Crissman, Lawrence W.

1967 'The segmentary structure of urban overseas Chinese communities'. *Man*, Vol. 2, No. 1, pp. 185-204.

Cushman, Jennifer & Wang Gungwu, eds.

1988 *Changing Identities of the Southeast Asian Chinese Since World War II*. Hong Kong: Hong Kong University Press.

De Uitkijk [Lookout]

1909-1936 *De Uitkijk* [Lookout]. Maandblad van de Nederlandsche Zeemans Vereeniging "Volharding" [a monthly review published by the Dutch seamen's association "*Volharding*"].

Dieleman, Frans

1993 'Multicultural Holland: myth or reality?' In King, ed., pp. 118-135.

Doomernik, Jeroen, Rinus Penninx & Hans van Amersfoort
1997   *A Migration Policy for the Future: Possibilities and Limitations.* Published by Migration Policy Group [Brussels].

Drury, Beatrice
1994   'Ethnic mobilisation: some theoretical considerations'. In Rex & Drury, ed., pp. 13-22.

EFCO (European Federation of Chinese Organizations)
1999   *The Chinese Community in Europe.* Printed in the Netherlands.

Entzinger, Han
1993   'Changing policy approaches and scenarios for the future'. In Entzinger et al., eds., pp. 149-164.

Entzinger, Han. Jacques Siegers & Frits Tazelaar, eds.
1993   *Immigrant Ethnic Minorities in the Dutch Labour Market, Analyses and Policies.* Amsterdam: Thesis Publishers.

Fa Yin [旅荷华人联谊会]
1996   "旅荷华人联谊会成立二十周年纪念特刊暨旅荷华人联谊会中文学校第十届毕业典礼纪念 特刊" [Special issue celebrating Fa Yin's 20th anniversary and the 10th graduation ceremony of Fa Yin Chinese school]. Printed in Amsterdam.

Fallers, L. A. ed.
1967   *Immigrants and Associations.* The Hague: Mouton.

Fei, Xiaotong [费孝通]
1992a "温州行" [Visit to Wenzhou]. In Fei, 1992b, pp. 285-304 (originally written in 1986).
1992b "费孝通学术著作自选集"[Self-selected Works of Fei Xiaotong]. Beijing: Beijing Normal University press.

Fijalkowski, Jurgen
1994   'Conditions of ethnic mobilisation: the German case'. In Rex & Drury, ed., pp. 123-134.

Fox, Richard G. ed.
1991   *Recapturing Anthropology, Working in the Present.* Santa Fe, New Mexico: School of American Research Press.

Freedman, Maurice
1967   'Immigrants and associations: Chinese in 19th century Singapore'. In Fallers, ed., pp. 17-48.
1979   *The Study of Chinese Society.* Stanford: Stanford University Press.

Galen, Kees van
1987   'Dorp zonder naam: de Chinezen uit Indonesie' [Village without name: the Chinese from Indonesia]. In Benton & Vermeulen, eds, pp. 132-146.
1989   *Geschiedenis van de Chung Hwa Hui (1911-1962): Indo-Chinese Studenten en Peranakan Politiek in Nederland* [History of Chung Hwa Hui (1911-1962): Indonesian Chinese students and Peranakan Politics in the Netherlands]. M. A. Thesis. Amsterdam: Instituut voor Moderne Aziatische Geschiedenis, Universiteit van Amsterdam.

Government Information Office, Executive Yuan, Republic of China, eds.
1988 *The Republic of China 1988, A Reference Book.* Taipei: Hilit Publishing Company.

Greeley, Andrew M.
1971 *Why Can't They be Like Us? America's White Ethnic Groups.* New York: E. P. Dutton & Co. Inc.

Groenendijk, C.
1987 'De rechtspositie van Chinezen in Nederland'[The legal status of the Chinese in the Netherlands]. In Benton & Vermeulen eds., pp. 85-117.

Guo Diqian [郭迪乾], Yun Changchao [云昌潮] & Lin Qian [林谦], eds.
1960 "泰国华侨社团史辑"[Historical documents of the Chinese associations in Thailand]. Bangkok: Zhongxing wenhua chubanshe.

Heek, F. van
1936 *Chineesche Immigranten in Nederland* [Chinese immigrants in the Netherlands]. Amsterdam: N. V. J. Emmering's Uitgevers MIJ.

HORECA Nederland (Koninklijk Horeca Nederland sector Chinees-Indische Bedrijven, Woerden & Hoge Hotelschool Maastricht)
1997 *Imago en Werkwijze Chinees-Indische Bedrijven, Onderzoek i.o.v. Koninklijk Horeca Nederland Sector Chinees-Indische Bedrijven* [The Image and Working Method of the Chinese-Indonesian Restaurants, A Study commissioned by the Chinese-Indonesian Restaurants Section of Royal Horeca in the Netherlands].

INFO Krant "半月报"
1984-1996 "半月报"[*De Chinese half-maandelijkse INFO Krant*; Chinese half-monthly INFO newspaper]. Published by the CCRM in Rotterdam.

Justitie, Ministerie van
1932 Memorandum, No. 43647. The Hague.

Katholiek Sociaal-Kerkelijk Instituut
1957 *De groep van Chinese afkomst in Nederland* [The group of Chinese origin in the Netherlands]. *Rapport* 168 [Report 168]. Printed in The Hague.

Kearney, M.
1995 'The local and the global: the anthropology of globalization and transnationalism'. *Annual Review Anthropology*. Vol. 24, pp. 547-565.

King, Russell
1993 'European international migration 1945-90: a statistical and geographical overview'. In King, ed., pp. 19-39.

King, Russell, ed.
1993 *Mass Migrations in Europe, the Legacy and the Future.* London: Belhaven Press.

Kleinen, John (working together with Martin Custers).
1987 'De Hoa's: Chinese vluchtelingen uit Vietnam' [The Hoas: Chinese refugees from Vietnam]. In Benton & Vermeulen, eds, pp. 170-180.

Koser, Khalid & Helma Lutz, eds.
1998 *The New Migration in Europe, Social Constructions and Social Realities.* Houndmills: Macmillan Press Ltd.

Kotkin, Joel
1993 *Tribes: How Race, Religion and Identity Determine Success in the New Global Economy*. New York: Random House.
KY "抗战要讯"[Kangzhan Yaoxun]
1937-1939 "抗战要讯"[Bulletin on resisting Japanese aggression]. Edited and published by The Dutch Chinese association to resist Japanese aggression and save China. The original copies are kept in the Library of the Sinology Institute, Leiden University, the Netherlands.
Lai, David Chuenyan
1988 *Chinatowns, Towns within Cities in Canada*. Vancouver: University of British Columbia Press.
Lever-Tracy, Constance, David Ip & Noel Tracy
1996 *The Chinese Diaspora and Mainland China, an Emerging Economic Synergy*. Houndmills: Macmillan Press Ltd.
Leydesdorff, Selma (translated by Frank Heny)
1994 *We Live with Dignity, the Jewish Proletariat of Amsterdam, 1900-1940*. Michigan: Wayne State University Press.
Li, Haoran [李浩然]
1996 "温州新跃迁"[New Growth of Wenzhou]. Shanghai: Shanghai shehui kexueyuan chubanshe.
Li, Minghuan [李明欢]
1989 "阿姆斯特丹唐人街的历史变迁"[A history of Chinatown Amsterdam]. In [Beijing] "华侨华人历史研究"[*Overseas Chinese History Studies*], 4: 31-39.
1990 'The Dutch are the European Chinese — Reflections'. In *Etnofoor* [Amsterdam], 2: 99-115.
1995a "当代海外华人社团研究" [A study of Contemporary Chinese Associations Abroad]. Xiamen: Xiamen daxue chubanshe.
1995b 'Living among Three Walls? The Peranakan Chinese in the Netherlands.' *Asian Culture* 19, pp. 43-54.
1996 '"To Get Rich Quickly in Europe!" a report of fieldwork in Wenzhou *Qiaoxiang*.' Paper presented for the workshop "European Chinese and Chinese Domestic Migration" at Oxford University.
1997 "温州华侨与温州建设" [Wenzhou emigrants and the development of Wenzhou]. In [Shanghai] "近代中国" [Modern China], 8: 27-39.
1998 'Transnational links among the Chinese in Europe: a study on European-wide Chinese voluntary associations'. In Benton & Pieke, eds., 1998: 21-41.
Li, Xuemin [李学民] & Huang Kunzhang [???]
1987 "印尼华侨史" [A History of the Chinese in Indonesia]. Guangdong: Guangdong gaodeng jiaoyu chubanshe.
Li, Yih-Yuan [李亦园]
1970 "一个移殖的市镇，马来亚华人市镇生活的调查研究"[An Immigrant Town: Life in an Overseas Chinese Community in Southern Malaya]. Taipei: Institute of Ethnology, Academia Sinica.

Liao, Jianyu (translated from English into Chinese by Li Xuemin & Chen Xunhua)
1986 "爪哇土生华人政治" [Peranakan Chinese Politics in Java]. Beijing: Youyi Chuban gongsi.

Lim, Linda Y. C., & L. A. Peter Gosling, eds.
1983 *The Chinese in Southeast Asia: Identity, Culture and Politics.* Singapore: Maruzen Asia. 2 volumes.

Lin, Sen [林森] & Chen Weichuan [陈位传]
1986 "海牙宫遇女皇 "[To be received by the Dutch Queen in The Hague]. In "山海经" [Popular legends], published in Hangzhou. No. 1.

Lipuma, Edward
1993 'Culture and the concept of culture in a theory of practice'. In Calboun et al., pp. 14-34.

Liu, Boji [刘伯骥]
1981 "美国华侨史续编"[A History of Overseas Chinese in the United States, A Continuation]. Taiwan: Liming wenhua shiye gongsi.

Liu, Hong
1998 'Old linkages, new networks: the globalization of overseas Chinese voluntary associations and its implications'. In *The China Quaterly*, September, pp. 582-609.

Live, Yu-Sion
1998 'The Chinese community in France: immigration, economic activity, cultural organization and representations'. In Benton & Pieke, eds., pp. 96-124.

Lü Ou Huaqiao fuyin budaohui [旅欧华侨福音布道会]
1994 "旅欧华侨福音布道会成立二十周年纪念专刊" (1974-1994) [Commemorative book of the twentieth anniversary of the founding of the association for overseas Chinese evangelical missions in Europe (1974-1994)]. No publishing house.

Mak, Lau Fong
1981 *The Sociology of Secret Societies: A Study of Chinese Secret Societies in Singapore and Peninsular Malaysia.* Oxford: Oxford University Press.

Massey, Douglas S., Joaquin Arango, Graeme Hugo, Ali Kouaouci, Adela Pellegrino and J. Edward Taylor
1994 'An evaluation of international migration theory: the North American case'. *Population and Development Review*, 20 (4), pp. 699-751.

McBeath, Gerald A.
1973 *Political Integration of the Philippine Chinese.* Berkeley: Center for South and Southeast Asia Studies, University of California.

Mei, Xuhua [梅旭华]
1997 "半个世纪的奋斗历程：旅荷华侨总会五十年" [Half a century of struggle: ACV is fifty years today]. In ACV, 1997, pp. 36-45.

Merton, Robert K.
1968 *Social Theory and Social Structure,* New York: the Free Press; London: Collier-Macmillan Limited. Enlarged Edition.

Merton, Robert K. (Edited and with an introduction by Aaron Rosenblatt and Thomas T. Gieryn)
1982   *Social Research and the Practicing Professions*, Cambridge & Massachusetts: Abt Books.
Merton, Robert K. & Alice S. Kitt
1950   'Contributions to the theory of reference group behaviour'. In Robert K. Merton & Paul F. Lazarsfeld, eds, pp. 40-105.
Merton, Robert K. & Paul F. Lazarsfeld, eds.
1950   *Continuities in Social Research: Studies in the Scope and Method of the American Soldier*, Glencoe, Ill.: Free Press.
Meyer, Han
1983   *Operatie Katendrecht* [Operation Katendrecht]. Nijmegen: SUN.
Montanari, Armando & Antonio Cortese
1993   'Third world immigrants in Italy'. In King, ed., pp. 275-292.
Niew, Shong Tong [饶尚东]
1991   "文莱华族会馆史论" [A History of Chinese Clan Associations in Brunei Darussalam]. Singapore: Singapore Society of Asian Studies.
Nonini, Donald M.
1997   'Shifting identities, positioned imaginaries: transnational traversals and reversals by Malaysian Chinese'. In Ong & Nonini eds., pp. 203-227.
Nonini, Donald M. & Aihwa Ong
1997   'Chinese transnationalism as an alternative modernity'. In Ong & Nonini eds., pp. 3-33.
OCEYB (Overseas Chinese Economy Year Book editorial Committee) [华侨经济年鉴编辑委员会]
1968-1997   "华侨经济年鉴" [Overseas Chinese Economy Year Book]. Taipei: OCAC (the Overseas Chinese Affairs Commission).
Ong, Aihwa
1997   'Chinese modernity: narratives of nation and of capitalism'. In Ong & Nonini eds., pp. 171-202.
1999   *Flexible Citizenship, The Cultural Logics of Transnationality*. Durham & London: Duke University Press.
Ong, Aihwa & Donald M. Nonini, eds.
1997   *Ungrounded Empires, The Cultural Politics of Modern Chinese Transnationalism*. New York, London: Routledge.
Pan, Lynn
1990   *Sons of the Yellow Emporor, A History of the Chinese Diaspora*. Boston: Little, Brown and Company.
Pan, Mingzhi [潘明智] ed.
1996   "华人社会与宗乡会馆" [Chinese Society and Their Traditional Associations]. Singapore: Lingzi dazong chuanbo zhongxin.
Park, R. E., & E. W. Burgess
1921   *Introduction to the Science of Sociology*.
Peng, Song Toh [彭松涛] ed.
1983   "新加坡社团大观" [Directory of Associations in Singapore]. Singapore: Historical Culture Publishers.

Penninx, Rinus. Jeannette Schoorl & Carlo van Praag
1993 *The Impact of International Migration on Receiving Countries: the Case of the Netherlands.* ᵃᵐ/Lisse: Swets & Zeitlinger.

ina's overseas Chinese policies.' *China Information,*

en in Nederland [The position of the Chinese in the : Documentatiecentrum voor het Huidige China, Rijksuniversiteit Leiden.
enton
Netherlands.' In Benton & Pieke, eds, 1998: 125-

stulli and Other Stories, Form and Meaning in Oral te University of New York Press.

ic minorities and the transformation of social a so-called multi-cultural society-the case of rury, ed., pp. 30-37.
ed.
Multi-cultural Europe. England: Ipswich book Co.

multi-cultural societies'. In Rex & Drury, ed., pp. 5-12.
1994b 'Conclusion: the place of ethnic mobilisation in West European democracies'. In Rex & Drury, ed., pp. 155-165.
Richardson, John G., ed.
1986 *Handbook of Theory and Research for the Sociology of Education.* New York: Greenwood Press.
Rijkschroeff, B. R.
1998 *Etnisch Ondernemerschap, de Chinese horecasector in Nederland en in de Verenigde Staten van Amerika* [Ethnic Entrepreneurship, the Chinese Catering Business in the Netherlands and in the United States]. Capelle a/d Ijssel: Labyrint Publication.
Robertson, Roland
1992 *Globalization, Social Theory and Global Culture.* London: Sage Publication Ltd.
Rotterdam Police Report
1930 *Rapport, Rotterdam Centraal Bureau, Vreemdelingendienst* [Report, Rotterdam Central Bureau, Aliens Departmen]. Agenda No. 87/20 / 1930. No. 2254/13766.
1933 *Rapport, Hoofdbureau van Politie, Centrale Recherche* [Report, Police Headquaters, Central Investigation Department]. No. 4187.
Sassen, Saskia
1988 *The Mobility of Labor and Capital.* Cambridge: Cambridge University Press.

Schierup, Carl-Ulrik
1994 'Multi-culturalism and ethnic mobilisation: some theoretical considerations'. In Rex & Drury, ed., pp. 38-47.
Schultze, Gunther
1994 'The importance of associations and clubs for the identities of young Turks in Germany'. In Rex & Drury, ed., pp. 135-142.
See, Chinben
1988 'Chinese organizations and ethnic identity in the Philippines'. In Cushman & Wang eds., pp. 319-334.
Sijde, R. R. van der
1983 'Chinese-Indische restaurants' [Chinese-Indonesian restaurants]. The Hague: Bedrijfschap HORECA Brochures, no. 129.
Sinn, Elizabeth, ed.
1998 *The Last Half Century of Chinese Overseas*. Hong Kong: Hong Kong University Press.
Skeldon, Ronald, ed.
1994 *Reluctant Exiles? Migration from Hong Kong and the New Overseas Chinese*. Armonk, NY: M. E. Sharpe.
Skinner, William
1957 *Chinese Society in Thailand: An Analytical History*. Ithaca: Cornell University Press.
1958 *Leadership and Power in the Chinese Community of Thailand*. Ithaca: Cornell University Press.
Stonequist, Everett V.
1965 *The Marginal Man, a Study in Personality and Culture Conflict*. New York: Russell & Russell.
Tan, Chee-Beng
1995 'Chinese Associations in Kapit'. *Asian Culture* 19, pp. 29-40.
Tan, Swan Bing
1986 'Geschiedenis en Ontwikkeling van de Peranakan in Nederland van 1911 tot 1940' [History and development of the Peranakan in the Netherlands from 1911 to 1940]. In *Eerste Minisymposium Vriendenkring Lian Yi Hui: Geschiedenis en Taal van de Peranakan in Nederland*. Printed in Rijswijk, Holland.
Thomas, William L. & Florian Znaniecki, Edited and abridged by Eli Zaretsky
1984 *The Polish Peasant in Europe and America*. Urbana & Chicago: University of Illinois Press. (Originally published in 5 volumes between 1918 and 1920.)
Thompson, Paul
1978 The Voice of the Past. Oxford: Oxford University Press.
1994 'Preface'. In Benmayor & Skotness, pp. v-vi.
Thompson, Richard H.
1980 'From kinship to class: a new model of urban overseas Chinese social organization'. *Urban Anthropology*, Vol. 9, No. 3, pp. 265-293.

Tian, Fang [田方 Chen Yiyun [陈一筠]
1986 "中国移民史论" [A Study of the Chinese Migration history]. Beijing: Zhishi chubanshe.

Tonkin, Elizabeth
1992 *Narrating Our Past, the Social Construction of Oral History*. Cambridge: Cambridge University Press.

Topley, M.
1967 'The emergence and social function of Chinese religious associations in Singapore'. In Fallers ed., pp. 49-82.

Townsend, James
1967 *Political Participation in Communist China*. Berkeley: University of California Press.

Tseng, Frank W. F.
1983 *Van Minderheid tot Minderheid: Etniciteit en Verandering onder Surinaamse Chinezen* [From minority to minority: ethnicity and change among Surinamese Chinese]. M. A. Thesis. Amsterdam: Universiteit van Amsterdam.

Tudder, Veronique de, Isabelle Taboade & Francois Vourc'h.
1994 'Immigrant participation and mobilisation and integration strategies in France: a typology'. In Rex & Drury, ed., pp. 116-122.

Union Report of the Dutch Central Association of Transport Workers
1927 *Het kleurlingenvraagstuk op de Nederlandsche vloot* [The problems of coloured workers in the Dutch fleet]. Hoofdbestuur van den Centralen Bond van Transportarbeiders.

Veblen, Thorstein
1928 *The Theory of the Leisure Class*. New York: Vanguard Press.

Vellinga, M. L. & Wolters, W. G.
1966 *De Chinezen van Amsterdam: de integratie van een ethnische minderheidsgroep in de Nederlandse samenleving* [The Chinese of Amsterdam: the integration of an ethnic minority group in Dutch society]. Amsterdam: Afdeling Zuid en Z. O. Azie van het Antropologisch Sociologisch Centrum van de Universiteit van Amsterdam.

Veraart, Jan
1993 'Young Turks in the Dutch labour market'. In Entzinger et al., eds., pp. 71-92.

Vermeulen, Hans, ed.
1997 *Immigrant Policy for a Multicultural Society: A Comparative Study of Integration, Language and Religious Policy in Five Western European Countries*. Published by Migration Policy Group [Brussels].

Voets, S. Y. & J. J. Schoorl
1988 *Demografische Ontwikkeling en Samenstelling van de Chinese Bevolking in Nederland* [Demographic Development and Composition of the Chinese People in the Netherlands]. Nederlands Interuniversitair Demografisch Instituut: Intern rapport nr. 54.

Vos, Jan
1994 'Illegal migrants in the Dutch labour market'. In Entzinger et al., eds., pp. 93-113.

Waldinger, Roger David
1990 *Ethnic Entrepreneurs: Immigrant Business in Industrial Societies*. California: Sage Publications, Inc.

Wang, Gungwu [王庚武]
1981 'Southeast Asian *Hua-Ch'iao* in Chinese history-writing.' *Journal of Southeast Asian Studies* 12:1, pp. 1-14.
1988 'The study of Chinese identities in Southeast Asia'. In Cushman & Wang eds., pp. 1-22.
1991 *China and the Chinese Overseas*. Singapore: Times Academic Press.
1993 'The status of overseas Chinese studies'. *Asian Culture*, No. 17, pp. 5-13.
1994 'Among non-Chinese'. In Tu, ed., pp. 127-146.
1998 'Upgrading the migrant: neither *Huaqiao* nor *Huaren*'. In Sinn, ed., pp. 15-33.

Wang, Gungwu [王庚武] ed.
1997 *Global History and Migrations*. Boulder, CO: Westview Prss.

Wang, Zhongming [王忠明] ed.
1985 "文成华侨历史资料" [Historical documents on Wencheng migrants abroad (1905-1984)]. Printed in Wencheng county.

Watson, James L.
1975 *Emigration and the Chinese Lineage: The Mans in Hong Kong and London*. Berkeley: University of California Press.
1977 'The Chinese: Hong Kong villagers in the British catering trade'. In Watson, ed., pp. 181-213.

Watson, James L. ed.
1977 *Between Two Cultures, Migrants and Minorities in Britain*. Oxford: Basil Blackwell. Reprinted in 1984.

Wenchengxian tongjiju [文成县统计局] ed.
1995 "文成统计年鉴 (1994)" [Statistical Yearbook of Wencheng County (1994)]. No publishing house.

Wenden, Catherine Wihtol de.
1994 'Changes in the Franco-Maghrebian association movement'. In Rex & Drury, ed., pp. 106-115.

Wickberg, Edgar
1988 'Chinese organizations and ethnicity in Southeast Asia and North America since 1945: a comparative analysis'. In Cushman & Wang ed., pp. 303-318.
1992 'Notes on some contemporary social organizations in Manila Chinese society'. In Baviera & See eds., pp. 43-66.
1993 'Chinese organizations in Philippine cities since world war II: the case of Manila'. *Asian Culture* 17, pp. 91-105.
1994 'Overseas Chinese adaptive organizations, past and present'. In Skeldon ed., pp. 68-84.

1996 'What is the future of the overseas Chinese *huiguan*'. *ISEAS Trends*, August 31-September 1.

Williams, Robin M.

1976 'Relative deprivation'. In Coser ed., pp. 355-378.

Witkamp, P. H.

1861 'Een chineesch letterkundige te Amsterdam'[A Chinese literary man in Amsterdam]. In *Het Nederlandsch Magazine (Nieuwe Serie)* [The Dutch Magazine (new series)]. Amsterdam, Gebr. van Es. Uitgegeven onder bescherming van H. M. De Koningin der Nederlanden [Amsterdam, Van Es Brothers, published under the protection of Her Majesty the Queen of the Netherlands].

Wong, Bernard P.

1977 'Elites and ethnic boundary maintenance: a study of the roles of elites in Chinatown, New York city'. *Urban Anthropology*. Vol. 6, No. 1, pp. 1-22.

1982 *Chinatown, Economic Adaptation and Ethnic Identity of the Chinese*. New York: CBS College Publishing.

Wu, Hua [吴华]

1975-1977 "新加坡华族会馆志" [Annals of Chinese *huiguan* in Singapore]. Three volumes. Singapore: Nanyang xuehui.

1980 "马来西亚华族会馆史略" [A Brief History of the Chinese *huiguan* in Malaysia]. Singapore: Southeast Asia Research Institute.

Wubben, Henk J. J.

1986 *"Chineezen en Ander Aziatisch Ongedierte": Lotgevallen van Chinese Immigranten in Nederland, 1911-1940* ["Chinese and other Asian vermin": the vicissitudes of Chinese immigrants in the Netherlands, 1911-1940]. Zutphen: De Walburg.

Xu, Bin [徐斌]

1956 "欧洲华侨经济" [Overseas Chinese Economy in Europe]. Taipei: Taiwan qiaowu weiyuanhui.

Yang, Shan [杨山]

1996 "华侨与华人的称呼是科学的概念" [The terms *Huaqiao* and *Huaren* are scientific concepts]. In Pan, ed., 1996: 37-46.

Yearbook of ROC

"中华民国年鉴" [Yearbook of the Republic of China]. Taipei: Zhonghua minguo nianjian chubanshe.

Yen, Ching-Hwang

1986 *A Social History of the Chinese in Singapore and Malaya 1800-1911*. Singapore: Oxford University Press.

1993 'Early Hakka dialect organizations in Singapore and Malaya 1800-1900'. *Asian Culture*, No. 17, pp. 106-126.

You, Hailong [游海龙] ed.

1980 "英国华侨手册" [Directory of the Chinese in the United Kingdom]. Published by Sing Tao Newspapers.

Yu, Zhong [余忠]

1977 "热烈庆祝旅荷华侨总会成立三十周年" [Warmly celebrate the thirtieth anniversary of ACV's founding]. In the first issue of ACV Bulletin, 17 August.

Zeijl, J. W. van

1971 *The Chinese Mother (1887-1962)*. Printed in England by C. A. Brock & Co. Ltd.

Zeven, Bart

1987 'Balancerend op de rand van Nederland: de Chinese minderheid in de jaren 1910-1940' [Balancing on the margin of the Netherlands: the Chinese minority during the years of 1910-1940]. In Benton & Vermeulen eds., pp. 40-64.

ZGQZXH [中国侨政学会, Zhongguo qiaozheng xuehui]

1956 "今日侨情" [Overseas Chinese Affairs Today]. Edited by Zhongguo Qiaozheng Xuehui. Taipei: Zhongguo Qiaozheng Xuehui.

Zhang, Zhicheng [章志诚]

1987 "瑞安丽岙华侨历史与现状" [Historical profile and contemporary situation of Rui'an Li'ao migrants abroad]. In Zhejiangsheng qiaoshi yanjiushi, pp. 31-61.

1990 "浙江瑞安白门乡华侨历史" [A history of Zhejiang Rui'an Baimen migrants abroad]. Typescript.

Zhejiangsheng qiaoshi yanjiushi [浙江省侨史研究室]

1987 "浙江华侨史料" [Historical documents on Zhejiang migrants abroad]. Unofficial publication.

Zhou, Nanjing [周南京] ed.

1993 "世界华侨华人词典" [Dictionary of Overseas Chinese]. Beijing: Beijing University Press.

Zhou, Wangsen [周望森] ed.

1995 "华侨华人研究论丛" [A Collection of Studies on Chinese Abroad]. Beijing: Zhongguo Huaqiao chubanshe.

1991 "青田石雕及其社会意义探析" [A study on Qingtian carved stone and its social historical significance]. In Chen ed., pp. 88-96.

Zhu, Jianhua, Xinshu Zhao, and Hairong Li

1993 'Public political consciousness in China'. In *Asian survey*, Vol. XXX, No. 10, pp. 992-1006.

Zhu, Li [朱礼] ed.

1996 "文成县志" [Wencheng county chronicles]. Beijing: Zhonghua shuju.

Zhujia [诸家]

1996 "有关海外华人称谓之议论" [Discussions on how to name the Chinese abroad]. In Pan, ed., 1996: 47-59.

Zinn, Dorothy Louise

1994 'The Senegalese immigrants in Bari: what happens when the Africans peer back'. In Benmayor & Skotnes eds., pp. 53-68.

Notes

Chapter 1

[1] One exception is the investigative report written by Frank Pieke (1988), which has been translated into Chinese by Zhuang Guotu and published in Taiwan. See the following paragraph.

[2] During my interview with Wubben, he made a further explanation as follows. Originally, his book was entitled *Lotgevallen van Chinese immigranten in Nederland, 1911-1940* (The experiences of Chinese immigrants in the Netherlands, 1911-1940). It was the publisher who had put the original title as a sub-title and used the quotation, i.e., "*Chineezen en ander Aziatisch ongedierte,*" as the title of the book and printed it in big, black characters. "The aim of the publisher was to make the book more attractive," Wubben said.

[3] For instance, after accepting the suggestion made by the report, the Dutch authorities agreed not to consider the Chinese immigrant community as one of the minorities that are backward and in need of special social support. However, they did provide them with some subsidies to improve their social position.

[4] According to his records, Pieke interviewed 43 Chinese from 26 families (Pieke, 1988: 226-230).

[5] LFCON is an association member of EFCO. In December 1996, the chairman of LFCON took the position of chairman of EFCO. He proposed the project and got the support of the two associations' committees. The project was sponsored by the Dutch institution *Amsterdam Centrum Buitenlanders* (Amsterdam Center for Foreigners) as well.

[6] In fact, Xu's book is based on another documentary book entitled *Jinri qiaoqing* (Overseas Chinese Affairs Today) published by an association called "the Chinese Institute of Overseas Chinese Policies" in 1956 in Taiwan (ZGQZXH, 1956).

[7] In total, 19 Zhejiang emigrants abroad have been invited as honorary members of the Center. Among them, two are living in the Netherlands, and 12 are living in other European countries.

[8] For instance, the Dutch Chinese association *Algemene Chinese Vereniging in Nederland* hosted the two leading cadres' visit to the Netherlands. During a dinner hosted by the association at which dozens of Wenzhou Chinese in the Netherlands were present, the visitors first explained their plan to improve the studies on Wenzhou emigrants abroad. Then, they asked all Wenzhou emigrants to make a donation to help the establishment of a research foundation in the name of the institute. The attendants donated a few thousand Dutch guilders in total on the spot. See the news report "Leading cadres of Wenzhou Overseas Chinese Research Institute came to visit the Netherlands," in ACV Bulletin, 3 February 1997.

[9] In the book, I wrote the only article that focussed on the Chinese associations in Europe, "Transnational links among the Chinese in Europe: a study on European-wide Chinese voluntary associations." It is an outcome of this study.

[10] *Zhujia* is a Chinese term meaning "a couple of scholars." This is a collection from which four brief articles are selected. These four articles all focussed on how to name

the Chinese abroad and show the diversity of opinions. The four authors are Chinese scholars who live in Brunei, Singapore, and the United States, respectively.

[11] It is worth noting that more than eighty per cent of the ethnic Chinese abroad have settled down in Southeast Asia. Most of them have regarded their adopted country as their fatherland. When discussing the general situation of the Chinese abroad, this important fact cannot be ignored.

[12] One typical example is the ethnic Chinese in today's Indonesia. In May 1998, when riots against the ethnic Chinese happened, only a few Chinese could escape from Indonesia even temporally.

[13] In his lecture given in "The Wertheim Lecture 1992" held by CASA (Center for Asian Studies Amsterdam), Anderson discussed the transnational phenomenon of "long-distance nationalism." According to Anderson, millions of "long-distance ethno-nationalists" "live their real politics long-distance, without accountability;" they "have no serious intention of going back to a home, which as time passes, more and more serves as a phantom bedrock for an embattled metropolitan ethnic identity" (1992:12). This description is of particular significance with regard to the Chinese immigrants in Western Europe today.

[14] It is worthwhile pointing out the following difference between the Chinese and English terms. In Chinese, the term *yimin* covers all the meanings expressed by the words migration, migrant, immigration, immigrate, immigrant, emigration, emigrate, and emigrant in English. Nevertheless, the Chinese term *yimin* has an added connotation not expressed in any of the English words. It also suggests a compulsory migration; in other words, people moving away from their homes because of official policy (Wang, 1998:16; cf. Tian & Chen, 1986). This is a principal reason that in China the special subject related to the Chinese abroad studies has been named as "*Huaqiao-Huaren* studies," rather than "Chinese migrants studies."

[15] On this point, the theoretical framework related to "symbolic capital" or "symbolic power" proposed by Bourdieu is a helpful concept of the social functions of my target (Bourdieu, 1986, 1990; Calboun, 1993; Lipuma, 1993). For the detailed discussion, please see Chapter VII.

[16] Interview with Mr. MH, 7 March 1995, in Amsterdam.

[17] The interviewee studied history in a university between 1954 and 1958. After graduation, he was an assistant professor in a university until he emigrated in 1964.

[18] Hong Kong is also an important area from which many Chinese in the Netherlands came. However, I could not do fieldwork in Hong Kong for the following considerations. Firstly, Hong Kong is an area of immigration, that is, many Hong Kong people immigrated into Hong Kong after the War, while their original hometown is in mainland China. Among the Hong Kong migrants in the Netherlands, a substantial part have their original hometown in the Shenzhen area. Secondly, my research budget was limited, which did not allow me to do more fieldwork than what has been done. However, I have noted that in the case of some ex-Hong Kong sojourners, their Hong Kong sojourn did affect their organizational motivations and activities in the Netherlands. Some examples will be discussed in later chapters.

Chapter 2

[1] As I have mentioned in Chapter I, before leaving China, many would-be emigrants looked to Europe as a whole, rather than to any specific European country, as their destination. After arriving in Europe, it was quite common for them to transfer from one country to another, and then to a third or even a fourth country, especially

in the initial period after their arrival (cf. Li, 1998: 27-35). Armed with this knowledge, it is clear that the emigration waves to the Netherlands very often cannot be
separated completely from the migration waves to other Western European countries, especially to England, France, and more recently Italy, Spain, and Portugal.

[2] Quoted from 'Holland' in *Ming Shi* [A History of the Ming Dynasty], an official
history book originally printed during the Qing Dynasty in 1739.

[3] I found interesting evidence of this: in 1861, the arrival of "a civilized Chinese"
in Amsterdam had surprised the townspeople. An article was written to describe this
unusual visitor, which said: it is normal for Amsterdammers to come across foreigners
very often while walking along the streets of Amsterdam, however, "you would be
surprised to meet any civilized Chinese within our city" (Witkamp, 1861:183).

[4] As it is commonly known, the Chinese presence in the East Indies preceded that
of the Dutch there. The 1930 census shows that among the Chinese in Java about
79% were descended from Chinese parents but born in the Netherlands East Indies,
and in the Outer Provinces of the East Indies this percentage was 48%. In aggregate,
this percentage is 63%. In other words, of the total of 1,190,014 Chinese inhabitants
of the Netherlands East Indies, 756,172 had been born in the Netherlands East Indies
(Cator, 1936:31, 39-40). These people were called the Peranakan — children of the
soil. Usually, the Peranakan Chinese spoke a modified form of Malay, wore local
clothing, prepared their food in Malay fashion and maintained active social relations
with their native neighbours, largely in accordance with local cultural rules. Nevertheless, it is very clear that they still identified themselves as Chinese and were
identified as Chinese.

[5] The results of the 1930 census of the Netherlands East Indies indicates that
"among the Chinese population 29 per cent is literate and 3.2 per cent knows how to
write the Netherlands language" (Cator, 1936:87).

[6] *Chung Hwa Hui* was an association organized by the Peranakan Chinese youth
who studied in the Netherlands. It was set up in 1911. Cf. Chapter III.

[7] In the relevant Dutch documents, *Guangdong* was spelled as *Kwantung, Kwangtung,
Koangtang*, or *Canton*; *Zhejiang* was spelled as *Chekiang, Chikwong*, or *Tchekiang*. All these
spellings can be found in the Chinese seamen's registers kept by the Dutch police or
by shipping companies in the 1930s. In order to avoid confusion, I have standardized
the spellings as Guangdong and Zhejiang in this dissertation.

[8] According to the standard Chinese language, the name of this district should be
spelled as Bao'an. In the relevant Dutch documents, however, following the Cantonese dialect used by the people who came from there, the name usually is spelled as Bo
On or Bo-on. In this dissertation I have standardized the spelling as Bo On.

[9] Since 1979, the Shenzhen Special Economic Zone has been designated and
established at the centre of Bo On county. Its new development and its effects on
migrant streams will be discussed later.

[10] It is said that since the beginning of the 20th century, there were some experienced Dapeng people who acted as brokers in Hong Kong to help their co-villagers
find a job in the Western shipping companies. Some had run their business so well
that they set up official employment agencies. It is noteworthy that these early brokers are acclaimed by their peer villagers today as the able pioneers who guided the
footsteps of their native villagers in the efforts of the latter to seek work abroad.

[11] The investigation of the Dutch seamen's trade union showed that a Dutch sailor
usually received a monthly pay packet of 91 to 100 guilders, but a similarly qualified
Chinese sailor only received 60 guilders; the Dutch boatswain could get 104.5 to 115
guilders monthly, but the Chinese boatswain only got 73 guilders. Meanwhile, claiming that the Chinese had their own eating habits as an excuse, the management of

Dutch shipping companies offered only 16.5 guilders per month to every Chinese seaman for food, but gave per Dutch seaman 24 guilders (see *De Uitkijk* [Lookout], 6 Aug., 1932).

[12] The details of the affairs can also be read in *De Uitkijk*, 11 Nov., 1911; *De Nederlandsche Zeeman* [The Dutch Seaman], January 1912. The Dutch seamen were highly incensed and very indignant by the appearance of Chinese seamen on the scene. In the newspaper published by the Dutch seamen's trade union, all Chinese seamen were sharply criticized as the Yellow Peril (*De Uitkijk*, 11 Nov., 1911; 19 Nov., 1926; *De Nederlandsche Zeeman*, 10 Dec. 1904; Jan. 1912). These poor Chinese seamen, however, simply wanted to earn money to support their families in their hometowns. All the slogans used by the Dutch seamen's trade union, such as "class consciousness," "unite with the Dutch workers to fight against capitalism," "protect seamen's primary rights" etc., were completely strange to these people, who had just left their villages where people had been used to a small-scale peasant economy for hundreds of years. Most Chinese seamen, I believe, did not even know there was a strike among the Dutch seamen, let alone that they were expected to support it.

[13] The Chinese seamen registered in the Dutch shipping companies (1898-1915)

Year	Total	Chinese	Chinese: total	Year	Total	Chinese	Chinese: total
1898	*	11	*	1907	15,146	116	0.8%
1899	9,105	109	1.2%	1908	15,321	92	0.6%
1900	9,833	335	3.4%	1909	15,948	259	1.6%
1901	11,593	312	2.7%	1910	17,135	196	1.1%
1902	11,695	227	2.4%	1911	18,559	765	4.1%
1903	12,815	245	1.9%	1912	20,939	1,254	6.0%
1904	13,319	217	1.6%	1913	23,152	1,701	7.3%
1905	13,204	144	1.1%	1914	26,072	2,100	8.1%
1906	13,620	148	1.1%	1915	25,503	2,165	8.5%

Source: *Aantallen monsteringen van Nederlanders en kleurlingen te Amsterdam* (1900-1915).

[14] In this part there are so-called *qiaoxiang* areas, i.e., specific emigration villages and towns, clustered in the region of Wenzhou port, but divided over Qingtian county, Wencheng county, and Rui'an county, and usually known as Wenzhou and Qingtian districts.

[15] The article written by Lin and Chen was published in a popular magazine named *Shanhai Jing*. The meaning of this Chinese magazine's title is "popular legends, folklore, or hearsay."

[16] This sort of belief that Qingtian and Wenzhou people were brought over to Europe by selling Qingtian carved stones is well known in the Wenzhou and Qingtian districts (cf. *Qingtian xian zhi*). Yet, I have my doubts. I believe that the number of Wenzhou and Qingtian people who relied basically on selling Qingtian carved stones to make their living in Europe must have been very limited. It is quite plausible that a few people did so at the beginning of their emigration, but it could not have lasted very long. To make a living by selling those carved stones means that they either had a large supply of stones with them or they could import new goods when they needed them. No documents have so far come to light which prove that either of these conditions existed at that time. Although it was more than anything else a fanciful story that their co-villagers were getting rich in Europe by selling Qingtian stones, such legends did provoke an emigration tide to Europe from the Wenzhou and Qingtian districts in the early 20th century.

[17] *Xiang* is a rural administrative unit between county and village.

[18] This investigation was conducted in 1985, by Wang Zhongming, a cadre of Wencheng *qiaolian* (returned overseas Chinese association of Wencheng). The report was printed in October 1985 as *Wencheng Huaqiao lishi ziliao* [Historical documents on Wencheng migrants abroad]. An unofficial publication.

[19] For instance, Chen Shihong is one. Using the savings he brought back from Europe, he bought a piece of land that was 8 *mu* in area. The other one is Zheng Jiatao. He bought a piece of land with an area of more than 10 *mu*.

[20] There are some publications on the topic of the peanut-Chinese. See van Heek, 1936; van Zeijl, 1971; Wubben 1986; Li, 1989; Chen, 1991; Pieke, 1995; Pieke & Benton, 1998. Individual reactions to peanut-Chinese were different. The Dutch authorities at that time "frowned on the 'economically useless' Chinese and the peanut-cake trade. The method of production was seen as unhygienic, and the sale as a thinly veiled form of begging" (Pieke & Benton, 1998:127). But some Dutch people were willing to help these Chinese. Father J. Dols and Mrs. Wilhelmina Johanna van Zeijl are two such individuals. When the Chinese were suffering in their most difficult years, Father Dols not only gave speeches asking all Dutch people to help the Chinese, but went with some Chinese on rounds to sell peanut-cakes in the streets. Never stinting in her hospitality to homeless Chinese in the Netherlands, Mrs. Wilhelmina Johanna van Zeijl was respected as a "Chinese mother" (van Zeijl, 1971).

[21] Interview with Mr. Hu Kelin, 29 September 1987, in Amsterdam.

[22] Personal correspondence from Mr. Cai Zexuan to me, dated 18 March, 1988.

[23] Interview with Mr. Hu Keli, 27 May 1987, in Leiden.

[24] Interview with Ms. LYX, 6 February 1996, in Wenzhou city.

[25] Interview with Mr. ChCh, 18 October 1987, in Amsterdam. Some research on this topic has only noted that "the Germans took no special measures against the Chinese during the occupation, despite their Nazi ideology" (Pieke & Benton, 1998:129), which gave people the impression that the Chinese immigrants in the Netherlands did not suffer much during the war. I simply cannot agree with this opinion. In fact, I was impressed by the psychological injury suffered by my interviewees in that war.

[26] *Qin peng hao you* is a popular Chinese term meaning relatives and good friends.

[27] The relevant numbers are provided by the Wencheng Police Office. See *Wencheng xian zhi* [Annals of Wencheng county], 1996:225-226.

[28] Only for a short period in 1962 did the Chinese government relax its vigilance especially along the Anglo-Chinese border, which resulted in the influx into Hong Kong of several thousand newcomers — most of whom were young people in their early twenties (Watson, 1984:188).

[29] During my interviews with some people of this group, if I asked them about their region of origin ("Where did you come from?") very often their immediate answer was "Hong Kong." Only when I asked them about their ancestor's place of origin did some mention another place. This is unusual behaviour among the Chinese.

[30] According to the original "reach-base" policy pursued by the Hong Kong government, all illegal immigrants from mainland China who had evaded capture at the border were allowed to stay and work in Hong Kong. Then they would be granted full Hong Kong citizenship without any problems. This policy was abolished on 1 October 1979.

[31] During my fieldwork in Shenzhen, I heard that before the 1980s there were some written or unwritten regulations to enact a severe penalty on those who had escaped to Hong Kong or dared to do so. For instance, whoever had escaped to Hong Kong would not be allowed to return home ever again; the potential escapees would be punished as soon as they were found; those who were arrested while

escaping would be sent to a labour-camp to remold their ideology; and the remittance sent by the escaped people could not be received by their family-members or relatives. All these punishments have been slowly abandoned since the reform movement.

[32] The 1967 riot in Hong Kong "began with demonstrations and work stoppages that turned into violent confrontation and terrorism. About 8,000 suspected bombs were reported and over 1,000 were found to be genuine. Fifteen persons were killed during the disturbance. The riot shook Hong Kong to its core, and many of the elite took flight." (Wong, 1992: 921)

[33] Up till 1963, more than two-thirds of the Wenzhou male adults in Singapore were carpenters.

[34] Interview with Mr. Yu Xinchou, 15 February 1996, in Wenzhou. In 1941 Mr. Yu emigrated from Wenzhou to Singapore and re-migrated to the Netherlands in 1965.

[35] Since some Peranakan Chinese did not register as *Chinese* after arriving in the Netherlands, the exact figure of Peranakan Chinese in the Netherlands should be higher.

[36] Quoted from an unofficial publication in Wenzhou. The figure has been confirmed by several native officials.

[37] Tan Kah Kee (1874-1961) was born in Jimei (a little village near Xiamen) in Fujian province, China. He went to Singapore in 1890, established his own factories in Singapore and Malaysia from 1904 on, and became a millionaire with his rubber business. In 1913, he began to donate money for the establishment of primary schools, middle schools, and vocational institutes in his hometown. In 1921, he established Xiamen University. At the same time, he also established several schools in Singapore and Malaysia for Chinese descendants. At a time when China was suffering from Japanese aggression, he became the leader of all overseas Chinese in Southeast Asia to resist the Japanese aggression and save China. After the establishment of the People's Republic of China, he returned to settle down in his hometown. He has also held many high positions in the central government of China.

[38] According to the late Mao Zedong (Mao Tse-tung): "In our country bourgeois and petty-bourgeois ideology, anti-Marxist ideology, will continue to exist for a long time [...] We still have to wage a protracted struggle against bourgeois and petty-bourgeois ideology. It is wrong not to understand this and to give up ideological struggle." Quoted from Mao Zedong: "Speech at the Chinese Communist Party's national conference on propaganda work" (12 March 1957). Beijing: People's press. First pocket ed., p. 26.

[39] Interview with Mr. MH, 8 October 1996, in Amsterdam.

[40] During the Cultural Revolution, in 1970, an order named as "six rules" was issued, first by the Guangdong provincial government, and then as a reference document by other provincial governments all over China. It contained the following rules: it is imperative to educate and to examine all cadres who have "overseas relations;" that is, "all cadres from various levels of government must stop any contacts with their relatives living in Hong Kong, Macao or abroad, no matter what their relatives are doing. Anyone who continues to keep contacts abroad will be expelled from the cadres' rank." And "from now on anyone who has overseas relations cannot be accepted as a cadre of the government." "All cadres' marriages should be examined to prevent producing new overseas relations." At that time, "having overseas relations" was nothing different from having reactionary political relations (consult *Shijie Huaqiao Huaren cidian* [Dictionary of Overseas Chinese], p. 201). From my interviews, I have heard countless such stories. There is no room here for detailed expo-

sitions. However, all Chinese who have experienced that period, including myself, will clearly remember the heavy social pressure upon those who had so-called overseas relations.

[41] Quoted from "Peng Guanghan reported what Comrade Deng Xiaoping said on 'having overseas relations is something excellent.'" In [Beijing] *Huasheng Bao* (Chinese Voice), 1 May 1983.

[42] "To celebrate Chinese New Year in Shanghai, Comrade Deng Xiaoping issued an important speech." In [Shanghai] *Jiefang Ribao* (Liberation Daily), 23 January 1993.

[43] During my interviews with the Chinese migrants or their relatives both in the Netherlands and in their original hometowns, I heard a lot of such stories:

(A) Mr. H went to Singapore by himself in the 1930s. His family (parents, brothers and sisters, and wife with a couple of children) had been left behind in a village of Wenzhou. In 1960, he re-emigrated to the Netherlands. Since the middle of the 1950s he has wanted his family to join him. Nevertheless, after a long process that lasted for several years, only his eldest son could get permission to go abroad in 1962. Others could not go abroad until the end of the 1970s, and some had to wait until the 1980s.

(B) Mr. Yu left Wenzhou and settled down in Singapore in 1941. After the birth of the People's Republic of China, in order to let his children receive Chinese education, he sent his three sons and one daughter (all were born in Singapore) to study in Wenzhou. In 1965, Yu re-migrated to the Netherlands knowing that the Chinese catering business was growing prosperously there. Then he asked his children (the eldest had graduated from middle school) to join him. This, however, appeared to be obstructed. Having consulted repeatedly with native officials, two sons obtained permission, but one son and one daughter were persuaded to stay in Wenzhou.

[44] Interview with Mr. ZZ, 28 January 1996. As a historian and acting general editor of Wenzhou Chronicles, he has collected relevant statistical figures from reliable official sources.

[45] The term *conspicuous consumption* was coined by Thorstein Veblen in *The Theory of the Leisure Class* (1928). The leisure class experiences pride in "wasteful" expenditures since wealth is honorific. For them, the consumption of goods is a symbol of "pecuniary strength and so of gaining or retaining a good name," and "it results in a heightening or reaffirmation of social status" (Merton 1968:123).

[46] In February 1996, during my fieldwork in Wenzhou, I observed the funeral rite for an expatriate Chinese dependent (*qiaojuan*) in Rui'an. The deceased was the 70-odd-year-old head of a family. Two of his sons and their families emigrated to France and set up a restaurant and a leather workshop there. The funeral rites began early in the morning in the centre of the village. Almost all villagers, around one thousand, came to pay their last respects to the departed man. Then hundreds of people accompanied the coffin to the tomb built on a stone mountain. When I saw the tomb, I almost could not believe my eyes. In order to protect the coffin, a crypt of around thirty square meters had been dug out. Outside the crypt, stones had been removed and a garden laid out. Moreover, around the tomb a wall had been built in the style of the Great Wall. After enjoying free cakes, cigarettes and drinks, all the villagers followed the family members back to the village. There a big free banquet began with 70 tables altogether (each table for about 10 persons). Something even more incredible happened in the middle of the banquet: one of the sons of the deceased walked from table to table distributing 100 yuan notes to all guests. "You should get wages for having dinner here," I was told. Then, some packaged food and whole boxes of

cigarettes were distributed, regardless of whether you wanted any and regardless of whether you smoked. "If you don't accept it, the host will be angry," I was warned. Afterwards I calculated the expenditures. I believe such a funeral must have cost at least 200,000 yuan, excluding the construction of the tomb.

[47] Naturally, for illegal migrants, wages will be much lower. It will be around 1,500 guilders per month for a cook and 800 for a waiter or waitress. Still, these wages are incomparable to the incomes in the migrants' hometowns, especially for migrants without family in Europe and who can therefore have free board and lodgings in the restaurant where they work.

[48] According to my informants, the cooks in European Chinese restaurants usually will be divided into three levels, such as *Dacu* (the chief cook); *Ercu* (the second cook) and *Sancu* (the assistant cook). Neither *Ercu* nor *Sancu* are required to have any special cooking skills, even *Dacu* can learn by on-the-job training. I believe this is the normal situation in most small-scale and some middle-scale Chinese restaurants in Europe. In the very large Chinese restaurants, only truly qualified *Dacu* will be employed.

[49] For instance, I was often asked: "Do you know when the Netherlands will have such an ad-hoc law?" One villager of Wenzhou told me very seriously: "We have heard that the Netherlands will announce a similar law very soon. Otherwise all Chinese restaurants have to close because the workers will all go to Italy for their residence permits." Another villager said somewhat angrily: "My son [an illegal migrant in the Netherlands] wrote me that the Dutch people are friendly, but the Dutch government is cold-blooded. It does not want to follow Italy. The Dutch government should do that. Both countries are in one Europe. Why are the immigrant policies so different?" (Interview with Lishan villagers, 7 February 1996).

[50] According to post-modern theorists, "the circulation of people, goods, and ideas creates a new transnational culture that combines values, behaviours, and attitudes from sending and receiving societies to create a new, largely autonomous social space that transcends national boundaries. This transnationalization of culture changes the context within which migration decisions are made" (Massey et al., 1994:737).

[51] As well as the labour migrants from the Wenzhou and Qingtian districts, there is another small group that came from mainland China: the Chinese scholars who stayed in the Netherlands after finishing their studies in the Netherlands or other Western countries; however, up to the end of the 1990s, their number is limited to a few hundred.

[52] It is said that the lady was a Chinese shopkeeper's wife, and her arrival did cause a lot of surprise and gossip within the Chinese community. The shop became crowded suddenly, many Chinese customers went there to see the shopkeeper's wife rather than to shop. ChB can remember it in detail even after half a century. Interview with Mr. ChB, 16 March 1988, in Amsterdam.

[53] Interview with Mr. LK, 31 October 1987, in Amsterdam.

[54] Cf. Wang, 1985: 4. The investigation includes Wencheng people who went to Southeast Asia and North America.

[55] In other words, the ratio of male to female was 304:100 in 1956; and changed to 116:100 in 1987 (Voets & Schoorl 1988: 12 & 16).

[56] The report counted each Chinese restaurant as one family because the investigators thought many Chinese restaurants are based on family business. See INFO Krant, 2 March 1987.

[57] The number was provided by a local *qiaowu ganbu* of Wenzhou on 28 January 1996.

[58] There are some differences between the dialects used in Wenzhou and Qingtian, but these dialects are mutually comprehensible.

[59] There is an interesting story that I often heard when I was doing my research in Wenzhou. At the end of the 1970s, a war between China and Vietnam broke out. Because the communication apparatus of the PLA (i.e., the Chinese People's Liberation Army) was very simple, all commands and information transferred between the units could be wiretapped by the Vietnamese Army. In order to maintain their secrecy, all telegraph operators had been replaced by soldiers who came from Wenzhou and Qingtian districts. They were trained to use their dialect to make communications between the units. It is said that due to the historical relationship between China and Vietnam, the Vietnamese Army could easily find people who understood the dialects used in south China, such as Cantonese, Hokkian or Hakka, but they could not find people who understood the Wenzhou dialect.

[60] Siauw Giok Tjhan (1914-1981) was a famous Peranakan Chinese. Before 1965, he was a Minister of Minority Affairs in one of the Indonesian Cabinets. During the last years of his life, he lived in Amsterdam. In an interview in Hong Kong in 1980, Siauw mentioned that there were twenty Peranakan Chinese in the Netherlands who had been promoted to a professorship. See Siauw Giok Tjhan: "Chinese in the Netherlands," reprinted in ACV Bulletin, 19 September 1983.

[61] For instance, during the mid-1980s, there was a discussion about whether the Chinese in the Netherlands should be recognized by the Dutch government as an official minority who are under some special protection by the government. One representative response from a Peranakan Chinese is as follows:

> Our Peranakan Chinese here have no necessity to ask for special protection from the government. But the restaurant Chinese may have a lot of troubles justifying them to ask for help. There is a great difference between the respective social status. The restaurant Chinese are the *minority* being in need of help. Not us. Definitely not!

However, a representative comment on Holland's Peranakan Chinese by other ethnic Chinese groups is as follows:

> Yes, they are highly educated, they are professionals, they have a higher status in the Netherlands, but they are not *really* Chinese.

[62] According to Tseng's study, in the early years of the 1980s the number of Surinamese-Chinese living in the Netherlands was between 3,500 and 4,000 (Tseng, 1983:69).

[63] When asked about why they gave up the attempts to run a business or shop in the Netherlands, the Surinamese-Chinese very often talked about the difficulties they encountered after their arrival in the Netherlands. Some representative responses are as follows:

> In Surinam, life was simple. Most of the people hardly know how to run a business well. But the situation in the Netherlands is different. It is too difficult for us Surinamese-Chinese to run any business in the Netherlands (interview with Mr. LQ, 5 December 1996, Amsterdam).

> The tax in the Netherlands is too high. We can never understand their system. No matter how much we have earned, all earnings have gone to pay the tax (interview with Mr. LG, 5 December 1996, Amsterdam).

> My husband was a very successful businessman in Surinam [...] But, we came here when we were old. We are tired of running any business here. Yet, the Dutch government is really kind. I never took any job since I came here, but I receive my living allowances from the Dutch government every month (interview with Mrs. LY, 12 October 1995, Amsterdam).

[64] Nevertheless, at the same time, the Dutch police (under the Ministry of Justice) complained that the Chinese Embassy often refuses to give the necessary cooperation

to repatriate illegal Chinese (e.g., see *NRC Handelsblad*, 9 October 1996). I believe the reasons are complex. After being found by the Dutch police, many illegal Chinese immigrants simply keep thinking that the longer they can stay in the Netherlands, the more chances they will find to change their illegal status. Thus, taking advantage of the contradictions among the three governments of mainland China, Taiwan and Hong Kong, some illegal Chinese refuse to tell where they come from. Then, no government of the three will accept them.

[65] Since being designated a Special Economic Zone, Shenzhen has changed from an emigration area to an immigration area. Most natives of Shenzhen have given up the desire of going abroad. Illegal migrants from Guangdong usually came from poor mountain areas located in north Guangdong.

[66] Since the Chinese government has announced clearly that whoever smuggled people abroad would be severely punished, most interviewees were reluctant to answer my questions related to the smuggling process. However, it is a well-known fact that some transnational smuggling networks exist.

[67] If the United States is the destination, the fee will be between 250 and 300 thousand Chinese dollars.

[68] In accordance with the *Wenzhou tongji nianjian* (1995) [Statistical Yearbook of Wenzhou (1995)], the annual average income per peasant in Wenzhou is 2,000 Chinese dollars.

[69] Practicing usury is forbidden in China. Yet, in those areas where smuggling groups are active, clandestine loan sharks can be found here and there. Some of them charge interests rates as high as twenty to thirty per cent per year.

[70] For instance, one of my respondents came from a teacher's family in Wenzhou. In July 1990, his parents borrowed 160 thousand Chinese dollars from usurers to send their only son to France. After spending a couple of months climbing over the mountains between China and Thailand and waiting in Bangkok, he flew to Hungary after receiving the necessary travelling documents. Then, after spending another couple of months in several Eastern European countries, he was at last smuggled in a private car to Paris in March 1991. In September 1991, he was luckily recruited by a French overseas mercenary unit. When I interviewed him, he had been in the unit for nearly five years. He told me that, although he dared not to spend any money frivolously and had to send all of his savings back home, his family still owed the usurers 110 thousand Chinese dollars.

[71] The number of this group is very vague and variable. In Western countries, since the illegal immigrants will not register in any official office, no concrete figure can be given. I have also tried to find out their number from their areas of origin, such as the Wenzhou and Qingtian districts, but this was not possible either, since the local governments of the *qiaoxiang* have announced some rules to stop clandestine emigration, and usually the family of the emigrant will not register at the local government as *qiaojuan* until the emigrant has got his/her living permit in their adopted country.

Chapter 3

[1] The association's name quoted here is copied from its constitution and from a report written by the Foreigners' Department, Central Bureau of the Police in Rotterdam (*Politie Rotterdam Centraal Bureau, Vreemdelingendienst*). Its Chinese name was spelled in accordance with the Cantonese dialect since most members were Cantonese speaking. However, in F. van Heek's book, the association's name was spelt *Wah Khioe Woei Koen* (1936:32).

[2] Historically speaking, I believe CHH is an important association that should not be completely ignored in the history of the Chinese association in the Netherlands. Nevertheless, being an association organized by some Chinese who were no-longer Chinese speaking, CHH has never been regarded as the pioneer of the Chinese associations in the Netherlands by most current Chinese association leaders. For instance, in 1990, I was asked to write the section on Chinese in the Netherlands for the *Dictionary of Overseas Chinese*. CHH was rejected since the editors regarded it as "an association belonging to the history of the Chinese in Indonesia."

[3] Since more than two centuries ago, the Malay Archipelago has been the principal destination of many Chinese emigrants. As early as around the turn of the 18th century, Chinese associations began to emerge in Southeast Asia, and spread very quickly. Being emigrants without any support or protection from the government of their motherland, consciously or unconsciously, as a strategy of survival in strange surroundings, the Chinese organized themselves in accordance with their traditional ties. They made use of links such as their clan bonds, their common origin, or their common dialect.

[4] In 1907, there were 15 THHK branches spread all over the Indies; in 1914, the number of THHK branches increased to 25.

[5] The principal purposes of THHK included reforming some old-fashioned customs and bad habits (especially as regards funerals and weddings); initiating welfare work for poor Chinese; setting up modern Chinese schools for the Chinese youngsters; protecting the legitimate rights and interests of Chinese in the Netherlands Indies; and strengthening ties with China. All these measures represented the fundamental requests of the common Chinese.

[6] Moreover, although THHK followed the Hokkian dialect (a dialect popularly used among the Chinese in the Netherlands East Indies) to spell its name, CHH spelled its name in accordance with standard Chinese, which reflected CHH's wider and more general national identification.

[7] It is said that the Dutch are the European Chinese. This was first spoken by the French and Germans to describe the Dutch as conservative people. While steam locomotives were busily running between the cities of other European countries, the Dutch were still enjoying the slow but reliable canal boat. Since the early part of this century, China has leapt from a feudal society to a republic, and the Netherlands has also achieved great economic success, which have changed many of the prejudices against the two peoples. The statement is still popular in the Netherlands, because the Dutch see it as an affirmation of their own hard-working, entrepreneurial spirit.

[8] Besides Oey Kang Soey, only a couple of persons who worked together with the Chinese workers could be identified as Peranakan Chinese: William Fung, born in Batavia, acted as secretary for the *Wah Kiu Wei Kun* in the 1930s; Sie Joen Kan, who received his Ph.D from Leiden and became a lawyer in The Hague, was invited by a Chinese association to be its advisor in 1940.

[9] It is important to add that many of CHH's members kept contacts with each other after their return to the Netherlands Indies. In August 1926, some active ex-CHH's members organized a *Chung Hwa Club* in the Netherlands Indies. Then, they went further to hold the well-known *Chung Hwa Congress* in 1927. It is clear that their feelings of belonging were rather towards the Indies than towards Holland or China.

[10] The name was spelled in the Cantonese dialect. It is *Huaqiao Huiguan* in standard Chinese.

[11] Interview with Mr. ChB, 16 March 1988, in Amsterdam. During the middle of the 1930s, Mr. ChB was the secretary of WKWK's branch in The Hague.

¹² The original document is kept by the Central Bureau of Police in Rotterdam. Agenda No. 87/20/1930; No. 2254/13766.

¹³ Ibid. According to Mr. ChB, among the Qingtian people, he was the only one selected as a staff member of a WKWK branch.

¹⁴ The relevant information is mainly drawn from the following documents: (a) Rotterdam Police Report, 1930; (b) Rotterdam Police Report, 1933; (c) Chen, 1991: 25-28.

¹⁵ In May 1996, I published an article in a Chinese newspaper in Holland. In that article, when describing the early history of the Chinese in Holland, I quoted some information from my interviews with an old man. In the quotation, I mentioned the man's real name and said he had been a boarding-house owner in the 1930s. To my surprise, the old man got very angry. He sent me a letter immediately. In the letter, he wrote: "In order *to redeem my reputation*, you should publish an open announcement in the same newspaper to proclaim that I have never been a boarding-house owner during the whole of my life." (my emphasis)

¹⁶ Quoted from *"Statuten van de Vereniging 'Chineesche Vereniging in Holland'"*: *Doel. Art. 3* (Constitution of the association "Chinese association in Holland": Intentions. Art. 3.)

¹⁷ Interview with Mr. Zhong, 19 October 1987, in Amsterdam. Zhong originally came from Bo On and was asked by his co-villager and the chairman of WKWK to be a member of WKWK soon after he jumped ship in Rotterdam in 1929.

¹⁸ The original text in Dutch is *"Als een volk zijn nationaliteitsgevoel verliest, dan worden zijn vrouwen misbruikt door Chineezen en ander Aziatisch ongedierte."* Since then, the derogatory term "Asian vermin" (*Aziatisch ongedierte*) now and then has been used by some Dutch persons to indicate Chinese immigrants in the Netherlands (cf. Wubben, 1986).

¹⁹ Also mentioned in Mr. ChB's letter, which was written on 15 May 1988 to the author (cf. footnote 12).

²⁰ Since working on this project, six of them have passed away.

²¹ In the middle of the 19th century, *Zhi Gong Tang* was first set up in San Francisco among the Chinese in the United States as a *Hongmen* secret society. At the end of the 19th century, because of affections towards Dr. Sun Yat-sen, *Zhi Gong Tang* was reformed as a nationalist association of overseas Chinese aimed at supporting the national revolution in China. Its branches spread all over. In Europe, *Zhi Gong Tang* set up its first branch among the Chinese in Liverpool at the turn of the 20th century (You, 1980:150). The exact date of the establishment of *Zhi Gong Tang*'s branch in the Netherlands is unknown. However, it was not earlier than the 1920s.

²² Its name in Dutch is *Het West-Europeesch Bureau van het Al-Chineesch-Zeemans-Verbond*. The relevant information is limited. During the early 1930s, the Chinese communist party sent someone to organize the Chinese seamen in the Netherlands. However, they could not achieve their aims because soon after they began to contact the Chinese seamen in Rotterdam, they were repatriated by the Dutch police. Meanwhile, some leaders of the Dutch Seamen Union also tried to unite the Chinese seamen. For instance, a booklet titled *Menschenhandel in Europa* (Human trade in Europe) was published in 1934. The booklet sharply criticized the human-trading business in Europe and asked to protect the Chinese seamen's rights and to unite all Chinese seamen. Although the publisher was the West-European Section of the All-Chinese Seamen Union, it was clear that the real editor was from the Dutch Seamen Union since all contents were in Dutch. Moreover, since almost no Chinese seamen read Dutch, they could not be influenced by the booklet.

²³ See the application form of WKWK to the Rotterdam police in 1930. The

original document is kept by the Central Bureau of the Rotterdam Police. Agenda No. 87/20/1930. No. 2254/13766.

[24] Interview with Mr. ChCh, 18 October 1987, in Amsterdam.

[25] Interview with Mr. HKL, 29 December 1996, in Leiden.

[26] Interview with Mr. LD, 5 September 1996, in Amsterdam.

[27] Interview with Mr. ChB, 16 March 1988, in Amsterdam.

[28] The Japanese army staged an incident at Lugouqiao near Beijing on 7 July 1937, which marked the beginning of the war between Japan and China.

[29] The exact date of the conference cannot be traced. Since it was in September 1937 that the Chinese Resistance Association made its first appeal to the Chinese in the Netherlands for donations to help China, I believe the association must have been established in August or early September 1937.

[30] Ms. Yang was a young heroine in the war. On 13 August 1937, the Japanese invaded Shanghai. The Chinese army rose in resistance. In the midst of a fierce battle, the Chinese flag was destroyed. To encourage the Chinese soldiers, Ms. Yang charged forward under a hail of bullets to bring a new Chinese national flag to the army. Her bravery was highly esteemed.

[31] *Het Verre Oosten Restaurant* was established in 1931. It had kept its position as one of a few distinguished Chinese restaurants in the Netherlands up till the 1950s. As was mentioned earlier, Kwok Shu Cheung, the owner of the restaurant, was also the chairman of WKWK in the late 1920s and the early 1930s.

[32] The three photos made at the meeting are considered historical documents.

[33] In my interviews, I heard many stories about returnees after the war. For instance, Mr. ZZY, a well-known head of the Bo On group in the Netherlands in the 1930s and 1940s, returned to his hometown soon after the end of the War. Disagreed with the Chinese Communist Party's policies in the land reform movement, he emigrated to Hong Kong in the early 1950s. In another example, soon after the War, going along with the trend of returning home, Mr. YY, a leader of a Zhejiang group in Amsterdam, brought the money he had saved for years back to his hometown to purchase land and houses there. Nevertheless, when he went back to Amsterdam to settle some final business, his properties in Wenzhou was confiscated in the land reform movement. Thence, he gave up his plan to return home and ended up staying in the Netherlands.

[34] To illustrate, Wong Sing, a powerful Chinese boarding-house keeper and shipping agent in Rotterdam in the 1920s and 1930s, advertised that "Chinese cooks, stewards, deck hands & stokehold crews, always on hand." Another influential Chinese shipping master proclaimed in his letter that "I have always a large number of seamen in hand" (Union Report, 1927:3-4).

[35] HORECA is a special Dutch abbreviation that means "hotel, restaurant and cafe."

[36] The office was set up in Jan van Nassau Straat 36, The Hague.

[37] Interview with Mr. CZX, 18 March 1988, in Amsterdam.

[38] Interview with Mr. MH, 2 September 1996, in Amsterdam.

[39] Further discussion on the Chinese religious associations of Rotterdam will be presented in Chapter IV:3. This is based on interviews with the initiators and consultations with the special issue published by *Lü Ou Huaqiao fuyin budaohui* in 1994.

[40] As an association aimed at establishing European links, it uses both English and Dutch names at the same time.

[41] Katendrecht is the area in which a well-known Chinatown was established in the 1930s.

[42] It was called Eurocup I then, now it is called the Champions League.

[43] Quoted from a remark made by Edgar van Lokven on 17 August 1998.

[44] In Edgar Wickberg's earlier articles, he had also used other classification models. For instance, in "Chinese Organizations and Ethnicity in Southeast Asia and North America since 1945: A comparative analysis," he employed a classification system of eight types, based upon their major purposes and the character of their membership: (1) clan and district associations, (2) trade associations, (3) professional organizations, (4) political associations, (5) educational and journalistic bodies, (6) recreational-cultural associations, (7) religious bodies, (8) community-wide coordinating and representative associations (including 'umbrella' organizations that represent other organizations in the community). See Wickberg, 1988: 304.

[45] "Kwangtung" is Guangdong.

[46] The "save China" associations were organized among the Chinese abroad after the establishment of the People's Republic of China. These associations were founded to "save China" from the rule of the Chinese Communist Party.
In accordance with the Yearbook of ROC published in 1951 (p. 685), the three groups and the respective statistics are as follows:

Guilds	1,309
Social associations	2,658
"Save China" associations	880

[47] "Anti-CPC/save China associations" are the former "save China associations."

[48] The statistics of 1990 are a good example. In 1990, according to the statistics counted and classified by the Overseas Chinese Affairs Commission in Taiwan, the overseas Chinese associations all over the world were classified as follows (Yearbook of ROC, 1991:493):

Community associations	568
Social associations	1,199
Regional associations	1,301
Surname associations	945
Guilds	627
Industrialists and merchants associations	1,412
Educational and cultural associations	658
Recreational associations	853
Youth associations	250
Women's associations	77
Anti-CPC and save China associations	172
Welfare associations	526
Religious associations	296
Non-governmental diplomatic associations	72
Others	137

[49] *Wu shu* is a Chinese traditional folk martial arts. Formerly, it was cultivated for self-defense. Now, it has developed as a form of physical culture.

[50] In 1996, some Dapeng people considered setting up their own co-villagers association in Germany. When asked whether their forthcoming association would become a branch of the *Tai Pang Gemeenschap in Europa*, the existing European-wide Dapeng association, one initiator simply told me that they regarded that association as an organization for Dapeng people in the Netherlands only (interview with Mr. LJ, 18 January 1997, in Dapeng Zhen). Cf. Chapter V: 3.

[51] For instance, *Tai Pang Gemeenschap in Europa* accepts its members only from those who emigrated from Dapeng, i.e., a district made up of six villages and one town. *Taiwan Shian-Chin in the Netherlands* is established on a province level. However, the Association for the Chinese from the Northeast China in the Netherlands asks that

the members come from the three Chinese provinces of Heilongjiang, Jilin and Liaoling.

⁵² See ACV Bulletin, 8 August 1994.

⁵³ Interview with Mr. ZJR, adviser of *Stichting Taiwan Shian-Chin in the Netherlands* (Association of Taiwan Fellow Provincials in the Netherlands), 13 December 1996, in Rotterdam.

⁵⁴ They are: *Stichting Familie Tang in Nederland* (Association of the Tang Family in the Netherlands]; *Stichting Familie Man* (Association of the Man Family); *Familie Pang vereniging in Nederland* (Association of the Pang Family in the Netherlands); *Vereniging Familie Choi in Nederland* (Association of the Choi Family in the Netherlands).

⁵⁵ The Cantonese surname "Tang" is pronounced "Deng" in standard Chinese; and "Man" is "Wen;" "Pang" is "Peng."

⁵⁶ Moreover, to further separate them from the natives, they stress the orthodox beliefs that they brought over from central China. That the Hakka people choose to title their association as *Tsung-Tsin* (*Congzheng* in standard Chinese), which simply means "to respect orthodoxy," reflects this group's consciousness. The Hakka's *Tsung-Tsin* association has a European-wide and even worldwide federation. The Hakka's *Tsung-Tsin* Association in Benelux is one branch of the Federation of Hakka *Tsung-Tsin* Associations in Europe, and the latter has also joined in the worldwide federation as a branch.

⁵⁷ Only those associations clearly registered as Chinese youth associations have been considered. Thus, there are Chinese sports clubs and recreational groups that have not been included in this group.

Chapter 4

¹ After-school Chinese schools teach their pupils Chinese language and culture on Saturday or Sunday, some on Wednesday afternoon as well, when Dutch primary schools are closed. Nowadays, among the 41 Chinese schools in the Netherlands, the large-scale schools located in big cities like Amsterdam and Rotterdam may have dozens of classes with several hundred pupils each, but some small ones only have ten-odd pupils each. Some Chinese schools are run by a Chinese association, and others are sponsored by their own management committee. In the latter situation, the school committee is sometimes regarded as an independent association.

² This figure was given by the chairman of ACV in 1997 (cf. ACV, 1997:3).

³ Concerning the early history of ACV, in addition to a rather limited number of written sources, the information mainly comes from the following interviews:

(A) Interview with Mr. Cai Zexuan (1910-1997). Cai came from Wenzhou to the Netherlands in 1936. He was one of the founders of ACV. From 1967 to 1972, he was its chairman. From 1980, he was an honorary chairman of ACV until he passed away in 1997. Between 1987 and 1996, I interviewed Cai many times. He always cordially agreed to be interviewed. Upon my request, in the summer of 1988, he wrote me three letters (without date) to tell me his personal experiences in the Netherlands. Some of his narratives relate to the history of ACV.

(B) Interview with Mr. Hu Kelin (1908-1998). Hu Kelin came from Wenzhou to the Netherlands in 1937. He was one of the founders of ACV. In 1978 and 1979, when the chairman of ACV was seriously ill, Hu Kelin was named acting chairman. From 1980, Hu was an honorary chairman of ACV until he passed away in May 1998. Between 1987 and 1996, sometimes in the Netherlands and sometimes in his newly built house located in his hometown in Wenzhou, I held many interviews with him. Although he was eighty-odd years old in the 1990s, his memory and his answers were still very clear.

(C) Interview with Mr. Mei Xuhua. Mei's father Mei Zhongwei (1906-1987) left Wenzhou for Southeast Asia in the early 1930s and re-emigrated to the Netherlands in 1940. The late Mr. Mei was one of the founders of ACV and was elected as its chairman between 1953 and 1956. Mei Xuhua himself came from China to the Netherlands in 1964 and joined ACV soon after his arrival. Between 1984 and 1987, Mei was the chairman of ACV. He has been an honorary chairman of ACV since 1993.

(D) Interview with Mr. Hu Zhiguang. Hu's father left Wenzhou for Singapore in 1940 and re-emigrated to the Netherlands in 1958. In 1962, Hu came to join his father in the Netherlands. Unlike his late father who had limited himself to his restaurant work, Hu is an enthusiast for social activities. Between 1981-1984 and 1988-1990, Hu was elected twice as the chairman of ACV. Hu has been an honorary chairman of ACV since 1993.

[4] Cf. Chen, 1991:20-21; 25-29. Among the twelve Chinese restaurants, six were located in The Hague, four in Amsterdam, and two in Rotterdam.

[5] The following quotation is translated from Cai Zexuan's letter, which was sent to me in 1988.

[6] According to Cai's narrative, his father died before he went abroad, and his mother and two brothers died during the war. Thus, Cai himself was not involved in the incident because he had no familymembers in China to whom he would have sent money.

[7] Another interviewee, Mr. Zhong Xinru (1903-1994), who was born in Bo On and arrived in the Netherlands in 1929, told me about this event as well. The basic version is similar. Zhong pointed out clearly that this event caused a strong aversion to the Chinese *Kuo Min Tang* Party among the Chinese in the Netherlands. Interview with Mr. Zhong Xinru, 19 October 1987, in Amsterdam.

[8] On 16 January 1947, Cai married a Dutch woman. He could clearly remember that it was a few weeks after his wedding day that he joined discussions with some friends about setting up an association.

[9] Cf. the article "Mr. Yu Zhong's Memorial Meeting Solemnly Held in his Hometown Wencheng County," in ACV Bulletin, 21 December 1981. I also got relevant information about Yu Zhong (1910-1981) from the interviews I held with his acquaintances, i.e., Cai Zexuan, Hu Kelin, Chen Bin, and Ms. Ma.

[10] According to Cai Zexuan, only nine people attended the preparatory work. However, according to Hu Kelin, there were nearly twenty initiators. Both of them gave me a list of names. Since most of them have passed away, however, it is not possible to check the truth.

[11] There are some other explanations about the meaning of the association's name. For instance, Mei (1997:36) explained that *Ou* was picked up from the name of Ou river, and Sea means the Wenzhou area is also next to the sea. However, Mr. Cai wrote me the following explanation: historically, the Wenzhou area was once under jurisdiction of a municipality called Ou Sea. Yet, someone told me that Ou Sea simply means that the Ou river flows to the great sea.

[12] A photo made of the meeting was found. On the back of the photo, someone wrote down the date of the meeting.

[13] The interview with Mr. Hu Kelin on 29 September 1987 in Amsterdam confirmed this; and the information was re-checked on 6 August 1996, in Utrecht.

[14] The Chinese pronunciations of the two characters, i.e., the *Ou* of *Ou Zhou* (Europe) and the *Ou* of *Ou Jiang* (Ou river), are the same, but the characters are different.

[15] Mr. Dai Zaipeng, came from Wenzhou and joined ACV in 1966; he also acted as ACV's accountant for about 15 years. In my interview with him (5 February 1996, in his hometown, Wenzhou), Dai stressed repeatedly that when Cheung became one of its leaders, the social status of ACV among the Guangdong Chinese rose significantly.

[16] This first complete, written constitution was published in the ACV Bulletin, 17 August 1977. This is the first issue of the ACV Bulletin.

[17] "Democratic centralism" is the organizational principle advocated by the Chinese Communist Party: centralism based on democracy and democracy under centralized guidance.

[18] Some of my interviewees did not agree that OSDA had sent a telegram to Beijing in 1949. The two founders, Hu Kelin and Cai Zexuan, said they could not remember whether there was such a telegram. Everyone, however, agreed that OSDA had expressed an obviously pro-Beijing orientation as soon as the People's Republic of China was established.

[19] According to Mei (1997:37), the first party held in the Netherlands to celebrate the National Day of the People's Republic of China was in 1952. Alternatively, the respondents Hu Kelin, Cai Zexuan and Zhong Xinru all recalled that it was in 1950. When I consulted Mei, he told me that he had heard several different years as well, from 1949 to 1952. He thought the Chinese in the Netherlands would not have been able to organize the party so soon after the founding of the People's Republic of China. Therefore, he personally selected 1952 as the right year. I myself respect the information from Hu, Cai and Zhong. First, the three of them attended the party themselves. Second, objectively speaking, since the Dutch government recognized the People's Republic of China in March 1950, then, taking those Chinese leaders' political orientation into consideration, it was possible and reasonable that some months later in that same year OSDA could have held a public party to celebrate the National Day of the People's Republic of China in Amsterdam.

[20] I first interviewed Mr. Hu Kelin on 29 September 1987, in Amsterdam; the second time was on 6 August 1996, in Utrecht.

[21] Interview with Zhong Xinru, 19 October, 1987, in Amsterdam.

[22] Some passports were suspended for a while, but some were suspended for years. The holders of these passports could not get them back until the Chinese Chargé d'affaires ad interim arrived in the Netherlands and lodged complaints with the authorities.

[23] Interview with Mr. G. J. Harbers, director of *Amsterdam Centrum Buitenlanders* (Amsterdam Center for Foreigners), 7 April 1995, in Amsterdam.

[24] At least four other Chinese interviewees who know about this case expressed their sympathy for the person. Since this is still a sensitive topic, to respect the confidentiality of all relevant informants, I will not disclose their names here.

[25] Mr. HZG, the first volunteer editor of the ACV Bulletin, told me about how he edited the ACV Bulletin in its beginning period: "We had no Chinese typewriter. The articles written by ourselves would be cut on stencils. Some articles were clipped from Chinese newspapers published in Beijing. I was in charge of the makeup of the pages. All was made by hand. I remember clearly that sometimes the size of one piece of newspaper clipping did not fit into a certain space of our page. Then, I had first to cut the piece of clipping to one line by one line, even one character by one character; and afterwards, to piece them together. The work was very hard." Interview with HZG, 25 March 1995, in Utrecht.

[26] On the other hand, some elder leaders were asked to take up a kind of honorary position: Yu and Cai, the two former chairmen and important initiators of ACV,

became advisers; Cheung, the former chairman of WKWK and vice-chairman of ACV, was nominated as an honorary chairman.

[27] During the 1950s and the 1960s, the chairman was usually chosen from among the dozens of activists. After ACV issued its Bulletin, usually one or two months before the committee selection, a note would be published to announce the voting date. All members were invited to attend the voting. Yet, from the fifth to the ninth election, each time there were only around one hundred to two hundred voters.

[28] Originally, it was planned to begin the voting procedure at noon on 11 March 1996 at the ACV's office. Nevertheless, from early morning, members started arriving. Around eleven, seeing that nearly one hundred persons were already in the ACV's office and more people were coming, it was decided that the voting procedure should begin one hour early. Since there was such an unexpected demand for ballots, the voting took a long time, and the results could not be announced until eight that evening.

[29] In 1996, when *Fa Yin* was going to celebrate its twentieth anniversary, I was asked to edit a special commemorative issue for the association. During the process of editing, I held several meetings with many of its members to recall the early history of *Fa Yin*; eventually, I interviewed 22 members individually. Based on this oral evidence and after reading the relevant reports published in various Chinese newspapers, I wrote an article to trace *Fa Yin*'s history between 1976 and 1996. This article has been discussed among the leaders and some active members of *Fa Yin*, and the basic facts described in the article were found to be correct. These investigations have composed the major basis of the following description.

[30] In fact, nobody could exactly say on which date *Fa Yin* was founded, although many of its earlier members remember that the association proclaimed its foundation in the early summer of 1976. On 25 July 1996, when a meeting was held to recall the early history of *Fa Yin*, the date of 18 June 1976 was accepted by all participants as the founding date of *Fa Yin* at the suggestion of the current chairman, Mr. But. Here I just follow their decision.

[31] According to the relevant record, 14 committee members made donations: Lin donated 7,000 guilders; Liang donated 2,500 guilders; and the donation made by each of the other 12 members was between a few hundred and two thousand guilders.

[32] Enkhuizen is 60 km north of Amsterdam, and Den Helder is 80 km north of Amsterdam.

[33] Mr. Liang stressed his will to me repeatedly during the interviews.

[34] For instance, the festival dinner is very often held in one of the best Chinese restaurants in Amsterdam. Each person is charged for 25 guilders for a ten-course meal.

[35] For instance, in 1995, the Amsterdam municipal committee agreed to give 70,000 guilders as a subsidy to the *Fa Yin* school.

[36] Mr. C. Y. But is one of the best-known Chinese restaurateurs in the Netherlands. Born in Dapeng in Guangdong province, But arrived in the Netherlands in 1970. He first worked as a cook in his sister's restaurant. In 1975, he set up his own Chinese restaurant. His business kept expanding in the 1980s. By the 1990s, he was the managing director of the Sea Palace floating restaurant (i.e., the biggest Chinese restaurant in the Netherlands) and of the hotel Falcon Plaza, both located in the centre of Amsterdam. At the end of 1994, *Fa Yin* was going to elect its fifth committee. Then, in order to obtain more support from Chinese businessmen, But was asked to chair the association even although he was not yet a member of *Fa Yin* at that time. But accepted the invitation (Cf. Chapter V).

³⁷ In addition, Mr. F. Bijdendijk, general director of *Het Oosten*, holds the position of treasurer; Mr. G. J. Harbers, director of ACB, is the secretary of the New Chinatown Foundation.

³⁸ Besides *Fa Yin*, the partners in this foundation include the following Chinese associations: LFCON (the National Federation of Chinese Organizations in the Netherlands); ACV; *Chen Hui* Foundation; two Chinese elders' associations, *Tung Lok* and *Chun Pah*; and the Association of Chinese Businessmen in Amsterdam.

³⁹ The relevant figures are quoted from the working paper New Chinatown Amsterdam, produced by the New Chinatown Foundation in September 1996.

⁴⁰ The Chinese name of CCRM is *Zhonghua huzhuhui* (Chinese Mutual Aid Association), which is rather different from its Dutch name. The reasons of these two different names will be discussed in the section (c). For convenience sake, in this text CCRM will be used.

⁴¹ Among Chinese Christians, the priest of the church would be respected by his followers as Father Priest or Master; and the priest's wife would be respected as *Shi Mu*, which can be translated as Mother Priestess or Female Master.

⁴² Interview with Mrs. Chan, 27 August 1996, in Rotterdam.

⁴³ In 1980, the Dutch government decided to set up a coordinated policy for the ethnic minorities in the Netherlands. In accordance with the official concept of ethnic minority defined by the Dutch government, the following groups are regarded as minorities: Surinamese, Antilleans and Arubans, Moluccans, Turks, Moroccans, Italians, Spaniards, Portuguese, Greeks, (former) Yugoslavs, Tunisians, Cape Verdians, Gypsies, recognized political refugees and tinkers (an indigenous semi-nomadic group that had been subject to a special government policy for a long time already). When the minorities policy was promulgated in 1980 these groups together totaled 450,000 people (Entzinger, 1993: 155).

⁴⁴ Interview with Mrs. Chan, 27 August 1996, in Rotterdam.

⁴⁵ In the interview with Mrs. Chan and Mr. Cheung, the coordinator of activities for CCRM, both of them stressed that Ms. Evenhuis is a prominent Dutch politician of great ability. A photo of Ms. Evenhuis was printed in the special issue published by CCRM to celebrate the tenth anniversary of its founding. Under the picture, there is a caption: Ms. Evenhuis, thank you very much for your heart-warming support in the last ten years (CCRM, 1994: *Foto-illustraties* [Photo-illustrations]).

⁴⁶ Most Chinese associations in the Netherlands have one Chinese name and one Dutch name. Because there are differences in the way of expressing things between the two languages, there may be some differences between the two names, as is the case with ACV and *Fa Yin*. Nevertheless, the CCRM's Chinese name is completely different from its Dutch name.

⁴⁷ In 1982, CRM and the Ministry of Public Health and Environmental Hygiene were combined into one ministry named the Ministry of Welfare, Public Health and Culture.

⁴⁸ It is worth pointing out that there is no other outsider who has paid enough attention to how the initiators of CCRM named the association. This fact, however, is a distinct example of CCRM's attempts to gain advantages from both the Chinese and the Dutch sides.

⁴⁹ Interview with Mrs. Chan, 27 August 1996, in Rotterdam.

⁵⁰ The five representatives of the relevant Dutch departments are: Mr. M. H. Custers from the Ministry of Home affairs, Mr. E. F. Stoove from the Ministry of Welfare, Public Health and Culture; Mr. C. V. D. Valk from the Ministry of Education, Ms. H. Evenhuis, a CDA member of Parliament, and Mr. P. Jonder, a representative of the Mayor of Amsterdam.

⁵¹ Cf. INFO Krant, 6 December 1985; CCRM, 1994:13.

⁵² Cf. INFO Krant, 21 February 1986.

⁵³ CCRM did not give a clear announcement about which *authority* had subsidized their buying of the building. However, it is said that a great part of the funding came from Taiwan.

⁵⁴ The building is located at Mathenesserlaan 481a, Rotterdam. According to a public report by CCRM, about two thousand Chinese made contributions. The balance sheet of buying and furnishing of the building published in INFO Krant is as follows (cf. INFO Krant 24 April 1987):

Items	Amount (Dutch guilders)	Remarks
Revenues	93298.5	Donations from Chinese all over the Netherlands
	50496.4	Subsidies from the authorities
Total	143794.9	
Expenditures	114116.95	To buy and renovate the house
	12401.1	To rebuild the basement of the house
	3358.88	All service charges and commission
	2812	To buy office furniture
Total	132688.83	
SURPLUS	11105.97	To support INFO Krant

⁵⁵ This announcement was published on the front page of each INFO Krant.

⁵⁶ Between 1992 and 1994, the INFO Krant increased to six pages for a while.

⁵⁷ *Chun Pah* is a Cantonese term meaning two evergreen trees, i.e., pine and cypress, which are likened to good health and long life.

⁵⁸ *Wai Wun* is a very traditional Cantonese term specially used as a poetic description of "sweet ladies."

⁵⁹ Between 1990 and 1991, *Chun Pah* set up its branches in the following six areas: Rotterdam, The Hague, Utrecht, Amsterdam, Eindhoven and Gelderland. Its seventh branch was set up in 1995.

⁶⁰ During 1996 and 1997, the news that CCRM was going to disband itself surprised many Chinese association leaders. Some did not believe it. Some regretted it. Some thought CCRM had exhausted its funding, because its backer, the Dutch political party CDA, is not in power any longer. Some sharply criticized a few leaders of CCRM and accused them of not daring to face the Chinese rank and file; it was said that these leaders had used the money from the sale of CCRM building — which was a donation from the Chinese people — for their private purpose. The establishment of the Reserve Fund by CCRM is a response to stop the gossip.

Chapter 5

¹ Interview with Mr. LT, 5 September 1996, in Amsterdam.

² Before the Second World War, there were several small Chinese shops and eating-houses located at Binnen Bantammerstraat of Amsterdam. It was called the China corner of Amsterdam.

³ Interview with Mr. LK, 11 April 1995, in Utrecht.

⁴ Name of the street where the Chinatown of Amsterdam has developed since the 1950s.

⁵ Usually, Mahjong is played with four persons at each table.

⁶ This demographic feature is similar to that of the Chinese communities in North

America, Australia and other European countries but different from those in Southeast Asia.

[7] "Concepts about a Chinatown vary from person to person, place to place, and time to time. A Chinatown may be conceived of as Chinese living quarters in a particular section of a city or as an agglomeration of Chinese restaurants, grocery stores, and other business, or as a concentration of both Chinese people and business in one area" (Lai, 1988:1). A small Chinatown like in Amsterdam is in fact a center of Chinese restaurants, Chinese stores, and some ethnic services, but it is not a concentrated Chinese housing quarter.

[8] The reasons why diversification is difficult are multiple. For instance, the Chinese migrants in the Netherlands are usually short of the necessary capital, not only economic capital, but also cultural capital like education, social networks and the necessary knowledge about the host society. In the whole of Western Europe, only in France did Chinese immigrants attain remarkable success in the diversification of their ethnic economy, although it is still far from the economic achievements accomplished by the ethnic Chinese in Southeast Asia. It is worth pointing out that most successful Chinese entrepreneurs in France emigrated from Indo-China and had vast experiences in business before their emigration. Also, the ethnic Chinese market itself in France is much bigger than that in the Netherlands.

[9] Among the Chinese immigrants in the Netherlands, working for a Western boss (including the Dutch and other Western people) is usually called "taking a Dutch job;" working in one of the Dutch government departments is called "taking a government job."

[10] For instance, an official of ACB made the following comment: "I have the impression that Chinese organizations in the Netherlands in general tend to rely too heavily on government funding. Most Dutch organizations do not receive government benefits but are still able to carry out their activities." Quoted from a remark made by Edgar van Lokven on 12 June 1998.

[11] Among the Chinese characters in common use, the pronunciation (in Cantonese) of seven Chinese characters is close to the pronunciation of "Dam."

[12] Interview with Mr. HY, 27 November 1995, in Rotterdam.

[13] In ancient China, under the traditional imperial examination system, *Zhuangyuan* is the title conferred on the one who came first in the highest imperial examination. In modern China, *Zhuangyuan* has been converted to name the best one in any field.

[14] The eight Chinese schools are located in The Hague, Rotterdam, Utrecht, Maastricht, Eindhoven, Roermond, Brunsum and Groningen. See ACV Bulletin, 30 August 1993.

[15] It is interesting to point out that some large-scale schools, e.g., *Fa Yin* Chinese School and Kah Wah Chinese School, do not nominate students for a *Dam Wah* Prize since they have their own reward system.

[16] Among the Turks and Moroccans, Islamic organizations have become the most numerous and important since the early 1980s.

[17] Dozens of small sports teams that have affiliated themselves with the nationwide Chinese sports federation CSFN do not register as an independent association.

[18] Interview with Mr. YHG, 26 January 1997, in Shenzhen.

[19] *Wu shu* is a kind of martial arts such as shadowboxing, swordplay, etc., formerly cultivated for self-defense, now a form of physical culture.

[20] Interview with Mr. MW, 15 October 1996, during "the eleventh Chinese sports meetings in the Netherlands," in Amsterdam.

[21] In 1985, a leading committee in the name of CSFN was founded. Then, in the same year, CSFN successfully held the first Chinese nationwide sports meetings in the

Netherlands. The association, however, did not officially register itself as a formal Chinese voluntary association at the Dutch registration office until 1988.

[22] Since this is still a disputed question, I will not publish the real names of all interviewees and the persons mentioned in the interviews.

[23] The interviewee is an old man and speaks Cantonese. He cannot give the full name of CSFN. Instead, he said that it is an association to let younger Chinese play "ball." This saying is popular among the Cantonese-speaking Chinese migrants who have less education.

[24] The Cantonese term *Wa Lai* is pronounced *Hua li* in standard Chinese.

[25] Interview with Ms. Mai, 18 September 1996, in the office of *Wa Lai*, Amsterdam. The full name of *Wa Lai*'s initiator is Ms. Mary van der Made-Yuen. Many Chinese call her *Mai Tai* in Cantonese. When translated into English, it is "Ms. Mai."

[26] She speaks Cantonese but not Putonghua (Standard Chinese).

[27] *Kah Wah* means "arouse the Chinese."

[28] The term is borrowed from Selma Leydesdorff. In her book on the Jewish proletariat of Amsterdam, she points out: "In Jewish tradition, there was a separate women's culture, in which the women helped each other and celebrated women's events among themselves. This world was entirely distinct from that of the men." (Leydesdorff, 1994: 144).

[29] Interview with Ms. Mai, 18 September 1996, in the office of *Wa Lai*, Amsterdam.

[30] Ms. Mai was educated in Christian schools of Hong Kong when she was a child. She spent her youth in France. She married a Dutch husband.

[31] According to the relevant statistics, in 1990 there are approximately 642,000 aliens in the Netherlands, though not all of them have gone through the process of immigration themselves. With regard to the number of foreign-born inhabitants and their immediate descendants, their number was estimated at 2.2 million in 1990, i.e., 15 per cent of the total population of the Netherlands (Penninx et al., 1993:1).

[32] The main clauses of this constitution were published in the first issue of ACV Bulletin, on 17 August 1977.

[33] Interview with Mrs. ChL, 27 August 1996, in Rotterdam.

[34] Having attended all relevant meetings held in 1987, I based my analysis on my own observations.

[35] Since the mid-1990s, the government funding changed from "institution funding" to "project funding." Few Chinese association leaders know how to work out an acceptable project.

[36] The relevant document is dated 28 October 1997.

[37] The Overseas Chinese Affairs Commission of the Republic of China was set up in 1926 by the Central Government. After 1949, OCAC came under the control of the Executive Yuan in Taiwan. OCAC "is devoted to the interests of Chinese nationals in foreign countries and areas [...] It has departments of administration, education, research, and general affairs" (Government Information Office, 1988:129). According to OCAC, Overseas Chinese include Chinese living abroad, naturalized citizens of Chinese descent, and persons of Chinese descent.

[38] After the founding of the Union of Chinese Associations in Europe, similar unions were set up under the "direction" of OCAC in Asia (in 1976), in Oceania (in 1977), in Africa (in 1978), and in America (in 1980). The 1976 meeting is considered the second annual meeting, although it officially proclaimed the founding of the association.

[39] Similar ruses have been adopted by the unions in the other continents.

[40] Cf. the article "While observing the changed situations, open up a new prospect

overseas," written by Zhang Xiaoyan (Chairman of OCAC) in Taipei: Zhongyang Daily, 12 May 1995.

[41] Ibid.

[42] Interview with LQ, 18 January 1997, in Dapeng.

[43] In *Shenzhen Qiaobao* (Newspaper of Overseas Chinese of Shenzhen), 22 February 1995.

[44] Interview with Mr. LKH, the chairman of Hong Kong Tai Pang Residents Association, 15 January 1997, in Dapeng.

[45] Interview with Mr. BCY, 30 December 1996, in Amsterdam.

[46] From my fieldwork in Hong Kong and Dapeng district, I found that the Hong Kong Taipang Residents Association has set up some special services for their emigrated co-villagers to visit their hometown, such as a special bus line going between Hong Kong and Dapeng and a hotel run by and for the Dapeng people.

[47] The Cantonese name Tang is pronounced Deng in standard Chinese.

[48] Interview with Mr. HZG (the Netherlands), 9 December 1996, in Amsterdam.

[49] Interview with Mr. HYS (Austria), 7 December 1996, in Amsterdam.

[50] According to the announcement presented at the fifth annual meeting of EFCO, 33 Chinese associations from ten European countries have paid their 1996 membership dues to EFCO. Their membership continued to 1997.

[51] Interview with Mr. MLS, 7 December 1996, in Amsterdam.

Chapter 6

[1] In the case of the Chinese community in the Netherlands, most business persons are Chinese restaurateurs.

[2] In the countries of Southeast Asia where the Chinese associations have a long history, one can observe that the chairman post of a well-known association is held in the hands of one person for twenty or more years. For instance, the "Hokkian Association of Singapore" is a well-known association with a history of more than one century. In 1930, Tan Kah Kee was elected as its chairman, and he did not give up this post until he retired to his hometown in mainland China in the early 1950s. Then from 1953 on Tan Lark Sye was chairman for twenty years until he died in 1972. After him, it is Wee Cho Yew who became chairman and up till now already more than a quarter of a century has passed (Li, 1995: 261).

[3] As was mentioned in Chapter IV, this Liang has no children. Since his wife died, he is alone and spends all of his time in the office of *Fa Yin*: to clean the office; to answer the telephone; to play cards or have chats with other Chinese visitors.

[4] Interview with Mr. KU, 4 June 1995, in Amsterdam.

[5] Interview with Mr. LW, 12 August 1997, in Amsterdam.

[6] Interview with Ms. LX, 10 July 1996, in Amsterdam.

[7] Interview with Mr. ZS, 13 September 1996, in Haarlem.

[8] Interview with Mr. YC, 10 September 1997, in Rotterdam.

[9] The foundation of this association has been set forth in Chapter III.

[10] Interview with Mr. Young, the chairman of CSFN and the major organizer of the 10th sports invitational tournament, 21 February 1998, in Amsterdam.

[11] Some donations were made directly for the ACV's celebrating activities without asking for any refunding. Some donations were refunded as advertisements since most committee members are business persons themselves.

[12] According to Yen, a representative selection procedure runs more or less as follows: on the selection day, members of the association were convened in the

clubhouse (or in some cases at the cemetery of collective ancestors). The names of the candidates were written on papers, which were rolled and put into a box or a brush-holder. A paper was taken out each time, and a pair of Poeh (lots) were thrown in the air in front of the deity of the association. If the Poeh turned out to be one flat and one convex, it was considered to have the blessing of the deity; if it did so three times consecutively, the candidate on the paper was considered to have been chosen by the deity, and his name would be announced on the spot as the new leader (Yen, 1993: 115-116).

[13] As a researcher and, moreover, an outsider at the meeting, I was asked to monitor and had a chance to see the whole process of voting.

[14] In accordance with the result of the voting, a vice-chairman should have gotten more than 250 ballots. But these four Guangdong people had polled less than two hundred votes.

[15] Interview with Mr. DL, 26 June 1995, in Amsterdam.

[16] Before the Second World War the situation was somehow different. The cases of WKWK and the Chinese Resistance Association described in Chapter III reveal the *compulsory power* of certain Chinese associations during that period.

[17] Translated from "*Fa Yin* Constitution," 1996 edition.

[18] Interview with Mr. WJ, 6 May 1995, in Amsterdam.

[19] Interview with the secretary of HCS, 22 October 1996, in Amsterdam.

[20] Interview with Ms. XH, 28 October 1996, in Amsterdam.

[21] Interview with Ms. TC, 27 August 1996, in Amsterdam.

[22] Interview with Ms. LH, 24 December 1995, in Amsterdam.

[23] Interview with Ms. TF, 22 August 1996, in Amsterdam.

[24] It seems that the organizers do not want their members to be members of both associations at the same time. In the winter of 1997, when one association changed its meeting date from Thursday to Wednesday, the other association made the same change.

[25] Interview with Mr. HC, 22 August 1996, in Amsterdam.

[26] Interview on 18 September 1996, in Amsterdam.

[27] Interview with the head of CCRM, 27 August 1997, in Rotterdam.

[28] Interview with the secretary of HCS, 22 October 1996, in Amsterdam.

[29] Interview with the vice-chairman of *Fa Yin*, 13 September 1996, in Amsterdam.

[30] Interview with Mr. ZJ, 1 February 1996, in Rui'an.

[31] Mr. LT simply regarded all Chinese immigrants who arrived in the Netherlands after the Second World War as "newcomers."

[32] Interview with Mr. LT, 5 September 1996, in Amsterdam.

[33] All of these are quoted from my research log.

[34] I was a visitor at that meeting. When asked how many members would normally attend such an annual members' meeting, the secretary told me that this meeting was very well organized so that there were more participants than in any annual meetings held in the former years.

Chapter 7

[1] Since early 1998, the mother tongue education policy in the Netherlands has become decentralized, i.e., it is up to the individual local governments to decide whether a Chinese school can obtain funding or not.

[2] LFCON: *Nieuwsbrief* (Newsletter), No. 10, March 1997, p. 7.

[3] In accordance with my interviews, the subsidy received by the teachers of Chi-

nese schools is called *che ma fei* in Chinese, which means to subsidize the teachers' travelling costs. Most teachers receive about two to three hundred guilders per month for giving courses for three to five hours per week.

[4] Cf. the policy of *Onderwijs allochtonen levende talen* (Teaching foreigners modern languages), first posed by the state secretary of *Ministerie van Onderwijs, Cultuur en Wetenschappen* (Ministry of Education, Culture and Sciences; OCW for short).

[5] Cf. *We hopen op steun en erkenning van de overheid zodat het Chinees onderwijs nog beter wordt*, in LFCON: *Nieuwsbrief* (Newsletter), No. 8, September 1996, pp. 5-11.

[6] CITO-2 stands for *Centraal Instituut Toets Ontwikkeling-2*. CITO is the abbreviation of the name of the institute responsible for the development of exams for different educational levels, but mainly for final exams of primary schools. The Level 2 corresponds to the level of a junior middle school.

[7] LFCON: *De resultaten van onderzoek naar de Chinese scholen* (The results of a survey of Chinese schools), in *Nieuwsbrief*, No. 8, September 1996, p. 5-11.

[8] According to the interview with the key organizer, Mr. ZY, the organizing committee was quite confident that the "Chinese culture camp," which is held once a year, would become a tradition in the Chinese immigrant community in the Netherlands.

[9] *Yao Yi* is a Chinese term meaning friendship.

[10] *Chen Hui* is a Chinese term meaning the first rays of the morning sun.

[11] *Taijiquan* is a kind of traditional Chinese fitness exercise to achieve harmony of body and mind.

[12] It is also named "tea party." All participants can chat freely and informally while drinking tea.

[13] For instance, between January and April 1998, one Chinese women's association in The Hague arranged eight programs for its members. Among them, two were lectures on health; five were about learning dancing, singing and making cakes; and one was a getting-together meeting. At the beginning of 1998, one Chinese women's association in Arnhem sent an announcement to its members about the programs of the coming year: on the first Monday of every month, a getting-together meeting with karaoke would be held; on the second Monday, a cooking class would be held; on the third Monday, there would be a class for learning standard Chinese by singing Chinese songs; and on the fourth Friday, "singing Cantonese opera."

[14] In 1997, another association named *Vereniging van Gediplomeerde Chinese Koks* (Association of Qualified Chinese Cooks) also held a course especially to teach the participants how to make excellent Indonesian cuisine. The teacher was an Indonesian cook of a specially high classification. Nearly fifty Chinese cooks followed the course. Among them, 37 finished all courses and received a diploma.

[15] The whole title of the research report is: *Imago Chinees Indische Bedrijven, Een onderzoek naar het imago van de Chinees Indische restaurants in Nederland* (Image of Chinese-Indonesian Enterprises, A research on the image of the Chinese-Indonesian restaurants in the Netherlands). Cf. HORECA 1997.

[16] Before the mid-1980s when there were few delegations that came from China to the Netherlands, it was an honour to be invited as a host. In the 1990s, with the significant rise in the number of delegations, some started to consider being a host organization as a burden.

[17] Interview with Mr. HZ, 22 December 1997, in Amsterdam.

[18] *Guanxi* is a popular Chinese term that means having special approaches and connections to reach one's objective.

[19] The 15th of the first lunar month is the Chinese Lantern Festival.

[20] Interview with Mr. WJ, 22 January 1998, in Amsterdam.

[21] The offices of these three associations are located not far from the office of LFCON.

[22] On this point, I appreciate the suggestions made by Dr. Hong Liu (Singapore National University). Discussions with him have helped me to develop the analysis of this topic.

[23] For instance, during my interviews with the relevant leaders, they often mentioned the fact that their associations are among the few that receive subsidies from the Dutch government. Also, in the relevant issues published by CCRM, ACV, and LFCON, all mentioned the dates and the amount of the subsidies they received from the Dutch government. In the special issue published by CCRM on the occasion of its tenth anniversary, it is stressed that it is through the efforts of CCRM that the Chinese associations in the Netherlands enjoy government funding (CCRM, 1994: 7-9). Nevertheless, in a special issue published by ACV on the occasion of its fiftieth anniversary, it claimed that it was through ACV's achievements that the Chinese associations are now receiving subsidies from the Dutch government (ACV, 1997: 42).

[24] There is an interesting example. Among the three Chinese elderly associations in Amsterdam, *Tung Lok* has received local government funding in 1996 and again in 1998. Thus, being very proud of the "achievements," the female chairperson of *Tung Lok* made her "announcement" publicly: *Tung Lok* is the only Chinese elderly association in Amsterdam that has been recognized by the municipality.

[25] This meeting has been held in Hangzhou (the provincial capital of Zhejiang), New York, Vienna, Paris, Hong Kong, among other sites.

[26] "Summary of minutes, Get-together Meeting of Prominent Zhejiang Migrants Abroad in 1996," in [Paris] *Ouzhou shibao* [Europe Times], 23 June 1996.

[27] Interview with a local official of Wencheng county, 13 February 1996, in Wencheng county.

[28] China's current leaders, Jiang Zemin and Zhu Rongji, once visited the Netherlands when Jiang was the mayor of Shanghai and Zhu was the vice-mayor of Shanghai. The photos in fact were taken at that time, i.e., before Jiang and Zhu became "the highest Chinese national leaders."

[29] *Mu*, a Chinese unit of area, is about 0.0667 hectares.

[30] In 1996, whenever an official delegation from Wenzhou visited the Netherlands, some Wenzhou Chinese would go to meet them to discuss this problem and lodged many complaints.

[31] After leaving the villages in Wenzhou where I did my fieldwork, I have kept in contact with some local villagers. The information quoted here came from the letters I received from them.

[32] Interview with one high-ranking official of Wenzhou municipality who headed a government delegation to visit the Netherlands, 19 September 1997, in Amsterdam.

[33] NPS is a branch of NOS (*Nederlandse Omroep Stichting*; Dutch Broadcasting Foundation).

[34] This program has been sponsored by a Dutch institution NPS. It started in December 1985. At the beginning, it broadcast news and relevant information only once a week, i.e., for half an hour every Monday night. From 1990, the broadcasting time increased to fifteen minutes every working day; from 1995, it increased to half an hour every working day.

Chapter 8

[1] In Indo-China, all Chinese associations as well as their schools, hospitals and charitable institutions were prohibited soon after the political changes in 1975. Since

the late 1980s, some ethnic Chinese have begun to re-organize activities but maintain a low social profile. In Indonesia, all Chinese associations were forced to stop activities after 1965. From the 1980s, some have been allowed to resume charitable activities but within a limited sphere. Nevertheless, after its ex-president Suharto stepped down in May 1998, the ethnic Chinese in Indonesia started to speak out after keeping silence for more than three decades. Moreover, some progressive persons have organized political parties and attempted to function as a potential political interest group. This recent development and its future trend are worthy of more scholarly attention.

[2] The relevant statistics are quoted from *Zhonghua minguo nianjian* [Year Book of the ROC], 1950, 1965, 1991 and 1997 editions. Cf. Li, 1995: 5-8.

[3] Sources: ibid. The numbers quoted here are just used for comparison purposes. However, I do not altogether accept the total number counted by OCAC. For instance, my own studies have shown that the total number of Chinese associations in Europe is much higher than the number provided by OCAC (cf. Li, 1995: 5-13).

[4] Interview with Mr. T. Chan, vice-chairman of the Chinese in Britain Forum, 5 July 1998, in Amsterdam.

[5] This is the first association established by Indochinese immigrants in Paris in 1982. In 1984, it changed its original name from "Association of French Residents of Chinese Origin" to "Association of French Residents of Indochinese Origin."

[6] Teochew (*Chaozhou* in standard Chinese) is a district located in the south part of Guangdong province of China.

[7] The opening ceremony of EFCO was held in Amsterdam in 1992. The annual meetings between 1993 and 1995 were held in Paris, Glasgow and Oslo.

[8] I was invited to attend the meeting. The relevant data are taken from my notes made at that meeting.

[9] In the present Philippines, some Chinese-school alumni associations are related to a given Chinese school. Others are related to a secondary school in Hong Kong, and still others centre on a secondary school in the Fujian province of China. Lions clubs and Chinatown fire brigades are local Chinese welfare or volunteer associations (cf. Wickberg, 1994: 82).

[10] However, regarding the membership of the Dutch professional associations, it should be noted that Peranakan Chinese professionals are in fact members of the respective Dutch associations. As already mentioned, the Peranakan Chinese, i.e., the Chinese immigrants who have come from Indonesia, are in general a highly educated group. The percentage of university graduates among them is quite high. Almost all of these Peranakan Chinese university graduates (medical doctors, medical specialists, pharmacists, scientists, engineers, dentists, economists, lawyers, etc.) are members of a Dutch professional association.

[11] Interview with Mr. DH, 7 April 1995, in Amsterdam.

[12] One potential aim of EFCO is to ask the Chinese government to accept its chairman as the appropriate delegate of the European Chinese.

Appendix III

[1] The Chinese associations names listed here are the names used by the associations themselves: most associations have their names both in Dutch and Chinese; some have their names in English and Chinese; and some have their names in Chinese only. For the last group, their names will be also given in Pinyin.

[2] All the initiators of this association have passed away, and none of the current members remember the exact year of its founding.

[3] This association was set up on 1 July 1964. Received recognition from the Dutch authorities concerned in June 1966, but stopped its activities at the end of the 1960s.

[4] In November 1997, the *Stichting* Fine Eastern Restaurants and The Asian Restaurants (set up in 1994) merged as one association, named Fine Eastern Restaurants in the Netherlands.

[5] This association stopped its activities between the late 1980s and the early 1990s, but was reorganized on 18 September 1996 in Rotterdam.

[6] After holding the first Chinese Sports Meeting in the Netherlands in October 1985 and continued to hold the Chinese sports meeting once a year, the Federation was officially set up and registered in 1988.

[7] Set up in 1987, but officially registered in March 1991.

[8] Cf. Footnote 4.

[9] The Buddha's Light International was set up on 16 May 1992 in Taiwan, China. By the end of the twentieth century, it has spread its branches to the whole of the Western Europe.

[10] On 19 November 1997, this association was formed by the merger of Stichting Fine Eastern Restaurants (set up in 1984) and The Asian Restaurants (set up in 1994).

[11] This association pronounced its establishment in December 1997, but held its official founding ceremony in April 1998.

Index